Dynamics of the Vietnam War

Jeffrey S. Milstein

Dynamics of the Vietnam War

A Quantitative Analysis and Predictive Computer Simulation

Ohio State University Press : Columbus

Manufactured in the United States of America

Library of Congress Cataloging in Publication Data
Milstein, Jeffery S
Dynamics of the Vietnam War.

Bibliography: p.
1. Vietnamese Conflict, 1961–
2. Digital computer simulation. 3. Electronic data processing—Multivariate analysis. I. Title.
DS557.A6M485 959.704'3'02854044 73-17351
ISBN 0-8142-0190-3

To my children—Steven, David, and Elise—and to all children, with the fervent hope that they may never experience war

Contents

	Acknowledgments	xi
	Introduction	xiii
Chapter 1	Theories Underlying Hawk and Dove Policy Models	3
Chapter 2	Data	18
Chapter 3	Methods of Analysis	29
Chapter 4	Tests of Crucial Hypotheses and Assumptions of U.S. Policy-makers about the Vietnam War	39
Chapter 5	Empirical Patterns of Interaction in the Escalation of the War	57
Chapter 6	Computer Simulation Predictions of the Escalation of the War	78
Chapter 7	Simulation Exercises of Alternative Hawk and Dove Policies	106
Chapter 8	The Vietnam War from the 1968 Tet Offensive to the 1970 Cambodian Invasion	128
Chapter 9	The Paradox of Waging War to Achieve Power	149
Chapter 10	U.S. Policy in Vietnam: Calculated or Miscalculated?	171
Chapter 11	Afterword: The 1973 Cease-Fire Agreement	186
	Appendix A: Content Analysis of Communications	199

Appendix B: Components of the Eight Communications Indices 207

Appendix C: Time Plots of Composite Indices and Individual Variables 211

Bibliography 247

Index 251

Illustrations

1	Misperception Leading to Escalation	9
2	Synthesized Mediated Stimulus-Response Model	12
3	Bootstrapping Predictions of Variables	35
4	The Escalation Cycle	61
5	Pattern of Military and Political Interaction	66
6	Bivariate Correlations in the "Peace Offensive" Pattern, 1965-67	69
7	Patterns of Interaction in Simulation Model	80
8-23	Graphs of Simulation Predictions	90
24	The Vietnam War as a Prisoner's Dilemma Game	107
25-31	Graphs of Simulation Predictions of Hypothetical "Dovish" Policy Alternative	114
32-38	Graphs of Simulation Predictions of Hypothetical "Hawkish" Policy Alternative	121
39	Major Relationships in the Vietnam War from the Tet Offensive to the Cambodian Invasion	145
40	Loss of Political Support in Pursuit of War Objectives	152
41	Trade-offs between Expected Net Benefits and Expected Net Costs of Waging War	153
42	Trade-offs of Elites and Masses between Expected Net Benefits and Expected Net Costs of Waging War	155
43	Expected Net Benefits and Real Net Costs	156
44	Real Net Costs and Individual's Indifference Map	157
45	Real Net Costs and Different Preference Systems of Elites and Masses	158
46	Increasing Real Costs and Different Preference Systems of Elites and Masses	160
47	Changes in Elites' and Masses' Preference Systems over Time	162
48	Primary Message Types	203

Tables

1	Winter-Summer and Spring-Fall Variables Used to Represent Seasonal Changes	24
2	Significance Levels of Correlation Coefficients	32
3	Regression Equation Model for Simulation Predictions	79
4	Measures of Goodness of Fit of Simulation Predictions	83
5	Mean Percentage Error of Simulation Predictions	85
6	Error Variance of Simulation Predictions/Total Variance	86
7	Exercises of Simulation with U.S. Commitments	109

Acknowledgments

This book has been a long labor, researched, written, and rewritten over a period of five years. I could not have completed it without the inspiration, help, criticism, and support of many people at various stages of the research and writing.

I thank first my wife, Jane Milstein, for her research and editorial assistance, as well as for her great patience and moral support.

I must also thank my friend William Charles Mitchell, who originated and programmed virtually the entire computer simulation program used in this research.

For early scholarly direction and criticism I am most grateful to Professors Robert C. North, Richard A. Brody, and William J. Paisley of Stanford University.

I am greatly indebted to those who have given me patient and effective computer programming and other research assistance over the years: Kenneth Fruit at Michigan State University; and Nathaniel Beck, Steven Dunning, Lloyd Etheredge, Jerry Eyster, Jong Lee, and Robert Luft at Yale University.

Translating theoretical ideas and the methods and initial results of empirical research into clear language that communicates not only to the specialist but also to the intelligent general reader is a difficult task for anyone. My own writing has benefited greatly from the editorial assistance I have had from Michelle Press, Robin Hamill, and June Guicharnaud of Yale University.

Typing and retyping a book manuscript is never an easy task, and I am grateful to Jackie Berman at Yale for her exact and patient work.

With the exception of an early version of Chapter 8, the research for, and the writing of, this book have been unsponsored, independent academic scholarship. My deepest gratitude goes to Stanford, Michigan State, and Yale universities for making this possible by giving me time and resources, particularly computer time. An early version of Chapter 8 was partially supported by Grant number 2635 from the National Science Foundation to the World Data Analysis Program at Yale University. The analysis and conclusions of this research are my own however, and do not in any way represent those of any department or agency of the United States government.

Finally, I wish to give my sincere thanks to Weldon Kefauver and the Editorial Board of the Ohio State University Press for publishing this book, and to Robert Demorest for his skillful editing and guidance during its publication.

Introduction

At the beginning of 1965 the Vietnam War was primarily a guerrilla war between the government of South Vietnam and the National Liberation Front, with the United States and North Vietnam primarily supplying advice and material support.* Within a few years the United States was embroiled in one of the largest and costliest wars of its history, exceeded in the number of casualties only by World War II, the American Civil War, and World War I. United States and North Vietnamese combat troops assumed the major burden of the fighting. The United States conducted massive bombing of North Vietnam. The Soviet Union and the People's Republic of China supplied the North Vietnamese with the most sophisticated weapons of modern war. Both sides made great human and material commitments, and suffered tens of thousands of casualties. And the country and people of Vietnam—both North and South—were devastated.

Yet despite the increased commitments of men and matériel, the military and diplomatic efforts, the violence, and the costs, neither side defeated the other militarily nor attained its primary goal: exclusive political control of South Vietnam.

This book is an analysis of the dynamics of the Vietnam War—what the general patterns of military and political interaction were during the war. The analysis is both theoretical and empirical, and uses statistical methods to examine monthly quantitative data systematically. The quantitative data represent monthly measures of military forces, actions and casualties; political support in Vietnam and in the United States; and of public statements about the war by leaders on both sides.

Effective policy depends in part upon the ability of policy-makers to predict the consequences of their actions. The ability to predict depends in turn upon having a valid theory or "model" of the relationship between actions and consequences—between means and ends. Policy-makers have asserted different models of the structure of relation-

*Throughout this study the political entities in Vietnam will be referred to by their commonly used names rather than by their legal names. "South Vietnam" is the Republic of Vietnam: "North Vietnam" is the Democratic Republic of Vietnam; and the "Viet Cong" is used synonymously with the National Liberation Front and the Provisional Revolutionary Government.

ships in the Vietnam War. Two such models became prominent: those represented in the so-called hawk and dove policy positions. Hawk and dove policy models represent "folk theories" about the conflict, i.e., sets of concepts and interrelations among them used by individuals to think about a problem. While hawk and dove folk theories predict the consequences of military actions in the war, the predictions of these two theories in general contradict each other.

How well the policy-makers were able to predict and evaluate the consequences of their own actions, and thus how valid folk theories that informed their policies were, has very important implications about the political process that underlies their policies and conduct of the war. If American policy-makers, for example, had accurately predicted that their policies and actions would not have achieved their policy objectives in Vietnam, and would have lead instead to the tragic consequences that did occur, one would infer very different motives and moral principles underlying their conduct of the war than one would if American policy-makers had made poor predictions about the consequences of their policies and actions. If the former were true, one might conclude that cynical calculation of international and domestic political advantage guided American policy in Vietnam. If the latter were true, one might conclude that American policies and actions in Vietnam were the inadvertant consequences of miscalculation. Thus, the models of the conflict that guided decision-making are of great concern to our understanding of the actions and policies chosen in the war.

In this book the models of the conflict held by the principal policy-makers are explicated from their public and private statements about the relationships that they assumed to exist between particular means and ends in the war. These models and the policies based upon them are analyzed theoretically and evaluated against factual criteria. Ineffective policies are shown to be based on invalid assumptions about the empirical relationships between policy means and ends.

Empirically valid relationships among military actions and political consequences in the war are represented as an interrelated set of time-lagged statistical equations in linear multiple regression form. These equations are used as the model for a computer simulation of the Vietnam War that makes predictions on a monthly basis of all the military and political variables in the model. These predictions reveal the implications not only of the actual policies that were followed during the war but of alternative policies recommended by both hawks and doves as well.

Finally, a basic political dilemma that confronted leaders on both sides of the war is analyzed theoretically and empirically—the trade-offs they had to make between extending their political power over others and retaining the political support that is the basis of their own power.

Dynamics of the Vietnam War

1

Theories Underlying Hawk and Dove Policy Models

Policy-makers engage in theorizing and model-building: they prefer certain goals and act to achieve them; they perceive relationships between their behavior and their goals; and they predict the expected consequences of alternative actions they consider. Such predictions may be of the form: "If I do A because x_1, x_2, x_3, . . . x_n are the way they are, then outcomes B_1, B_2, B_3, . . . B_n will follow." In short, policy-makers act on the basis of expectations derived from past experience, and these expectations are synthesized into models. The theories and models that can be explicitly analyzed are those that come from the policy-makers' own private and public statements and those inferred from their behavior in different situations.

Policy models that have been asserted by leaders on the same side of the Vietnam War are in some cases as different from each other as they are from those of leaders on the other side. Policy-makers have been divided in their views of the relationships between means and ends in the war. Two basic orientations toward the conflict that have emerged on each side are popularly referred to as "hawk" and "dove."

Hawk and dove policy models are folk theories about international behavior in a limited conflict that contain simplified versions of certain psychological and behavioral theories. In particular, these policy models are related to theories of political behavior. "Politics" can be partially defined as the distribution of values over which there is conflict, "power" as the process of achieving values by changing or continuing (i.e., controlling) the behavior of those with whom one is in conflict. In international relations, because legitimate authority is rarely recognized, the behavior of another actor is changed either by obtaining his voluntary compliance through the use of persuasion or bargaining or his involuntary compliance through the use of coercion. Against this theoretical background hawk and dove policy models can be seen as competing theories of behavior compliance and modification: the hawk model emphasizes controlling the adversary's behavior by threatening or using coercive punishments; the dove model emphasizes the use of promises and rewards, including self-restraint, to attain voluntary compliance.

Both theories predict the consequences of escalating or deescalating hostile actions against an adversary. Both assume a limited conflict in which it is not military capability but the *will* to pursue policy objectives by coercive means that determines behavior and outcomes. Thus, hawk and dove models deal with questions of commitments to strategic goals, not battlefield tactics. In a battlefield situation the application of superior military force to destroy an enemy's manpower and weaponry may well be the most efficacious means of controlling an adversary. In a protracted, limited war, as in Vietnam, however, it is not possible to destroy the enemy's total military strength because of physical and political reasons. It is not necessary to destroy a country in order to defeat it. Even major wars have involved losses of less than 11 percent of the total population of the warring nations—not enough to render a country ineffective but, demonstrably, enough to convince the leaders to stop the fighting.[1] The implicit rules of limited wars limit destruction of the enemy's military capabilities even more. Thus, the most central concerns of the conduct and termination of limited wars are issues of will, commitment to political objectives, and other psychological factors in decision-making and conflict behavior.

The major theoretical focus of hawk and dove models is similar to that of deterrence theory. The main difference is that hawk and dove policy models of limited wars are concerned with how to diminish and end a war once one is involved in one—the hawks by winning it, the doves by stopping it to end the violence—whereas deterrence theory is concerned primarily with preventing a war from starting. Prior to involvement in a war, the primary concern of dove models also is how to avoid war, whereas hawk models are more concerned with how wars might be used to achieve desired goals.

Once involved in a limited war, the hawk theory predicts that escalation will *reduce* an enemy's hostile behavior. The dove theory predicts that escalating one's own hostile actions will *increase* the enemy's. The dove theory maintains that to persuade an adversary to reduce his hostile actions, one must reduce one's own toward him. The hawk theory asserts that such deescalation would only lead the enemy to take advantage of the respite and escalate his hostilities.

Both theories contain crucial assumptions and hypotheses about how people behave in a limited conflict. To understand the theoretical bases of these policies, let us look briefly at the simplified versions of some general theories of human behavior that are contained in the hawk and dove policy models.

LEARNING, STRESS, AND EXCHANGE THEORIES

Hawk and dove policy models draw upon simplified versions of three general theories of human behavior: learning theory, stress theory, and exchange theory.

The main assumption drawn from *stress theory* is that a person acts to reduce stresses, tensions, and pressures that result when external conditions upset his equilibrium. This theory pays particular attention to "irrational" behavior, in which relief from tension, rather than maximization of values, is sought. Examples of stress theories are Howard and Scott's[2] theory of the stress resulting from being unable to cope with a problem, and frustration-aggression theory, in which frustration is conceptualized as tension due to blocked impulses.[3] Stress theory explains one major motivation of behavior.

From *learning theory* (in particular, operant-conditioning) hawk and dove models take the assumption that people modify their behavior on the basis of their past experience. They perform more and more frequently behavior associated with subsequent rewards and perform less and less frequently behavior associated with subsequent punishments. What constitutes a reward or punishment may be inherent in the individual[4] or group or established by external norms.[5]

In some of their hypotheses hawk and dove models implicitly assume rational actors. *Exchange theory* is a variant of the rational theories of human behavior, which provide still another explanation of what motivates behavior. Rational theories assume that people try to get at the least cost more of what they value. People are assumed to have sets of goals consistently ordered in terms of their relative value to the individual. People pursue goals through the exchange of actions that each values differently. In trying to obtain these goals, people make comprehensive searches for all possible instrumental actions (subject to time and information costs), calculate the probabilities of each action's success, and then select the action or set of actions that maximizes the values of the actor. Exchange theory assumes interaction between two or more rational actors. Goals sought are instrumental or terminal, and include compliance, power, status, wealth, knowledge, loyalty, and well-being.[6]

These three general theories in their simplified forms are similar and complementary in many respects. All three posit that people act in order to obtain something they want (rewards, values, or relief from stress) and to avoid or minimize things they do not want (punishments, stresses, or costs). Thus, all three theories assume that human behavior is purposive. The motivating mechanisms in the three theories are similar conceptually. Increasing a stress can be considered punishing; reducing a stress (or any other punishment), rewarding.

The hawk and dove versions of these theories posit that the acts of one side in a conflict that are negatively valued by the other (e.g., hostile or violent acts) are stress-producing or punishing. The behavior of the punished side would then tend to be extinguished, because people seek to avoid punishment (according to learning theory) and minimize costs or negative values (exchange theory). Similarly, positively valued acts (e.g., those perceived as friendly) can be considered stress-reducing or rewarding. Behavior thus rewarded would tend to be reinforced and repeated, because people seek rewards, to reduce stress, and to maximize values. In general, hawk and dove models consider rewards and punishments to be political, military, or economic.

These three basic theories are not altogether compatible. A major difference lies in their predictions concerning human behavior in a conflict. Stress theory hypothesizes that a person under severe stress is not likely to make a rational choice, because high degrees of stress impair the ability to learn, to order priorities consistently, to perceive accurately, and to seek and consider all relevant information. Thus, under conditions of high stress, it is possible that an individual would choose an action that increased rather than decreased the punishment he experienced. Exchange theory, as a theory of rational action, assumes that goals will be consistently ordered, regardless of the amount of stress. Learning theory assumes that all relevant information about contingent rewards and punishments is present.

These three general theories explain different aspects of behavior, and thus their theoretical assumptions are different. Learning theory assumes there are few behavior alternatives, but that rewards can vary greatly. Rational theories, on the other hand, assume a great number of possible behaviors, but a restricted number of rewards. Ideally, one would like to combine these theories into a more general theory containing many behavior alternatives and many reward alternatives. Hawk and dove models draw upon a simplified version of such a combined general theory.

It is not surprising that folk theories have adopted simplified versions of general behavioral theories, for educated policy-makers have had some exposure to the formal theories. Prescriptive rational decision-making models, for example, have been explicitly held as a norm by some U.S. policy-makers, and systems analysis and operations research have been incorporated into some aspects of military policy-making. In addition, exponents of rational theories believe they should be applied in policy-making. Leading learning theorists (e.g., B. F. Skinner) have asserted that learning theory can be applied to human behavior.[7] Osgood claims that people can learn reinforcement contingencies. A first actor can condition the behavior of a second by making his behavior contingent upon that of the second. This principle can be applied to the deescalation of a conflict.[8]

In using parts of learning, stress, and exchange theories, hawk and dove policy models, assume that the actor is a unit, conceived as a policy-making group or individual leader who chooses actions for the nation. Moreover, it is assumed that the behavior of one actor is responsive to the behavior of another actor. These assumptions of responsive unitary actors do not explicitly take into account other plausible explanations of national decision-making and action, especially those that consider complex organizational processes and bureaucratic and domestic politics.[9] The use of learning, exchange, and stress theories to explain and predict the behavior of unitary national actors assumes that the stresses, values, rewards, and punishments ascribed to the unitary actor are more important in determining national behavior than the interests of lower-level bureaucrats and politicians. No theoretical conceptualization is "true" in a metaphysical sense. The purpose of constructing a theory is to derive explanations and predictions the validity of which can then be tested against the facts. Hawk and dove models assume unitary responsive national actors. The following analyses make this same assumption in order to test the adequacy of these models.

THEORETICAL EXPLANATIONS OF INTERACTION

Hawk and dove models not only use simplified versions of learning, stress, and exchange theories to explain what motivates and conditions a single actor's behavior, but they also use the notion of linking the behavior of two or more actors to explain dynamic interaction. The behavior of each actor is considered a stimulus to the other actor, and each is conceptualized as responding to the behavior of the other. It will be useful to review briefly the theoretical concepts of interaction upon which the simplified hawk and dove folk theories are based, and how the concepts derived from learning, stress, and exchange theories are incorporated into theories of conflict interaction.

Stimulus-Response Models

In the simplest *models*, international conflict is conceptualized as a fight. An actor is considered to react without thinking to the attack of another actor who is trying to control his behavior. He responds to hostility with increased hostility, and a combative cycle ensues.[10]

In a fight both self and mutual control is diminished in a spiraling pattern of escalation. This process can be represented as a simple reciprocated stimulus-response pattern, i.e., each actor's behavioral response is a stimulus to the other actor: Stimulus from Actor A → Response from Actor B (= Stimulus) → Response from Actor A, and so on.

Since this process is conceived as automatic, with the actions of each actor serving as starting points for the opposing actor's counter-actions, each step in a fight should be predictable (increasingly violent actions), and only rising costs or destruction of one or both of the actors could terminate the fight.

Mediated Stimulus-Response Models

The second general type of model, the *mediated stimulus-response model*, includes the class of variables included in learning, stress, and exchange theories. Explanations of the relationship between the behavior to which an actor is subjected and the behavior that actor subsequently exhibits include characteristics of the actor. The simplest representation of this model is the S-O-R paradigm, which indicates that response (R) is affected by the stimulus (S) as mediated by attributes of the actor or organism (O) producing the response.[11]

Since the theories most relevant to policy-making conceive of the individual decision-maker as the actor or "organism" in the S-O-R paradigm of international conflict, these theories emphasize psychological attributes as mediating factors, including perception, evaluation, intention, and learning.[12]

Two synthetic concepts that summarize many of the psychological functions attributed to individual decision-makers in the S-O-R model have been developed by Thomas and Znaniecki[13] and refined by March and Simon,[14] Snyder et al.,[15] and Brody.[16] These are the "definition of the situation" and the "definition of policy."

In *defining the situation*, an actor observes his environment (including the behavior of other actors) and receives information from it (including communications from other actors). He decodes and interprets this information, and forms an image of the environment and the actors in it congruent with his past experience. This process is affected by the actor's values, personality traits, past experience, learning, memory, and situational factors such as stress, threat, and time constraints.

In *defining policy*, an actor is motivated to achieve what he perceives as desirable and to avoid what he considers undesirable. The motivations are a function of the actors' habits, values, perceptions of possible success, and specific incentives.[17] An actor selects actions on the basis of perceived associations between specific behaviors and desired rewards[18] in order to narrow the gap between the situations preferred and the ones perceived.[19]

In both definition of situation and definition of policy, perception plays a key role in determining an actor's response to a given stimulus. Misperception of a stimulus, such as the behavior of the adversary, may lead an actor to respond inappropriately to the stimulus.[20]

One source of misperception is cognitive rigidity.[21] For example, a dogmatic unchanging image of an enemy leads to inaccurate perceptions of his behavior or his intentions. An enemy might attempt to deescalate a conflict, but that attempt may not be perceived because of an unchanging hostile image of that enemy. Thus, policy-makers might fail to respond to peaceful overtures and instead increase the intensity of their violent behavior.

In their studies on the outbreak of World War I, Holsti, North, and Brody[22] and Zinnes[23] found that policy-makers on one side perceived the behavior of their adversary to be more hostile or threatening than it was intended to be. This misperception led to increased hostile intent and more violent behavior. When this misperception occurred on both sides of the conflict, an escalating conflict spiral ensued. This process may be diagrammed as in Figure 1, in which misperception

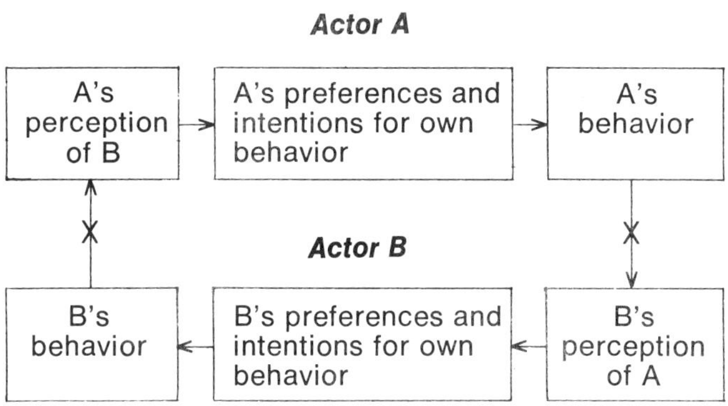

Figure 1. Misperception Leading to Escalation

is indicated by an arrow broken by an X. Thus, misperceptions can be not only perpetuated but magnified and built upon when they occur on both sides of a conflict.

Other mediating factors include bureaucratic commitments. Policies made within the framework of large bureaucratic organizations tend to be relatively resistant to change. Bureaucrats have their own interests dependent on policies to which they have committed themselves, e.g., officers in the U.S. Air Force are generally committed to the use of air power. Even if a deescalation by North Vietnam were accurately perceived by top policy-makers, preferences in the U.S. Air Force for continued use of air power would make a cessation of all bombing less likely.

The intervening variables represented by the "O" in the S-O-R model clearly make for a more comprehensive and valid representation of reality. As will be shown, hawk and dove models sometimes incorporate such mediating factors. The importance attached to these factors, especially to enemy perceptions and preferences, however, affects the ability of hawk and dove models to explain interactions.

Linked Mediated Stimulus-Response Models

Linked mediated stimulus-response models ($S_A \rightarrow O_A \rightarrow R_A \rightarrow S_B \rightarrow O_B \rightarrow R_B$) also take interdependence into account. Rapoport[24] theorizes that in a "game" the outcome of a conflict depends not only upon the outputs or attributes of either actor but also on their interdependent expectations of what the opponent's behavior in a given situation will be. When both actors in a "prisoner's dilemma" game try to maximize their own values by exploiting the other's cooperation, the empirical result is a long series of exploiting choices by both actors in which neither cooperates with the other.[25] The effect is analogous to escalation that leads to counterescalation, in which neither side is willing to risk cooperation because each fears exploitation by the other.

Another model of interaction[26] consists of a pair of simultaneous differential equations of the form $dx/dt = ky - ax + g$ and $dy/dt = lx - by + h$. Richardson was concerned with the rate of increase in arms budgets, but one could substitute armed hostilities. The rate of increase in hostilities is a function of the sensitivity (k and l) of one actor to the other actor's level of hostility, times that level (x and y), minus a fatigue or cost factor (a and b), times the current level of each actor's own hostile behavior (x and y), plus the amount of grievance toward the other actor or commitment to political goals (g and h). Richardson's concepts of sensitivity and grievance, which in his model determine the course of the interaction, are similar to mediating psychological factors conceptualized by other theorists.

The parameters k or l in the Richardson equations could theoretically represent perception as well as sensitivity or propensity to react to enemy behavior. Boulding[27] has shown in an analysis of the Richardson equations that the rate of increase in hostility depends upon this reaction coefficient. Lagerstrom,[28] in an analysis of simultaneous differential equation models of the Richardson type, has demonstrated that a spiraling arms race or escalation of hostilities will occur when the product of the reaction coefficients of the two sides in a conflict is greater than one. Thus, an explanation of escalating conflict behavior predicted in the Richardson model is misperception of the behavior of the adversary. This interpretation of the parameters k and l of the Richardson model is more satisfying than one in which there is a parameter with no empirical referent, because perception is a concept that can be operationalized and measured.[29]

A model proposed by North[30] represents most of the mediating variables posited by the foregoing theorists: S (stimulus) → r (perception or definition of the situation) → s (preference or definition of policy) → R (response). This theoretically comprehensive model of conflict interaction forms the basis for a synthesized mediated stimulus-response model of the escalation of the Vietnam War diagrammed in figure 2. The conceptual components of the "definition of the situation" and the "definition of policy" are indicated for only one actor. In this diagram each actor in the conflict is conceptually linked to the other through outcomes that are dependent upon the behavior of both, and through each actor's perceptions of outcomes and of the behavior of the other actor. Reflecting the work of the theorists mentioned above, this S-O-R model was constructed as an example of the theoretical factors that must be taken into account to explain the dynamics of interaction.

Given the nature of the data publicly available, including the formerly top-secret "Pentagon Papers," it is impossible to operationalize and to test systematically all the links in this model, particularly the relationships among the psychological variables. However, this synthesized model of mediating mechanisms operating in dynamic interaction is an example of the way in which the complexity of conflict interactions can be represented, and provides a comparison to the theoretically simpler hawk and dove policy models. Keeping in mind this brief discussion of the simplified versions of learning, stress, and exchange theories and of general models of dynamic interaction, we shall now turn to the specific details of hawk and dove models as they relate to escalation and deescalation.

HAWK AND DOVE POLICY MODELS

The hawk policy prescription for reducing enemy violence in a limited war has been to increase one's own violent actions. The hawks' hypothesis is that, in the face of escalated violence, the enemy's motivation to continue the war at an intensified level will be reduced. The theoreti-

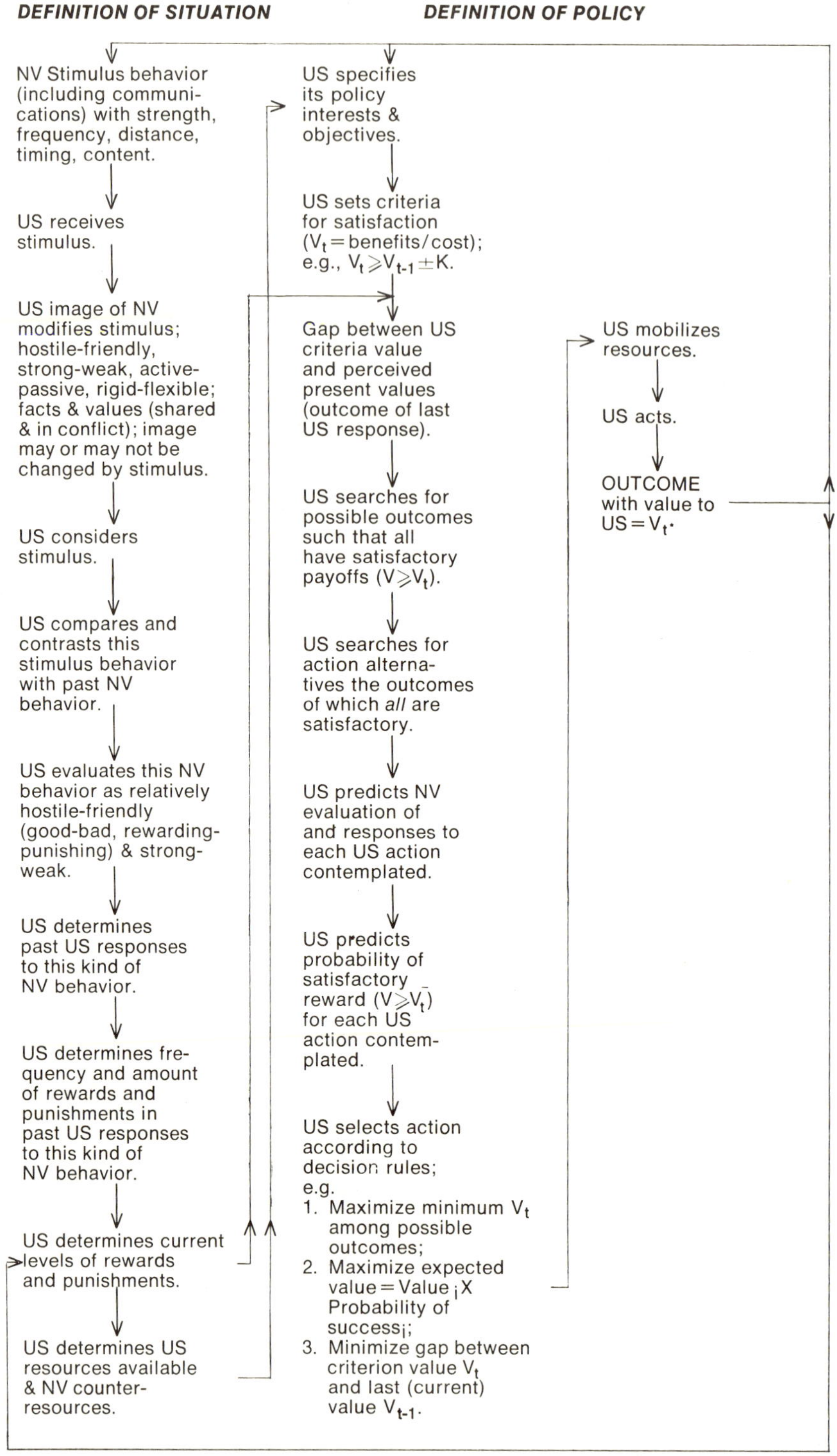

Figure 2: Synthesized Mediated Stimulus-Response Model

cal reason for an enemy to deescalate is that beyond some tolerable point the punishment, stress, and costs resulting from the escalated violence would, in the enemy's mind, outweigh any possible future reward (e.g., future political control over disputed territory and people). Thus, following learning theory as well as exchange theory, the hawks hypothesize that in the face of overwhelming punishment the enemy's violent behavior will be extinguished. The hawks assume that the enemy will make the same evaluation of punishments and rewards regarding the violence to which it is subjected and the worth of its political objectives as would the actor applying the punishment in the same situation.

The dove policy model maintains that, to reduce enemy violence, one should reduce one's own violent actions toward him; for even though an enemy's capabilities to engage in violence will remain intact, his motivation to use them will be reduced. Theoretically, by deescalating violence against an enemy, one reduces the punishments, stresses, and costs he bears. From the viewpoint of exchange theory, such a reduction induces an enemy to deescalate his own hostile efforts because he can continue to pursue his long-range political objectives, but at less cost to himself, if he reduces his own hostile efforts. The dove's hypothesis is that the enemy will act to be cost/effective, and therefore continue to reciprocate a deescalation of hostilities.

From the viewpoint of learning theory, reciprocal deescalation is relatively rewarding to an enemy and to oneself (less punishment is inflicted upon both and both can pursue their own objectives using relatively less effort and fewer resources). As each side reduces its hostilities still further in response to its enemy's decreasing violence, these reductions would become mutually reinforcing.[31]

The dove policy model has two different sets of basic assumptions: one is strictly normative, the other is empirical and pragmatic. Different doves consider their importance differently. The basic normative assumption of the dove policy model is: (1) violence is morally wrong. Other more pragmatic assumptions of the dove model are: (2) increased violence is ineffective in changing the behavior of an enemy because potential political power is more rewarding to him than present or anticipated increases in hostile actions are punishing to him; (3) actors can be flexible about their political objectives and hostile behavior; (4) political objectives are not worth unnecessary costs; (5) attempts to recoup past losses are not worth additional costs; (6) mutual reduction of violence is desirable and advantageous to both sides; and (7) an enemy will recognize a unilateral attempt to deescalate violence as an implicit bargaining bid for him to reciprocate. The dove model therefore assumes that it is better and more rational to minimize violence and costs to both sides as long as a conflict continues.

A basic theoretical counter-hypothesis that the hawk model makes is that the doves' proposal to reduce one's own violence in order to reduce the enemy's reduces the enemy's stresses, punishments, and costs, and thus constitutes a relative reward for his *current* behavior (at the current level of violence, rather than at the reduced level), gives him the impression he is succeeding, and reinforces that behavior. Thus, the hawks maintain, the enemy would continue the existing level of hostilities, taking advantage of a unilateral reduction of violence.

The dove model counters this argument by maintaining that the enemy will not view a reduction in punishment to be a reward for his current violent behavior, because he will realize that he can have the relatively more valuable reward of being able to continue striving for his goal in a most cost/effective way if he reduces the level of his violent behavior. Continuing to strive for a goal, but at reduced costs, the doves argue, would be perceived by the enemy as more valuable than some temporary gain derived from exploiting a deescalation, for such exploitation would surely lead to reescalation, and therefore lose its value very quickly.

The doves go on to criticize the hawk model for its unrealistic assumptions about the enemy's motivations and calculations: first, for considering that strongly held long-term national commitments are of less value than the material costs and stresses of war presently endured; and second, for assuming that the enemy will value its past commitments and costs less than its present punishments when deciding whether to discontinue its behavior because of current punishments.

The hawks criticize the dove model for assuming that the enemy will be subjectively hurt less than oneself if commitments and costs are increased, and also for assuming that the enemy will accurately perceive the intent of deescalation as an effort to decrease violence on both sides, rather than as a trick or as a sign of a basic weakness to be exploited.

The doves counter that this problem can be dealt with through diplomatic channels, and that the hawk position too may assume inaccurate perception on the part of the enemy. For example, the increase in stress accompanying escalated violence may lead the enemy to misperceive the balance of capabilities, and the increased punishment incite him to renew his determination and counterescalate in continued pursuit of his long-range objectives.

The doves have still more theoretical reasons for criticizing the hawk proposal that escalation will cause the enemy to deescalate. It may be true that when an enemy is punished for a given level of armed hostility, his violent behavior *at that level* will be extinguished. However, in a limited war that has already escalated, it is unlikely that the enemy will give up his ultimate political objective. Therefore, in the face of escalation that makes the achievement of his goal more distant, it is more likely that his violent behavior at the current level will be extinguished, and his efforts *escalated* if he perceives he has the capability to do so. Therefore, instead of deescalating, the enemy may either try harder in the same mode of behavior, or try something else. ("Something else" may include shifting from conventional to protracted war, e.g., to terrorism, assassination, and guerrilla attacks; shifting the site of combat, e.g., to Cambodia, Laos, or North Vietnam; or shifting the major combatants in the war, e.g., "Vietnamization"). Only when all else fails is it likely that the long-range political objective will be given up. Thus the question of which side has more "will" is dependent upon a comparison of the basic long-term political commitments of both sides.

A major distinction between the two policy models is what each considers to be of paramount importance in a violent conflict. As noted above, many doves assume that the reduction of violence is good in itself, and that policy objectives can be pursued through less violent means. Many doves further maintain that mutual violence is ineffective, and therefore senseless. Hawks assume that achieving policy objectives is most important, even if violence has to be used to do this. Moreover, the hawk model usually maintains that superior force will be effective in achieving policy objectives. The hawks perceive conflict as a zero-sum game: "If you win the objective (political power or territory), I lose it" (although in the Vietnam War "winning" was sometimes defined as "not losing"). Doves perceive conflict as containing a major non-zero-sum element: "If we both reduce our violence, we will both be better off."

The potential intensity of violence is a major factor in determining whether reducing conflict is considered valuable in itself. Most people consider the avoidance of a thermonuclear war to be a good in itself or a positive-sum benefit. There is less agreement about the value of avoiding violence in a limited war, especially when hawks perceive not only a positive value (the political objective) to be gained by fighting, but the additional value of possibly deterring similar wars (e.g., other wars of national liberation) or another war with the same adversary. The dove model makes an assumption analogous to that of deterrence theory, which states that mutual annihilation is less preferable than any other policy objective (save possibly being annihilated alone).

A further distinction between hawks and doves is what they intend

2

Data

The first step in the empirical analysis of alternative policy models is to construct quantitative indices to measure the concepts in the policy-makers' models and in the theoretical models of the war with which we shall deal. Some of these indices are single variables, others are weighted sums of two or more variables. The indices were constructed to obtain reliable and valid indicators of theoretical concepts, to transform certain information into a form appropriate for quantitative analysis, and to make the models and analysis more parsimonious.

The monthly data used in this study were chosen to represent military strength, military efforts, consequences of these efforts, political support, and public communications of leading policy-makers that express their perceptions and preferences regarding the war. The data are all public and thus allow independent analysis.[1] The data are limited, however. Some information of theoretical interest has probably never been collected; some necessary data are simply not available; and as revealed by the unusual publication of the *Pentagon Papers*[2] in the summer of 1971, some of the most relevant information has been classified secret by the U.S. government. This classified information includes the policy analysis and written thoughts of government officials as well as military data combined for geographical units within South Vietnam.

Nonetheless, the available data are rich enough to analyze the most significant aspects of the war; the escalation and counterescalation of commitments from 1965 through 1967, the political and military consequences of those commitments, and the change in the course of the war following the Tet offensive in 1968.

The recent availability in the *Pentagon Papers* of documents that were once top secret will help to inform the interpretation of public statements made by top officials in the U.S. government.

CONSTRUCTION OF MILITARY, PUBLIC OPINION, AND SEASONAL INDICES

Valid indicators of theoretical concepts are important to policy-makers as well as to social scientists. For example, the U.S. Department of Defense reportedly constructed an "index of victory" consisting of the numbers of North Vietnamese and Viet Cong killed, hamlets pacified, Communist troops infiltrated and recruited, and miles of roads cleared in South Vietnam (*Wall Street Journal*, 27 Oct. 1967, p. 1). An index of two or more variables is more reliable than a single-variable index because it is less subject to fluctuations due to random error and to the same biases producing nonrandom error. Indices can thus reflect more accurately than individual variables the abstract concept implied in a theory.

Differences and proportional differences between the values of one month and the next, as well as absolute values, are used for all variables except public statements. Differences reflect the incremental nature of decision-making, e.g., the additional number of troops committed in a given month. Increments in hostile behaviors are the components of the general upward trend in hostilities that is termed escalation. The determinants of the size of these increments can be useful in explaining the escalation of the war. The use of proportional differences, a form of logarithmitic transformation of the data, is based on the concept that larger changes in a particular variable—bombing of North Vietnam, for example—are possible once a high-enough level of activity has been reached with the same effort required by smaller changes at lower levels of activity. The addition of 100 bombing sorties over North Vietnam was a major decision in 1964, but a bureaucratic one in 1967. It is more relevant to speak of a 10 percent increase in bombing missions than of the absolute increase.

Variables and Indices of Military Efforts

1. *North Vietnamese and Viet Cong military strength* is represented by *troop levels*. Recruitment and infiltration are indicated by the *change* from one month to the next in the reported number of Viet Cong and North Vietnamese troops in South Vietnam, including main force divisions, regiments, and battalions, Viet Cong guerrilla platoons, Viet Cong administrative and logistical personnel, but *not* political cadres or irregular self-defense militia.

2. *United States military effort* is indicated by the changes in U.S. commitments, a weighted sum equal to .025 times the number of U.S. troops in South Vietnam, plus 50 times the number of U.S. ground operations of battalion-size or larger, plus .67 times the number of U.S. bombing sorties over South Vietnam, plus the number of hundreds of short tons of cargo sealifted to South Vietnam by the U.S. Military Sea Transport Service.[3]

3. United States military action is also indicated by the number of *U.S. bombing sorties over North Vietnam*. For 1965 the number of bombing sorties is used. After 1965 the U.S. government reported mis-

sions rather than sorties. Accounts from the field suggest that each mission had an average of three sorties; therefore, for 1966 and 1967, three times the reported number of bombing missions is used.

Like all data used in this study, data on the bombing of North Vietnam come from public sources; these officially released figures, however, may require some qualification. After the bombing was halted in November 1968, it would be expected that more bombing missions would be flown over the South because of the additional planes available. However, the number of bombing sorties over South Vietnam before and after November 1968 is fairly constant, the number remaining about the same as for the previous year. The seasonal pattern in the number of sorties is also consistent with previous years. Since it is now acknowledged that the United States bombed the Laotian part of the Ho Chi Minh trail, one might infer that all or most of the planes that once were used over North Vietnam were shifted to bombing the North Vietnamese in Laos. Otherwise, most of those airplanes would be idle, an unlikely event during a war. Thus, the bombing "halt" of November 1968 appears to have been a geographic shift, rather than a halt. Information is not available as to whether bombing missions over Laos were included in the public statistics on bombing of North Vietnam.

The number of bombing missions at any time depends on the numbers of planes, bombs, and pilots available. Public data on these latter variables, however, are not available. Thus, other variables on which public data are available will be used in the analysis to predict the number of U.S. bombing missions.

Indices of the Consequences of Military Action

4. *U.S. casualties* are measured by ten times the number of U.S. troops killed in action, plus the number of wounded requiring hospitalization, plus half the number wounded not requiring hospitalization.

5. *North Vietnamese and Viet Cong attrition* is measured by 2.5 times the reported number of Communist troops killed, plus 3 times the total number of weapons captured, plus the number of Communists captured.

6. *South Vietnamese casualties* are indicated by four times the total number of South Vietnamese troops reported killed in action (including regular troops of the Army of the Republic of Vietnam [hereafter abbreviated as ARVN], Regional Forces, and Popular Forces) plus the number reported seriously wounded.

7. The *kill ratio*, the number of Viet Cong and North Vietnamese

troops killed in action divided by the number of U.S. plus South Vietnamese troops killed, is an index that the U.S. Department of Defense reportedly used as an indicator of relative progress in the war. The number of "third nation" (e.g., South Korean) troop casualties is not included in this index because these data were not reported for the entire period under study.

Variables and Indices of Political Support

8. *U.S. domestic support for the Johnson administration* is indicated by the difference between the percent who approve and who disapprove of the way Johnson handled his job as president. These data come from the American Institute of Public Opinion and were measured in their "Gallup Poll" each month during the period studied. Gallup Poll data on the way Johnson handled the situation in Vietnam were not available on a monthly basis until July 1965. However, the correlation between disapproval of Johnson's handling of his job as president and of the situation in Vietnam from July 1965 to December 1967 is very high, .89 . Similarly, approval of President Johnson on these two items correlated .80 .

9. Data on the number of *Viet Cong and North Vietnamese defectors* (called *hoi chanh* or "ralliers") were collected by the U.S. Department of Defense and used as an indicator of Communist morale. It is assumed here that the greater the number of defectors, the lower the Communist troop morale.

10. *Confidence in the government of South Vietnam* by the people of that country is one of the key measures of the war's progress. In a "war of national liberation" the achievement of political objectives is primary, and military actions are only a means to winning the confidence of, and control over, the people.

It is very difficult to measure directly the confidence the South Vietnamese people have in their government. In the politically treacherous situation in South Vietnam, people are most reluctant to reveal their true opinions about the government to strangers who might ask direct questions about them, for a stranger might be suspected of being an agent of one side or the other. Thus, we need to develop an unobtrusive measure of popular confidence in the South Vietnamese government (Webb et al., 1966).

The measure used in this study is the value that people in the urban money economy placed on the South Vietnamese government's *piastre* currency in terms of the U.S. dollars it could buy as compared with its value in terms of the goods and services it could buy.

To construct this index, we first take the mid-month selling price (in dollars) of the piastre by hand-payment in the Saigon black market, i.e., dollars/piastre. This represents the value of the piastre in terms of the more stable liquid asset of U.S. dollars. We then adjust this value of the piastre in terms of dollars by the economic factors of money supply (M.S.) and consumer prices (C.P.), i.e., the value of the piastre in terms of goods and services.

The purchasing power or value of one piastre in terms of goods and services is 1/Consumer Prices. Thus, according to the quantity theory of money (Friedman, 1968), in an underdeveloped country like South Vietnam, the total value in goods and services of all piastres circulating in the domestic economy is Money Supply/Consumer Prices, i.e., M.S./C.P.

As American personnel and dollars in South Vietnam increased, the money supply in South Vietnam increased, driving up consumer prices because of increased demand for South Vietnamese goods and services, and thus also tending to decrease the value of the piastre in terms of goods and services. The American influx also had the effect of increasing demand for the piastre, since purchases of goods and services were made in piastres.

When we take the ratio of the black market dollar value of the piastre, i.e., (Dollars/Piastre), to the total value of the piastre money supply in the economy, i.e., (Money Supply/Consumer Prices), we have the relative preference of the South Vietnamese people for the liquid asset of U.S. dollars as compared with their preference for goods and services. Since people can more easily flee with their wealth in the form of dollars than as goods and services, the assumption of this measure is that the less confidence the South Vietnamese people have in their government, the greater the proportion of their wealth they will tend to hold in U.S. dollars and the smaller the proportion of their wealth they will prefer to hold as goods and services. Therefore, the measure used in this study is:

$$\textit{Popular Confidence} = \left(\frac{\textit{Dollars}}{\textit{Piastre}}\right) \bigg/ \left(\frac{\textit{Money Supply}}{\textit{Consumer Prices}}\right)$$

or the equivalent,

$$\left(\frac{\textit{Dollars}}{\textit{Piastre}}\right) \times \left(\frac{\textit{Consumer Prices}}{\textit{Money Supply}}\right)$$

This index is correlated .92 with the black market value of the piastre over the sixty-nine-month period from January 1965 through September 1970.

Data on the black market value of the piastre are quoted at least twice monthly by financial firms in Hong Kong who have agents in Saigon. These data are publicly available and were collected from a money dealer in San Francisco. Data on South Vietnamese consumer prices and money supply are publicly available in various issues of the *International Financial Statistics* published by the International Monetary Fund.

Indices of Seasonal Changes

The Vietnam War was affected by seasonal variations. Monsoon or dry weather affected the number of U.S. bombing missions, the number of ground operations either side could initiate, and the movement of troops and supplies from North Vietnam to South Vietnam. Ideally, one would like to test with local rainfall and cloud data the degree to which season affected military activities in various parts of Vietnam. However, public local weather data for North Vietnam are not available. Although regional weather data are available for the South, they are not useful for correlation with activities in North Vietnam, since the monsoon seasons in North and South Vietnam do not coincide. Moreover, regional weather variations cannot be correlated with the data on military activities combined at the national levels, the only military activity data publicly available.

11-12. In lieu of actual weather data throughout the war, four "dummy" variables are used to represent seasonal variations. The first two dummy variables are called *winter-summer* and *spring-fall*, and are represented by sine curves given the monthly values shown in table 1.

13. The third dummy variable, a seasonal variable corresponding to the *best flying weather over North Vietnam*, is represented by the following values: July = 1, August = 3, September = 1, remaining months = 0.

14. The fourth is a dummy variable reflecting the *holiday activities* of Christmas and Tet: December = 1, January = 2, remaining months = 0.

CONSTRUCTION OF INDICES OF PUBLIC POLICY STATEMENTS

Public statements made by major policy-makers in the United States, South Vietnam, North Vietnam, and the National Liberation Front

TABLE 1

WINTER-SUMMER AND SPRING-FALL VARIABLES USED TO REPRESENT SEASONAL CHANGES

	Jan.	Feb.	Mar.	Apr.	May	June
Winter-Summer	10.0	8.65	5.0	0.0	-5.0	-8.65
Spring-Fall	0.0	5.0	8.65	10.0	8.65	5.0
	July	Aug.	Sept.	Oct.	Nov.	Dec.
Winter-Summer	-10.0	-8.65	-5.0	0.0	5.0	8.65
Spring-Fall	0.0	-5.0	-8.65	-10.0	-8.65	-5.0

comprise the communications data. All statements made during the years 1965, 1966, and 1967 that appeared in the *New York Times Index* were content-analyzed according to a coding scheme in which speakers' *preferences* and *perceptions* concerning forty-one separate items were separately recorded. The coding scheme (presented in Appendix A) measures on an ordinal scale the speakers' public preferences for increasing, continuing unchanged, or decreasing the particular behaviors or events referred to in the statements. Speakers' perceptions of these same behaviors or events were also measured on an ordinal scale as certainly decreasing, possible decreasing, remaining unchanged, possibly increasing, or certainly increasing. These data were collected on a daily basis and combined into monthly totals. For the three years (1965 through 1967) 1,857 separate statements, including 3,941 specific perceptions and preferences, were coded.

The forty-one topics were combined into the following eight communication indices: (1) North Vietnamese and Viet Cong leaders' preferences regarding their own military and political activities; (2) their perceptions of U.S. and South Vietnamese military and political activities; (3) their preferences for negotiation; (4) their preferences for particular outcomes and goals; (5) U.S. and South Vietnamese leaders' perceptions of North Vietnamese and Viet Cong military and political activities; (6) their preferences regarding their own military and political activities; (7) their preferences for negotiation; and (8) their preferences for particular outcomes and goals. The components of these communications indices are fully described in Appendix B.

These indices are sums of measures on those of the forty-one specific items relevant to each of the eight general topics. Depending upon the nature of the statement, either the frequency of statement, the frequency times the typical comment, or the frequency times the difference between preference and perception is used as the measure. For example, the United States never expressed a preference for increasing North Vietnamese troop strength in South Vietnam. However, the *frequency* of statements preferring decreased North Vietnamese troop strength is indicative of the salience of North Vietnamese troops to the U.S. decision-makers. Many topics were discussed too infrequently to permit adequate measures of perceptions or preferences.

The coding of preferences and perceptions as ordinal values raises the problem of combining them with the interval data derived from counting the frequency of each topic. The problem was minimized, however, in several ways. First, the coder of the public statements was instructed to evaluate the strength of preference or perception as a linear continuum. Second, because only three or five ordinal classifications were used, the ordinal-to-interval transition is reasonable. Third, several measures were combined into a single index; thus, errors were not systematic and could be expected to cancel each other. Treating the perception and preference indices as if they were interval data allows the use of the product-moment correlation and regression analysis when relating these communications indices with other interval data, such as military casualties.

RELIABILITY AND VALIDITY OF THE DATA

As in any empirical research, there is some "slippage" between the theoretical concepts and their operationalization. The main question is whether the variables are valid measures of the theoretical concepts. Confidence in the validity of the "hard" data (i.e., military actions and Gallup Poll data) is greatest; however, even these are not above question. The military data, since they come from unclassified sources, may cover up what was "really" happening; as in the previously cited example, data on U.S. bombing of North Vietnam may have included bombing of the Ho Chi Minh Trail in Laos as well. However, to the extent that policy-makers themselves relied on the data used in this study, the pragmatic validity of the data is enhanced. For example, even if the number of Communist troops in South Vietnam was inaccurate (and there is evidence that these figures were rough estimates), if the Johnson administration responded to those figures by deciding to increase U.S. military strength, then even those inaccurate data should help explain U.S. behavior. An additional problem is that the public military data on Vietnam are aggregated for the whole country, an aggregation that may cover up differences in the type of warfare in specific locales: guerrilla war in some areas, conventional war in others, and some combination of the two in still other areas.

There is also the problem of deliberately falsified information. One particular variable should be mentioned in this regard, since it occurs so often in general discussion of the subject: the number of Viet Cong and North Vietnamese troops reported killed may be exaggerated, as have been estimates of enemy casualties in most wars. There may be a tendency by U.S. forces to count all Vietnamese killed who were not part of the South Vietnamese armed forces as "enemy." "Body counts" were not often literally that, according to independent observers. Double counting frequently occurred, and sheer guesses were often made by artillery crews and bomber pilots. On the other hand, there were no doubt Viet Cong and North Vietnamese killed by bombs or artillery shells who were never counted. General Giap, the North Vietnamese defense minister, reportedly remarked to a correspondent for the Milanese magazine *L'Europeo* that 500,000 North Vietnamese had been killed in the entire war through the spring of 1969, a figure that was very close to the U.S. government tally of 500,509 North Vietnamese and Viet Cong killed from 1 January 1961 to 30 May 1969 (Ayres, *New York Times*, 1 June 1969).

These data need not be absolutely accurate to be useful, however. In this research trends over time are of interest and importance. Thus, relative changes from month to month are probably more significant than absolute numbers. In addition Communists reported killed and American casualties (a more reliable figure) correlate .92 within the same month. Both variables indicate the intensity of the fighting, and deaths resulting from firefights probably are proportional over the long term. If one wishes, then, to ignore Communist casualty figures, the intensity of the war during this period can still be measured by counting U.S. and South Vietnamese casualties.

Despite the difficulties mentioned above, the validity problems posed by the hard data are relatively minor. For the military variables the operational definition is very close to the conceptual definition, e.g., military effort. Gaps between operational measures and concepts are larger in the political support variables. That the number of Viet Cong defectors indicates Communist morale has face validity; but it is, admittedly, based on intuition. The use of the Saigon black market value of the piastre, adjusted for consumer prices and money supply, as an indicator of the popular confidence in the government of South Vietnam is a more indirect measure. The reasoning behind the use of the adjusted piastre value is that an indirect measure of people's confidence in a government is how much they value its paper currency as compared to some more universal standard of wealth. Both of these indicators do, however, provide "unobtrusive measures," which Webb and his associates (1966) have convincingly demonstrated to be superior to more direct measures, such as survey questions, especially when a normative response bias can be anticipated. In the treacherous political situation in South Vietnam, the most invalid measure of popular support for either side is probably the direct survey question, which has been used by CBS News (CBS News, 1967) and the U.S. Information Agency.

The communications data pose even more serious problems. The reliability of the content analysis is open to question because the tabulation of statements is based to some extent on the subjective judgment of the coder. Initially, two coders independently coded a subsample of the communications. On this small subsample 100 percent agreement was achieved. Thereafter, a single coder coded the statements from the *New York Times Index*. The great volume of the work (1,857 separate statements) made it impractical for a second coder to code all the statements.

The publication of the "Pentagon Papers" has brought into serious question the validity of the public statements of preferences and perceptions of U.S. leaders. One might speculate that the public statements of the leaders of North and South Vietnam are equally misleading. One of the most significant revelations of the "Pentagon Papers" is that U.S. leaders consciously attempted to keep the truth about their deepening involvement in the Vietnam War from the American people, press, Congress, and foreign allies, as well as from the foe in Vietnam. The "Pentagon Papers" are themselves an incomplete set of secret government documents during the Vietnam War, for the papers came principally from sources in, or in contact with, the Office of the Secretary of Defense. Later memoirs, diaries, secret documents, and transcripts of private meetings and telephone conversations from other parts of the U.S. government, especially the Office of the President, will no doubt reveal much more about the thinking that formed Vietnam policy.

However, the public statements of policy-makers on both sides of the war are not without value. These are the statements to which the public responded, on which world opinion focused, and to which the opposing side paid at least some attention. It is thus of interest to see what relationship these public statements of perceptions and preferences had to actual behaviors and outcomes of the war.

1. The source of the military data is table 6, Unclassified Statistics on Southeast Asia, U.S. Department of Defense, Office of Assistant Secretary of Defense (Comptroller), Directorate for Information Operations. These data are the only public complete time series on military activities in the war. They are selective in the choice of activities measured and reported, and may be biased. They do represent the Defense Department's view of what was happening in the war. The use of these data for research and policy evaluation is in no way an endorsement of the activities reported in the data.

Computer-readable copies of any data used in this study will be made available by the author to readers or researchers requesting them. Requests should be addressed to International Relations Archive, Inter-University Consortium for Political Research, P.O. Box 1248, Ann Arbor, Michigan 48106.

2. The *Pentagon Papers* as published in the *New York Times* (New York: Bantam Books, Inc., 1971). Subsequent citations will appear in the text, abbreviated to "NYT, *PP*," with page references.

3. Since the impact of each component of an index is proportional to the variance due to that component and not due to the mean, weightings are chosen so that the product of weighting and standard deviation are of the relative magnitude desired for each component in the index. This procedure accounts for some of the unusual coefficients. The weightings are the subjective judgments of the researcher.

3

Methods

Four techniques of data analysis are used in this study.

GRAPHS

All variables were graphed through time and against each other. These graphs facilitate the visual recognition of patterns in the data. The human eye and brain are superior to computers for recognizing patterns, discrete and continuous, linear and nonlinear. For example, visual inspection of the time plots reveals that there were three phases of the Vietnam War from 1965 through 1967: January–November 1965, December 1965–January 1967, and February–December 1967. During each phase the minimum monthly casualty figures are higher than the maximum casualties of the previous period. In January 1968 a new phase began with the Tet offensive.

CORRELATIONS AND SERIAL CORRELATIONS

The second analytic technique is the calculation of correlations among the variables, including reciprocal time lags and leads. Variations in one variable may be systematically related to variations in another variable, with no delay or with a delay of some given amount of time. For example, not only is the relationship between U.S. bombing and Communist troop commitments in the same month examined, but also the relationship of bombing to the commitment rate in a subsequent month. If bombing affected North Vietnamese troop commitments, the effect would not be observed until later months because of the time required—as long as five months—for troops to go from North to South Vietnam.

In this same example the relationship of Communist troop commitments to bombing in subsequent months is also examined. In analyzing a dynamic process like the Vietnam War, empirical data can help one infer which of two variables changes in response to prior changes in the other. For example, did increases in U.S. bombing in North Vietnam precede increases in Communist troop commitments in South Vietnam or vice versa?

If one considers the Vietnam War as a time series experiment (Campbell and Stanley, 1963), variations in a dependent variable may be considered due to previous or simultaneous variations in a logically related independent variable. The statistical method of reciprocal serial (lagged) correlation can help determine the sequence of changes in pairs of variables that are both observed over time (Campbell and Clayton, 1961). When changes in one variable occur earlier than changes in a second variable, one may infer that the first is responding to the second. Of course, there may be alternative explanations. Previous changes in a third variable may be affecting both the second and first variables. A time series experiment differs from a true experiment in that such alternative explanations cannot be ruled out.

In the method of serial correlation, if two variables are observed to change continuously over time, and if past values of one (x) are more highly correlated with present values of a second (y) than past values of the second (y) with present values of the first (x), i.e., when $r_{x_{t-n}y_t} > r_{y_{t-n}x_t}$, then changes in the first variable (x) can be considered to have occurred prior to changes in the second (y). The time lag between changes in two variables is determined by choosing the time lag (n) giving the highest correlation between the two variables, i.e., when $r_{x_{t-n}y_t}$ is at its maximum. In this study, when the highest correlation between two variables is in the same month, time precedence is assumed on theoretical grounds.

Partial correlation techniques are not used to determine time or "causal" sequence (Blalock, 1964) because measurements of all variables over time are available, thus providing more information on the time sequences of variations than "causal" modeling techniques assume one has.

The concept of "cause" commonly includes three components: time precedence of the cause before the effect, concomitant variation of the two, and an assumed logical or metaphysical relationship between the cause and the effect. Serial correlation can be used to analyze time precedence and concomitant variation. However, since no statistical method can specify logical or metaphysical relationships, one should be aware that alternative explanations involving some third variable are not ruled out by serial correlations. Serial correlation allows one to observe reciprocal relationships between two variables and to measure the strength of such relationships. It is an appropriate technique for inferring time precedence since expected time lags in variations between military and political variables used in this study are commensurate with the monthly intervals between observations.

Outlying values cause a problem in interpreting the general relationship between variables. If outlying values are included in calculating correlation coefficients, they may lead one to infer a relationship that is in fact true only because of the outlying values. If outlying values are omitted from the calculation, the relationship is not all-encompassing. Mathematical transformations could be used for each variable in an attempt to construct a more normal distribution before correlating variables, but this raises serious problems of substantive interpretation.

Visual inspection was used to check bivariate relationships for outlying values, shape of the curve, and scatter. In this way the human eye and brain are used in conjunction with correlation and regression coefficients to recognize patterns and identify significant relationships. The researcher decides whether the inclusion or exclusion of outlying values makes a difference in general relationships. If outlying values are excluded, general propositions are qualified accordingly (Conn and von Holdt, 1965; Hall et al., 1968).

Given the nature of the data in this study, the use of statistical tests of significance is problematical. Some would argue that such tests are appropriate only with a randomly drawn probability sample (Morrison and Henkel, 1969). The data in this study are not a random sample. However, they are a sample of all observations possible with different operational measures. They are also a sample of months taken from the entire Vietnam War. Because the data are a sample in this sense, and because inferences are drawn from them about conceptual relationships, statistical significance tests may be appropriate.

The level of statistical significance varies with the sample size (Friedheim and Kadane, 1970). The data here represent a relatively small number of observations for each variable (thirty-six for the pre-Tet offensive period). If more monthly data were gathered, the level of statistical significance would increase.

The historical context of each data point in these time series can be independently assessed. For example, the small number of U.S. bombing missions over North Vietnam in January 1966 was associated with the Johnson administration's "peace offensive." Thus, the substantive as well as statistical significance of general relationships and of exceptions to them can be independently evaluated, increasing the chances for making valid statements about what happened in the war.

Thus, the statistical significance of a correlation coefficient or *t*-ratio is left an open question. The reader may judge for himself the importance of a reported correlation by its size, which is an estimate of the strength of association between variables. As a working rule of thumb, the estimated strength of association considered "significant" enough to support a hypothesis and be reported in the text is equal to, or greater than, an absolute value of .30 for a correlation coefficient and 2.1 for a *t*-ratio. Thus, as a minimum standard, 9 percent of the variance in one variable must be accounted for by the variance in the second variable.

Where outlying values distort the bivariate correlation (thereby overestimating the strength of association), the values are not reported. Where outlying values lead to an underestimate of the strength of association, the outlying values are excluded and the recomputed correlation coefficient is reported.

The strength of association selected as a minimum ($r \geq .30$; t-ratio of regression coefficient/standard error ≥ 2.1) is comparable to a statistically significant correlation at the .05 level if the data were a probability sample of 33 observations randomly drawn from some hypothetical universe ($N = 33$ when time lags of 3 months are used with 36 observations). The values of r shown in table 2 are reported by Hays (1963, p. 531) as necessary for rejection of the null hypothesis that $r = 0$ with 33 randomly selected observations:

TABLE 2

SIGNIFICANCE LEVELS OF CORRELATION COEFFICIENTS

Significance Level	Two-tailed	One-tailed
.05	.34	.29
.01	.44	.40
.001	.54	.51

Correlation analysis is used to test the hypotheses of the decision-makers, to suggest variables to be used in the construction of indices, and to estimate the strength of theoretical and empirical relationships. It is supplemented by the third analytic technique, regression analysis.

REGRESSION ANALYSIS

Regression analysis is a statistical technique for estimating the coefficients of the specific independent variables used to explain and predict a specific dependent variable. The coefficients are calculated using a "least-squares" criterion in order to get a best fit to the data. In a typical linear multiple regression equation of the form $Y_i = a_i + b_1x_1 + b_2x_2 + \ldots + b_nx_n + E_i$, the regression coefficient b_i for each independent variable x_i indicates how much the dependent variable Y_i will change with a unit change in x_i under the assumption that other independent variables in the equation are held constant. The error term, E_i, represents all other factors affecting the variation in the dependent variable besides those specified in the equation. The predicted monthly value of the dependent variable Y_i in a regression equation is calculated by multiplying the value (in the previous month indicated by the lag) of each independent variable (x_i) and its respective regression coefficient (b_i), and then adding these products for all the independent variables (through x_n) to the constant term a_i. Predictive models consist of several regression equations, in which each "endogenous" independent variable (the values of which are determined by the other variables in the model) is treated as a dependent variable in a separate equation.

In the predictive multiple regression models in this study, past values of independent variables predict present values of dependent variables. Time-lagged relationships are of from one to five months. Reciprocal predictive loops within the same month are avoided in specifying the models. Four "exogenous" seasonal variables also appear in the models as independent variables to represent the effect of weather changes and the Christmas-Tet holiday period. Other variables in the system are not used to explain these exogenous variables, for their values are independent of the other variables in the model.

The problem of *multicollinearity* must be considered in selecting independent variables for the regression equations. If independent variables are themselves highly associated, it is difficult to measure their separate effects on the dependent variable because of measurement and sampling error. Multiple regression measures the change in the dependent variable caused by a change in one of the independent variables while simultaneously controlling for the values of the other independent variables. However, it is impossible to keep the values of one independent variable constant while varying the values of another independent variable with which it is highly correlated.

For this reason independent variables that logically might be included in regression equations were excluded if their correlation with another substantively relevant independent variable was greater than .70 . Below this degree of intercorrelation, the problem of multicollinearity is not severe. In a few cases two highly correlated independent variables are included in a regression equation because substantive knowledge of the particular process requires it. In these cases the size of the regression coefficients measuring their "independent" effects on the dependent variable may not be correct. The substantive validity of the model is enhanced, however, as is its predictive validity (measured by the square of the multiple correlation coefficient, R^2).

The square of the multiple correlation coefficient, R^2, indicates the amount of variance accounted for in the dependent variable by the independent variables in a multiple regression equation. It is a measure of the ability of the equation to predict the dependent variable in that it measures the "goodness of fit" of the monthly values of the dependent variable predicted by the equation with the actual historical monthly values of the dependent variable.

The R^2 is thus a measure of the proportional reduction in the error in predicting the monthly values of the dependent variable as compared to the prediction that the value of the dependent variable in each month is the mean value of that variable over all the months.

COMPUTER SIMULATION

The fourth analytic technique is computer simulation. This technique is used to predict future values of military and political variables under existing and alternative policies.

Regression analysis is a form of prediction in which each dependent variable is predicted from known values of independent variables. Regression analysis, however, does not allow one to make repeated predictions farther and farther into the future because future values of the independent variables are unknown. However, an interrelated set of regression equations in which present values of dependent variables are sufficiently and consistently dependent on past values of independent variables can make repeated predictions to extrapolate the entire system of variables into the future in a step-by-step (or month-by-month) way.[1]

This repeated prediction is done by simulating the future values of the endogenous independent variables in the following way. The Vietnam War model consists of an interrelated set of regression equations, including the specification of time-lagged relationships. Using actual data from the Vietnam War (e.g., the values of each variable during the thirty-six months of 1965 through 1967), the regression coefficients and constants are estimated (as described in the above section on multiple regression analysis). Using only the *initial* real values of each variable from the first month of each of these time series (i.e., only one real data point for each variable) and these estimated regression coefficients and constants, the set of regression equations is solved. The solutions are the predictions of the values of the dependent variables for the second month. These predicted values of the variables —rather than their actual values for that second month—are then used with the same regression coefficients and constants to predict the value of each variable for the third month. This "bootstrapping" technique is repeated again and again to make month-by-month predictions. These predictions can be continued beyond the period from which the regression coefficients were estimated from the known data.

In this way predictions are made as the implications of the relationships specified in the model continue to unfold. As past values of independent variables predict present values of dependent variables, present values of these dependent variables—used as independent variables in other equations—are used to predict future values of other dependent variables. Thus, the implications of the complicated interdependent relationships among the variables can be foreseen, provided that these relationships continue to hold in the future as they have in the past.

This bootstrapping procedure is illustrated in figure 3. In this example

$$\hat{Y}_{1_{t+1}} = a_1 + b_1 x_{1_t} + b_2 x_{2_t} + b_3 x_{3_t} + E_1 \qquad (1)$$

$$\hat{x}_{1_{t+1}} = a_2 + b_4 x_{4_t} + b_5 x_{5_t} + b_6 x_{6_t} + E_2 \qquad (2)$$

$$\hat{Y}_{1_{t+2}} = a_1 + b_1 \hat{x}_{1_{t+1}} + b_2 \hat{x}_{2_{t+1}} + b_3 \hat{x}_{3_{t+1}} + E_1 \qquad (3)$$

Figure 3. Bootstrapping Predictions of Variables

in Equation 1, the second month's value of Y_1 (at time $t+1$) has been predicted (indicated by the symbol ^) using the first month's *actual* value of X_1 (at time t). However, the *predicted* value of X_1 for the second ($t+1$) month (derived from Equation 2) is used to predict the value of Y_1 for the third ($t+2$) month, as shown in Equation 3. In the same way, after the second month, all endogenous variables are predicted from previous predictions, month after month.

This method of simulation is a stringent test of the predictive validity of a model, for though the simulation method uses the regression coefficients that represent the relationships among variables for a whole time period (e.g., 1965–67), one begins by making predictions by this bootstrapping method, using only the first months' real data for each of the endogenous variables in the system. All the data beyond the first month are predicted by the equations in the model. Moreover, by the third month in the simulation, all data points being predicted are based on previously predicted values of the variables in the system.

This simulation method is straightforward when variables are dependent only on past values of independent variables. A problem arises when one variable is dependent on another variable in the same time period, i.e., with no lag. Regression analysis would use a set of simultaneous equations if two variables were hypothesized to affect each other reciprocally within the same time period. However, a large system of simultaneous equations might present problems of stability (e.g., error terms cannot be assumed to be uncorrelated with the independent variables in each equation [Blalock, 1964]). Systems of simultaneous equations would also require a difficult parameter calculation to prevent a biased estimation of parameters. One possible solution is the development of a nonreciprocal (i.e., hierarchical or recursive) system of variables. A recursive system allows a relatively simple estimate of parameters, and hence calculation of predictions, but requires a hierarchy of variables to be theoretically specified for nonlagged relationships between variables. For example, in a recursive model, if one month's U.S. troop commitments are used to predict the same month's Communist troop commitments, then the latter cannot be used to predict the former. However, *previous* values of Communist commitments could be used to predict current U.S. commitments. Although the specification of a hierarchy of hypothesized causation within the same time period may seem artificial, it can be justified on the basis of other information available about policy-making in the Vietnam War (e.g., the "Pentagon Papers"), as well as for theoretical reasons.

The hierarchy used here is designed to be substantively and theoretically plausible, to account for the greatest amount of explained variance in the regressions, and to provide the best simulation. In this model, troop commitments are at the top of the concurrent hierarchy, followed by combat activities, then military outcomes (such as casualties), then changes in popular support and confidence, and finally communication variables indicating leaders' publicly stated perceptions and preferences. Within a single month, for example, an increase in Communist commitments can be related to a later increase in U.S. commitments (airborne troops could go into action in South Vietnam one week after the decision was made to commit them from the United States). These developments can be related to subsequent increased bombing, increased casualties, and to changes in the number of Communist defectors, South Vietnamese popular confidence, and U.S. popular approval of the president. Finally, at the bottom of the hierarchy of variables that might relate to each other in the same month are the decision-makers' public statements of perception or preference. These public statements were placed last because policy-makers probably can react more quickly with verbal statements than they can with military actions.

Computer simulation offers several advantages over regression analysis. First, simulation allows predictions to be made farther and farther into the future beyond the time point for which actual data are available. Second, it allows complex interaction effects to become apparent over time even though only linear additive regression models are considered. Simulation is a more realistic way to study interaction in international relations than multiplicative regression models because the assumptions made in the use of multiplicative terms are difficult to support (e.g., that the rate of increase in a dependent variable is proportional to the product of two independent variables).

Third, ascribing significance to a Vietnam War model consisting of a set of regression equations demands a stringent test of the model. This more stringent test is provided by the simulation. If the simulation does not accurately predict the values of the variables, then the model has not uncovered the underlying relationships. If the simulation makes accurate predictions despite the possibly increasing error terms in the equations, as the bootstrapping process proceeds, it has passed a stringent test indeed. Accurate prediction from a simulation is a better indicator of the predictive validity of a model than is an examination of the variance explained by the regression equations of the model because of the complex interactions among the variables in a simulation. Thus, simulations may allow one to draw inferences about the phenomena that could not otherwise be drawn.

Once an accurate predictive model has been developed, it can be used to explore the probable consequences of *experimental changes* in selected variables. Policy-makers, for example, might wish to determine probable outcomes of alternative strategies before actually implementing any one of them. Computer simulation can make such forecasts as long as the relationships among the variables in the system remain constant. What would have happened, for example, if President Johnson had continued the peace overtures of December 1965–January 1966, the period of the thirty-eight-day bombing halt and of major diplomatic activity? An answer can be found in a *computer simulation exercise* of the model. The simulation is exercised by making the experimental variable exogenous in the system, i.e., allowing it only the specified experimental values rather than the values it would otherwise take on as a dependent variable in the system.

The results of the computer simulation exercises of hawk and dove policy alternatives is reported in chapter 7. This research was undertaken in an exploratory spirit. That computer simulations of alternative futures in the Vietnam War have evinced any validity at all is startling and provocative, both for its practical and for its intellectual implications.

1. This technique is similar to methods used in numerical analysis for the solution of differential equations, and was developed for use in this research by my computer scientist colleague William Charles Mitchell.

4

Tests of Crucial Hypotheses and Assumptions of U.S. Policy-makers about the Vietnam War

In chapter one we discussed the *theoretical* structure of assumptions and propositions that generally underlie hawk and dove policy models. In this chapter we shall investigate the *empirical* validity of selected crucial *policy* assumptions and predictions by principal U.S. policy-makers upon which U.S. policy and conduct of the war were based.

There are two important reasons for studying the crucial assumptions and predictive hypotheses of policy-makers' own "folk models." First, if principal policy-makers *believe* them to be true, this in itself influences the formulation of policy and the conduct of the war. Second, by determining whether or not important assumptions and hypotheses are empirically valid, we can understand why certain outcomes in the war followed certain policy decisions whereas others did not.

The reason we focus on U.S. policy-makers' models of the war is that the public disclosure of the once top-secret "Pentagon Papers" allows us to examine in some detail the beliefs of U.S. leaders about the war. Ideally, one would like to acquire a similar set of policy papers of the North Vietnamese and Viet Cong to determine their beliefs about the war, and to test their assumptions against empirical data. This remains a task for future research.

UNITED STATES POLICY ASSUMPTIONS AND HYPOTHESES

The primary assumption of U.S. policy-makers that motivated U.S. involvement in the Vietnam War was a folk model called the *domino theory*. This theory assumed that the Communist government of the People's Republic of China, through its support of wars of national liberation, was set upon a course of expanding its power and influence throughout Asia and the Pacific. These "people's wars" were those fought by guerrilla insurgents against existing non-Communist regimes. The crucial assumption of the domino theory was that if South Vietnam should "go Communist," other Southeast Asian countries would inevitably follow. The reasoning behind this assumption was that if the United States should fail to meet its commitments in South Vietnam, Communists throughout the world, but particularly in Southeast Asia, would conclude that it would not meet its anti-Communist commitments elsewhere, and the Communists would consequently challenge pro-U.S. non-Communist regimes in other countries. If South Vietnam went Communist, a whole set of strategic international linkages would be challenged, first in Southeast Asia, then Japan and South Asia, then the Middle East, and finally Europe. Based on the analogy of Nazi Germany's behavior prior to World War II, the domino theory argued that to stop this series of challenges to its vital interest, the United States would eventually be pushed into a third world war. The folk theory implied that to prevent this chain of events, the United States must thwart the Communist take-over of South Vietnam (NYT, *PP*, p. 27).

Whether or not the People's Republic of China was bent on expansion during the early 1960s is a question that can be answered only by historical evidence, much of which (e.g., policy papers) is not available to U.S. scholars at this time. Any Communist Chinese plans for expansion have no doubt been modified by the thwarted Communist coup in Indonesia in 1965, by the Great Proletarian Cultural Revolution that began in 1966, by Chinese fears of Soviet military attack since 1969, and by the beginnings of a Chinese-American détente in 1972.

The assumptions that countries in Southeast Asia and the rest of the world would fall like dominoes if the United States did not prevent a Communist take-over of South Vietnam and that the United States would be pushed into a third world war are not subject to scientific empirical test, since the events referred to in the assumptions have never occurred. History has provided no data on what would have happened had the United States *not* intervened in Vietnam. Thus, we cannot know in any scientific sense whether this crucial assumption upon which U.S. Vietnam policy was based was actually true. What is of significance is that U.S. policy-makers *believed* it to be true, and thus this folk theory directly motivated the formulation of U.S. policy in Vietnam.

Using empirical data, we shall now test crucial assumptions and hypotheses that guided U.S. policy in Vietnam. These are clustered into four main categories: (1) the effectiveness of U.S. air power against North Vietnam; (2) the effectiveness of U.S. ground forces in South Vietnam; (3) the effects of U.S. military commitments on South Vietnamese political stability and popular confidence; and (4) the effects of U.S. commitments and actions in Vietnam on public opinion and popular support in the United States.

We shall now look at these testable assumptions and hypotheses in more detail, examine the way in which they were articulated by principal U.S. policy-makers, and determine their validity by testing them against empirical data from the period during which the major escalation of the Vietnam War occurred, January 1965 to December 1967.

United States Bombing of North Vietnam

United States leaders at first assumed that the *threatened* use of massive U.S. military power, including large-scale bombing, would persuade North Vietnam to relinquish its support and direction of the Viet Cong's insurgency in the South, since the North Vietnamese presumably could not win against superior American military power.

Historically, the use of military coercion against North Vietnam began with the covert operations undertaken as "Operation Plan 34A" from February to August 1964. The operation's implied message to North Vietnam was that they should cease their support of the Viet Cong insurgency in the South or bear the consequences of massive (and presumably devastating) U.S. military force in North Vietnam. (NYT, *PP*, chap. 5) The operations included sabotage and psychological operations against North Vietnam. (McNamara Memorandum to Johnson, "Vietnam Situation," 21 December 1963, NYT, *PP*, p. 273. The covert operations are described on pp. 301-6.)

Since these covert operations against North Vietnam failed to persuade its leaders to halt their support of Viet Cong guerrilla insurgency in the South, U.S. policy-makers initiated a policy of bombing North Vietnam. As originally conceived, these air attacks were designed to increase the costs to North Vietnam of its aid to the Viet Cong. The assumption of U.S. leaders was that these added costs would be sufficiently great to break the *will* of the North Vietnamese to continue supporting the Viet Cong. The bombing attacks against North Vietnam were not at first designed to affect significantly North Vietnam's *capability* of continuing its support for the Viet Cong guerrilla war in South Vietnam.

As early as 22 January 1964, the chairman of the Joint Chiefs of Staff, General Maxwell D. Taylor, recommended to Secretary of Defense McNamara that the United States "must therefore be prepared fully to undertake a much higher level of activity, not only for its beneficial tactical effect, but to make plain our resolution, both to our friends and to our enemies." The activities included "conduct[ing] aerial bombing of key North Vietnam targets, using U.S. resources under Vietnamese cover, and with the Vietnamese openly assuming responsibility for the actions" (NYT, *PP*, pp. 276–77). United States policy-makers thus defined the stakes in the Vietnam War as a test of wills, designed partially to prove the credibility of U.S. commitments.

President Johnson and his closest advisers (the "principal" makers of U.S. Vietnam policy, according to the "Pentagon Papers"—McGeorge Bundy, William P. Bundy, Henry C. Lodge, Robert McNamara, John McNaughton, Walt W. Rostow, Dean Rusk, and Maxwell Taylor[1])—assumed that an escalation of the bombing of North Vietnam would, in the words of Maxwell Taylor, "persuade or force the D.R.V. [North Vietnam] to stop its aid to the Vietcong and to use its directive powers to make the Vietcong desist from their efforts to overthrow the government of South Vietnam" (briefing paper, 27 November 1964, NYT, *PP*, p. 326) In the concrete terms stated by Assistant Secretary of Defense McNaughton on 6 November 1964, North Vietnam must:

> (1) Stop training and sending personnel to wage war in SVN and Laos.
> (2) Stop sending arms and supplies to SVN and Laos.
> (3) Stop directing and controlling military actions in SVN and Laos.
> (4) Order the VC and PL [Pathet Lao] to stop their insurgencies and military actions.
> (5) Remove VM [Viet Minh] forces and cadres from SVN and Laos.
> (6) Stop propaganda broadcasts to South Vietnam. . . .
> (NYT, *PP*, p. 367)

The type of bombing effort planned, as outlined by William P. Bundy in a final draft position paper on 29 November 1964, was a program "of graduated military pressures directed systematically against the DRV. Such a program would consist principally of progressively more serious air strikes, of a weight and tempo adjusted to the situation as it develops. . . . " (NYT, *PP*, p. 375)

The assumption of the principal U.S. policy-makers was that the North Vietnamese would break under the pressure of American air power. Yet the Central Intelligence Agency, the Defense Intelligence Agency, and the State Department's Bureau of Intelligence and Research felt that the chances for this were small. North Vietnam is composed primarily of decentralized, self-sufficient agricultural villages, and is therefore not as vulnerable to devastation by bombing as would be a highly centralized industrial economy (NYT, *PP*, p. 331). From another point of view, the Joint Chiefs of Staff felt that only quick massive bombing—rather than calculated limited bombing—would convince the North Vietnamese leaders that "the U.S. intends to use military force to the full limits of what military force can contribute to achieving U.S. objectives in Southeast Asia" (NYT, *PP*, p. 330). Undersecretary of State George Ball also expressed doubt that bombing North Vietnam would accomplish U.S. policy objectives (NYT, *PP*, p. 325).

Even within President Johnson's closest circle of advisers, there were some doubts about how effective the bombing of North Vietnam would be. The historical evidence suggests that bombing was pursued despite these doubts because of the perceived lack of alternatives on how to strengthen the South Vietnamese government and avoid its defeat by the Viet Cong and the North Vietnamese (NYT, *PP*, p. 344).

The U.S. air war against North Vietnam was launched first on 4 August 1964. The bombing was initiated in response to a North Vietnamese PT boat attack on 2 August against the U.S. destroyer *Maddox*, which was operating in the Gulf of Tonkin on an intelligence patrol related to South Vietnamese commando raids on North Vietnam. The *Maddox*, joined by the destroyer *C. Turner Joy*, was attacked again by torpedo boats on 4 August, and within twelve hours of the time word of the attack reached Washington, reprisal bombing raids were launched from U.S. carriers in the Gulf of Tonkin. The U.S. destroyers may have been mistaken for South Vietnamese vessels escorting South Vietnamese commando raids on North Vietnamese installations. The attacks on the destroyers were, in any case, quickly taken by United States decision-makers as justification for launching the retaliatory raids against North Vietnam that had long been planned (NYT, *PP*, chap. 5).

The continual bombing of North Vietnam, although planned by U.S. policy-makers in the latter part of 1964 (an original bombing scenario was outlined on 23 May 1964 [NYT, *PP*, p. 343]), was not begun until February 1965. In reprisal for a Viet Cong attack on the U.S. military advisers' compound at Pleiku, South Vietnam, on 6 February 1965, U.S. Navy jets, in an operation named "Flaming Dart I," bombed and rocketed North Vietnamese barracks and staging areas at Donghoi (NYT, *PP*, p. 343).

A second and heavier U.S. bombing attack against North Vietnam, "Flaming Dart II," occurred on 11 February 1965, in reprisal for a guerrilla attack on an American barracks at Quinhon, South Vietnam. On 13 February 1965 President Johnson ordered the beginning of "Operation Rolling Thunder," which began on 2 March 1965. This operation was to become the gradually escalating air war against North Vietnam (NYT, *PP*, p. 343).

Within a month and a half the primary objective of Operation Rolling Thunder had changed. At first at attempt to break the *will* of the North Vietnamese in their support of the war in South Vietnam, the operation's objective became the destruction of North Vietnam's *capability* of supporting such a war. This shift occurred in March 1965 as the North Vietnamese showed no diminution in their determination to continue supporting the Viet Cong (NYT, *PP*, p. 398). Thus, the bombing was aimed at strategic targets such as petroleum storage facilities, at military targets, and at the North Vietnamese transportation system that carried men and supplies through North Vietnam and Laos. By the summer of 1965 the objective of the bombing had become to reduce the flow of men and supplies from North to South Vietnam (NYT, *PP*, p. 468).

Operationally, then, the success or failure of the bombing in fulfilling U.S. policy objectives can be measured by the number of North Vietnamese troops, arms, and supplies sent from North to South Vietnam, and the number of Viet Cong guerrillas trained by the North Vietnamese. The assumption by U.S. policy-makers that bombing North Vietnam would persuade its leaders to cease their support of the Viet Cong can thus be tested by correlating the monthly number of U.S. bombing missions over North Vietnam with the number of North Vietnamese and Viet Cong troops reported to be in South Vietnam.

The empirical data from January 1965 to December 1967 show that, contrary to the hawkish assumptions of the principal American policy-makers, the number of Communist troops in South Vietnam *increased* with the number of U.S. bombing sorties over North Vietnam (the correlation is .82 with a one-month lag). Even the *rates* of Communist troop commitments in South Vietnam increased proportionally with the *rate* of U.S. bombing missions over North Vietnam (the correlation is .44 with a two-month lag). Thus, although the U.S. made more costly to the North Vietnamese their support of the war in the South, their *capability* of continuing such support was not destroyed. The *psychological* effect of the escalation in the bombing was to strengthen the *will* of the North Vietnamese and increase their determination to continue the war. The net effect of the bombing was thus the intensification of North Vietnamese efforts in the war, including their escalation of troop commitments. This finding thus supports the prediction of the dove folk theory that escalation would lead to counterescalation, and refutes the contrary hawk theory.

There is evidence of a nonstatistical nature that shows this process of reciprocal escalation and counterescalation. The U.S. State Department had evidence of a major increase in infiltration from North to South Vietnam during 1964. After the Tonkin Gulf incident, Ambassador Taylor reported the appearance of North Vietnamese regulars in October 1964 (NYT, *PP*, p. 338). A Central Intelligence Agency and Defense Intelligence Agency memorandum reported the presence in February 1965 of a regular North Vietnamese regiment of the 325th People's Army of Vietnam division. This regiment was accepted into the Communist order of battle in Kontum province in April 1965 after the sustained bombing of North Vietnam had begun (NYT, *PP*, p. 409).

There is additional evidence that the bombing strengthened North Vietnamese determination in the war. The director of the Central Intelligence Agency, John A. McCone, in a 2 April 1965 memorandum to Secretaries Rusk and McNamara, McGeorge Bundy, and Ambassador Taylor, wrote "I have reported that the strikes to date have not caused a change in the North Vietnamese policy of directing Viet Cong insurgency, infiltrating cadres and supplying material. If anything, the strikes to date have hardened their attitude" (NYT, *PP*, p. 440).

An intensive study sponsored by the Defense Department in the summer of 1966 arrived at the same conclusion: the bombing of North Vietnam had "no measurable effect" either on North Vietnamese will or capability to support and direct Communist insurgencies in South Vietnam and Laos[2] (NYT, *PP*, p. 505). Forty-seven top scientists participated in this study through the Institute for Defense Analysis. Entitled "The Effects of U.S. Bombing on North Vietnam's Ability to Support Military Operations in South Vietnam: Retrospect and Prospect," the study identified two implicitly assumed sets of causal relationships in then current official thinking about the bombing:

> 1. That by increasing the damage and destruction of resources in NVN, the U.S. is exerting pressure to cause the DRV to stop their support of the military operations in SVN and Laos; and
> 2. That the combined effect of the total military effort against NVN—including the U.S. air strikes in NVN and Laos, and the land, sea, and air operations in SVN—will ultimately cause the DRV to perceive that its probable losses accruing from the war have become greater than its possible gains and, on the basis of this net evaluation, the regime will stop its support of the war in the South. (NYT, *PP*, p. 506)

The study goes on to state:

> These two sets of interrelationships are assumed in military planning, but it is not clear that they are systematically addressed in current intelligence estimates and assessments. Instead, the tendency is to encapsulate the bombing of NVN as one set of operations and the war in the South as another set of operations, and to evaluate each separately; and to tabulate and describe data on the physical, economic, and military effects of the bombing, but not to address specifically the relationship between such effects and the data relating to the ability and will of the DRV to continue its support of the war in the South. (NYT, *PP*, p. 506)

This study points out that although it was assumed that military punishment would break the will of the North Vietnamese to continue their support of the war in the South, there existed no adequate methodology to determine how much bomb damage would do so. Bomb damage can be systematically quantified; there were no systematic indicators of North Vietnamese determination. Thus, according to this study, "there is no firm basis for determining if there is *any* feasible level of effort that would achieve these [U.S.] objectives" (NYT, *PP*, 506-7).

The Institute for Defense Analysis study also offered some explanation of why U.S. bombing of North Vietnam had not been effective:

> Although the political constraints seem clearly to have reduced the effectiveness of the bombing program, its limited effect on Hanoi's ability to provide such support cannot be explained solely on that basis. The countermeasures introduced by Hanoi effectively reduced the impact of U.S. bombing. More fundamentally, however, North Vietnam has basically a subsistence agricultural economy that presents a difficult and unrewarding target system for air attack.
>
> The economy supports operations in the South mainly by functioning as a logistic funnel and by providing a source of manpower. The industrial sector produces little of military value. Most of the essential military supplies that the VC/NVN forces in the South require from external sources are provided by the USSR and Communist China. Furthermore, the volume of such supplies is so low that only a small fraction of the capacity of North Vietnam's rather flexible transportation network is required to maintain the flow. (NYT, *PP*, pp. 502-3)

Thus, North Vietnam was an inappropriate target for strategic or interdiction bombing because, according to the "Pentagon Papers," such bombing "assumed highly industrial nations producing large quantities of military goods to sustain mass armies engaged in intensive warfare" (NYT, *PP*, p. 469).

The Institute for Defense Analysis study went on to explain why U.S. bombing had not weakened the will of the North Vietnamese:

> . . . Initial plans and assessments for the ROLLING THUNDER program clearly tended to overestimate the persuasive and disruptive effects of the U.S. air strikes and, correspondingly, to under-estimate the tenacity and recuperative capabilities of the North Vietnamese. This tendency, in turn, appears to reflect a general failure to appreciate the fact, well-documented in the historical and social scientific literature, that a direct, frontal attack on a society tends to strengthen the social fabric of the nation, to increase popular support of the existing government, to improve the determination of both the leadership and populace to fight back, to induce a variety of protective measures that reduce the society's vulnerability to future attack, and to develop an increased capacity for quick repair and restoration of essential functions. (NYT, *PP*, pp. 505-6)

An even earlier study by the Defense Intelligence Agency in November 1965 had informed Secretary McNamara that although bombing had reduced industrial performance in North Vietnam, "the primarily rural nature of the area permits continued functioning of the subsistence economy," and that "the air strikes do not appear to have altered Hanoi's determination to continue supporting the war in South Vietnam" (NYT, *PP*, p. 469).

The ineffectiveness of the bombing of North Vietnam was explained in a very different way by the generally more hawkish Joint Chiefs of Staff. In a memorandum to Secretary McNamara on 10 November 1965, the Joint Chiefs stated: "We shall continue to achieve only limited success in air operation in D.R.V./Laos if required to operate within the constraints presently imposed. The establishment and observance of de facto sanctuaries within the D.R.V., coupled with a denial of operations against the most important and war supporting targets, precludes attainment of the objectives of the air campaign." They added, "Now required is an immediate and sharply accelerated program which will leave no doubt that the U.S. intends to win and achieve a level of destruction which they will not be able to overcome" (NYT, *PP*, pp. 475-76).

Among the conflicting opinions and policy recommendations presented by different agencies and advisers, President Johnson selected a general pattern of gradual escalation in the bombing. Although neither hawks nor doves believed that gradual escalation would be effective in achieving U.S. objectives, the policy represented an essentially political compromise reached by a very politically conscious Lyndon Johnson. Not until the Tet offensive of January–February 1968 demonstrated how ineffective the Johnson administration's Vietnam policy had been was there a reversal of bombing policy. A cutback of bombing to the twentieth parallel in North Vietnam on 31 March 1968 was part of the effort to commence negotiations to end the war. The bombing of North Vietnam was halted by the Johnson administration in October 1968, when the deescalation of bombing proved successful in persuading the North Vietnamese to agree to begin formal negotiations. Thus, the assumptions of the dove folk theory concerning the effects of bombing North Vietnam proved more nearly correct than did the hawkish assumptions that were implemented during most of the Johnson era.

Effects of U.S. Ground Forces in South Vietnam

President Johnson's decision in April 1965 to commit U.S. ground troops to offensive action in South Vietnam was a reversal of an American policy held since the Korean War: that the U.S. should avoid another land war in Asia. His decision was formalized in the National Security Action Memorandum 328, on 6 April 1965. The memorandum included presidential approval of an 18,000- to 20,000-man increase in U.S. military support forces, the deployment of two additional Marine Battalions and one Marine Air Squadron, and "a change of mission for all Marine Battalions deployed to Vietnam [two were deployed in March 1965] to permit their more active use under conditions to be established and approved by the Secretary of Defense in consultation with the Secretary of State" (NYT, *PP*, pp. 382-83).

The reason for this major decision to commit U.S. ground combat forces in Vietnam was the failure of the bombing to make the North Vietnamese cease their support of the war in the South. As spelled out in the "Pentagon Papers":

> Official hopes were high that the Rolling Thunder program would rapidly convince Hanoi that it should agree to negotiate a settlement to the war in the South. After a month of bombing with no response from the North Vietnamese, optimism began to wane.
>
> The U.S. was presented essentially with two options: (1) to withdraw unilaterally from Vietnam leaving the South Vietnamese to fend for themselves, or (2) to commit ground forces in pursuit of its objectives. A third option, that of drastically increasing the scope and scale of the bombing, was rejected because of the concomitant high risk of inviting Chinese intervention. (NYT, *PP*, p. 383)

Thus, the Johnson administration committed U.S. forces to a ground war in Asia believing that those forces could achieve its objectives in Vietnam. The purposes of this troop commitment were to convince the North Vietnamese that their winning over the combined forces of the U.S. and South Vietnam was impossible and therefore to persuade them to cease their support of the Viet Cong. Ambassador Taylor wrote on 17 April 1965:

> However, it is becoming increasingly clear that, in all probability, the primary objective of the GVN [Government of South Vietnam] and the USG [United States Government] of changing the will of the DRV to support the VC insurgency cannot be attained in an acceptable time-frame by the methods presently employed. The air campaign in the North must be supplemented by signal successes against the VC on the South before we can hope to create that frame of mind in Hanoi which will lead to the decisions we seek. (NYT, *PP*, p. 445)

Thus, U.S. aims in March 1965, according to Assistant Secretary of Defense McNaughton, included: "70%—To avoid a humiliating U.S.

defeat (to our reputation as a guarantor). 20%—To keep SVN (and the adjacent) territory from Chinese hands. 10%—To permit the people of SVN to enjoy a better, freer way of life" (NYT, *PP*, p. 432). If the North Vietnamese could not be persuaded to cease their efforts, the purposes of the large U.S. ground effort in South Vietnam included: "To defeat the VC on the ground" (NYT, *PP*, p. 436).

Initially, the strategy adopted to prevent a Viet Cong victory was an enclave strategy. However, after Viet Cong victories in May and June 1965, the United States adopted a strategy of "search and destroy," the objective of which was "to take the war to the enemy, denying him freedom of movement anywhere in the country . . . and deal him the heaviest possible blows" (NYT, *PP*, p. 403). As described by Secretary McNamara in a memorandum to President Johnson on 20 July 1965, U.S. combat forces were "by aggressive exploitation of superior military forces . . . to gain and hold the initiative . . . pressing the fight against VC-DRV main force units in South Vietnam to run them to ground and destroy them" (NYT, *PP*, p. 457). Thus, the strategy chosen to defeat the Communists was one of attrition, or the so-called "meat-grinder" strategy (NYT, *PP*, pp. 501-2).

The basic assumption of the principal policy-makers in the Johnson administration was that in the face of supposedly superior American combat forces in South Vietnam, the North Vietnamese would realize that they could not win and would thus cease their efforts in South Vietnam. Walt W. Rostow, chairman of the State Department's Policy Planning Council, wrote to Secretary McNamara on 16 November 1964: "We must make clear that counter escalation by the Communists will run directly into U.S. strength on the ground; and therefore the possibility of radically extending their position on the ground at the cost of air and naval damage alone, is ruled out" (NYT, *PP*, p. 418).

The empirical data from January 1965 through December 1967 show that the above assumption of the Johnson administration was incorrect. Rather than deterring additional Communist troop commitments in South Vietnam or reducing their number through attrition, the escalation of U.S. troops, supplies, and combat operations in South Vietnam was followed by a concomitant North Vietnamese and Viet Cong *counterescalation* of troop commitments (the correlation coefficient is .94).

Counterescalations of Communist troop commitments and Communist counteroffensives necessitated round after round of additional U.S. combat troop commitments. President Johnson willingly granted General Westmoreland an 18,000–20,000 man increase in April 1965; in July 1965, 44 battalions were granted for a total of 193,887 troops (NYT, *PP*, pp. 384-85). In November 1965 General Westmoreland requested a total of 375,000; in December 1965, 443,000; in January

1966, 459,000; in August 1966, 542,588. In March 1967 General Westmoreland asked for 200,000 more troops, but this request was scaled down to 30,000 new men (NYT, *PP*, pp. 460-61).

It was not until March 1968, when General Westmoreland requested an additional 206,756 men in the wake of the devastating Communist Tet offensive of January and February, that the continued build-up of American ground forces in Vietnam was halted by President Johnson in a major policy reversal. The president sent just 30,000 more men to Vietnam, recalled General Westmoreland, and announced that he would neither seek nor accept the nomination of his party for reelection.

Thus, the hawkish U.S. policy of escalation was met by Communist counterescalation. In the end it was not the North Vietnamese and Viet Cong but the Americans who were forced for military and political reasons to halt the escalation spiral.

U.S. Bombing of North Vietnam and Popular Confidence in the South Vietnamese Government

Throughout the Vietnam War, a major objective of U.S. policy-makers was the establishment and maintenance of a stable anti-Communist government in South Vietnam that could and would actively prosecute the war against the Viet Cong and North Vietnamese. This proved to be a difficult goal after the fatal coup against Ngo Dinh Diem in November 1963. A great deal of political instability followed Diem's assassination, taking the form of coups, plots, cabinet shake-ups, mass demonstrations, and general turmoil. United States policy-makers were greatly displeased by this political instability, fearing that the Viet Cong would take advantage of the situation to strengthen their own political position. The political conflict among different factions of non-Communists in South Vietnam weakened the cooperation necessary for successful conduct of the war against the Communists.

An excellent example of the desire of principal U.S. policy-makers for political stability in South Vietnam is found in Ambassador Maxwell Taylor's remarks to the "young Turk" leaders of a coup against the High National Council and the civilian government of Tran Van Huong in December 1964. Among those present were two later presidents of South Vietnam, Nguyen Cao Ky and Nguyen Van Thieu. Ambassador Taylor is quoted in an airgram to the State Department, on 24 December 1964, as saying:

> . . . I told you all clearly at General Westmoreland's dinner we Americans were tired of coups. Apparently I wasted my words.

> Maybe this is because something is wrong with my French because you evidently didn't understand. I made it clear that all the military plans which I know you would like to carry out are dependent on governmental stability. Now you have made a real mess. We cannot carry you forever if you do things like this. . . . (NYT, *PP*, p. 379)

Late 1964 and early 1965 saw continued political turmoil in South Vietnam and many military defeats of the South Vietnamese government's forces. In response to this situation, U.S. policy-makers sought to decrease political divisiveness and increase the military and political effectiveness of the South Vietnamese government, including its popular appeal and support. Ambassador Maxwell Taylor presented an approved U.S. government statement and program to the South Vietnamese government at the end of November 1964. It stated:

> It was the clear conclusion of the recent review in Washington of the situation in South Vietnam that the unsatisfactory progress being made in the Pacification Program was the result of two primary causes from which secondary causes stem. The primary cause has been the governmental instability in Saigon, and the second the continued reinforcement and direction of the Viet Cong by the Government of North Vietnam. It was recognized that to change the downward trend of events, it will be necessary to deal adequately with both of these factors.
>
> In the view of the United States, there is a certain minimum condition to be brought about in South Vietnam before new measures against North Vietnam would be either justified or practicable. At the minimum, the Government in Saigon should be able to speak for and to its people who will need special guidance and leadership throughout the coming critical period. The Government should be capable of maintaining law and order in the principal centers of population, assuring their effective execution by military and police forces completely responsive to its authority. . . . (Gravel ed., *PP*, p. 343)

The program went on to say:

> Better performance in the prosecution of the war against the Viet Cong needs to be accompanied by actions to convince the people of the interest of their government in their wellbeing. Better performance in itself is perhaps the most convincing evidence but can be supplemented by such actions as frequent visits by officials and ranking military officers to the provinces for personal orientation and "trouble shooting." The available information media offer a channel of communication with the people which could be strengthened and more efficiently employed. The physical appearance of the cities, particularly Saigon, shows a let-down in civic pride which, if cor-

> rected, would convey a message of governmental effectiveness to their inhabitants. Similarly, in the country an expanded rural development program could carry the government's presence into every reasonably secure village and hamlet.
>
> If governmental performance and popular appeal are significantly improved, there will be little difficulty in establishing confidence in the government. . . . (Gravel ed., *PP*, p. 345)

In return for greater propaganda efforts by the South Vietnamese government, the U.S. government offered to begin bombing the Laotian corridor and North Vietnam, actions the South Vietnamese generals had sought since July 1964. (Gravel ed., *PP*, p. 328).

> . . . While the Government of Vietnam is making progress toward achieving the goals set forth above, the United States Government would be willing to strike harder at infiltration routes in Laos and at sea. . . .
>
> . . . If the Government of Vietnam is able to demonstrate its effectiveness and capability of achieving the minimum conditions set forth above, the United States Government is prepared to consider a program of direct military pressure on North Vietnam as Phase II. . . .
>
> . . . As contemplated by the United States Government, Phase II would, in general terms, consititute a series of air attacks on North Vietnam progressively mounting in scope and intensity for the purpose of convincing the leaders of North Vietnam that it is to their interest to cease aid to the Viet Cong and respect the independence and security of South Vietnam. . . . (Gravel ed., *PP*, p. 344)

Thus, aside from its military objectives in North Vietnam, the U.S. bombing that commenced on 6 February 1965 had as one of its primary objectives the improvement of political stability and popular confidence in South Vietnam. Secretary McNamara stated this objective clearly and publicly: "It was also anticipated that these air operations would raise the morale of the South Vietnamese people who, at the time the bombing started, were under severe military pressure" (McNamara, *New York Times*, 26 August 1970).

The assumed relationship between U.S. bombing in North Vietnam and popular confidence in the South Vietnamese government was thus a crucial hypothesis in the folk theory held by principal U.S. policymakers. We can test this assumption empirically using monthly data between January 1965 and December 1967 on the number of U.S. bombing missions over North Vietnam and the index of popular confidence described in chapter 2 (i.e., the dollar value of the South Vietnamese piastre on the black market times the index of consumer prices divided by the money supply). Using multiple regression analysis and controlling for autocorrelation in the popular confidence index by using the previous month's value of the index, the empirical test shows that there is *no* systematic relationship between the number of bombing missions over North Vietnam in one month and popular confidence in the South Vietnamese government the following month. Thus, the empirical evidence refutes the policy assumption that the bombing of North Vietnam would systematically contribute to the achievement of U.S. political objectives in South Vietnam.

U.S. Ground Forces and Popular Confidence in the South Vietnamese Government

Since the bombing of North Vietnam did not have the sustained effect of bolstering the morale of, and public confidence in, the government of South Vietnam, one might also question the effectiveness of the build-up of U.S. ground forces in accomplishing the same purpose. The original commitment of U.S. Marine combat forces in February 1965 had as one of its main objectives bolstering the morale of the South Vietnamese government and increasing its willingness to continue the fight against the Communists (Gravel ed., *PP*, p. 432). Was this policy successful?

A multiple regression analysis of empirical data from January 1965 through December 1967 shows that, when controlling for auto-correlation in the popular confidence index, there is *no* systematic relationship between the monthly commitment of U.S. troops, supplies, and combat operations, and popular confidence in the South Vietnamese government the following month. Thus, the empirical evidence again refutes the folk theory that U.S. military forces would systematically contribute to the strengthening of popular confidence in the South Vietnamese government.

U.S. Commitments in Vietnam and Public Opinion in the United States

The principal U.S. policy-makers were incorrect in their predictions concerning the military and political effectiveness of bombing North Vietnam and committing U.S. ground forces to combat in South Vietnam. Yet they continued these policies despite the contrary warnings of their own intelligence agencies and other respected analysts. Why they continued to do so may be explained by a fourth major assumption of the Johnson administration: based on the historical precedent of the political events in the United States following the Communist takeover of mainland China, an administration perceived by the American public as being "soft on Communism" would be punished politically (Ellsberg, 1971). Conversely, the Johnson administration believed in the U.S. public's willingness—even its insistence—that its government take the necessary measures to prevent a Communist take-over in South Vietnam.

It is doubtful that President Johnson believed that the American public wholeheartedly endorsed a policy of perpetually escalating U.S. military commitments in South Vietnam. In early 1965 President Johnson launched the air war before committing U.S. ground combat forces because, according to the "Pentagon Papers," the American public "would find an air war less repugnant than a ground war" (NYT, *PP*, p. 329). The public consensus since the Korean War was that the United States should not again become entangled in a land war in Asia. Thus, when the president ordered on 6 April 1965 an increase in U.S. ground forces and approved their use in offensive operations, it was noted in National Security Action Memorandum 328:

> The President desires that with respect to the actions in paragraphs 5 through 7 [military support force increase, deployment of additional U.S. Marines, and permission granted to the Marines to be more aggressive in their missions], premature publicity be avoided by all possible precautions. The actions themselves should be taken as rapidly as practicable, but in ways that should minimize any appearance of sudden changes in policy, and official statements on these troop movements will be made only with the direct approval of the Secretary of Defense, in consultation with the Secretary of State. The President's desire is that these movements and changes should be understood as being gradual and wholly consistent with existing policy. (NYT, *PP*, p. 443)

This example of minimum public disclosure is representative of a pattern of official secrecy concerning the extent of U.S. military, economic, and political involvement in Vietnam. Such official secrecy suggests that the Johnson administration had at least some awareness of the American public's distaste for a policy of gradually escalating U.S. military commitments in Vietnam. One may infer, however, that President Johnson believed that the U.S. public was, on balance, favorable to a firm policy of resistance toward Communists, since he frequently cited public opinion polls that showed public support for his Vietnam policy.

A statistical analysis of monthly data from January 1965 through December 1967 comparing the percentages of the American public approving and disapproving President Johnson's handling of his job (as measured in the American Institute of Public Opinion's "Gallup

Poll") with the index of U.S. military commitments in Vietnam shows a very strong *negative* relationship: the more U.S. troops and supplies sent to Vietnam in one month and the more combat in which the troops engaged, the *less* support the president received from the American people in the following month (the correlation coefficient is —.93).

This loss of political support for President Johnson was accompanied by a loss of support for his Vietnam policy. From July 1965 to December 1967 the American Institute of Public Opinion regularly assessed domestic public reaction to the way President Johnson was handling his job as president and to his handling of the Vietnam War. During this period public evaluation of the president's general performance and of his Vietnam policy were highly correlated: the percentages of those who disapproved of the president and his Vietnam policy correlated .89; the percentages of those who approved of the president and his Vietnam policy correlated .80 .

Thus, the Johnson administration was incorrect in its crucial assumption that the American public would approve a policy of gradual escalation in Vietnam. In its evaluation of the war the American public's greatest consideration was its monetary and human costs, rather than its value in defeating Communism. The most significant costs to the American people were the number of American "boys" killed and wounded in Vietnam. The correlation between American casualties in Vietnam and the margin of approval for President Johnson and his Vietnam policy is very strongly negative ($r = —.77$). The more casualties incurred, the more the public disapproved of the president and his Vietnam policy. Why the costs of waging war in Vietnam led to a decline in domestic political support will be further analyzed in chapter nine.

In concluding this chapter, we should note that the principal policymakers of the Johnson administration held and acted upon hawkish assumptions or "folk models" of the interrelationship between international politics and domestic politics that were in many respects as incorrect as their assumptions about the dynamics of international politics. President Johnson's failure to foresee that escalation of the Vietnam War would lead to a loss of political support for his presidency was as significant as his failure to foresee that bombing North Vietnam would not lead to greater popular confidence in the South Vietnamese government or that the Communists would be able to equal his escalation rather than surrender to it. Although President Johnson may gradually have been made aware by dissenting advisers and agencies that his hawkish folk models were invalid, he nonetheless continued to be guided by them in his direction of American policy in Vietnam.

1. Although not one of President Johnson's closest advisers, General William Westmoreland was one of the people who most influenced U.S. policy in Vietnam. General Earl G. Wheeler as chairman of the Joint Chiefs of Staff, and John A. Mc-Cone, director of the CIA, also played significant roles in influencing U.S. policy in Vietnam during the Johnson administration.

2. This study, conducted at the Jason Division of the Institute for Defense Analysis in Wellesley, Massachusetts, from June through August 1966, was under the leadership of Dr. Jerrold R. Zacharias of the Massachusetts Institute of Technology. The idea for a summer seminar of scientists and academic specialists to study technical aspects of the war had been suggested by Dr. George B. Kistiakowsky and Dr. Carl Kaysen of Harvard and Dr. Jerome B. Wiesner and Dr. Zacharias of M.I.T. These men were given briefings by high officials from the Pentagon, the C.I.A., the State Department, and the White House, and were provided with secret materials. Assistant Secretary of Defense John McNaughton was the overseer of the project (NYT, *PP*, pp. 483-84).

5

Empirical Patterns of Interaction in the Escalation of the Vietnam War

Held up to the light of empirical data, the models of the war held by U.S. policy-makers were clearly inadequate. Convinced that their own decisions and actions would alone determine the outcome of the war, they generally failed to consider adequately not only the reactions of their opponents but the fact that the outcomes of war are dependent upon the actions of both sides. Thus, this tragic war was conducted, at least partially, on the basis of invalid assumptions and models.

To predict accurately the consequences of policy decisions and actions, a valid model of the conflict is needed. It is essential, for example, to find out what factors were or were not systematically related to each other, i.e., the general empirical patterns of actions, reactions, and consequences during the conflict. Using the statistical methods of correlation and regression analysis, this chapter will demonstrate such major patterns of interaction during the Vietnam War's escalatory period from 1965 through 1967.[1]

MUTUAL ESCALATION

The main discernible pattern of behavior in this war was mutual escalation. In 1964 U.S. military commitments to South Vietnam were substantial, but limited to providing equipment, funds, and advisers. At the end of 1964 there were 23,000 U.S. military personnel in South Vietnam. Except for the Tonkin Gulf incident, U.S. airpower had not been used against the North.

North Vietnamese support of the Viet Cong in the south was also limited in 1964 to supplies and to men who for the most part had been South Vietnamese members of the Viet Minh and who had moved to the North after the 1954 cease-fire. Only in late 1964 did regular North Vietnamese soldiers begin infiltrating into the South. Their number is estimated to have been 12,000, at the least, by the end of 1964 (less than 10 percent of the total Communist troop strength in South Vietnam at the time) (Sharp and Westmoreland, 1969, p. 3). Large numbers of regular troops of the North Vietnamese Army apparently were sent into the South only after the United States went beyond previous tacit limits and bombed North Vietnam in the Tonkin Gulf incident of August 1964. Indeed, the role of the North Vietnamese prior to 1965 may have been similar to that of tht U.S. "advisers" to the South Vietnamese army.

The Tonkin Gulf incident itself was used by the Johnson administration as an occasion for U.S. escalation that had, in fact, been in the planning stages for months (NYT, *PP*, chap. 5, especially pp. 286-88). In other words, the deteriorating situation that U.S. and South Vietnamese policy-makers perceived at the end of 1964 and the beginning of 1965 led them to escalate the war to avoid a Communist victory. This situation was vividly described by Admiral U. S. G. Sharp, the U.S. commander in chief in the Pacific:

> During January and February 1965 the general situation in South Vietnam continued to worsen, the military threat increased, political tensions in Saigon deepened, and morale plummeted. It became increasingly apparent that the existing levels of United States aid could not prevent the collapse of South Vietnam. Even as deliberations on how best to deal with the situation were in progress within our government, the Viet Cong launched a series of attacks on American installations in South Vietnam. These attacks indicated that North Vietnam was moving in for the kill. It appeared that they would succeed, perhaps in a matter of months, as things were developing. Acting on the request of the South Vietnamese government, the decision was made to commit as soon as possible 125,000 United States troops to prevent the Communist takeover.
>
> At the same time President Johnson indicated that additional forces would be sent as requested by the Republic of Vietnam and the Commander of the United States Military Assistance Command, Vietnam (Sharp and Westmoreland, 1969, pp. 4-5).

This pattern of escalation at the beginning of 1965 was repeated throughout the period from 1965 through 1967. Thus, in response to these Communist troop increases and to thwart a Communist military victory and political take-over in South Vietnam, the Johnson administration committed U.S. troops and supplies and ordered bombing sorties in South Vietnam and battalion-size or larger ground operations.[2]

$$\underset{R^2 = .90}{U.S.\ Commitments} = \underset{(2{,}400)}{-23{,}000} + \underset{(.01)}{.164}\ N.V. + V.C.\ troops_{t-1} \qquad (1)$$

Furthermore, the U.S. bombing of North Vietnam was intensified as well, in response to the increasing numbers of North Vietnamese and Viet Cong troops sent to the South. This, of course, was meant to prevent the defeat of South Vietnamese forces by compelling the North Vietnamese to stop sending their troops and supplies into the

South. And that positive relationship between Communist troop commitments and U.S. bombing missions over North Vietnam still holds even when taking into account the winter-summer seasonal variation that affects flying weather, as well as the momentum of the U.S. bombing policy.

$$\begin{array}{lll} \textit{U.S. bombing sorties} = & -\,2{,}900 & +\ .64\ \textit{U.S. bombing N.V.}_{t\text{-}1} \\ \quad \textit{over N.V.} & (1{,}400) & \quad (.10) \\ R^2 = .91 & & +\ .021\ \textit{N.V.} +\ \textit{V.C. troops}_{t\text{-}1} \\ & & (.007) \\ & & -\ 110\ \textit{Winter-Summer} \\ & & (34) \end{array} \qquad (2)$$

As already discussed in detail in chapter 4, the main objective of the U.S. bombing of North Vietnam was to decrease infiltration of North Vietnamese troops and supplies into the South. But that objective was *not* achieved. Indeed, the results were quite the contrary: the North Vietnamese and Viet Cong counterescalated by committing more of their troops to South Vietnam in response to increased U.S. bombing of the North.

$$\begin{array}{lll} \textit{N.V.} + \textit{V.C. troops} = & 194{,}000 & +\ .0099\ \textit{U.S. bombing} \\ \quad R^2 = .67 & (8{,}000) & \quad (.0012)\ \ \textit{sorties over N.V.}_{t\text{-}1} \end{array} \qquad (3)$$

One might conclude, in fact, that the U.S. bombing of North Vietnam provoked the North Vietnamese to increase their commitments in the South. According to the theory of cognitive congruence, one might speculate that North Vietnamese leaders came to value success in their struggle in the South in proportion to the costs of the punishments they suffered in the North as a result of their participation in the South. In other words, the continual bombing of North Vietnam that occurred from February 1965 through October 1968 (and intermittently until it was continual again starting in the spring of 1972)—escalating the war geographically and in destructive power—was a key factor in the spiraling escalation of North Vietnamese troop support to the Viet Cong in South Vietnam.

That the North Vietnamese considered the bombing of the North a provocative escalatory action is further indicated by their insistence that the bombing be the only issue on the agenda at the start of the Paris negotiations in May 1968.

Another reason for the North Vietnamese and Viet Cong's escalating their own troop commitments in the South was to offset the American escalation of troop, supply, and battle commitments there. Because American troop commitments and the American bombing of North Vietnam were so highly inter-correlated ($r = .92$ within the same month), we cannot simultaneously measure their relative impact on Communist troop escalations using the statistical methods of multiple regression. However, since at the beginning of 1965 the Communists were on the verge of winning a military victory and causing the collapse of the South Vietnamese government, we may infer that they increased their troop commitments in the South because the American escalation of troop and combat commitments threatened the victory they expected. Thus, we can specify equation 4 and measure the impact of U.S. commitments on Communist troop increases.

$$\underset{(6{,}000)}{\textit{N.V. + V.C. Troops} = 183{,}000} + \underset{(.3)}{4.5}\ \textit{U.S. Commitments}_{t\text{-}2} \qquad R^2 = .87 \tag{4}$$

The military consequence of troop escalations on both sides was the intensification of fighting and hence an escalation of both U.S. casualties and Communist attrition.[3]

$$\textit{U.S. Casualties} = \underset{(650)}{-890} + \underset{(.03)}{.44}\ \textit{U.S. Commitments} + \underset{(47.)}{150.}\ \textit{Spring-Fall} \qquad R^2 = .83 \tag{5}$$

$$\textit{N.V. + V.C. Attrition} = \underset{(1{,}600)}{5{,}700} + \underset{(.08)}{.84}\ \textit{U.S. Commitments} \qquad R^2 = .75 \tag{6}$$

Increases in U.S. commitments, including battalion-size operations and tactical bombing within South Vietnam, did achieve the objective of General Westmoreland's "meatgrinder" strategy—that of inflicting heavy casualties on the North Vietnamese and Viet Cong. However, the hawkish assumptions of that strategy proved invalid; indeed, rather than wear down the Communist forces, it led the Communists to replace their forces instead. For although North Vietnamese and Viet Cong manpower was not limitless, it was not exhausted either; and apparently, they were willing to continue to accept high casualties.

The very high correlation between U.S. casualties and North Vietnamese and Viet Cong attrition ($r = .92$) indicates not only that the escalating combat resulted in proportionally escalating combat losses on *both* sides, but also that during this 1965-67 period the intensity of the fighting on both sides could be measured using U.S. casualties alone.

South Vietnamese casualties were not as highly correlated with U.S. casualties ($r = .22$) or with Communist attrition ($r = .29$) as these latter two variables were with each other. Since firefights between opposing military forces usually result in casualties on both sides, these findings indicate that U.S. troops took on most of the direct combat with the Communist forces during the 1965-67 period, leaving the South Vietnamese troops mainly responsible for maintaining the security of pacified areas.

As U.S. casualties increased, the U.S. bombing of North Vietnam increased proportionately ($r = .86$ with a three-month lag). One major objective of the intensified bombing was, in the words of General Westmoreland, "the destruction of war-supporting activities which would assist us directly in the prosecution of the ground battle in the South" (Sharp and Westmoreland, 1969, p. 98). However, in attempting to reduce Communist military effectiveness and hence U.S. casualties, the escalation cycle was repeated: increased bombing of North Vietnam, Communist troop increases, U.S. troop increases, and increased casualties. Thus the vicious cycle went on and on.

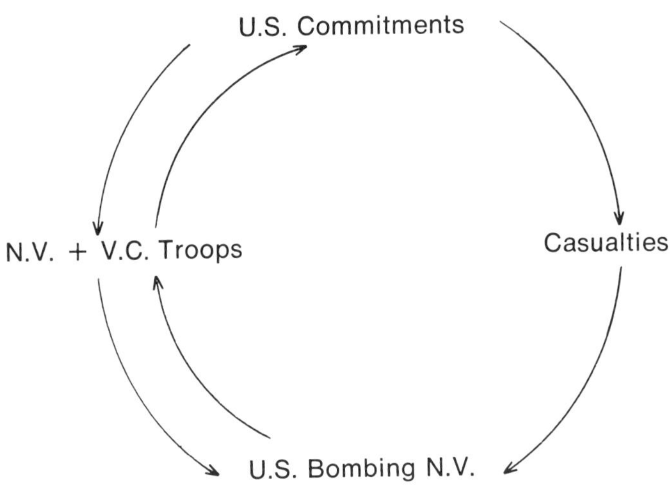

Figure 4. The Escalation Cycle

U.S. PUBLIC OPINION

Although relating to domestic politics in the United States, public support for President Johnson and his administration's Vietnam policy was another crucial element in the dynamics of the Vietnam War; and the leaders on both sides realized that fact. To the North Vietnamese and Viet Cong leaders, American public opinion was of strategic importance to the achievement of their objectives in Vietnam. They expected that in this protracted war that was costly to the United States, they could outlast the American determination to go on because they were fighting in their own country, whereas the Americans were fighting in a country that was of peripheral interest to the national security of the United States. Moreover, they believed that American popular support for the war would eventually fall to the point that the U.S. government would be forced to withdraw from Vietnam as the French had from Indochina in 1954.[4]

It is now clear that the North Vietnamese and Viet Cong were correct in their expectation that as the U.S. commitments of troops, supplies, and combat in South Vietnam continued to escalate, U.S. public opinion support for President Johnson and his Vietnam policy would fall.

$$\textit{Percentage of U.S. Public Supporting President Johnson} = \underset{(2.4)}{53.6} - \underset{(.0001)}{.0019}\ \textit{U.S. Commitments}_{t\text{-}1} \qquad R^2 = .88 \tag{7}$$

Since the escalating troop and battle commitments resulted in more Americans killed, as well as greater amounts of tax dollars spent on the war, higher taxes to finance the war, and increased inflation, which was fed by the government's initial deficit war spending and its resultant excessive demands on the U.S. economy, the American people steadily withdrew their support from, and voiced their opposition to, the Johnson administration and its Vietnam War policy. Indeed, public opinion support for President Johnson fell so low by March of 1968 (36 percent) that had he then sought a second full term, he would have faced less chance of reelection than any incumbent American president since 1948 and possibly since 1932.

In sum, President Johnson tried but failed to lead American public opinion to support his Vietnam policy. The less public support he had, judging from the polls, the more he and his administration publicly stated their preferences for increasing American military commitments in Vietnam ($r = -.30$ with a one-month lag). Yet as he made more and more military commitments, he lost more and more support.

The Johnson administration thus found itself in a dilemma partly of its own making. To save the South Vietnamese government from military defeat and political collapse at the hands of the North Vietnamese and the Viet Cong, President Johnson felt he had to commit an increasingly large number of U.S. troops to combat in South Vietnam. And to help the American and South Vietnamese troops defeat the Communists, he and his administration felt they had to intensify the bombing of North Vietnam. The Communists met these escalations with counterescalations of their own. Thus, the war was stalemated at increasingly greater levels of violence and casualties, and American public support for the war continued to decline.

POPULAR SUPPORT FOR THE VIET CONG

Yet another essential factor with regard to the dynamics of the war was the decline in popular support for the Viet Cong. In a "war of national liberation," the insurgents depend upon the local populace for military recruits, food supplies, information, and compliant behavior that may be based on threat, coercion, exchange for services, or ideological zeal. Such "cooperative" behavior is their political power, and insurgents depend upon it for their own protection from the political authorities they oppose, as well as for their continued operation.

Local people may cooperate with insurgents for a variety of reasons: the fear of being harmed by the insurgents if they do not; a possible gain in social or economic advantages if they do; or perhaps a true belief in the insurgents' cause. During a war, however, there is one determining factor for the behavior of local people: they will cooperate with whoever they think can most reliably offer them protection from harm, whether they be insurgents or the political authorities they are fighting. Survival—for oneself, one's family, and one's way of life—is the primary motivation in such situations. People will give their services, their goods, their money, their loyalty, and even a sense of legitimacy to those who they think can reliably protect them, and will even fight along with them for what they see as self-protection, whatever the demands.

When such demands are no longer seen as legitimate, local people will withdraw their compliance, if they get the chance, and will cease to cooperate. In other words, when insurgents cannot be relied upon to protect a population, the population will defect.[5]

Thus, we can measure the loss of popular support for the Viet Cong by counting the number of military and political defectors ("hoi chanh" or "ralliers") from it each month, because most of these "ralliers" to the South Vietnamese were Viet Cong, rather than North Vietnamese.

Of course, their number was partly determined by the size of the Viet Cong forces; for as the war escalated and the Viet Cong forces increased, the number of Viet Cong defectors inevitably rose as well—

and sometimes for quite simple, personal reasons. Merely wanting to return to their homes and families to help plant or harvest the crops is one example, for the season of the year is also a determining factor.

$$\textit{N.V. + V.C. Defectors} = \underset{(500)}{-1{,}100} + \underset{(.002)}{.011}\ \textit{N.V. + V.C. Troops} + \underset{(16)}{48}\ \textit{Spring-Fall} \qquad R^2 = .47 \tag{8}$$

Still, season and number of Viet Cong troops are only a partial explanation for the number of Viet Cong defectors. As the war escalated, it took an increasingly heavy toll in North Vietnamese and Viet Cong attrition. And as attrition increased, many of those who had joined the Viet Cong came to realize that the Viet Cong was not protecting them and therefore defected in ever larger numbers.

By looking at the determinants of the monthly proportion of North Vietnamese and Viet Cong who defected—i.e., the ratio of defectors to total North Vietnamese and Viet Cong troops—we can show that attrition among the Viet Cong was a significant factor in its own right, and not just a result of increased Viet Cong forces. In the following regression equation, attrition and season are significant factors, but U.S. commitments are not.

$$\left(\frac{\textit{N.V. + V.C. Defectors}}{\textit{N.V. + V.C. Troops}}\right) = \underset{(.0010)}{.0037} + \underset{(.000065)}{.00013}\ \textit{Spring-Fall} + \underset{(.00000009)}{.00000017}\ \textit{N.V. + V.C. Attrition} - \underset{(.000000095)}{.000000033}\ \textit{U.S. Commitments}_{t\text{-}1} \qquad R^2 = .29 \tag{9}$$

Thus, although we cannot simultaneously measure the independent effects of both troops and attrition on North Vietnamese and Viet Cong defections because of their being so highly intercorrelated, we can measure the effect of attrition alone when controlling for season.

$$\textit{N.V. + V.C. Defectors} = \underset{(270)}{430} + \underset{(.013)}{.061}\ \textit{N.V. + V.C. Attrition} + \underset{(17)}{32}\ \textit{Spring-Fall} \qquad R^2 = .44 \tag{10}$$

We may therefore conclude that the escalation of the fighting and the number of casualties had a negative effect on the political support for the Viet Cong that paralleled the negative effect it had on political support for the Johnson administration in the United States.[6]

POPULAR CONFIDENCE OF THE SOUTH VIETNAMESE IN THEIR GOVERNMENT

We now come to the question of the South Vietnamese popular confidence in their government, which in this study is measured by an index of the ratio of the black-market value of the South Vietnamese piastre in terms of dollars to the value of the piastre in goods and services, i.e. [(Dollars/Piastre) / (Money Supply/Consumer Prices)].[7]

Using this index as a measure, we can see that South Vietnamese popular confidence varied during the 1965-67 escalatory period of the war. Except for an abrupt rise in July 1965, when American troops first began offensive combat operations against the Communists, popular confidence generally dropped until it reached a low point in May 1966. It rose, in general, from then until it reached a high point in August 1967, whereupon it began to fall once more, never again reaching that height.

Since it is based on economic components, this indicator is highly autocorrelated and thus demonstrates a high degree of inertia. When controlling for such autocorrelation in regression equations, U.S. commitments in South Vietnam, U.S. bombing in North Vietnam, and North Vietnamese and Viet Cong troops, taken individually, have no significant effect on the index in question. Thus, its variation appears to be independent of the steady escalation of the war.

SUMMARY OF MILITARY AND POLITICAL INTERACTION

The main pattern of military and political interaction during the 1965-67 escalatory period of the Vietnam War is illustrated in figure 5. Reciprocal escalation between U.S. troop and combat commitments in South Vietnam and the U.S. bombing of North Vietnam, on the one hand, and that of North Vietnamese and Viet Cong troops, on the other, led to increasingly heavy American and North Vietnamese and Viet Cong casualties. The U.S. commitments reduced political support in the United States for the Johnson administration and its Vietnam policy; the attrition suffered by the North Vietnamese and Viet Cong reduced the Viet Cong's popular support. Thus, in seeking to gain military and political control of South Vietnam, both sides lost militarily as well as politically.

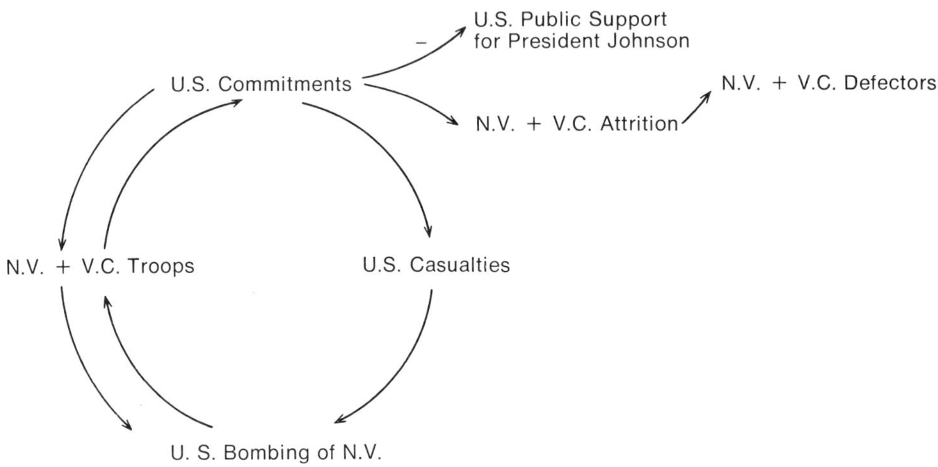

Figure 5. Pattern of Military and Political Interaction

This pattern of interaction was unrelieved until the Communist Tet offensive, which began in January 1968, forced the Johnson administration to review its entire Vietnam policy, reduce and then halt the bombing of North Vietnam, and move to start negotiating with the North Vietnamese and Viet Cong in Paris.[8]

PUBLIC STATEMENTS OF POLICY-MAKERS

The subsidiary patterns of interaction between public rhetoric and military actions during this 1965-67 period remain to be analyzed. To begin with, the public statements of policy-makers on both sides were elements in the domestic and international politics of the war. Public statements directed toward domestic audiences and foreign allies were used to justify policies and gain support for them. Those directed at adversaries were used to threaten or promise, and sometimes to bargain tacitly.

Since such public statements were heeded by leaders on both sides, as well as by those leaders' own people and allies, they constituted political acts during the war, even though they were often misleading and sometimes outright lies, as may be seen, for example, by comparing many public statements of American policy-makers with their private secret memoranda published in the *Pentagon Papers.*

In analyzing the patterns of relationships between the public statements of policy-makers and their actual behavior during the war, one finds a basis for such domestically important political phenomena as the "credibility gap" during the Johnson administration and the failure of the two sides to negotiate a deescalation of the war during the 1965-67 period.

As was explained in chapter 2, eight communications indices were constructed from a systematic content analysis of the public statements made by the policy-makers on both sides (U.S. and South Vietnamese; North Vietnamese and Viet Cong). These statements were coded from the *New York Times Index* for the entire period of 1965-67. The indices were constructed to measure each side's publicly stated preferences for its own military and political activities; perceptions of the opposing side's military and political activities; preferences for negotiations; and preferences for advantageous outcomes in the war.[9]

"PEACE OFFENSIVES"

The major pattern of relationships of the public rhetoric on both sides to their military actions, and to the political consequences of such actions, may be described as the so-called peace offensive—a term first used by President Johnson in describing the intensified diplomatic efforts that accompanied the thirty-eight-day halt in the bombing of North Vietnam during December 1965 and January 1966. It was characterized by what appeared to be public attempts to persuade the adversary to enter into negotiations that would deescalate or end the war in order to stop the terrible destruction and loss of life. The peace offensive pattern of public rhetoric, however, occurred throughout the 1965-67 period.

A main characteristic of the various peace offensives was that, in general, they were designed as attempts to assuage the negative international and domestic political reactions to the escalation and conduct of the war as much as they were attempts to seriously negotiate a compromise to end the war. Each side, through its military efforts, demonstrated that it sought to win militarily and politically, or at least to avoid being defeated. More than a call for serious negotiation of a compromise settlement, the public rhetoric of the leaders on both sides consisted generally in thinly disguised exhortations for the adversary to renounce its own objectives and military efforts. Knowing that such exhortations would probably go unheeded, the policy-makers responsible for them were more likely playing a cynical domestic political game with their own constituents and an international political game with nonbelligerents in deference to "world opinion" than seriously seeking a compromise that would end the war.

United States rhetoric with regard to negotiating was intended as much for dovish political opponents of the Johnson administration, U.S. allies, neutrals, and nonbelligerent Communist states as for the North Vietnamese and Viet Cong. Indeed, as to the former, such public statements were most likely meant to have the effect of assuaging opposition, showing determination, explaining policy, and bringing them over to the Johnson administration's point of view.

Documentary evidence for this interpretation of U.S. peace offensives includes the following quotation from a memorandum in the "Pentagon Papers," written by Secretary McNamara on 20 July 1965:

> Together with the above military moves, we should take political initiatives in order to lay a groundwork for a favorable political settlement by clarifying our objectives and establishing channels of communications. At the same time as we are taking steps to turn the tide in South Vietnam, we would make quiet moves through diplomatic channels (a) to open a dialogue with Moscow and Hanoi, and perhaps the VC, looking first toward disabusing them of any misconceptions as to our goals and second toward laying the groundwork for a settlement when the time is ripe; (b) to keep the Soviet

Union from deepening its military [*sic*] in the world until the time when settlement can be achieved; and (c) to cement support for U.S. policy by the U.S. public, allies and friends, and to keep international opposition at a manageable level. Our efforts may be unproductive until the tide begins to turn, but nevertheless they should be made. (NYT, *PP*, p. 458)

The series of bivariate correlations illustrated in figure 6 demonstrates the general "peace offensive" pattern during the 1965-67 period, as well as the linkages of this pattern to the military escalation and its political consequences during this same period.

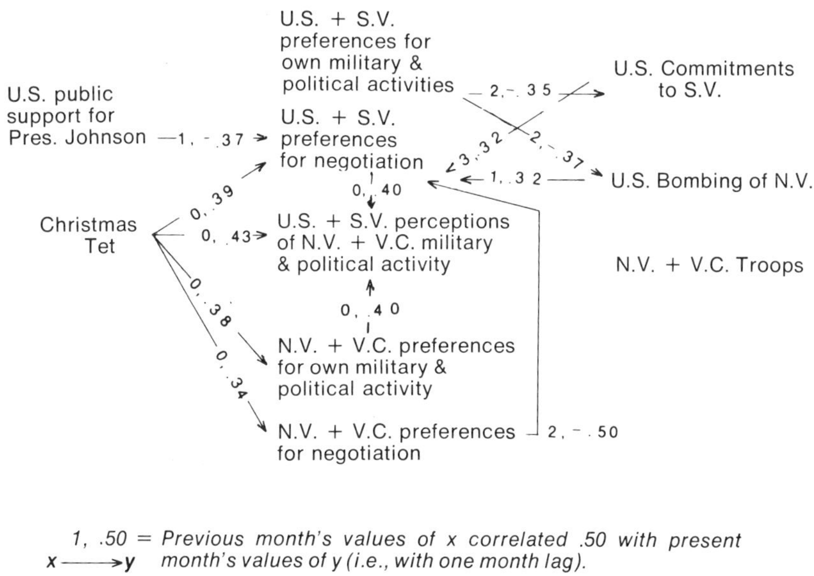

Figure 6. Bivariate Correlations in the "Peace Offensive" Pattern, 1965-67

Following decreases in American public support for President Johnson and his Vietnam policy ($r = -.37$ with a one-month lag), increases in U.S. troop and combat commitments in South Vietnam ($r = .32$ with a three-month lag), and in U.S. bombing of North Vietnam ($r = .32$ with a one-month lag), U.S. and South Vietnamese leaders tended to increase the frequency of their public statements expressing preference for a negotiated settlement of the war. Moreover, these statements tended to occur during the Christmas-Tet holiday season ($r = .39$). Such findings suggest that, motivated in part to counter dovish criticism of its Vietnam policy, the Johnson administration took the occasion of the Christmas-Tet holiday season to demonstrate its peaceful spirit by increasing the number of its public statements regarding its desire to end the war by negotiations.

The first peace offensive after the sustained bombing of North Vietnam had begun occurred in May 1965. President Johnson's personal message of 10 May 1965 to General Maxwell Taylor, the U.S. ambassador to South Vietnam, clearly illustrates the pattern of the peace offensive approach that the Johnson administration followed throughout the escalatory phase of the war. The holiday period on this occasion was Buddha's birthday rather than Christmas or Tet.

> I have learned from Bob McNamara that nearly all Rolling Thunder operations for this week can be completed by Wednesday noon, Washington time. This fact and the days of Buddha's birthday seem to me to provide an excellent opportunity for a pause in air attacks which might go into next week and which I could use to good effect with world opinion.
>
> My plan is not to announce this brief pause but simply to call it privately to the attention of Moscow and Hanoi as soon as possible and tell them that we shall be watching closely to see whether they respond in any way. My current plan is to report publicly after the pause ends on what we have done. . . .
>
> You should understand that my purpose in this plan is to begin to clear a path either toward restoration of peace or toward increased military action, depending upon the reaction of the Communists. We have amply demonstrated our determination and our commitment in the last two months, and I now wish to gain some flexibility. . . . (*New York Times*, 28 June 1972, p. 18)

That the Johnson administration was also heeding its hawkish constituents is shown by its attempt to "soften up" the Communists by escalating combat in the South and bombing in the North prior to these public statements. For the hawks had argued that the U.S. could offer to cease its bombing in the North in exchange for a Communist capitulation and a halt in their military efforts in the South.

On the other hand, the North Vietnamese and Viet Cong leaders also tended to use the Christmas and Tet holiday season as an occasion to increase the frequency of their publicly stated preferences for negotiation ($r = .34$). Moreover, the Communists generally made similar statements following periods in which they had inflicted relatively heavy casualties on the South Vietnamese forces that were engaged in efforts to "pacify" and secure the countryside. Thus, the Communists also sought to negotiate when they were in a position of strength, as well as to reduce their public statements regarding their preferences for outcomes in the war of advantage to themselves.

$$\begin{aligned} \textit{N.V. + V.C. Public Preferences for Negotiation} = & -25 + .018\ \text{S.V. } \textit{Casualties}_{t\text{-}3} \\ & \ \ (7) \quad (.006) \\ & + 7.2\ \textit{Christmas-Tet} \\ & \quad (2.3) \\ & - .55\ \textit{N.V. + V.C. Public Statements} \\ & \quad (.25)\ \textit{about Favorable Outcomes} \end{aligned} \qquad (11)$$

$R^2 = .41$

However, the North Vietnamese and Viet Cong leaders, like their U.S. and South Vietnamese counterparts, appeared to follow a mixed declaratory policy; for on both sides increased publicly stated preferences for negotiations were uncorrelated with statements preferring their own military and political activities. In other words, both sides were as likely as not to be publicly stating their preferences for increasing their own military and political activities in South Vietnam during the same month that they were publicly stating their desire for negotiating.

Furthermore, both sides were likely to increase their troop commitments in South Vietnam, and the United States to increase its bombing of North Vietnam, during the same month that their respective leaders stated their growing desire for negotiations. In addition, the United States tended to *increase* its commitments in South Vietnam ($r = —.35$ with a two-month lag) and its bombing in North Vietnam ($r = —.37$ with a two-month lag) following the U.S. and South Vietnamese leaders' publicly stating their preferences for *decreasing* their military and political activities in South Vietnam. Thus, by not matching their actions to their words, each side would reinforce the other's distrust and fear of being exploited.

The sincerity of all statements preferring negotiation were therefore continually suspect. Each side believed that the other was taking advantage of holiday cease-fires to resupply and reinforce their own troops. For example, within the same months that the U.S. and South Vietnamese leaders increased their publicly stated preferences for negotiation, they also publicly expressed their belief that the North Vietnamese and Viet Cong were increasing their military and political activity in South Vietnam ($r = .40$), and this most particularly during the Christmas-Tet holiday periods ($r = .43$).

Now, in point of fact, the public statements of U.S. and South Vietnamese leaders asserting that North Vietnamese and Viet Cong military and political activity in South Vietnam was increasing were actually uncorrelated with Communist troop increases. Rather, they were apparently responses to public *statements* of North Vietnamese and Viet Cong leaders conveying their preferences for increased military and political activities ($r = .40$). And although Communist troop increases were uncorrelated with such statements, the statements also tended to increase during the Christmas-Tet holiday periods ($r = .38$).[10]

North Vietnamese President Ho Chi Minh's 1966 poetic New Years' message printed in *Nhan Dan* is an example of the bellicose rhetoric of the holiday periods:

> May the South shine with new victories,
> With many more Dautieng, Baubang, Pleime, Danang. . . .
> May the North fight heroically,
> The higher the American aggressors escalate,
> The heavier their defeats.
> Let all our compatriots unite and be of one mind,
> Whether at the front line or in the rear
> Let our people redouble their efforts,
> Emulating in production and rushing forward to the fight
> Against the U.S. aggressors, for national salvation, our
> Victory is certain.

This poem (reprinted in the *New York Times*, 2 Jan. 1966, p. 22), directed to a domestic North Vietnamese audience, appeared little more than a month after Ho and Premier Pham Van Dong had expressed their desire for negotiation in a personal interview with Amintore Fanfani, then Italy's foreign minister, and Giogio La Pira, professor of Roman law and former mayor of Florence. The meeting took place on 11 November 1965, and was reported in the *New York Times* on 18 December 1965. The following are excerpts from their statements:

> . . . In order for the peace negotiations to come about, there will be necessary (a) a cease-fire (by air, by sea, by land) in the entire territory of Vietnam (North and South); the cessation, that is, of all belligerent operations (including therefore also the cessation of debarkation of further American troops); (b) a declaration according to which the Geneva agreements of 1954 will be taken as the basis for the negotiations—a declaration made up of the four points formulated by Hanoi, points that are in reality the explanation of the Geneva text and which therefore can be reduced to a single point: application in other words of the Geneva accords.
>
> . . . The government in Hanoi is prepared to initiate negotiations without first requiring actual withdrawal of American troops.

Ho Chi Minh also added: "I am prepared to go anywhere; to meet anyone" (Fanfani, p. 3).

During the holiday period a year later, in a personal interview with

Harrison Salisbury, reporter and associate editor of the *New York Times*, Premier Pham Van Dong of North Vietnam again stated simultaneously both his desire for deescalating and ending the war and his determination to continue the fighting if necessary:

> "The moment the United States puts an end to the war, we will respect each other and settle every question. Why don't you [the U.S.] think that way?"
>
> At another point he said that with a cessation of hostilities, "we can speak about other things." He added: "After this there will be no lack of generosity on our part—you may be sure of that."
>
> At the same time the Premier stressed again and again that North Vietnam was prepared to fight 10 years, 20 years, or any number of years in support of its sovereignty and independence in its "sacred war."
>
> "We are determined to fight on until our sacred rights are recognized.
>
> "The big question is to reach a settlement which can be enforced.
>
> "The party which has to make first steps is Washington. We have no doubt on this point. If this does not come about today, it will come tomorrow. It's no use to make haste, the questions will be put wrongly and we will have to wait again. So let the situation ripen.
>
> "We are prepared for a long war because a people's war must be a long war, a war against aggression has to be a long war. Nobody knows how long it will be. It lasts until there is no more aggression.
>
> "How many years? What I used to tell our friends was that the younger generation will fight better than we—even kids so high. They are preparing themselves. That's the situation.
>
> "How many years the war goes on depends on you and not on us." (Salisbury, 4 January 1967, pp. 1-2)

Such belligerent rhetoric on the part of the North Vietnamese and Viet Cong leaders during peace offensives was probably meant as a bargaining counter to U.S. attempts to apply military pressure to the Communists prior to U.S. peace offensives—itself a move designed to coerce the Communists to negotiate a settlement on U.S. terms. According to the "Pentagon Papers," U.S. conditions for a negotiated settlement, at least in the spring of 1965, "were not 'compromise' terms, but more akin to a 'cease and desist' order that, from the D.R.V./VC point of view, was tantamount to a demand for their surrender," albeit "discreet and relatively face-saving" (NYT, *PP*, pp. 388, 458). Indeed, Secretary McNamara outlined the desired outcomes of any negotiated settlement that the Johnson administration considered fundamental and acceptable in a memorandum dated 20 July 1965. The terms would have amounted, in effect, to a Communist capitulation:

(a) VC stop attacks and drastically reduce incidents of terror and sabotage.
(b) DRV reduces infiltration to a trickle, with some reasonably reliable method of our obtaining confirmation of this fact.
(c) U.S./GVN stop bombing of North Vietnam.
(d) GVN stays independent (hopefully pro-U.S., but possibly genuinely neutral).
(e) GVN exercises governmental functions over substantially all of South Vietnam.
(f) Communists remain quiescent in Laos and Thailand.
(g) DRV withdraws PAVN forces and other North Vietnamese infiltrators (not regroupees) from South Vietnam.
(h) VC/NLF transform from a military to a purely political organization.
(i) U.S. combat forces (not advisors or AID) withdraw.

(NYT, *PP*, p. 458)

The North Vietnamese and Viet Cong leaders thus matched American toughness in starting negotiations with their own toughness with statements expressing their determination to continue their part in the war and not capitulate.

Each side interpreted the other side's toughness at the time of peace offensives as a sign of insincere negotiating tactics. United States and South Vietnamese leaders, expecting that their attempts to initiate negotiations would be unsuccessful, and fearing that the Communists would take advantage of them during holiday lulls in the fighting, tended to focus their attention on the belligerent public statements of the North Vietnamese and Viet Cong leaders rather than the more conciliatory statements supporting negotiations to end the war. Moreover, since Communist troop commitments were uncorrelated with North Vietnamese and Viet Cong leaders' publicly expressed preferences for negotiation, Communist troop increases would as likely as not have occurred within the same month that Communist preferences for negotiations were being publicly announced. Under pressure from its hawkish critics not to trust the Communists nor to risk American lives by letting up the military pressure on them, the Johnson administration tended to pay heed to the belligerent rhetoric of the Communist leaders and plan for the worst. By citing Communist intransigence, and thus temporarily relieving the dovish political pressure to negotiate instead of fighting, the Johnson administration used the peace offensives to "clear the decks" for intensified reescalation of the war (NYT, *PP*, p. 388).

That President Johnson viewed Communist offers of negotiation as requests for surrender is illustrated by his statement in a public speech at Johns Hopkins University on 7 April 1965, to the effect that the United States was bombing North Vietnam "to convince the leaders of North Vietnam—and all who seek to share their conquest—of a simple fact: We will not be defeated. We will not grow tired. We will not withdraw, either openly or under the cloak of a meaningless agreement" (Johnson, 7 April 1965).

During peace offensives the Communists also were presented with double messages by the U.S. and South Vietnamese leaders, who were often making *their* belligerent statements about increasing their own military and political activity at the same time as they were publicly stating their preferences for negotiating an end to the war, since such public statements were uncorrelated. Moreover, given the fact that U.S. troop commitments to South Vietnam and the bombing of North Vietnam were uncorrelated with U.S. and South Vietnamese leaders' public statements expressing a preference for negotiations, American intentions were even more ambiguous, since American troop commitments and the bombing of the North were as likely to increase as decrease during the same month that U.S. and South Vietnamese leaders increased their publicly expressed desires to negotiate. The contradiction between American words and deeds was probably designed to show U.S. determination to continue its military efforts until the Communists capitulated.[11] Thus, wishing to give an image of strength and determination but suspicious of American intentions, North Vietnamese and Viet Cong leaders accused not only U.S. leaders of being insincere but the "peace offensives" as being trickery designed to take advantage of them. As a result, both sides were more polarized and intent on continuing the fighting; for, in fact, U.S. and South Vietnamese public statements expressing a preference for negotiations decreased subsequent to increased numbers of similar public statements by the North Vietnamese and Viet Cong ($r = -.50$ with a two-month lag).

In other words, with each side distrusting the enemy, afraid of being taken advantage of, desiring that the other side capitulate under the cover of a negotiated settlement of the war, the peace offensives failed to achieve a negotiated end to the fighting.

The main reason for the "peace offensive" rhetoric's failure to end the war was that, although each side had an incentive to reduce the intensity of the conflict and hence its own military and economic losses, the respective leaders desired the initial objective (i.e, political control of South Vietnam) even more. Although a cessation of hostilities was attractive to both sides, both wanted it on their own terms. Distrustful of the enemy, neither side wanted peace at the cost, or even apparent cost, of capitulation. Indeed, both felt the need to justify the heavy costs they had already brought upon themselves, and the respective leaders were willing to bear ever greater losses in order to inflict ever greater punishment on the enemy, believing at each escalatory step that they could force the other side to capitulate. Refusing to concede victory or apparent victory to the enemy, each side felt impelled to press ahead and failed to recognize that its own escalation would provoke counterescalation, not capitulation, on the part of the enemy. Thus, both sides were confounded in their attempts to halt the spiral of increasingly intense warfare in Vietnam.[12]

1. The regression coefficients (*b*) state (within some stated standard error (*SE*)) the magnitude of the effect of an independent variable on a dependent variable. The sign of the regression coefficient indicates the direction of the effect (plus or minus). These equations can be used to predict the value of a dependent variable given the value of the independent variable, assuming that the value of the independent variable stays within the range of the values it has had in the past and from which these regression equations were derived.

The proportional reduction in the error of the prediction of a dependent variable, as compared with the error associated with using the mean value as the predicted value, is measured by the square of the multiple correlation coefficient, or R^2.

Values for all variables in the regression equations are monthly. Values are within the same month except those marked "*t*-1," which are of the previous month, and "*t*-2," which are the values from two months before.

The first-order autocorrelation term (i.e., the dependent variable with a one-month lag) is included in the specification of the regression equations for those dependent variables which for theoretical or substantive reasons we would expect to display a great deal of "inertia." For example, the number of troops one month is dependent upon the previous month's number, because this variable is necessarily additive. The number of bombing missions flown one month is not dependent in the same way on the number flown the previous month; they need not be additive. The number of bombing missions, however, does display a great deal of autocorrelation because of bureaucratic inertia and the momentum of the bombing policy: once the bombers and pilots were in Southeast Asia, there was a great deal of incentive to use them if possible unless limited by political decisions.

The specification of the regression equations is informed by theoretical and substantive considerations, however, and autocorrelation terms will not always appear in the regression equations when substantive or theoretical terms take precedence in the specification. Additional U.S. troop commitments, for example, were made not primarily because U.S. troops were already in Vietnam but in response to additional North Vietnamese and Viet Cong troops.

2. Even though U.S. commitments are highly autocorrelated, we know that their increase was due more to Communist troop increases than to mere momentum. Hence, the specification of equation 1.

3. United States commitments are more highly correlated with U.S. casualties and N.V. + V.C. attrition than are N.V. + V.C. troops. Because U.S. commitments and N.V. + V.C. troops are so highly correlated, we cannot include them both in a multiple regression to determine their separate but simultaneous effect on

U.S. casualties and N.V. + V.C. attrition. Hence, U.S. commitments are specified in regression equations 5 and 6.

4. President Johnson was also aware that American public support for his Vietnam policy was of crucial importance to his international and domestic political plans. In fact, he frequently quoted the results of public opinion polls, which he sometimes carried in his coat pocket when they were favorable to him and to his Vietnam policy. As noted in chapter 4, he did his utmost to lead the American people to support his policy; and he controlled the flow of information to the Congress and public with regard to the full extent of the actual commitments made to South Vietnam as a result of his policy, as well as the costs of those commitments. For example, in order to avoid congressional and public debate about his policy and commitments, he chose to finance the war initially through huge budget deficits rather than ask the Congress for a necessary tax increase. This deficit financing of the war eventually lead to very serious domestic and international economic problems for the United States, including rapid inflation and a deficit in its international balance of payments.

5. Defection is literally "voting with one's feet." Defections from the Viet Cong often occurred when South Vietnamese government forces demonstrated local military superiority and overran Viet Cong areas.

6. This ironic effect of both sides' escalation of the war will be further analyzed in chapter 9.

7. The development of this indirect index is described in chapter 2.

8. The patterns of interaction after the Tet offensive, including the withdrawal of U.S. ground troops from Vietnam during the Nixon administration, are analyzed in chapter 8.

9. See Appendix A, "Content Analysis of Public Communications."

10. During the same holiday periods, however, Communist leaders might also make statements indicating their willingness to negotiate, so that by contrast to their stated determination to fight on in the war, their proposals for peace on North Vietnamese and Viet Cong terms would appear more acceptable to U.S. and South Vietnamese leaders and not a sign of Communist weakness.

11. This pattern of relationships between public statements of the policy-makers of the United States and U.S. troop commitments in South Vietnam, as well as the bombing of North Vietnam, suggests an explanation of the "credibility gap" that developed during the Johnson administration. The American public heard the Johnson administration publicly saying one thing (that it preferred to reduce American military efforts in Vietnam) and saw it doing another: making larger American troop and combat commitments in South Vietnam and intensifying the bombing of the North ($r = -.35$ and $-.37$ respectively with two-month lags). Moreover, the public realized that no correspondence existed between the administration's publicly stated preferences for negotiating an end to the war and its preferences for increasing American military efforts in Vietnam. It is little wonder, then, that the American people came to question the truthfulness of the Johnson administration's public statements.

12. Even later high-level negotiations between the United States and North Vietnam such as those occurring from October to December 1972 reflect this pattern of each side's wanting to end the war on its own terms, being frustrated by the other side, and reescalating the war.

6

Computer Simulation Predictions of the Escalation of the War

Discovering and analyzing the general empirical patterns of political and military interactions help us not only to understand the dynamics of the war but also to construct predictive models based upon those patterns. Predictive models have practical significance and at the same time fulfill one of the major purposes of scientific inquiry:

> The purpose of science is to describe the world in an orderly scheme or language which will help us to look ahead. We want to forecast what we can of the future behavior of the world; particularly we want to forecast how it would behave under several alternative actions of our own between which we are usually trying to choose. (Bronowski, p. 70).

In this chapter a model, using the computer simulation method described in chapter 3 and constructed from relationships empirically validated in chapter 5, will be used to predict (as if we were in March 1965) the course of the war during the 1965-67 escalatory period and beyond. In the next chapter we will use this model and computer simulation method to make predictions of what the course of the conflict might have been under hypothetical alternative hawk and dove policies.

REGRESSION EQUATION MODEL

The model used in the computer simulation consists of the eight interrelated regression equations shown in table 3. The dependent variables in these equations are the components of the primary pattern of mutual escalation analyzed in chapter 5. They include: North Vietnamese and Viet Cong troops, U.S. troop and combat commitments in South Vietnam, U.S. bombing sorties over North Vietnam, U.S. casualties, North Vietnamese and Viet Cong attrition, U.S. public support for President Johnson, North Vietnamese and Viet Cong defectors, and the popular confidence of the South Vietnamese people in their government. The empirical relationships represented in this model are diagrammed in figure 7.

As discussed in chapter 3, a model constructed of interrelated regression equations can be used to make predictions by means of computer simulation when the model meets certain criteria. These include time-

TABLE 3

REGRESSION EQUATION MODEL FOR SIMULATION PREDICTIONS

$$\textit{N.V. + V.C. Troops} = \underset{(5{,}000)}{194{,}000} + \underset{(0.3)}{4.1}\ \textit{U.S. Commitments}_{t\text{-}3} \tag{1}$$

$$\textit{U.S. Commitments} = \underset{(1{,}900)}{-\ 3{,}100} + \underset{(.011)}{.027}\ \textit{N.V. + V.C. Troops}_{t\text{-}1} + \underset{(.06)}{.82}\ \textit{U.S. Commitments}_{t\text{-}1} \tag{2}$$

$$\textit{U.S. Bombing N.V.} = \underset{(1{,}400)}{-\ 2{,}900} + \underset{(.10)}{.64}\ \textit{U.S. Bombing N.V.}_{t\text{-}1} - \underset{(34)}{112}\ \textit{Winter-Summer} + \underset{(.007)}{.021}\ \textit{N.V. + V.C. Troops}_{t\text{-}1} \tag{3}$$

$$\textit{U.S. Casualties} = \underset{(650)}{-\ 890} + \underset{(47)}{150}\ \textit{Spring-Fall} + \underset{(.03)}{.44}\ \textit{U.S. Commitments} \tag{4}$$

$$\textit{N.V. + V.C. Attrition} = \underset{(1{,}600)}{5{,}700} + \underset{(.08)}{.84}\ \textit{U.S. Commitments} \tag{5}$$

$$\textit{Percentage of U.S. Public Supporting President Johnson} = \underset{(2.4)}{53.6} - \underset{(.0001)}{.0019}\ \textit{U.S. Commitments}_{t\text{-}1} \tag{6}$$

$$\textit{N.V. + V.C. Defectors} = \underset{(270)}{430} + \underset{(0.013)}{0.061}\ \textit{N.V. + V.C. Attrition} + \underset{(17)}{32}\ \textit{Spring-Fall} \tag{7}$$

$$\textit{Popular Confidence of the South Vietnamese} = \underset{(320)}{410} + \underset{(.07)}{.87}\ \textit{S.V. Popular Confidence}_{t\text{-}1} + \underset{(.0054)}{.0065}\ \textit{U.S. Commitments}_{t\text{-}1} \tag{8}$$

lagged relationships, nonreciprocal specification of relationships within the same time period, and feedback relationships. In addition, the greater the amount of statistical variance explained (i.e., the greater the R^2) in all of the variables, the more accurate will be the predictions for all the variables in the model.

In order to make predictions using this computer simulation method, each independent variable used to predict some dependent variable (except the exogenous seasonal independent variables) must itself be predicted as a variable dependent upon some other independent variables. In this way, a new value for each variable is predicted each month, and these new values are used to predict the following month's values of all the variables.

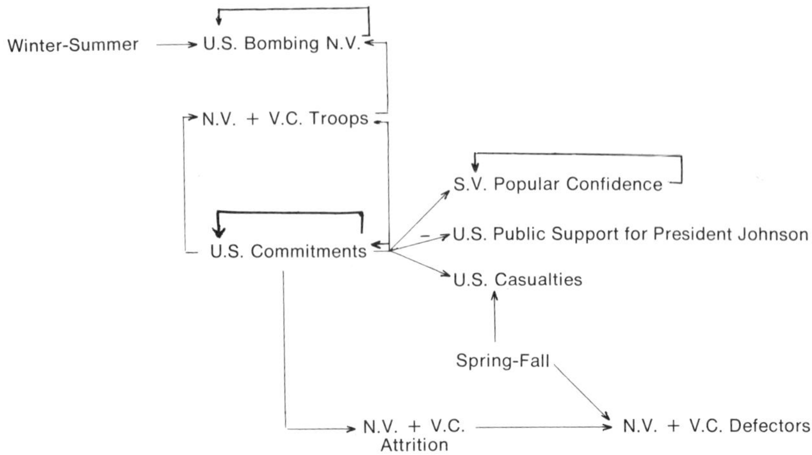

Figure 7. Patterns of Interaction in Simulation Model

In order to achieve a high multiple correlation coefficient for each variable (since the success of the simulation predictions for all variables depends upon the accuracy of the predictions for each variable), some of the equations specified in this model include autocorrelation terms, i.e., the past value of the dependent variable itself. In each such equation, (U.S. commitments, U.S. bombing, South Vietnamese popular confidence) the inclusion of the first order autocorrelation term is theoretically justified, because of the "inertia" or "momentum" of these variables.

In the equations for U.S. commitments and U.S. bombing of North Vietnam, intercorrelated independent variables are specified. Their inclusion is justified on theoretical grounds, since U.S. commitments and bombing were determined by policies and actions of both sides. Moreover, inclusion of collinear independent variables in these cases contributes to a greater amount of statistical variance explained in the dependent variables.

One will note in equations 1 and 2 in table 3 that U.S. commitments and North Vietnamese and Viet Cong troops determine each other with a time lag for both. The purpose for this specification is to provide feedback in the model. In regression analysis, predictions of the dependent variable are based on *given* updated values of the independent variables. In computer simulation, however, after the initial values are given, all predicted values in following months are themselves based upon *prior predictions* of the independent variables. Thus, for simulation purposes, a model without feedback in which, for example, variable

A determines variable B, and variable B in turn determines variable C, i.e., $A \rightarrow B \rightarrow C$, will not work, for we will not be able to predict the next month's value of A. What we must do instead is construct models in which feedback relationships are specified, e.g., in which variable B or variable C determines variable A, i.e., $A \leftrightarrow B \rightarrow C$ or $A \rightarrow B \rightarrow C \rightarrow A$. When $B \rightarrow A$ or $C \rightarrow A$ relationship is lagged in time, we can predict the next month's value of A, and thus do another round of predictions of B and C as well. This is the "bootstrapping" process described in more detail in chapter 3. The chief advantage of constructing models that include feedback relationships is that using the computer simulation technique, one can continue to make predictions indefinitely into the future of each variable in the model. We shall now turn to the predictive results of the simulation of this model.

RESULTS OF THE SIMULATION OF THE 1965-67 ESCALATION

Using just the initial values of January, February, and March, 1965, the simulation of the model made predictions for each month from April 1965 on. In general, the simulation predicted the major trends of the escalation of the war from April 1965 through December 1967. The predicted values of the variables show a realistic stability, i.e., they do not diverge rapidly from the actual values or oscillate widely from one month to the next.[1]

A comparison of the graphs of the values predicted by the simulation (noted by "0's" on the graphs) and of the actual values of the variables (noted by "X's") (see figures 8–15) shows a good duplication of the actual escalatory trends in U.S. commitments and casualties, U.S. bombing of North Vietnam and North Vietnamese and Viet Cong troops and attrition. Moreover, the steep drop in U.S. public support for President Johnson is clearly seen in the computer simulation. The predictions also represent the "peaks" and "valleys" in the variations of U.S. bombing of North Vietnam, U.S. casualties, and defections from the Communists, even though the predictions may not go as high or as low as the actual values of these variables. The "peaks" and "valleys" in the predicted values of these variables reflect seasonal changes and show a regular yearly phase component that matches that in the actual values of the variables. To test whether this model and simulation represent nothing more than a linear time trend and a yearly phase, a separate regression analysis and simulation were done in which each dependent variable was predicted only by the two independent variables of a linear time trend and the month. The average explained variance (R^2) was only 35 percent in the regression equations, suggesting that the phase component in the simulations is not a regular curve such as a sine wave. Thus, the other variables in the simulation model are necessary to explain the escalation of the Vietnam War. The predictions of South Vietnamese popular confidence do show a decline and rise, but do not reflect the steepness of the actual decline, the sharp rise starting in June 1966, and the abrupt fall starting in September 1967. This lack of correspondence between the simulation predictions and actual values of this variable is further evidence that, as reported in chapter 5, U.S. commitments did not have a significant systematic effect on South Vietnamese popular confidence, even though for lack of an alternative determinant, the computer simulation model was specified in this way.

We can evaluate the accuracy of the simulation predictions by comparing them with the actual monthly values for each variable and to the values estimated by the ordinary regression technique. In ordinary regression the actual monthly values of the independent variables are used to make the estimate of the dependent variables. By contrast, in the simulation, only the predicted monthly values of the independent variables from April 1965 on are used to make additional predictions of the dependent variables.

Table 4 provides six different measures of the goodness of fit of the values predicted by the simulation to the actual values and to the values estimated by the ordinary regression technique.

In table 4 we see in column 2 that, when compared with the actual values, the mean error of the simulation predictions ranged from a remarkably low 4 percent for the number of N.V. + V.C. troops to a very large 843 percent for U.S. bombing sorties over North Vietnam.[2]

The mean error of the estimates made using ordinary regression analysis (shown in column 3) range from a low of 5 percent for the number of N.V. + V.C. troops and South Vietnamese popular confidence to a high of 455 percent for U.S. bombing sorties over North Vietnam.

Thus, when comparing the errors in the simulation prediction with the errors in the ordinary regressions in column 4, we see that the predictions made by the computer simulation using only the initial data from January through March 1965 average only 35 percent more error than do the estimates made by ordinary regression, which continually uses the previous month's actual values for the estimates it makes.

When comparing the variance explained by the simulation predictions (in column 6) with the variance explained by regression analysis (column 5), we see that for seven of the eight variables, the simulation predictions are nearly as accurate as the estimates made by regression

TABLE 4

MEASURES OF GOODNESS OF FIT OF SIMULATION PREDICTIONS

Variables	(1) $\frac{\Sigma \text{Prediction}}{\Sigma \text{Actual}}$	(2) Mean Percent Prediction Error = $\frac{\sum \frac{\lvert\text{Actual-Prediction}\rvert}{\text{Actual}}}{N}$	(3) Mean Percent Regression Error = $\frac{\sum \frac{\lvert\text{Actual-Regressed}\rvert}{\text{Actual}}}{N}$	(4) $\frac{\text{Prediction Error}}{\text{Regression Error}} = \frac{\Sigma\lvert\text{Actual-Prediction}\rvert}{\Sigma\lvert\text{Actual-Regressed}\rvert}$	(5) Explained Variance of Regression = $R^2 = \frac{\sum\left[\text{Regressed} - \left(\frac{\Sigma \text{Actual}}{N}\right)\right]^2}{\sum\left[\text{Actual} - \left(\frac{\Sigma \text{Actual}}{N}\right)\right]^2}$	(6) Explained Variance of Prediction = $R^2 = \frac{\sum\left[\text{Prediction} - \left(\frac{\Sigma \text{Actual}}{N}\right)\right]^2}{\sum\left[\text{Actual} - \left(\frac{\Sigma \text{Actual}}{N}\right)\right]^2}$
1 N.V. + V.C. attrition	1.01	.21	.18	1.15	.71	.68
2 S.V. popular confidence	.99	.10	.05	2.05	.82	.37
3 U.S. commitments	1.01	.15	.09	1.75	.98	.95
4 U.S. casualties	1.01	.41	.36	1.15	.80	.80
5 U.S. bombing N.V.	1.04	8.43	4.55	1.85	.90	.80
6 U.S. public support for L.B.J.	.99	.72	.64	1.14	.86	.84
7 N.V. + V.C. defectors	.98	.34	.33	1.02	.37	.36
8 N.V. + V.C. troops	1.01	.04	.05	.68	.86	.92

N.B.: Σ = Sum
Prediction = Values predicted by computer simulation
N = Number of months
Regressed = Values estimated by ordinary regression
Actual = Actual monthly values

analysis. Indeed, the simulation predictions of the number of North Vietnamese and Viet Cong troops are better than the regression estimates. The average explained variance for the simulation predictions is 72 percent, compared with 79 percent for the regression estimates. Thus, on the average, the simulation predictions explain only 7 percent less variance than do the regression equations. This is remarkable when we consider that the simulation predictions were made up to thirty-three months beyond the initial actual values.

The predictive capability and stability of the simulation predictions is evidence that the regression equation model and the empirical patterns upon which the simulation is based have incorporated a substantial part of the systematic dynamics of the Vietnam War. The stringent test that the simulation technique gives the model lends strong support to the validity of the relationships incorporated in that model.

The two exceptions to the good predictive results of the computer simulation are the predictions of South Vietnamese popular confidence and North Vietnamese and Viet Cong defectors. The relatively poor predictive results for these two variables suggests that there are other important factors determining these two variables that were not included in the model. For the majority of the variables in this model, however, the ability of the computer simulation to predict values accurately during the 1965-67 period is striking.

One will recall from the discussion of the computer simulation method that the predictions for the 1965-67 period are based on the regression coefficients derived from the data from the entire period, but using only the actual data from the first three months of this 36-month period to start the generation of the predictions. The "bootstrapping" method of computer simulation, however, can continue to generate predictions for each variable beyond the last month of the period from which the regression coefficients were derived. We will now turn our attention to the predictions beyond 1967—through September 1970—to determine the accuracy of the predictions of the computer simulation when based upon the initial actual values from the first three months of 1965.

Because data were not available after December 1967 for North Vietnamese and Viet Cong troops, we shall confine the evaluation of the predictions made by the computer simulation in the period following 1967 to the seven variables for which comparable data are available.

Table 5 shows the mean percentage error of the predictions made by the computer simulation for the periods of April 1965–December 1967, April 1965–September 1970, and January 1968–September 1970.[3] The predictions made for this last period are based solely on the regression coefficients derived from the 1965–67 period, and the data from January–March 1965.

TABLE 5

MEAN PERCENTAGE ERROR OF SIMULATION PREDICTIONS

$$\frac{\sum \frac{\text{ACTUAL-PREDICTION}}{\text{ACTUAL}}}{\text{N}}$$

Variable	April 1965- December 1967 (N = 33)	April 1965- September 1970 (N = 66)	January 1968- September 1970 (N = 33)
N.V. + V.C. attrition	.21	.31	.40
S.V. popular confidence	.10	.44	.77
U.S. commitments	.15	.23	.31
U.S. casualties	.41	.57	.73
U.S. bombing N.V.	8.43	6.49§	.10*
U.S. public support for President Johnson	.73	.97‖	1.63†
N.V. + V.C. defectors	.34	.44	.55
N.V. + V.C. troops	.04	...‡	...‡

*January 1968 — October 1968 only
†January 1968 — December 1968 only
‡Data not available for comparison after January 1968
§April 1965 — October 1968 only
‖April 1965 — December 1968 only

Table 5 shows that the average error of the predictions made by the computer simulation increase as one extends the predictions farther from the initial starting point, i.e., the first three months of 1965. The average error is increased from the minimum of 16 percent for U.S. commitments to a maximum of 90 percent for U.S. public support for President Johnson. However, the error in the predictions for 1968 up to the time of the bombing halt were actually much less than they were during the 1965-67 period (733 percent better)!

Table 6 shows another measure of the goodness of fit for the simulation predictions for the 1965-67 and 1968-70 periods—the ratio of the error variance of the predictions to the total variance of the variables. Error variance is a measure that is less sensitive to the magnitude of the actual values than is the mean percentage error. The error variances for the period from 1968 on are much greater than those for the 1965-67 period.

What these measures show is that computer simulation that is based on the structure of relationships in the war for the 1965-67 period is not, in general, able to make very accurate predictions for the period of 1968 on, particularly when the simulation is based on the actual values of only the first three months of 1965, when U.S. military com-

TABLE 6

ERROR VARIANCE OF SIMULATION PREDICTIONS/TOTAL VARIANCE

$$\frac{\sum(\text{ACTUAL-PREDICTION})^2}{\sum \dfrac{(\text{ACTUAL-}\overline{\text{ACTUAL}})^2}{N}}$$

Variable	April 1965-December 1967 (N = 33)	April 1965-September 1970 (N = 66)	January 1968-September 1970 (N = 33)
N.V. + V.C. attrition	.32	.98	1.99
S.V. popular confidence	.63	2.56	9.36
U.S. commitments	.05	.59	3.04
U.S. casualties	.20	.69	1.05
U.S. bombing N.V.	.20	.19§	.67*
U.S. public support for President Johnson	.16	.16‖	.87†
N.V. + V.C. defectors	.64	.76	1.07
N.V. + V.C. troops	.08	...‡	...‡

*January 1968 — October 1968 only
†January 1968 — December 1968 only
‡Data not available for comparison after January 1968
§April 1965 — October 1968 only
‖April 1965 — December 1968 only

mitments in South Vietnam and bombing of North Vietnam were very small and just beginning to build up.

In figures 16 through 23 we can see the results of the computer simulation predictions for the entire 66-month period graphed. The graphs show shape and sources of errors calculated in tables 5 and 6. The computer simulation failed to predict, for example, the decline in South Vietnamese popular confidence after the Communist Tet offensive in January 1968. The computer simulation shows a continuing rise in U.S. commitments to South Vietnam, although in reality those commitments started to decline after they reached their peak in May 1968 during the Communist spring offensive that was beaten back. The computer simulation predicted a continuation of the seasonal variation in the pattern of U.S. bombing of North Vietnam, although with diminishing numbers of bombing sorties. These predictions were fairly accurate for the first ten months of 1968, but the simulation failed to predict the halt in the bombing of North Vietnam starting at the end of October 1968. The computer simulation did predict the continued decline in popular support for President Johnson, although it missed the big upsurge of support for him in April 1968 after he announced that he was limiting the bombing of North Vietnam, asking the Communists to negotiate in Paris, and not running for reelection to the presidency. Subject to seasonal variations, the computer simulation predicted a gradual increase in the number of North Vietnamese and Viet Cong defectors, but failed to predict the great reduction in Communist defectors in preparation for, and during, the Communist Tet and spring offensives of 1968, and the huge upsurge of defections from the Communists in the wake of the failure of that peak Communist military effort. And finally, the computer simulation predicted a gradual increase in both U.S. casualties and North Vietnamese and Viet Cong attrition subject to seasonal variations, but missed the huge upsurge in these casualties that occurred at the time of the Communist Tet and spring offensives in 1968.

In this review of when the computer simulation predictions begin to be less accurate, we can identify a common element: the change in the overall system of military and political interaction that was initiated and associated with the Communist Tet offensive of 1968. The inability of the computer simulation to make accurate predictions in the post-Tet period, when the regression model is based upon data and the interrelationships among variables in the pre-Tet period, is strong evidence that the military and political interactions in the Vietnam War did change in significant ways starting at the time of the Tet offensive. Thus, if its formerly accurate predictions diverge from reality, the computer simulation can be used as a diagnostic tool to discover whether, when, and how a system of interaction has changed. We will analyze the new system of interaction in the post-Tet period in chapter 8. We shall now turn briefly to consider the problem of modeling unstable systems that the Tet offensive has presented to us.

MODELING UNSTABLE SYSTEMS

System instability—the change in relationships among the same variables over time—poses a difficult problem for the analyst or policy-maker who wishes to use computer simulations to make forecasts. Particularly for forecasts upon which policy decisions are to be based, one must have a model that remains valid over time. This poses a particular dilemma for policy-makers: their own decisions that attempt to establish a new policy and break with an old pattern of action may themselves break the overall pattern of relationships in the system of interaction, and make the prediction of reactions and consequences less accurate than otherwise would be the case.

To construct a model with good predictive ability even when the processes under study change, one can include only those relationships that do remain stable over time, if there are any. One can also attempt to construct a more comprehensive model including new variables that account for changes in the relationships among other variables. For example, if analysts for policy-makers in both Washington and Hanoi knew what the relationships were between their own behavior and that of their adversary, they might advise their respective policy-makers to take advantage of those relationships by changing the pattern of their own behavior. If this advice were followed, the system of interaction would change. If one knew which contingency plans (such as those included in the "Pentagon Papers") were proposed and which accepted as guiding future policy and actions, one would include that information in a more comprehensive model to increase the accuracy of that model's predictions even under altered circumstances. One would expect more rapid and greater changes in the structure of a conflict system if both sides were analyzing behavioral interrelationships and modifying their behavior accordingly, much like two hunter-killer submarines chasing each other in the darkness of the ocean depths.

If it is not possible to build a more comprehensive model, one might construct a discontinuous one, i.e., one submodel for one time period, another for a different time period. To predict with a discontinuous model, however, one has to know somehow which subsystem one is in to use the appropriate submodel. One's only guide is to make alternative predictions with the different submodels, and then to revaluate their accuracy once actual data become available. This requires careful judgment and information that is independent of the model itself.

Thus, empirical patterns that are incorporated into systematic models can help us look ahead and guide our decisons and actions. The methods used in this research—correlation and regression analysis and computer simulation—can be an enormous aid in analyzing patterns of interaction and foreseeing the implications of those patterns. It must be realized, however, that the utility of these methods is limited by the stability of those patterns over time.

1. In the following graphs, the actual values of each variable for each month are represented by X; the values predicted by the simulation of the composite empirical model are represented by 0.

The predictions are made using only three initial data points (January through March 1965) and the set of regression coefficients for each dependent variable listed in chapter 6. These regression coefficients were derived only from 1965-67 data. Thus the predicted values for 1968 and onward are pure prediction. The predicted values for 1965-67 are predictions from the empirical relationships and three initial values of each variable. For this reason, the first three values are not predicted or shown on the graphs.

An X and not a 0 is printed on these graphs when the predicted and actual values for that month are nearly the same. The actual values are not printed when no actual data were collected, as in 1968 for some variables. Because these values have been scaled for analytic purposes, the values printed on the vertical axis are not absolute values but relative values for that index.

2. The large percentage error in the number of U.S. bombing sorties over North Vietnam is partly artifactual. The bombing halt in January 1966 makes the ratio of the difference between actual and predicted to actual number very large for that month.

3. Because the new Nixon administration started in January 1969, U.S. public opinion support for the president is calculated only through December 1968. Because U.S. bombing of North Vietnam was halted for some time after October 1968, the calculations for this variable are made only through October 1968.

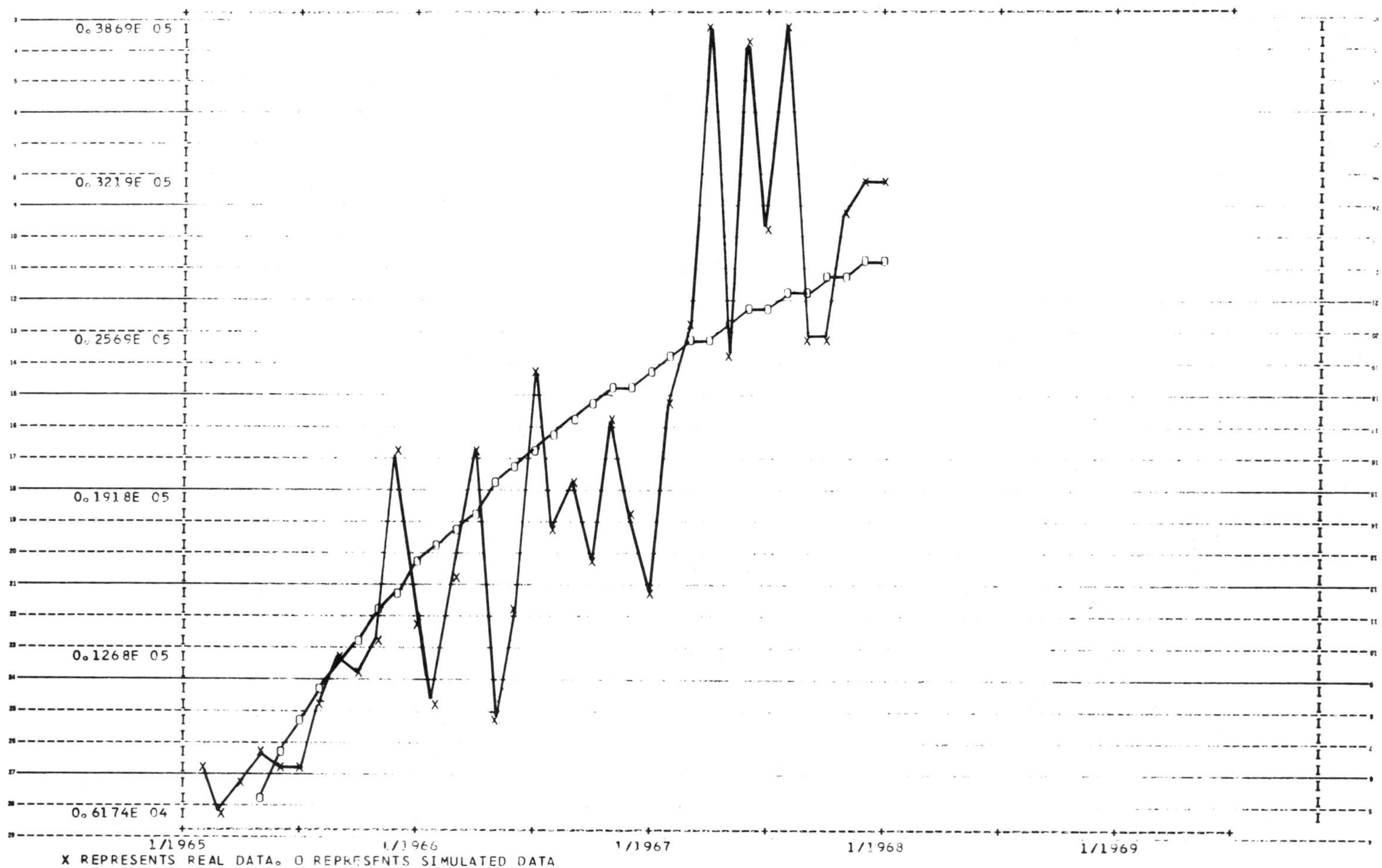

Fig. 8. N.V. + V.C. attrition

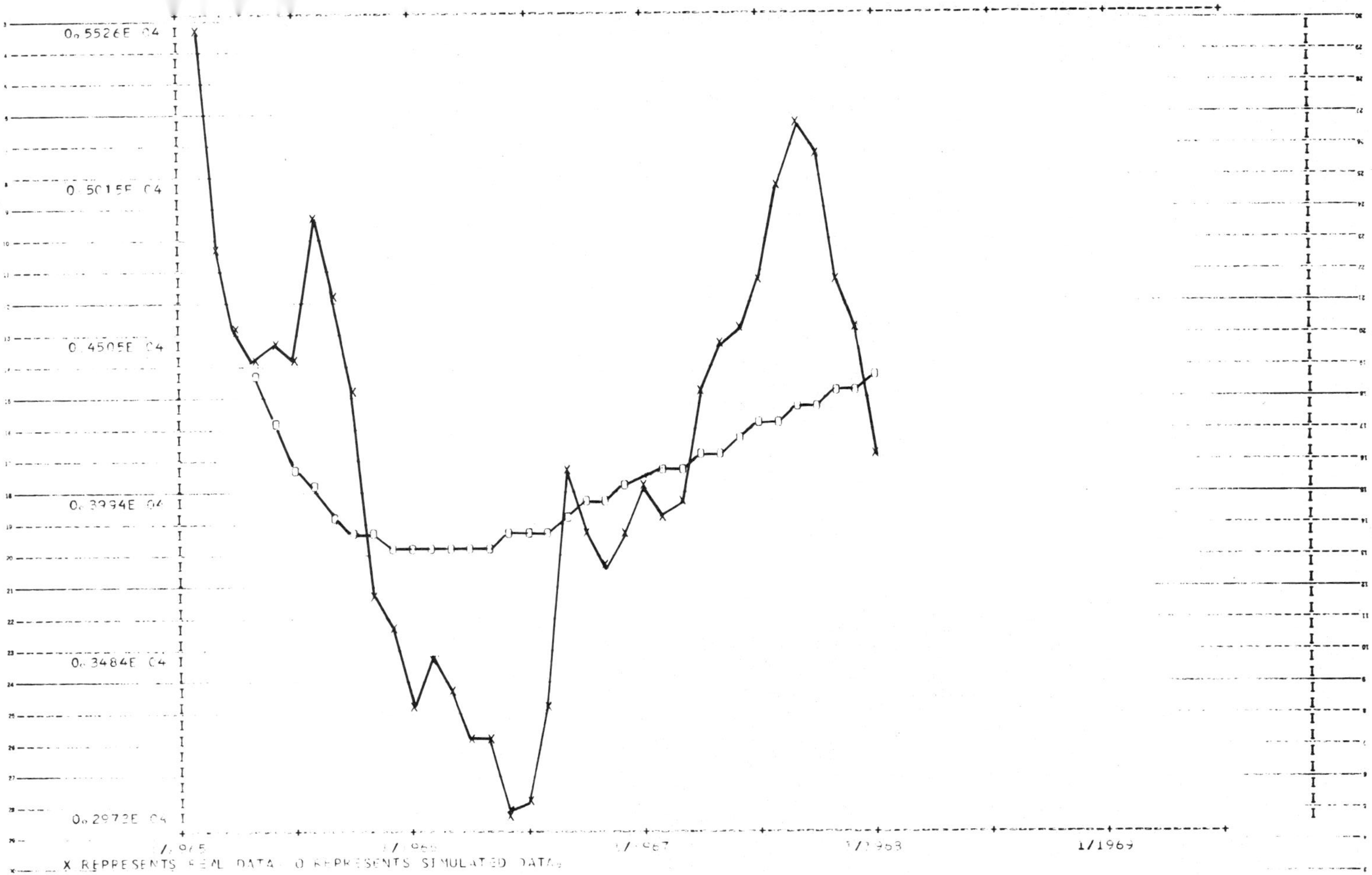

Fig. 9. S.V. popular confidence

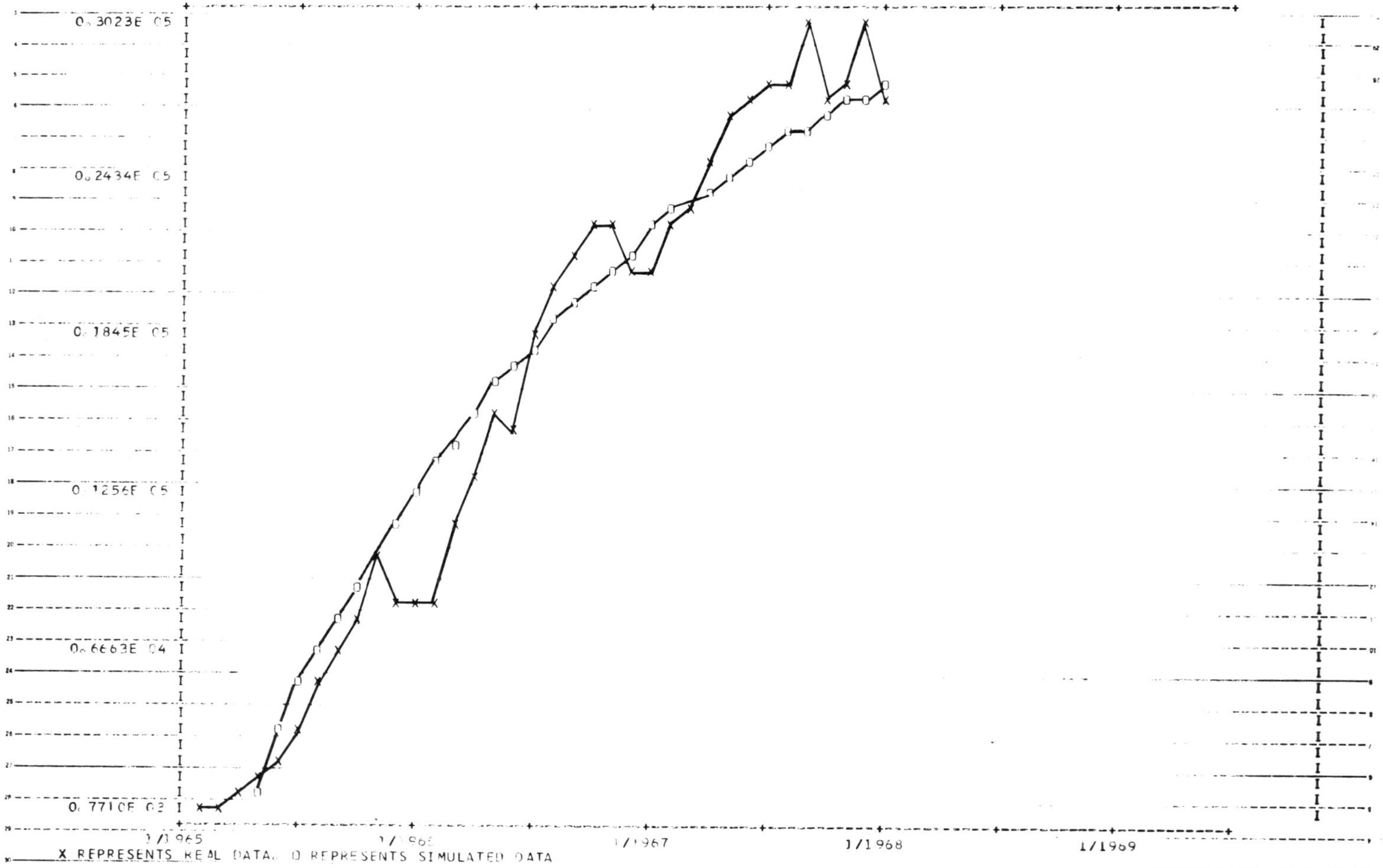

Fig. 10. U.S. commitments

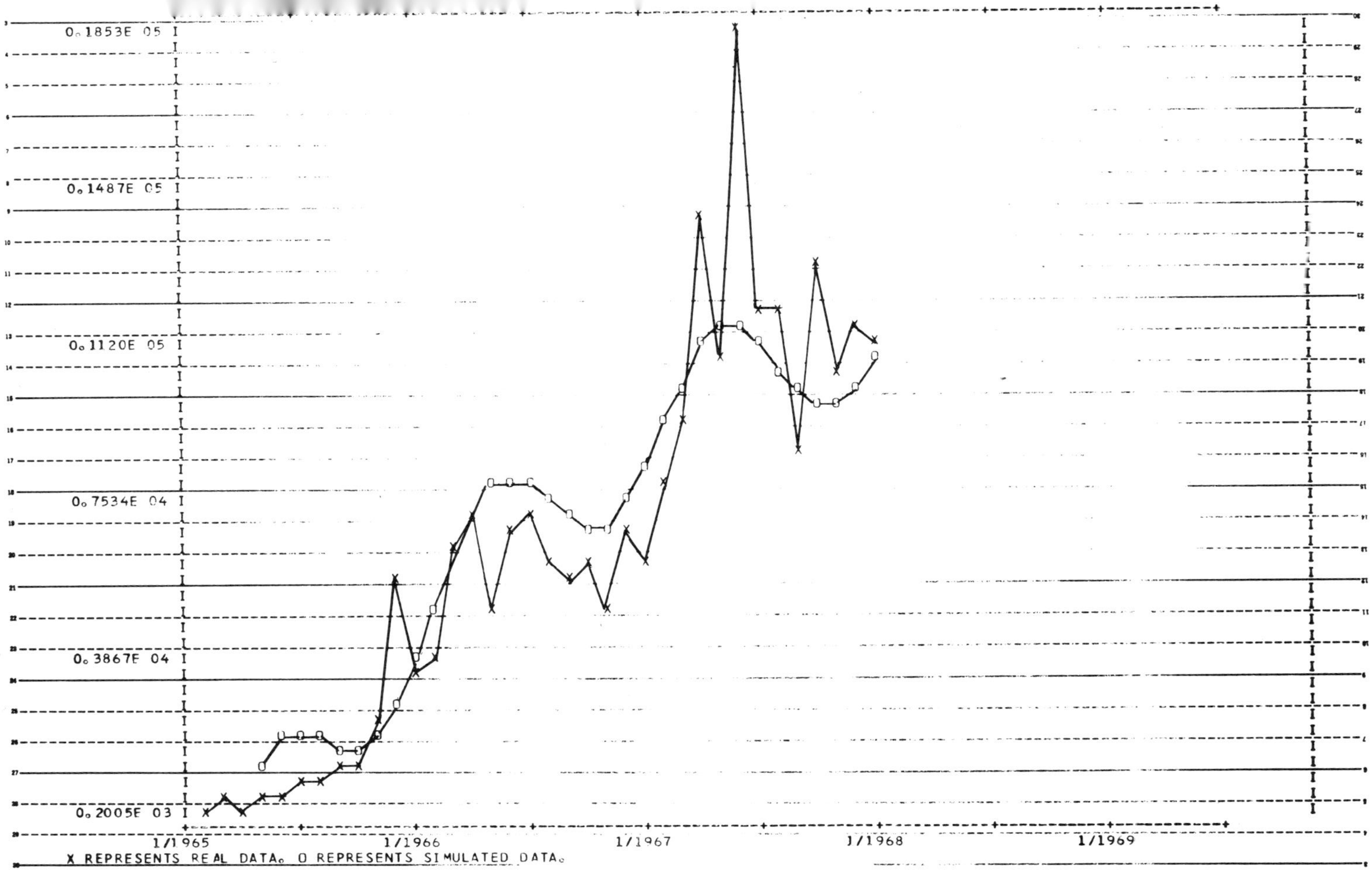

Fig. 11. U.S. casualties

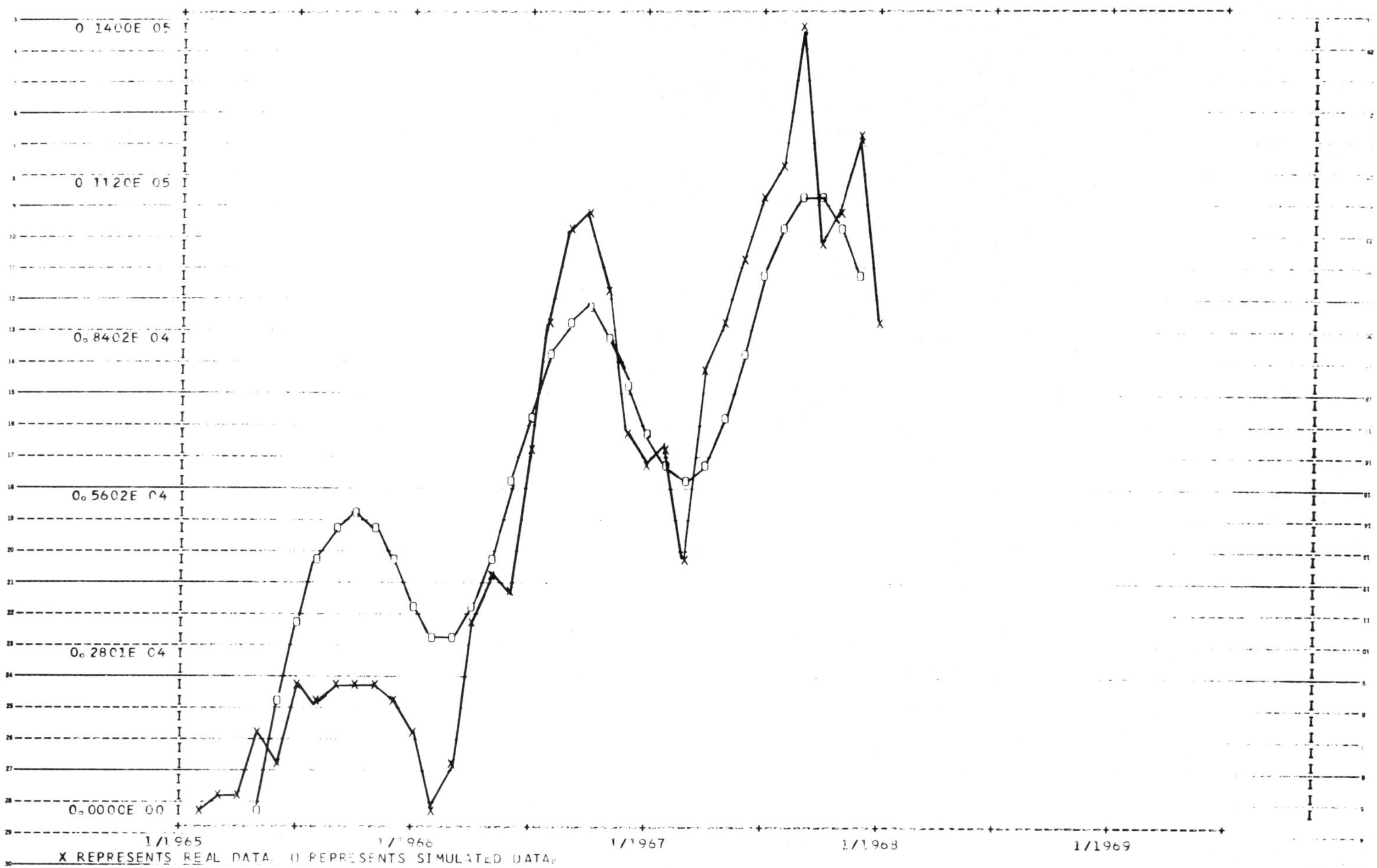

Fig. 12 U.S. bombing of N.V.

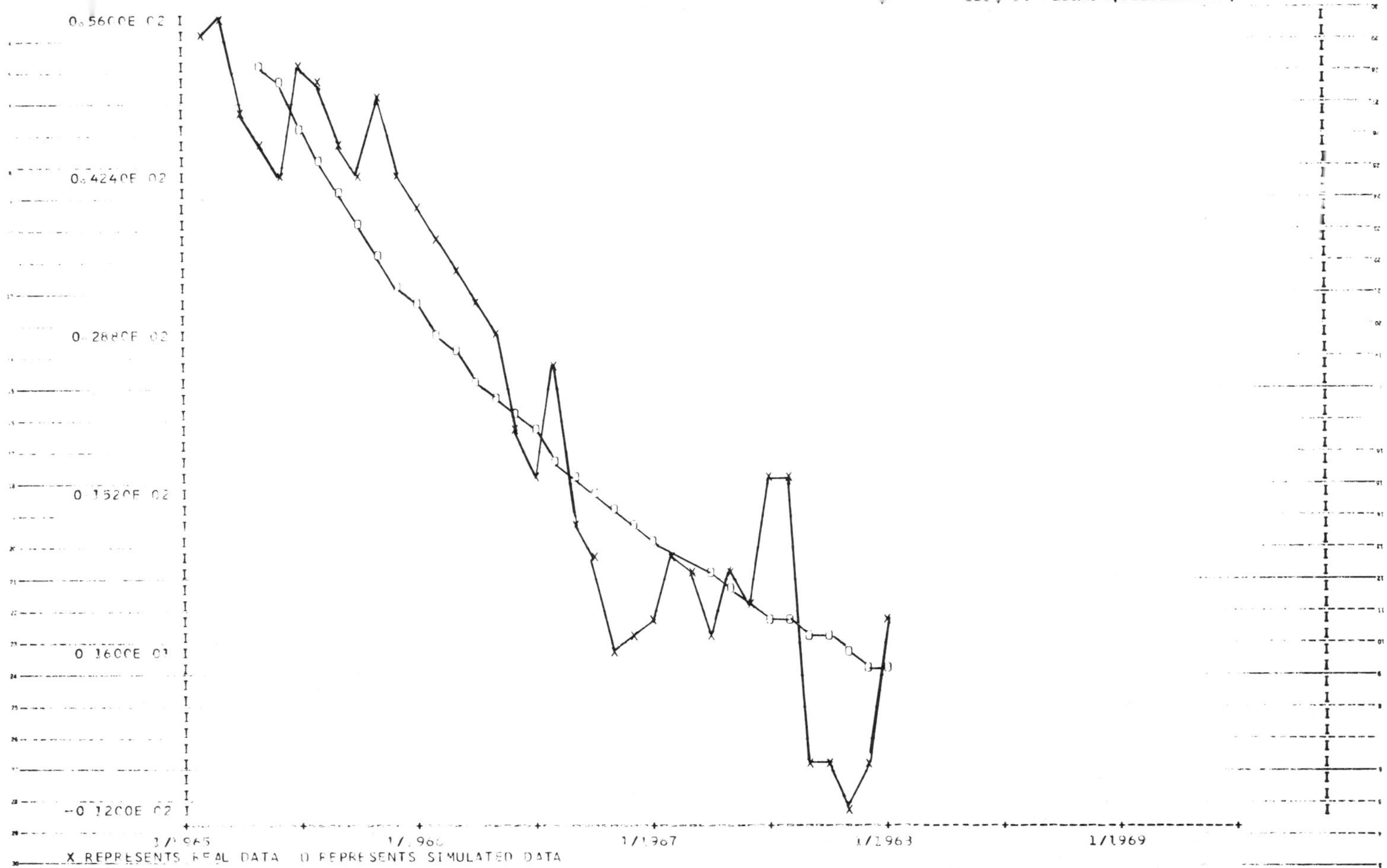

Fig. 13. U.S. public support for the president

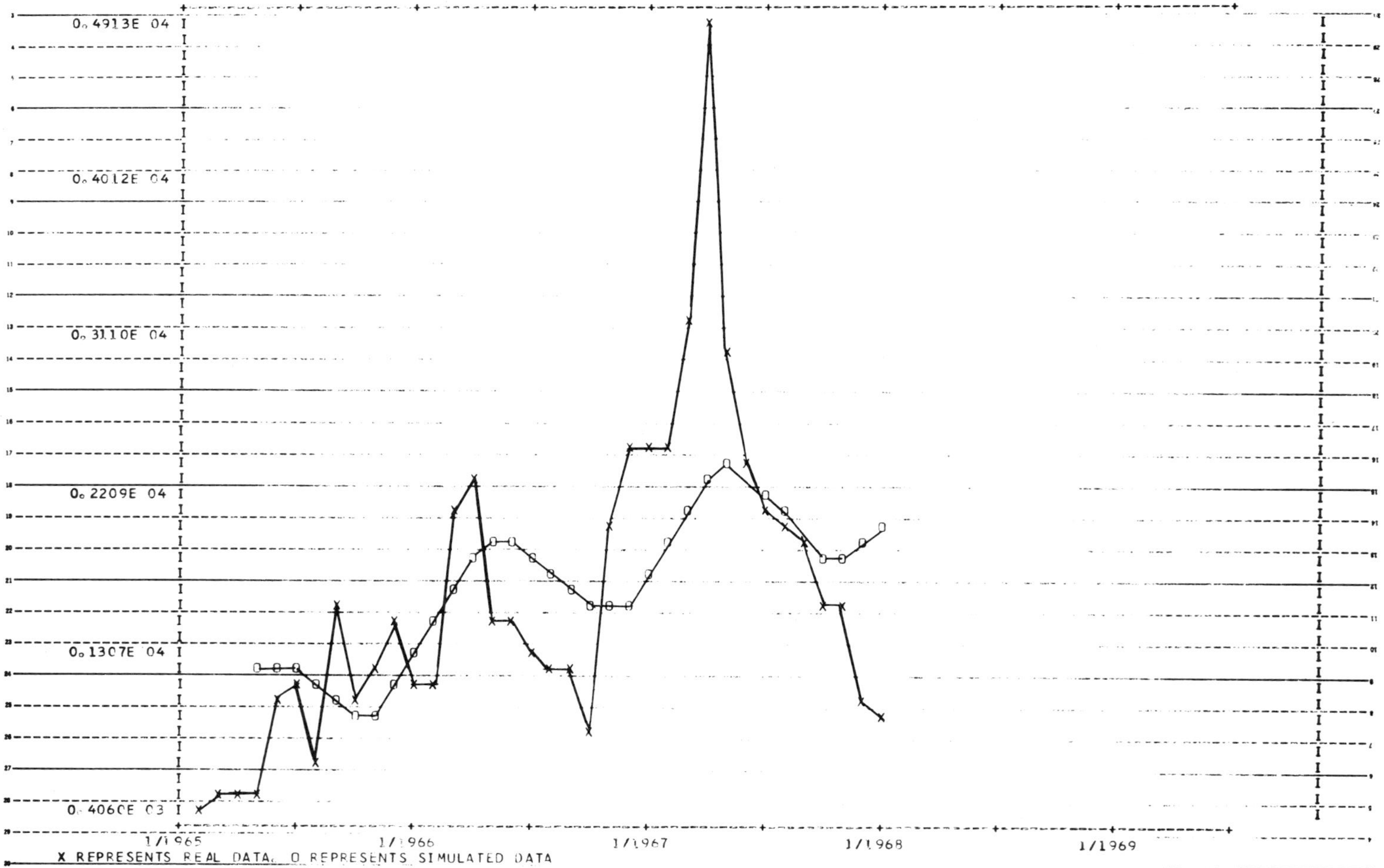

Fig. 14. N.V. + V.C. defectors

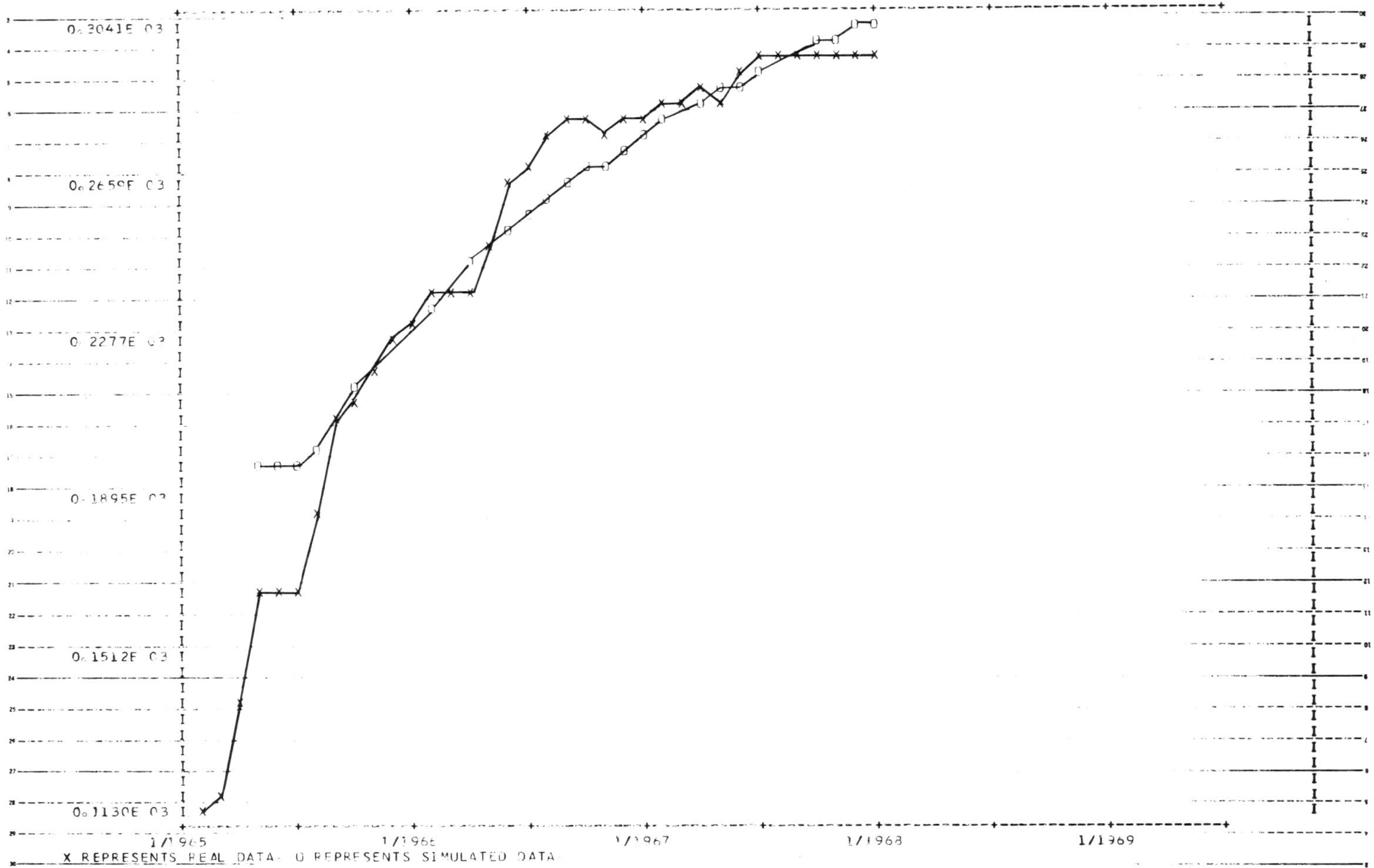

Fig. 15. N.V. + V.C. troops

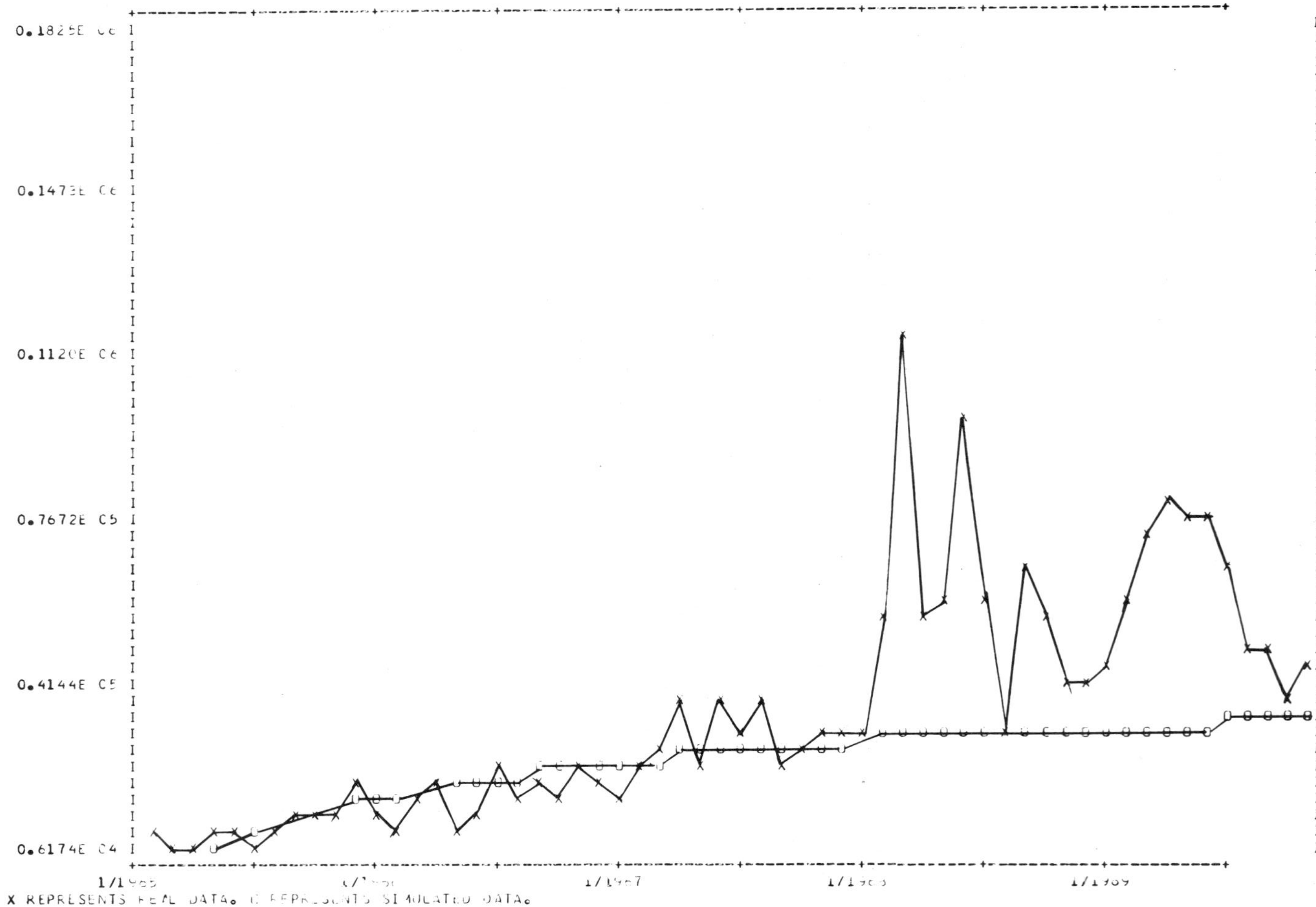

Fig. 16. N.V. + V.C. attrition

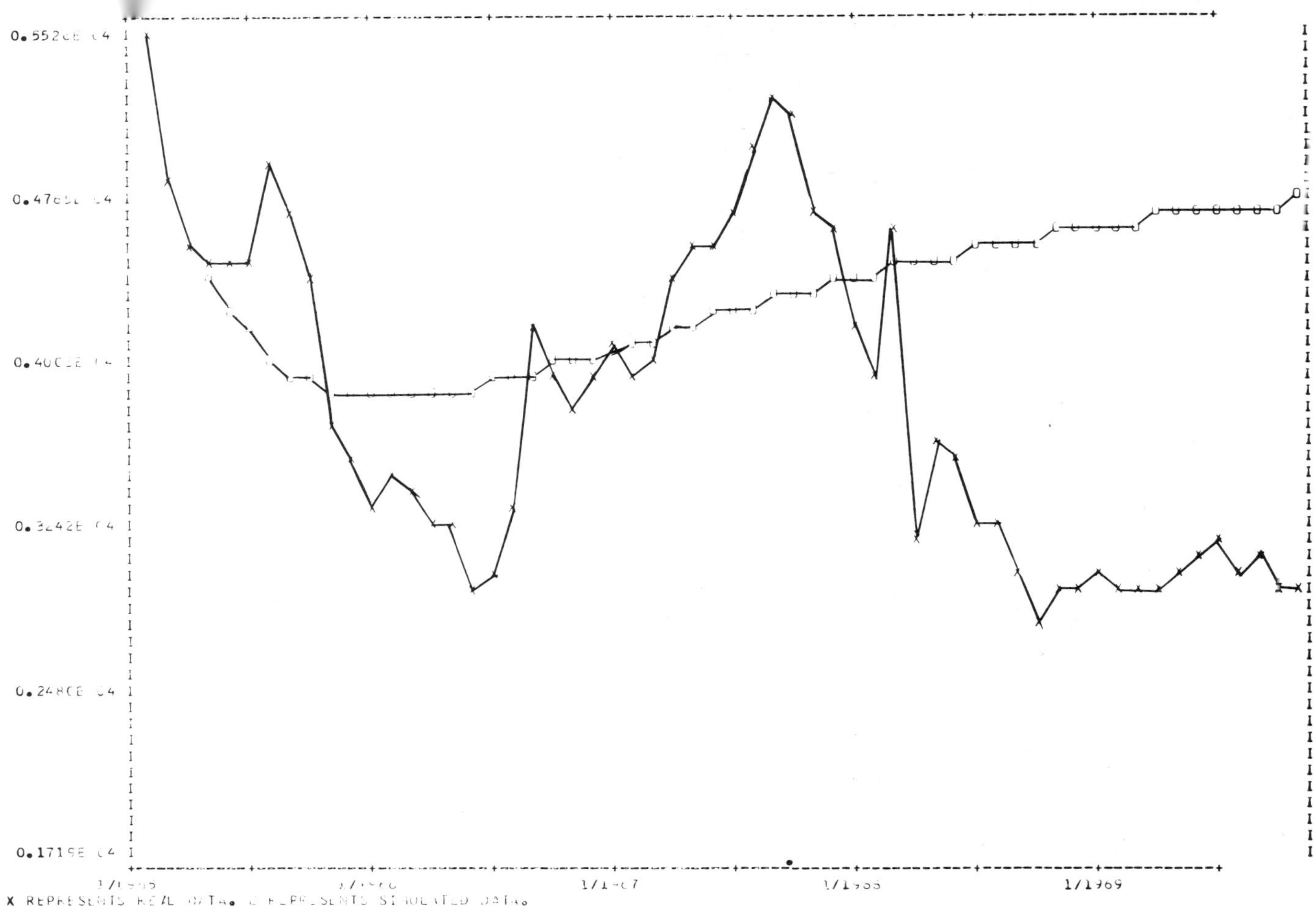

Fig. 17. S.V. popular confidence

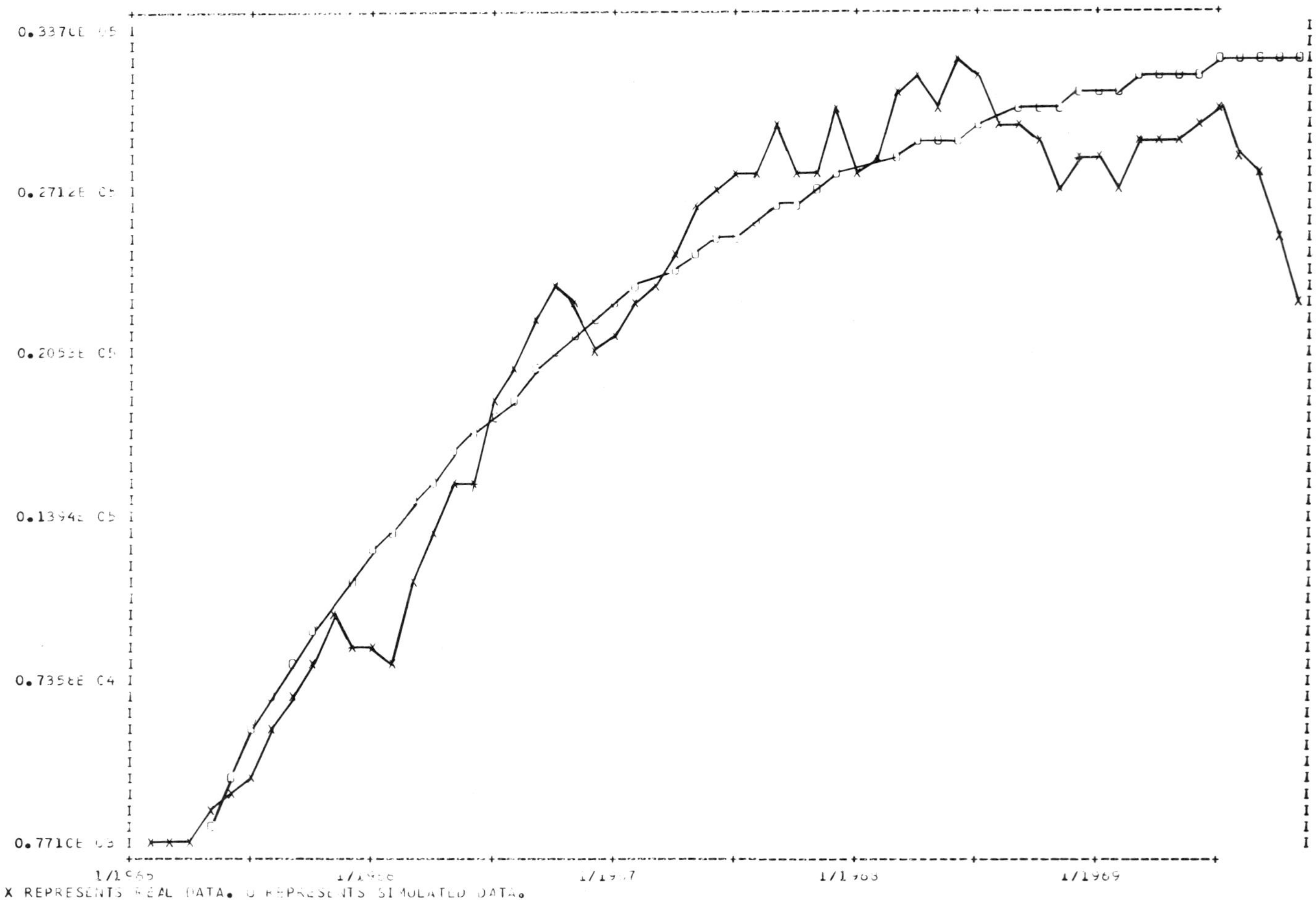

Fig. 18. U.S. commitments

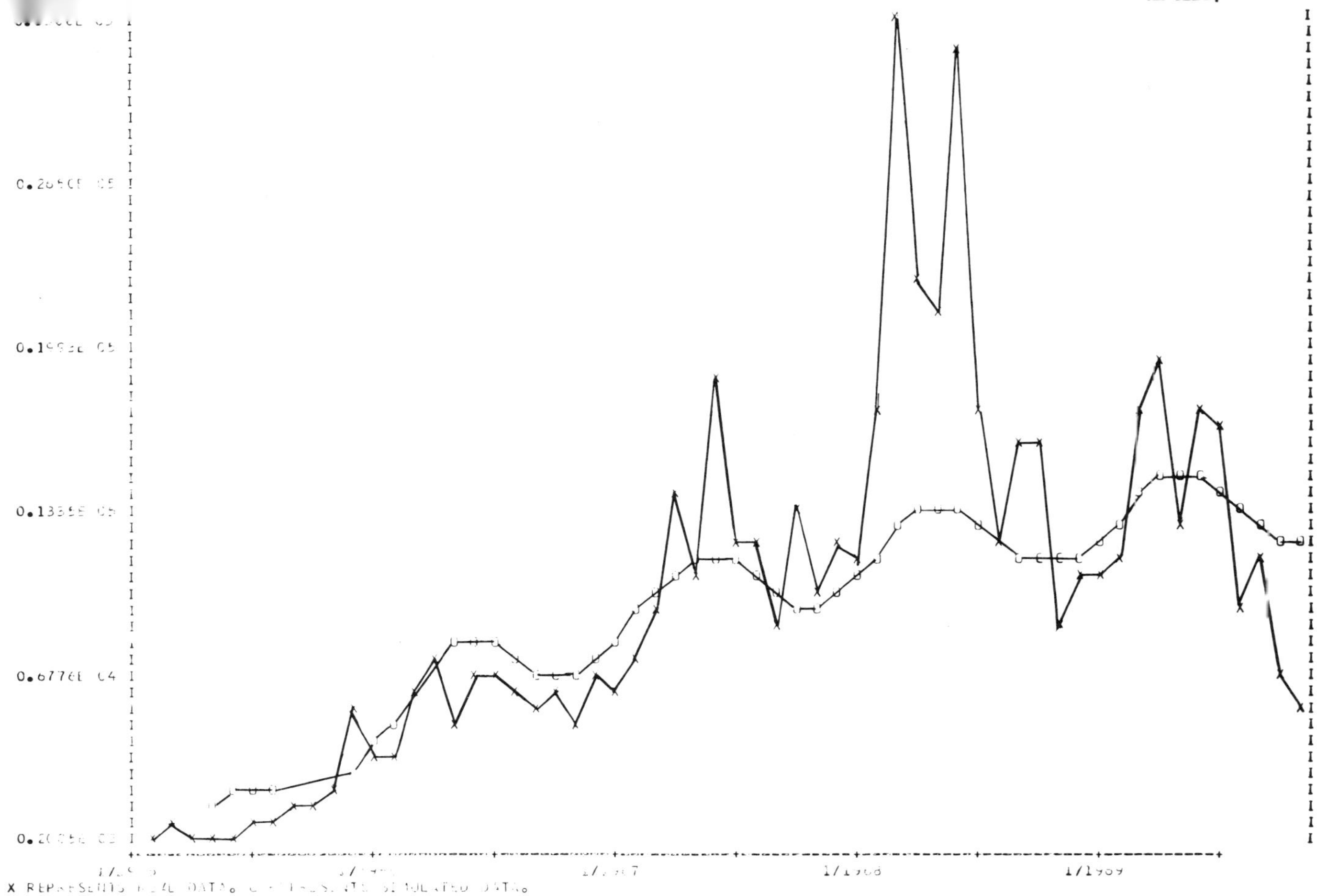

Fig. 19. U.S. casualties

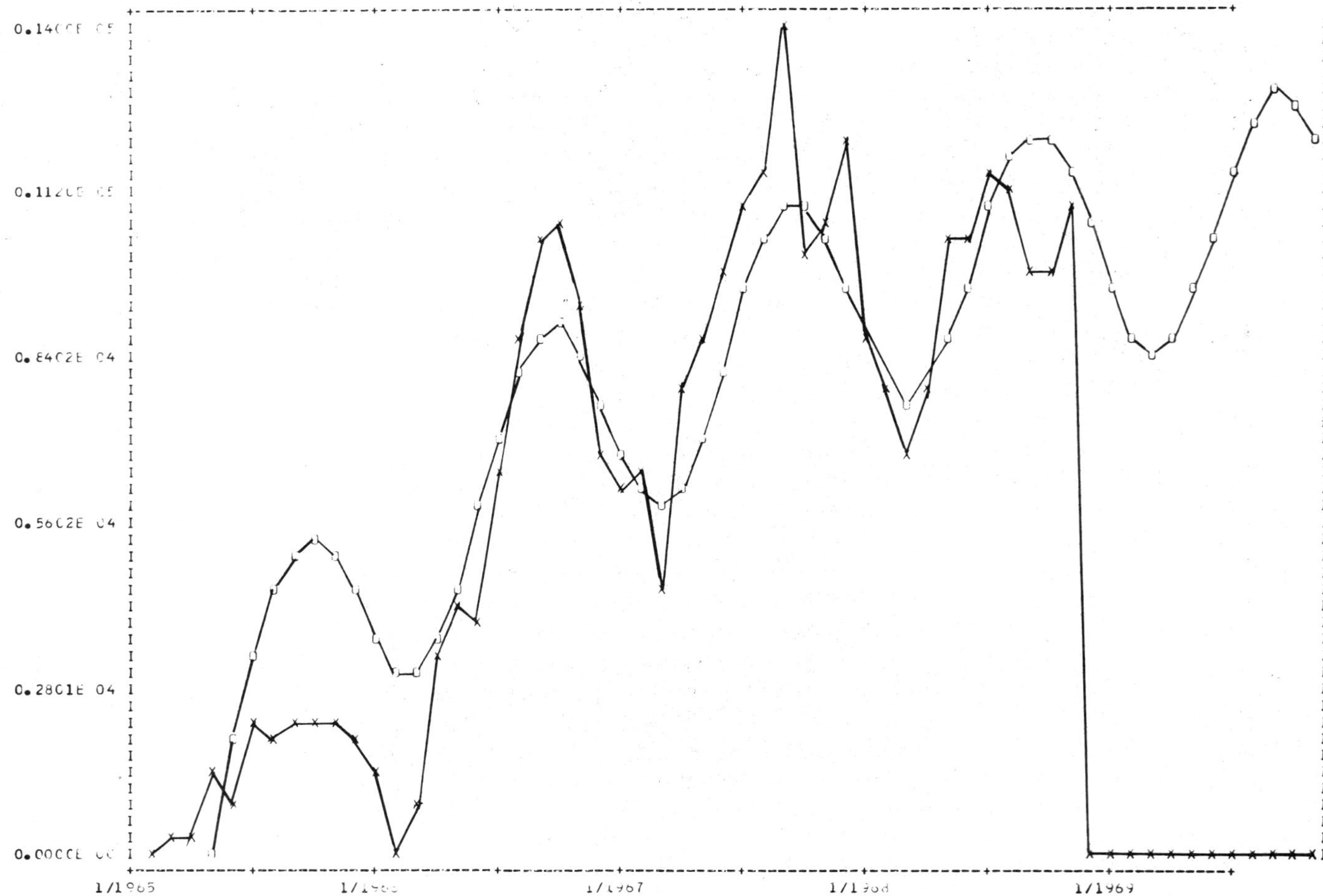

X REPRESENTS REAL DATA. O REPRESENTS SIMULATED DATA.

Fig. 20 U.S. bombing of N.V.

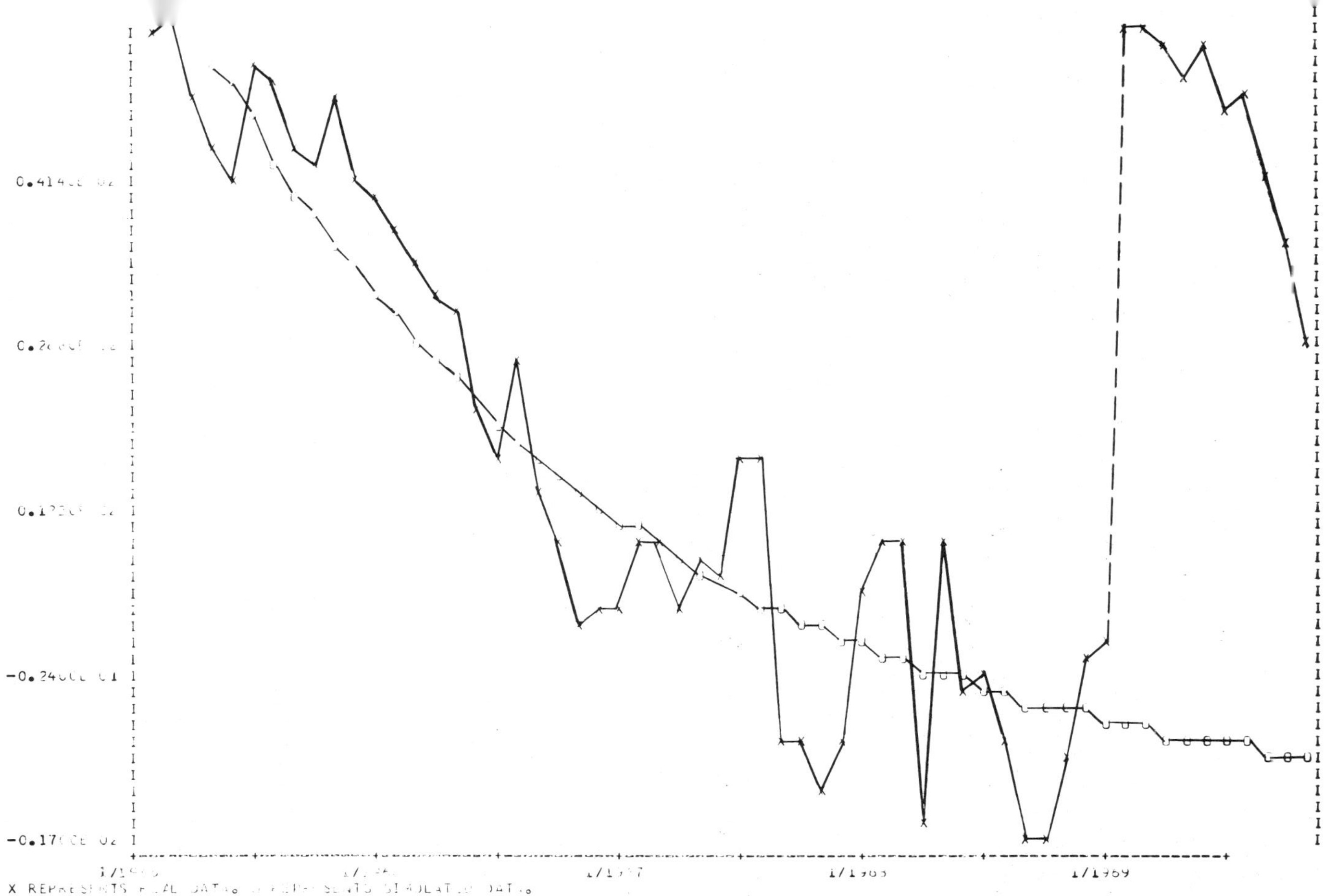

Fig. 21. U.S. public support for the president

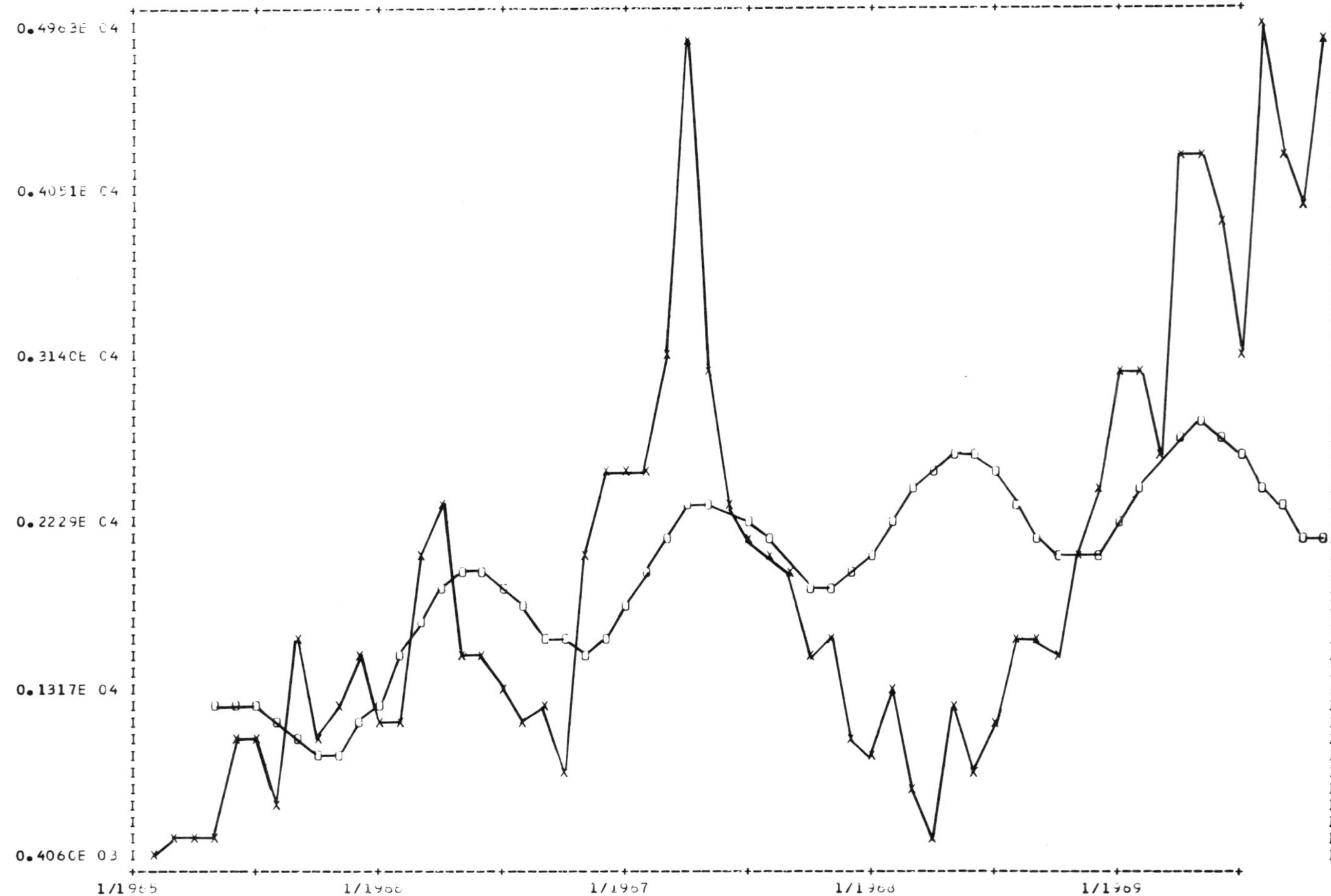

X REPRESENTS REAL DATA. O REPRESENTS SIMULATED DATA.

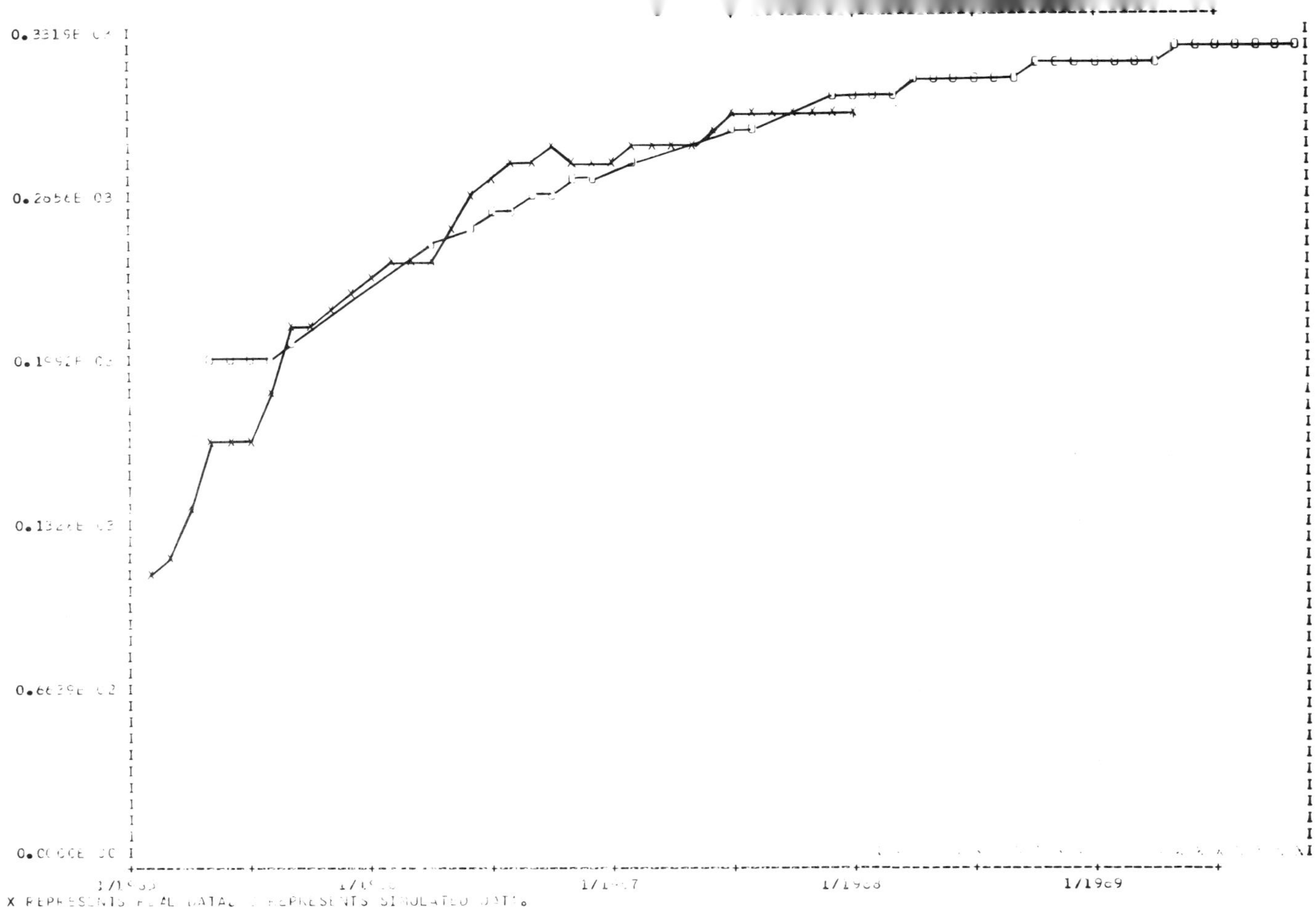

Fig. 23. N.V. + V.C. troops

7

Simulation Exercises of Alternative Hawk and Dove Policies

Once a computer simulation of a model of the dynamics of the Vietnam conflict has been successful in making stable and reasonably accurate predictions, one can use it to explore changes that occur in the predicted values of dependent variables as one changes a single independent variable in a known way. Such an exercise is analogous to the experimental manipulation of a single variable.

EXERCISING THE SIMULATION TO EXPLORE ALTERNATIVE POLICIES

When the experimental variable in the simulation exercise represents an action that policy-makers themselves can directly control, then the simulation exercise is a way to forecast and explore possible outcomes of alternative policies. During the period in which the relationships among the variables remain stable, we can use such simulation exercises to explore what effect hypothetical policies and actions would have had on the course of the conflict.

Forecasting the different consequences of various possible actions is one of the principal purposes and uses of scientific inquiry. Informed by such forecasts, decisions could be made and actions taken that impose minimum costs on all concerned. The analysis necessary to make appropriate forecasts is surely less costly than the actual military and political commitments made on an experimental basis. The reversal of actual commitments has been extremely difficult even when their consequences have been unsatisfactory.

HAWK AND DOVE EXERCISES OF THE SIMULATION

As an exercise of the computer simulation, we will here explore what might have been the consequences of both relatively more hawkish and dovish U.S. policies in Vietnam. Focusing on U.S. commitments to South Vietnam, which include U.S. troops, supplies, battalion-size or larger combat operations, and bombing sorties within South Vietnam, we will see what the consequences for all other variables in the system would have been had U.S. policy been to make U.S. commitments to South Vietnam the following multiples of what they actually were: 0.25, 0.5, 1.5, 2.0, and 2.5. We can perform these exercises by making

U.S. commitments an exogenous variable, i.e., by controlling the monthly values of U.S. commitments, rather than allowing them to be dependent upon other variables in the system, as is done in the regular simulation.

The results of each simulation exercise are valid only under the assumption that the structure of relationships among the variables in the simulation model would be the same under the altered policy as it was under the actual policy carried out during the war. We can show that this assumption of unchanged structure during the simulation exercises is theoretically valid.

Let us represent the Vietnam War during the 1965–67 period as a two-person zero-sum Prisoner's Dilemma game in which policy choices become obvious over time, as shown in figure 24.

FIGURE 24

THE VIETNAM WAR AS A PRISONER'S DILEMMA GAME

		North Vietnamese and Viet Cong	
		Escalate	Deescalate
U.S. and South Vietnamese	Escalate	3rd, 3rd	1st, 4th
	Deescalate	4th, 1st	2nd, 2nd

The preference orderings of the four outcomes that would result from the different joint actions of the two sides are indicated first for the United States and South Vietnamese, and then for the North Vietnamese and Viet Cong.

According to this model, each side wants most to win by escalating its own military efforts while its enemy deescalates theirs and wants least to be taken advantage of in this way. Each side's second choice is to reduce its costs in the war by deescalating, but only if the other side also deescalates. And each side's third choice is to escalate its military efforts and costs in order to win, even though the enemy does the same in response.

If each side in the war had based its policy on the assumptions of a hawkish folk-model, they would have assumed that by escalating their military efforts, their adversary would be forced to deescalate theirs, i.e., they would have made the assumption of a *negative* relationship. According to the Prisoners' Dilemma model of the conflict, however, each side would eventually escalate if the other did, since mutual escalation is more preferable (ranked third) than having one's own deescalation be exploited by the other side (ranked fourth).

As we have seen in the empirical analysis, the actual pattern of conflict during the 1965-67 period of the war was mutual escalation, i.e., a *positive* relationship, as predicted by the dovish folk-model. In the exercise of the two alternative hawkish policies, this same positive relationship between the military efforts of both sides would continue to hold, and thus the results of the simulation exercises would be valid.

The exercises of the dovish alternative policies should also be valid. In these exercises we are defining the policies in which U.S. military commitments are less than they in fact were as relatively deescalatory. Now the hawkish folk-model assumes that if one deescalates, the enemy will try to take advantage of that deescalation and escalate their own military efforts, i.e., it makes the assumption again of a *negative* relationship. The dovish folk-model, on the other hand, assumes that if one side deescalates, the other side will also do so, i.e., it again makes the assumption of a *positive* relationship.

Theoretically, this positive relationship assumed by the dovish folk-model should hold during the deescalation situation for the same reason it held during the escalation situation: for each side, mutual deescalation is more preferable (ranked second) than is having one's deescalation exploited by the other side (ranked fourth). Neither side would continue to deescalate unless the other side also did. Thus, if each side perceived that its deescalation were being exploited, it would soon revert to escalation, since mutual escalation (ranked third) is preferable to being exploited (ranked fourth). The pattern of interaction between the two sides would therefore be a positive relationship. If each side's deescalation is not exploited, then mutual deescalation will occur, its being preferred by both sides (ranked second) to mutual escalation (ranked third). Mutual deescalation also involves a positive relationship between the actions of the two sides.

Because the structure of the model used in these simulation exercises specifies a positive relationship between the actions of the two sides in the Vietnam War, the results of these exercises should be valid. The model and the results of the exercises would be invalid only in the unlikely event that one side continued to deescalate over a long period of time in spite of the fact that over the same period of time its enemy continued to exploit that deescalation by escalating instead.

The results of the simulation exercises are given in table 7. In this table the effects of the specific changes in U.S. commitments on the seven other variables in the system are compared as the ratio of the sum of the predicted values to the sum of the actual values. The table also shows the ratio of the sum of the values predicted in the regular simulation in which no changes were made in U.S. commitments (i.e., the simulation predictions that appear in chapter 6) to the sum of the actual values.

TABLE 7

EXERCISES OF THE SIMULATION WITH U.S. COMMITMENTS

Variables	Regular Simulation	0.25 x Actual	0.50 x Actual	1.5 x Actual	2.0 x Actual	2.5 x Actual
	$\frac{\Sigma \text{ Predictions}_s}{\Sigma \text{ Actual}}$	$\frac{\Sigma \text{ Predictions}_e}{\Sigma \text{ Actual}}$	$\frac{\Sigma \text{ Predictions}_e}{\Sigma \text{ Actual}}$	$\frac{\Sigma \text{ Predictions}_e}{\Sigma \text{ Actual}}$	$\frac{\Sigma \text{ Predictions}_e}{\Sigma \text{ Actual}}$	$\frac{\Sigma \text{ Predictions}_e}{\Sigma \text{ Actual}}$
N.V. + V.C. attrition	1.010	.458	.640	1.366	1.730	2.093
S.V. popular confidence	.991	.877	.913	1.058	1.130	1.203
U.S. casualties	1.012	.148	.432	1.571	2.141	2.710
U.S. bombing of N.V.	1.050	.647	.776	1.290	1.548	1.805
U.S. public support for the president	.985	2.218	1.812	.188	- .624	- 1.436
N.V. + V.C. defectors	.978	.574	.707	1.239	1.504	1.770
N.V. + V.C. troops	1.004	.815	.877	1.123	1.247	1.370

Σ Predictions_s = sum of predictions made in regular simulation for 33 months
Σ Predictions_e = sum of predictions made in exercise of simulation for 33 months
Σ Actual = sum of actual values for 33 months

Since the sum of the predictions made in the regular simulation were a maximum of 5 percent different from the sum of the actual values, we can focus our comparison of the results of the exercises on the ratio of the sum of the simulated values to the sum of the actual values. This ratio will be only slightly different from the ratio of the sum of the predictions in the exercises to the predictions made in the regular simulation, and is useful to compare the exercises with each other as well as with the actual values.[1]

In general, the exercises of the computer simulation follow the trends of the regular simulation. (See figures 25-31, which show the results of the exercise in which U.S. commitments are one-quarter of what they actually were, and figures 32-38, which show the results of the exercise in which U.S. commitments are two and one-half times what they actually were.) The results of the exercises are in conformance with the prediction of the dove folk-theory: when U.S. commitments are reduced from what they actually were, the military variables of North Vietnamese troops, U.S. casualties, North Vietnamese and Viet Cong attrition, and U.S. bombing of North Vietnam are also reduced. North Vietnamese and Viet Cong troops are not reduced by as great a percentage as are U.S. commitments, indicating the presence of Viet

Cong forces even with no American forces present. Popular confidence in the South Vietnamese government is also reduced, as are defectors from the Viet Cong, although the impact on the latter is proportionally greater than the impact on the former.

Thus, according to this exercise of the computer simulation, had the United States conducted the war less intensely and with fewer military commitments, the Communists would also have done so, and military casualties on both sides would have been many fewer. However, politically, the Viet Cong would have benefited and the South Vietnamese government suffered from such a dovish U.S. policy. President Johnson, however, would have enjoyed a much greater margin of popular support in the United States from such a dovish policy—a margin that, in the most dovish policy tested here, would have been 40 percent as compared with a negative 8 percent by November 1967. Such a margin of popular approval would in all probability have allowed him to seek and be reelected to the presidency.

In the hawkish policy exercises in which U.S. commitments were increased over what they actually were, the consequences again conform more to the predictions of the dove than of the hawk folk-theory: North Vietnamese and Viet Cong troops also increase (although their increases are not proportionally as great as are increases in U.S. commitments). U.S. casualties are increased at an even greater rate than are U.S. commitments, and North Vietnamese and Viet Cong attrition and U.S. bombing of North Vietnam are also increased. Larger U.S. commitments increase popular confidence in the South Vietnamese government (20 percent when U.S. commitments are 2.5 times their actual value), and increase North Vietnamese and Viet Cong defectors even more (77 percent in the same exercise). Thus, a more hawkish U.S. policy would have hurt the Viet Cong politically more than it would have helped the South Vietnamese government.

These findings are evidence that the main political influence of the United States on the people of South Vietnam has been more a negative one of working against the Viet Cong through destruction and attrition, than it has been a positive one of building the confidence of the South Vietnamese people in their government. Thus, U.S. military power has more influenced people to withhold support from the Viet Cong for fear of their own lives than it has influenced them to support the government in Saigon. United States coercion and violence have apparently reduced the legitimacy ascribed to the Viet Cong by reducing the credibility of their claim that they can protect the people. On the other hand, the relatively small impact of U.S. coercive power on South Vietnamese popular confidence may be due to the fact that a significant number of the South Vietnamese people are not willing to ascribe legitimacy to a government whose American ally has caused massive civilian destruction, loss of life, and disruption. Thus, more hawkish U.S. policies were more likely than more dovish U.S. policies to avert a Communist political take-over in South Vietnam.

According to the computer simulation exercises, in response to greater U.S. military commitments, the Communists would also have increased their commitments. American escalation accompanied by a Communist counter-escalation would have produced the major domestic political impact of a more hawkish American policy: an even more precipitous decline in President Johnson's domestic political support than actually occurred. In the most hawkish of the computer simulation exercises analyzed here, his margin of political support would have been *negative* as early as March 1966 (instead of the actual negative margin that first occurred in August 1967); and by December 1967 it would have been a *negative* 93 percent (i.e., 3.5 percent of the people for Johnson, 96.5 percent against).

Thus, according to these exercises of the computer simulation, more dovish policies than were actually in effect during the 1965-67 period would have resulted in fewer U.S. military costs and a more favorable political outcome in the United States for President Johnson, but a less desirable political outcome in South Vietnam. On the other hand, more hawkish policies during this period would have resulted in a more favorable political outcome in South Vietnam for the Johnson administration, but greater military costs (especially in terms of U.S. casualties), and a much more rapid political decline for President Johnson.

The results of the simulation exercises do demonstrate the very real *dilemma* faced by U.S. policy-makers: each general policy alternative—escalation or deescalation—involves the trade-off of some military and political benefits to achieve others. More dovish policies would have achieved fewer military casualties and greater political support for the president at the cost of a greater risk that South Vietnam would be "lost" to the Communists. More hawkish policies, on the other hand, would have been more likely to defeat the Communists, but at the costs of more American casualties and political disaster for the president in the United States. A deescalation policy may have had political disadvantages in Vietnam, but the domestic political disadvantages of a policy of escalation are probably more crucial to the president. This may be the reason President Johnson eventually changed his policy from one of escalation to one of deescalation in the spring of 1968. He changed too late to reverse the public's repudiation of him and his Vietnam policy, but his experience apparently impressed his successor. President Nixon's policies of temporarily continuing the bombing halt, withdrawing most U.S. troops, negotiating with the Communists in Paris, and trying to "Vietnamize" the war were clearly geared toward reducing American military casualties and gaining domestic approval in the United States.

A policy of "Vietnamization" and reduction of U.S. military commitments in South Vietnam poses the dilemma shown in these computer simulation exercises. The reduction of U.S. military commitments weakened popular confidence in the South Vietnamese government. Moreover, the military forces of the South Vietnamese government had been unable to contain the Communists without American help.

We shall now turn to an analysis of the empirical patterns in the war during the period following the Communist Tet offensive. In this period President Johnson began to de-Americanize the war, and President Nixon withdrew U.S. troops in similar attempts to cope with this political-military dilemma. In chapter 9 we will return to a theoretical analysis of the policy dilemma the Vietnam War posed to the president.

1. To calculate the ratio of the sum of the predictions of an exercise to the sum of the predictions made in the regular simulation, for any variable, simply divide the ratio of the sum of the predictions in the exercise to the sum of the actual values by the ratio of the sum of the predictions in the regular simulation to the sum of the actual values.

2. Negative U.S. casualties in the exercises can be interpreted as being essentially zero.

GRAPHS OF SIMULATION PREDICTIONS OF HYPOTHETICAL HAWK AND DOVE POLICY ALTERNATIVES

The following graphs are the values of selected variables which are predicted by exercising the computer simulation. The predicted values of the selected variables under the hypothetical policy changes are indicated by zero (0). The actual values of the variables in each month are indicated by X.

The values predicted by the computer simulation of different policy alternatives can be compared with each other, with the actual values, and with the values predicted by the regular computer simulation shown in chapter 6.

Figures 25 through 31 represent a dovish policy alternative (U.S. commitments to South Vietnam = 0.25 × actual); figures 32 through 38, a hawkish policy alternative (U.S. commitments to South Vietnam = 2.5 × actual).

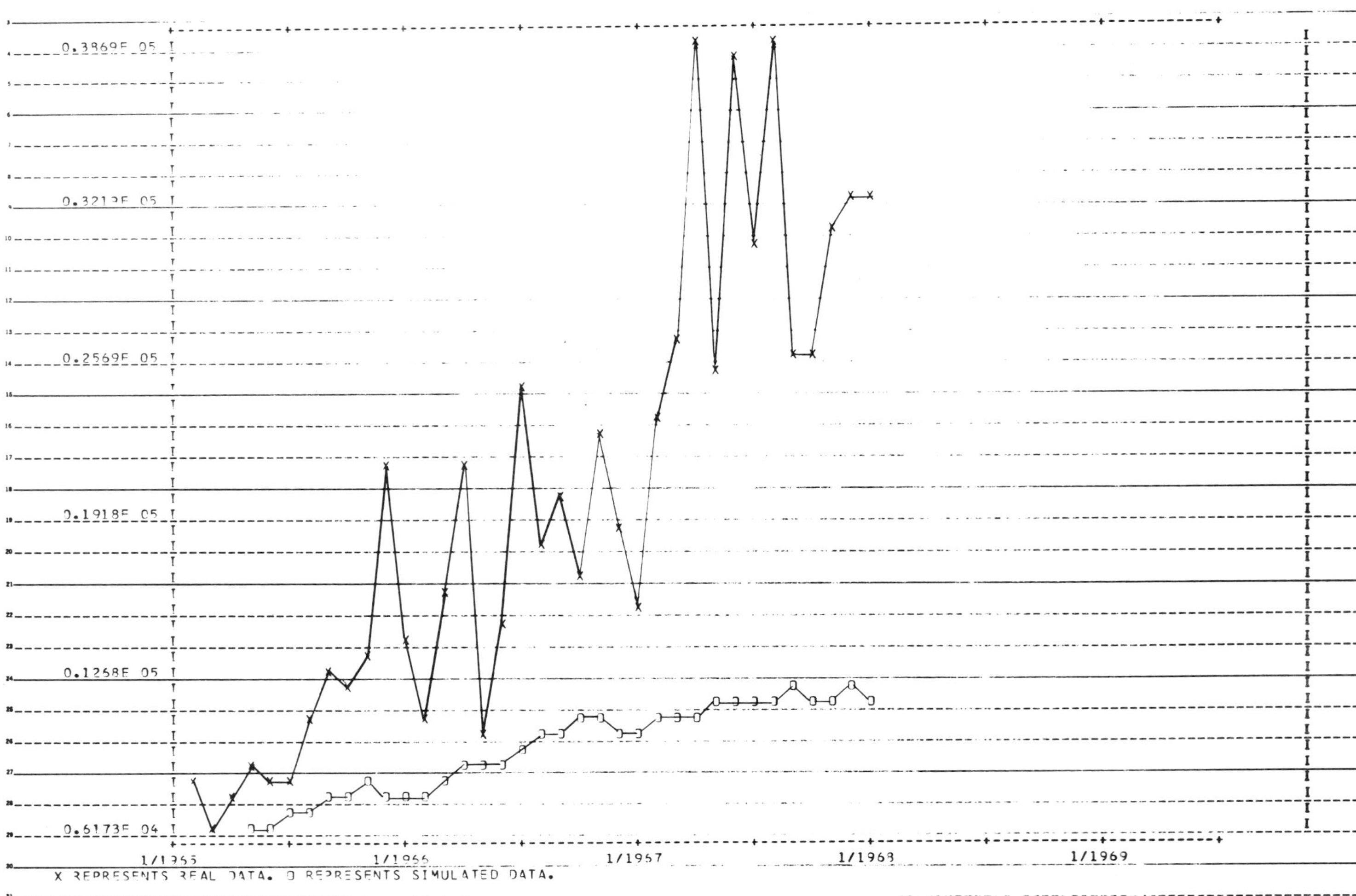
0.3869E 05
0.3213E 05
0.2569E 05
0.1918E 05
0.1268E 05
0.6173E 04
1/1965
1/1966
1/1967
1/1968
1/1969
X REPRESENTS REAL DATA. O REPRESENTS SIMULATED DATA.

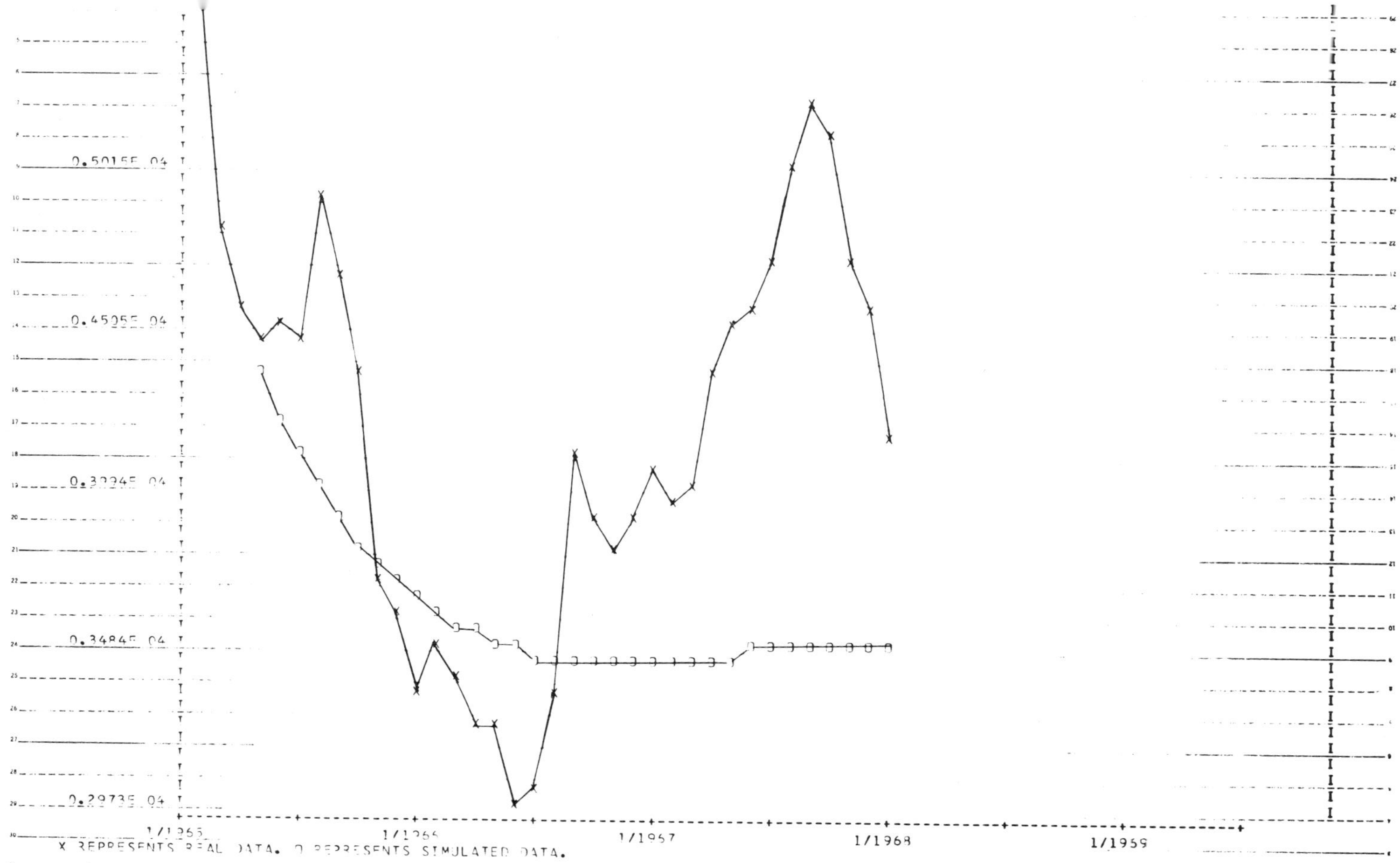

Fig. 26. S.V. popular confidence

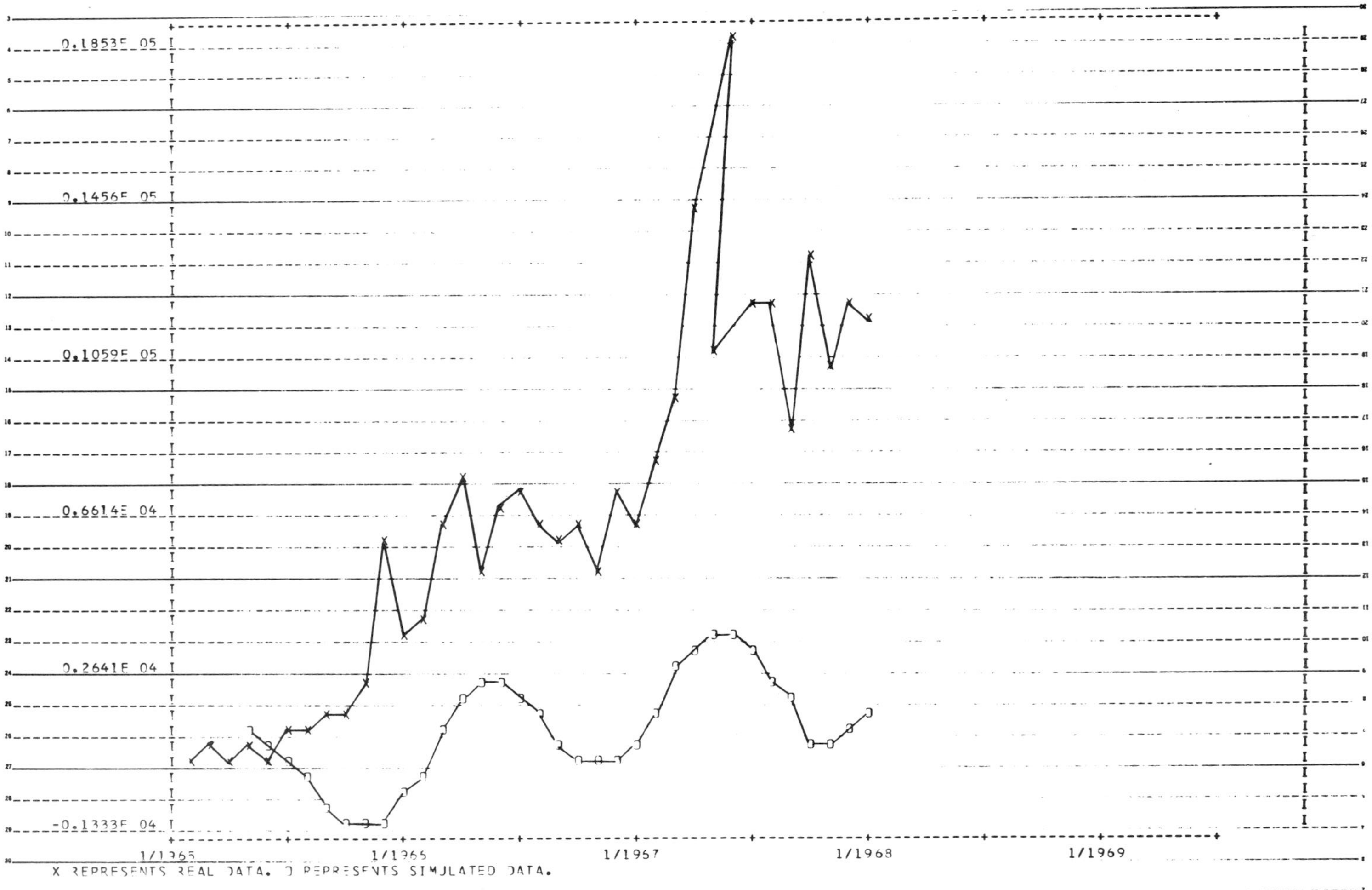
0.1853E 05
0.1456E 05
0.1059E 05
0.6614E 04
0.2641E 04
-0.1333E 04
1/1965
1/1966
1/1967
1/1968
1/1969
X REPRESENTS REAL DATA. O REPRESENTS SIMULATED DATA.

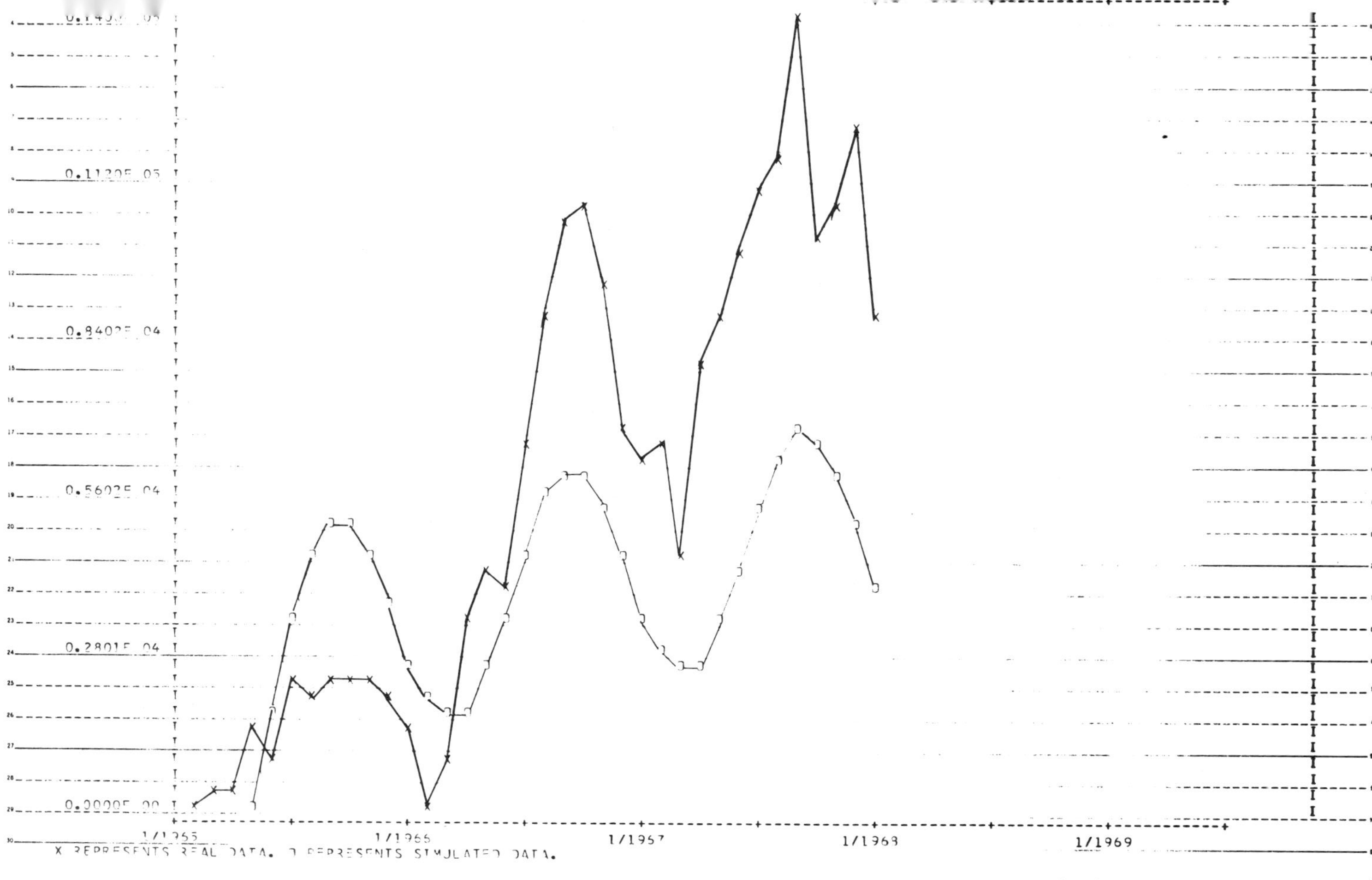

Fig. 28. U.S. bombing of N.V.

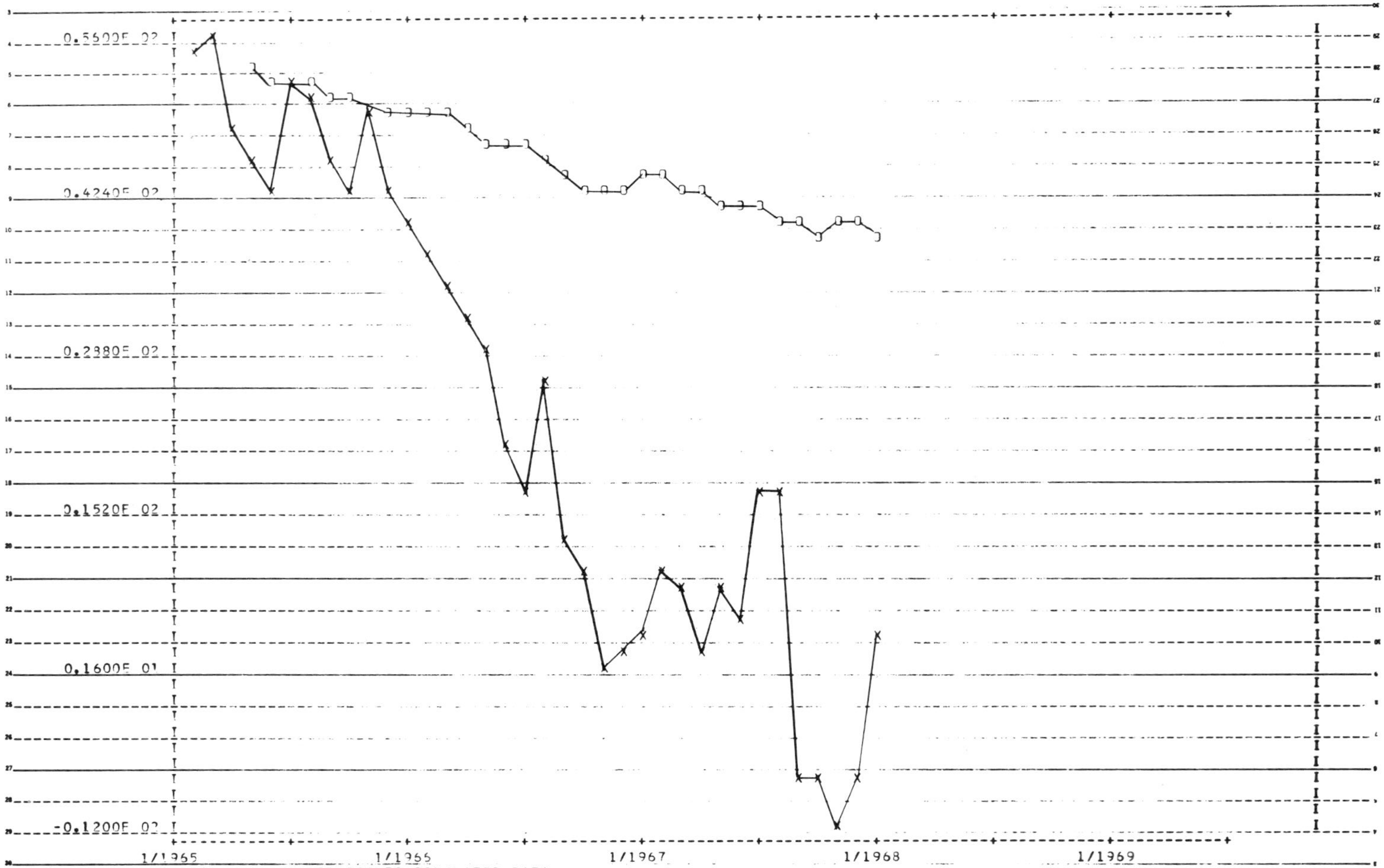

X REPRESENTS REAL DATA. O REPRESENTS SIMULATED DATA.

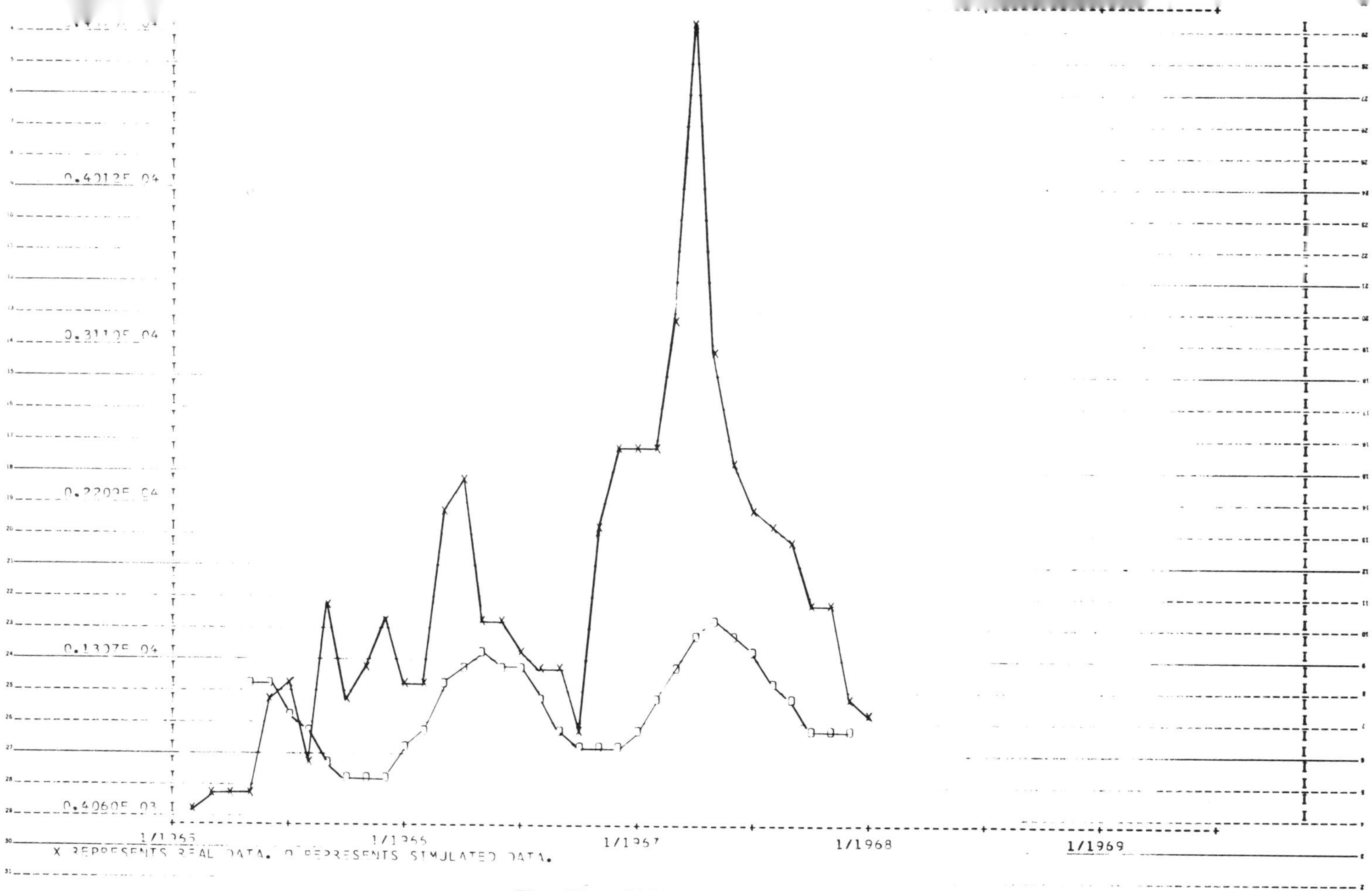

Fig. 30. N.V. + V.C. defectors

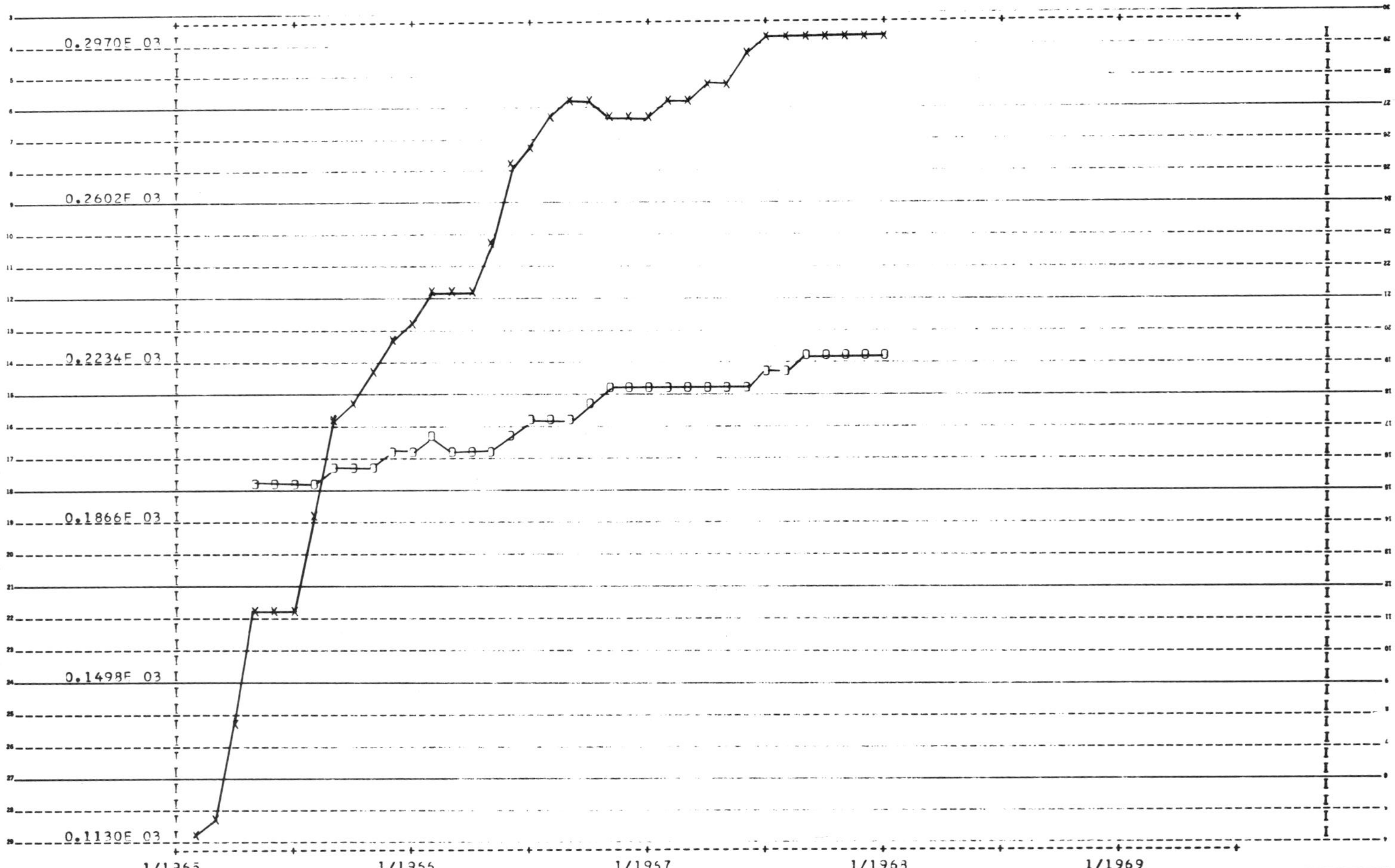

X REPRESENTS REAL DATA. O REPRESENTS SIMULATED DATA.

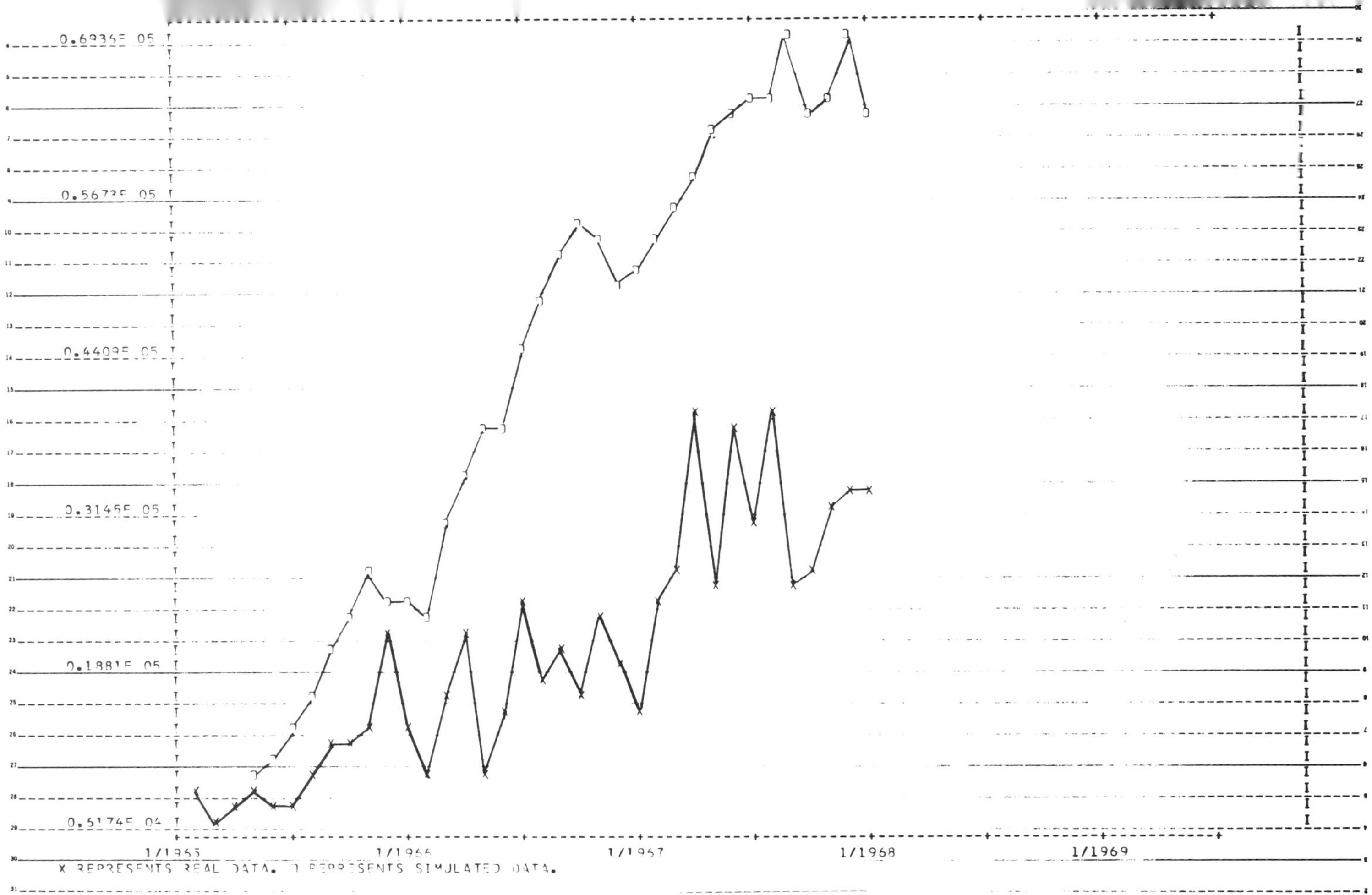

Fig. 32. N.V. + V.C. attrition

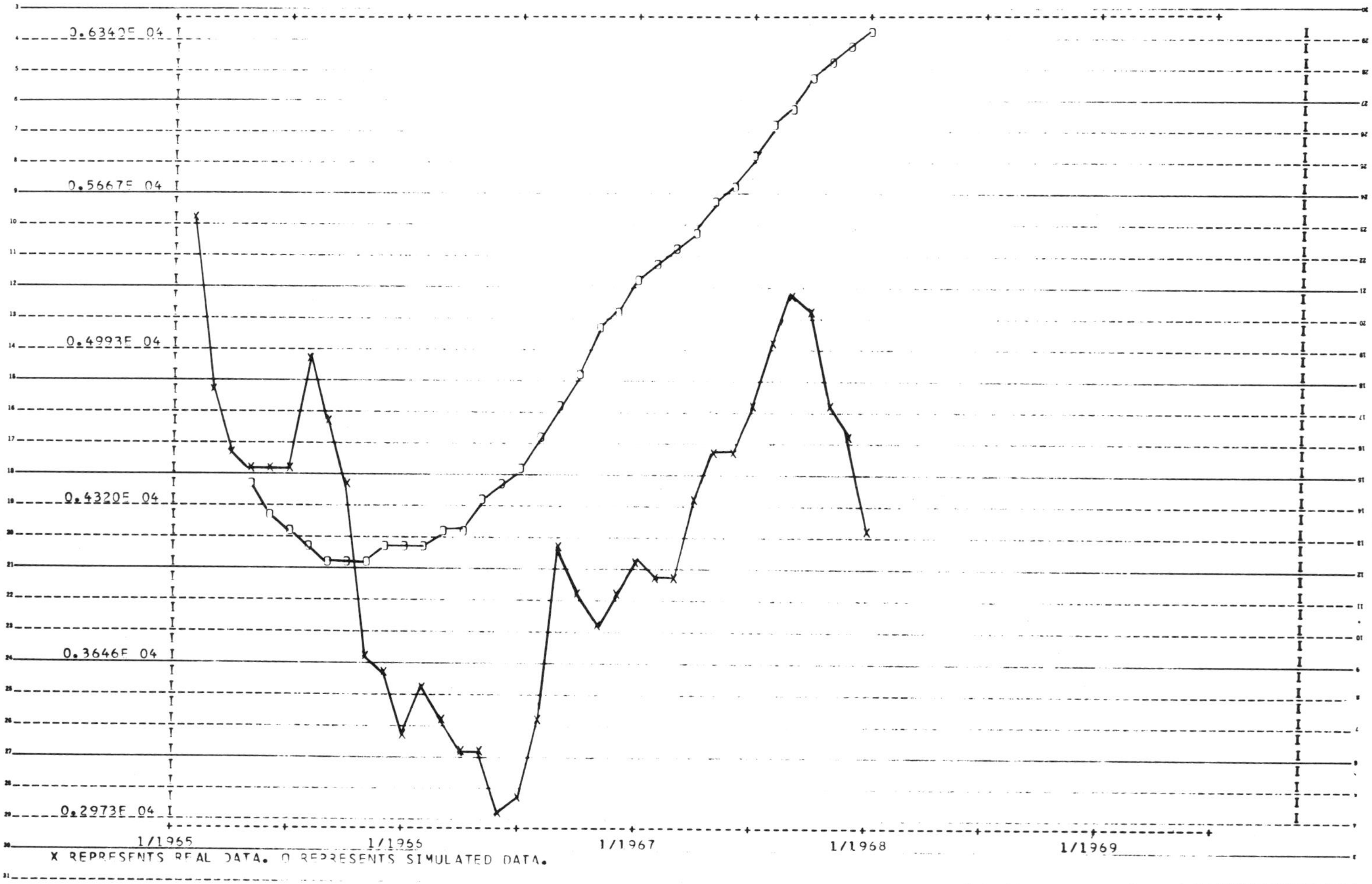

Fig. 33. S.V. popular confidence

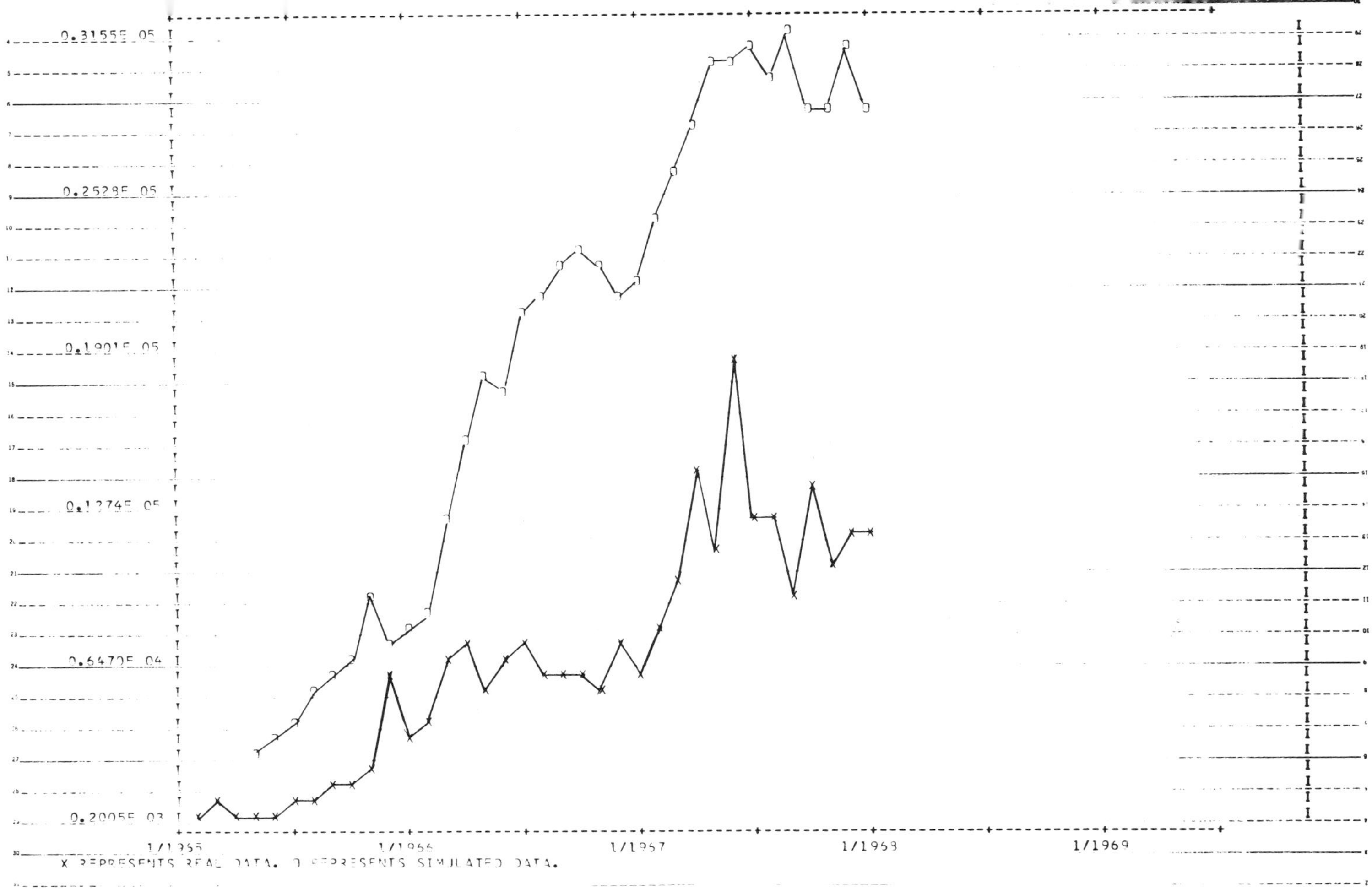

Fig. 34. U.S. casualties

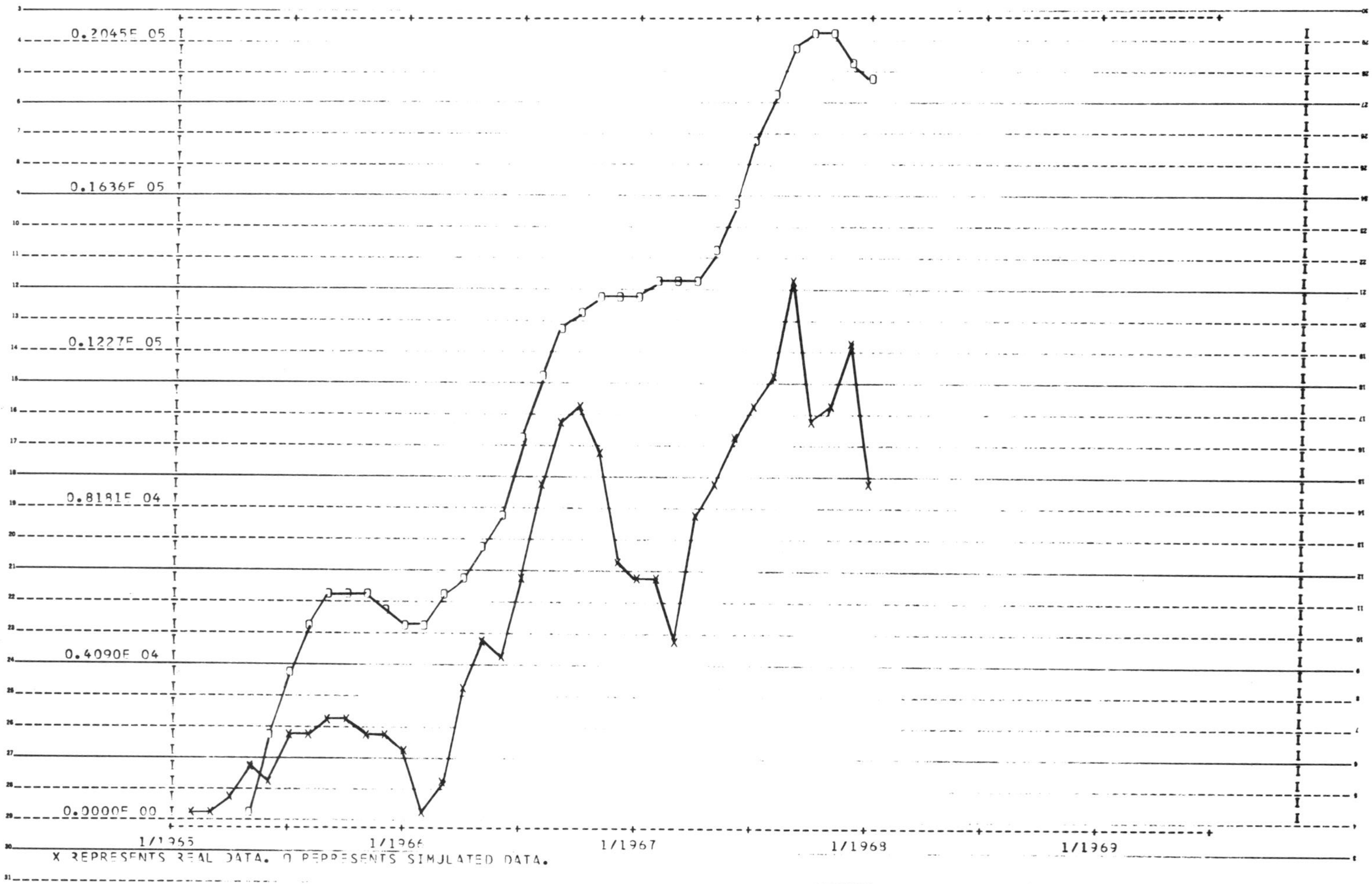

Fig. 25 U.S. bombing of N.V.

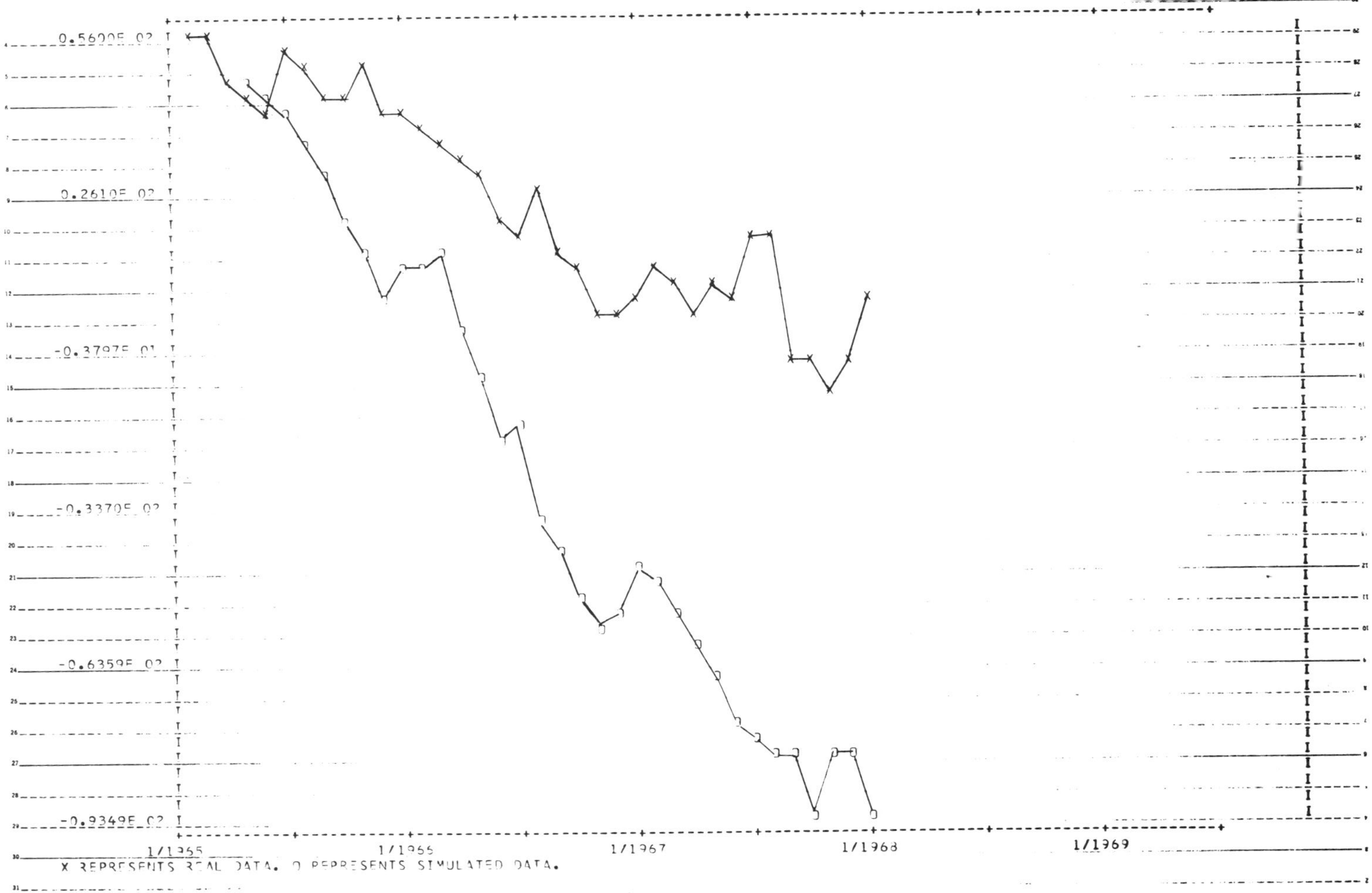

Fig. 36. U.S. public support for the president

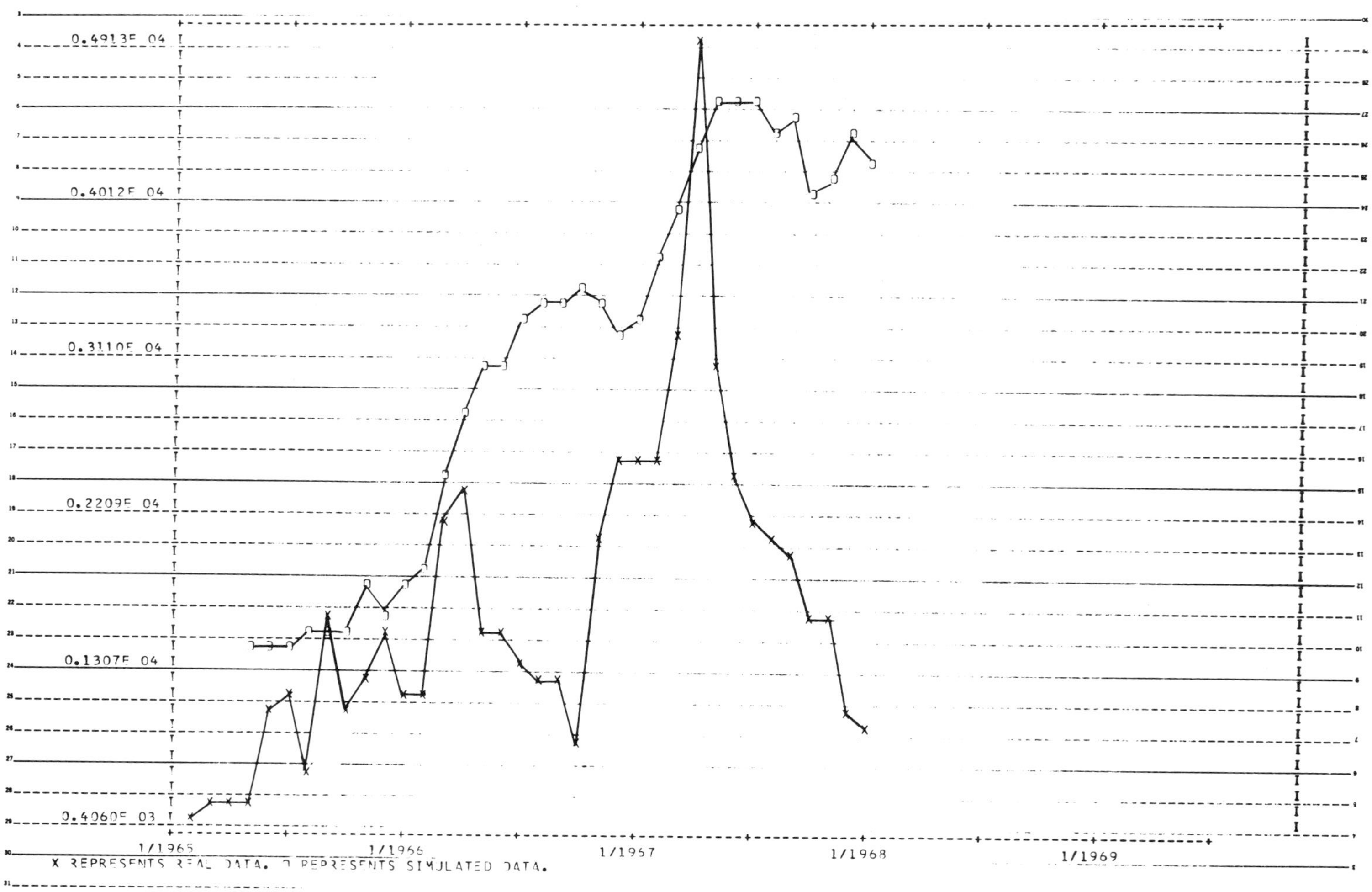

Fig. 27 N.V. + V.C. defectors

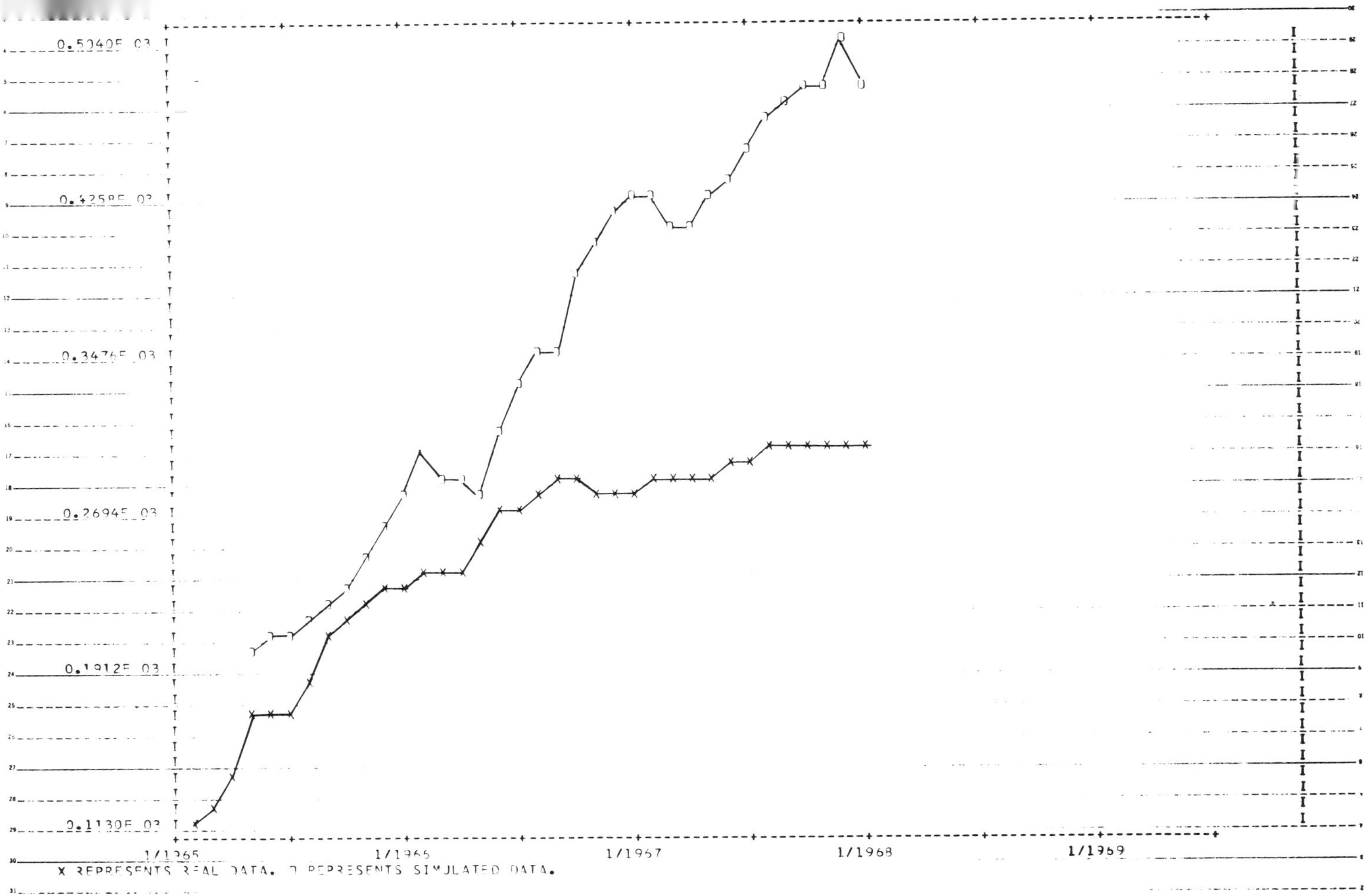

Fig. 38. N.V. + V.C. troops

8

The Vietnam War from the 1968 Tet Offensive to the 1970 Cambodian Invasion

The Communist Tet offensive started at the end of January 1968 and marked a climax and turning point in the Vietnam War. The North Vietnamese and Viet Cong forces made numerous coordinated attacks throughout all of South Vietnam, temporarily occupied some major towns and parts of cities in South Vietnam, and severely disrupted the South Vietnamese government's "pacification" program in the countryside.

The Tet offensive, however, was tremendously costly to the North Vietnamese and Viet Cong. They suffered tens of thousands of military casualties, including at least one top field commander. The political organization of the Viet Cong was severely hurt when thousands of local political cadre who had "surfaced" during the Communist offensive were subsequently killed or captured after the offensive was defeated and they lost the protection of their military forces.

Despite its tremendous military and political costs to the Communists in Vietnam, however, the Tet offensive was a great international political success for the Communists. The Tet offensive clearly demonstrated that the intervention of more than a half-million American troops and the massive bombing of North Vietnam had failed to defeat the Communists or to prevent them from launching major offensives. It thus forced the Johnson administration to reevaluate its entire Vietnam policy. Starting in March 1968, U.S. policy in Vietnam began to change. General Westmoreland was recalled from Vietnam to be army chief of staff on 22 March 1968. High past and current officials of the U.S. government advised President Johnson to deescalate the war. And on 31 March 1968 President Johnson announced that he would limit the bombing of North Vietnam and not seek reelection. The United States negotiated with the North Vietnamese to halt the bombing and to convene formal talks among all parties to the conflict in Paris. The United States began to "de-Americanize" the war, and halted the bombing of North Vietnam on 31 October 1968. On 5 November 1968 Richard Nixon was elected the new president of the United States.

The Nixon administration launched its "Vietnamization" policy, gradually withdrawing American ground combat troops from Vietnam, strengthening the South Vietnamese ground forces, and shifting the main effort in the ground fighting against the Communist forces to the South Vietnamese while supporting them with American logistical, air, and naval power.

Thus, in many important respects the period of the war that began with the Tet offensive was qualitatively different from the escalatory period that preceded it. This qualitative change can be seen in the change in the structure of relationships among many of the important variables in the war, as made evident in the computer simulation. For example, using the multiple regression model based on the structure of relationships existing from 1965 through 1967, the simulation was unable to predict the huge upsurge in casualties at the time of the Tet offensive or the halt in the bombing in North Vietnam.

The beginning of the shift in the structure of the war can be seen in the October through December 1967 values of what was a leading indicator of the Tet offensive—North Vietnamese and Viet Cong defectors. The actual number of Communist defectors declined during those months even though the simulation predicted an increase based on the past structure of relationships. The novel element that contributed to the decline in Communist defectors was probably Communist preparations for the Tet offensive. The expectation of a victorious offensive probably persuaded many would-be defectors among the Communist ranks not to defect.

The halt in the bombing of North Vietnam, the withdrawal of American ground combat troops from South Vietnam, and the Paris talks did not bring peace to Vietnam, however. Indeed, the invasion into Cambodia by U.S. and South Vietnamese troops in May 1970 marked another turning point in the war—its overt spread throughout Indochina. The invasion into Cambodia was followed by two other significant invasions—the unsuccessful South Vietnamese invasion of North Vietnamese–controlled areas in Laos in February 1971 and the major North Vietnamese invasion of South Vietnam that began in April 1972—an offensive that was responded to by the resumption of U.S. bombing of North Vietnam. Since the invasion into Cambodia broke a deescalatory trend in the war, it will be useful to analyze the empirical pattern of relationships in the war during the two-and-a-quarter-year period from the Tet offensive to the Cambodian invasion to help us evaluate the policies initiated during that period and continued beyond it.

DATA

The data used are monthly values of variables that indicate seven major concepts relevant to the war policies of the belligerents during the period from the Tet offensive to the Cambodian invasion. The data are corrected for the number of days in a month where such correction is appropriate.[1] These concepts and variables are:[2]

1. "Vietnamization"
   a. South Vietnamese ground operations of battalion size or larger
   b. $\left(\frac{\text{South Vietnamese ground operations}}{\text{U.S. ground operations}}\right)$
   c. $\left(\frac{\text{U.S. troops killed}}{\text{South Vietnamese troops killed}}\right)$
2. U.S. Actions
   a. Bombing missions in North Vietnam
   b. Bombing attack sorties in South Vietnam
   c. Helicopter attacks
   d. U.S. troop levels and monthly changes
   e. U.S. ground operations of battalion size or larger
3. "Pacification" or Security from North Vietnamese and Viet Cong Attack
   a. Viet Cong abductions of civilians
   b. Viet Cong killings of civilians
   c. Viet Cong terrorist incidents
   d. Viet Cong and North Vietnamese armed attacks
4. Military Outcomes
   a. U.S. troops killed
   b. South Vietnamese troops killed
   c. North Vietnamese and Viet Cong troops killed
5. Popular Confidence in the South Vietnamese Government
   a. Adjusted black market piastre value in Saigon, i.e.,

$$\left[\left(\frac{Dollars}{Piastre}\right) \Big/ \left(\frac{Money\ Supply}{Consumer\ Price\ Index}\right)\right]$$

6. Viet Cong Political Support
   a. Military and political defectors from the Viet Cong
7. U.S. Public Opinion
   a. Percentage approving President Johnson's handling of his job as president and President Nixon's handling of the Vietnam War

FINDINGS

American policy after the Tet offensive—decreasing U.S. military operations and withdrawing American troops—depended for its success upon the achievement of three conditions: (1) "*Vietnamization*," i.e., the South Vietnamese government's assumption of the major military efforts in the war; (2) "*pacification*," *i.e.*, the South Vietnamese government's securing the population from North Vietnamese and Viet Cong attacks; and (3) the *confidence* of the South Vietnamese people in the stability of the South Vietnamese government.[3] We will here explore the relationships of these three conditions to each other and to U.S. actions, military casualties, and political effects in the United States and among the Viet Cong.

VIETNAMIZATION

President Nixon stated that the withdrawal of U.S. troops from Vietnam required Vietnamization. To evaluate this policy, therefore, it is important to determine the extent to which the South Vietnamese forces took over the combat burden as the Americans withdrew. In addition, we must determine how the South Vietnamese government forces reacted to North Vietnamese and Viet Cong actions.

In this study Vietnamization is measured in three ways. The first is simply the number of battalion-size or larger ground operations[4] initiated by the South Vietnamese forces. When measured in this way, Vietnamization was independent of North Vietnamese and Viet Cong armed attacks of the previous month, and independent of U.S. ground operations as well. However, South Vietnamese ground operations increased with Viet Cong terrorist incidents within the same month.[5]

$$\underset{\textit{ground operations}}{\textit{South Vietnamese}} = 570 + \underset{(0.9)}{2.0}\ \textit{V.C. terrorist incidents} \quad (R^2 = .16) \qquad (1)$$

The second operational measure of Vietnamization is the ratio of South Vietnamese ground operations to U.S. ground operations. This measure incorporates the concept of the relative combat efforts made by the South Vietnamese as compared with those made by the Americans. Measured in this way, the regression equations show that Vietnamization was retarded by increased numbers of Viet Cong abductions of civilians and by increased rates of U.S. troop withdrawals.

$$\left(\frac{\textit{S.V. ground operations}}{\textit{U.S. ground operations}}\right) = 12 - \underset{(.001)}{.004}\ \textit{civilians abducted by V.C.}_{t\text{-}1} \quad (R^2 = .21) \qquad (2)$$

$$\left(\frac{\textit{S.V. ground operations}}{\textit{U.S. ground operations}}\right) = 8.8 - \underset{(.00005)}{.00021}\ \textit{monthly change in number of U.S. troops} \quad (R^2 = .37) \qquad (3)$$

Declining popular confidence in the South Vietnamese government seems to have spurred the government to increase its military efforts relative to that of the Americans, probably in an attempt to demonstrate the government of South Vietnam's own ability to fight the Communists and build popular confidence in that ability.

$$\left(\frac{S.V.\ ground\ operations}{U.S.\ ground\ operations}\right) = 24 - \underset{(.00010)}{.00098}\ popular\ confidence_{t\text{-}1} \quad (R^2 = .78) \tag{4}$$

Considered at the same time, increased numbers of Viet Cong terrorist incidents spurred Vietnamization, whereas increased numbers of regular North Vietnamese and Viet Cong armed attacks retarded Vietnamization.

$$\left(\frac{S.V.\ ground\ operations}{U.S.\ ground\ operations}\right) = 7.2 + \underset{(.01)}{.05}\ V.C.\ terrorist\ incidents - \underset{(.003)}{.01}\ N.V. + V.C.\ armed\ attacks_{t\text{-}1} \quad (R^2 = .62) \tag{5}$$

The number of civilians killed by the Viet Cong seems to have had no systematic effect one way or the other on Vietnamization.

U.S. Troops Killed/South Vietnamese Troops Killed: A Measure of Vietnamization

The ratio of U.S. troops killed to South Vietnamese troops killed is another indicator of Vietnamization. It measures the relative amount of combat with the North Vietnamese and Viet Cong. As Vietnamization increases, this ratio decreases.

The bivariate regressions show that as the rate of U.S. troop withdrawals increased, the casualty ratio declined. As one would expect, the ratio also decreased with more South Vietnamese ground operations and with fewer U.S. ground operations and air attacks in the South.

$$\left(\frac{U.S.\ troops\ killed}{S.V.\ troops\ killed}\right) = .49 + \underset{(.000002)}{.000007}\ monthly\ change\ in\ number\ of\ U.S.\ troops \quad (R^2 = .33) \tag{6}$$

$$\left(\frac{U.S.\ troops\ killed}{S.V.\ troops\ killed}\right) = .71 - \underset{(.0001)}{.0003}\ S.V.\ ground\ operations$$

$$(R^2 = .21) \qquad (7)$$

$$\left(\frac{U.S.\ troops\ killed}{S.V.\ troops\ killed}\right) = .23 + \underset{(.001)}{.003}\ U.S.\ ground\ operations$$

$$(R^2 = .16) \qquad (8)$$

$$\left(\frac{U.S.\ troops\ killed}{S.V.\ troops\ killed}\right) = .11 + \underset{(.000004)}{.00002}\ U.S.\ bombing\ attack\ sorties\ in\ S.V.$$

$$(R^2 = .61) \qquad (9)$$

U.S. ACTIONS

United States disengagement from Vietnam was initiated by the Johnson administration's realization that its past policy of escalating American commitments to South Vietnam, increasing U.S. combat operations, and bombing North Vietnam had been unsuccessful in achieving the American military objective of defeating the North Vietnamese and Viet Cong armed forces. When General Westmoreland requested more than two hundred thousand additional American troops after the 1968 Tet offensive, a complete reevaluation of American policy was made because the request for more troops asked for more of the same measures that had been shown to be unsuccessful.[6]

U.S. Troops in South Vietnam

What were the determinants of the number and the change in the number of U.S. troops in Vietnam from the Tet offensive to the Cambodian invasion? One could hypothesize that U.S. public opinion influenced the number of U.S. troops and the rate of their withdrawal. President Nixon stated that Vietnamization also affected the rate of U.S. troop withdrawals, as did North Vietnamese and Viet Cong hostile actions.

Bivariate regressions of operational indicators of the above variables with monthly changes in the number of U.S. troops (i.e., the *rate of change*) in Vietnam show that increased numbers of South Vietnamese ground operations, indicating greater Vietnamization, did increase the rate of U.S. troop withdrawals.

$$\textit{Monthly change in number of U.S. troops} = 19{,}000 - \underset{(.8)}{3.}\ \textit{S.V. ground operations}$$

$$(R^2 = .29) \qquad (10)$$

Viet Cong killing of civilians in South Vietnam and other Viet Cong terrorist incidents, indicating the degree of pacification, were independent of the rate of U.S. troop withdrawals, as was the monthly percentage of the U.S. public that approved of the way the president handled his job. The latter finding indicates that troop withdrawal decisions were not continually influenced by U.S. public opinion on a monthly basis, although they might have been from a longer time perspective. The decisions themselves covered troop withdrawals implemented over a number of months.

When the ratio of U.S. troops killed to South Vietnamese troops killed declined (an indicator of the decreasing fraction of combat engaged in by the United States as compared with the South Vietnamese), the monthly rate of U.S. troop withdrawals increased.

$$\textit{Monthly change in number of U.S. troops} = -\ 19{,}000 + \underset{(14{,}000)}{34{,}000} \left(\frac{\textit{U.S. troops killed}}{\textit{S.V. troops killed}} \right)$$

$$(R^2 = .19) \qquad (11)$$

U.S. troop levels were independent of the number of South Vietnamese ground operations, Viet Cong killing of civilians, and other Viet Cong terrorist incidents. Thus, North Vietnamese and Viet Cong activities and the progress of Vietnamization did not systematically determine U.S. troop levels month after month.

United States troop levels did decrease as the ratio of U.S. troops killed to South Vietnamese troops killed in the previous month decreased. Since the ratio of troop casualties is a good indicator of the actual combat engaged in by the United States as compared with South Vietnamese forces, it is apparent that South Vietnamese forces took over more and more of the combat as U.S. troops withdrew.

$$\textit{Number of U.S. troops} = 420{,}000 + \underset{(36{,}000)}{190{,}000} \left(\frac{\textit{U.S. troops killed}}{\textit{S.V. troops killed}} \right)_{t\text{-}1} \qquad (R^2 = .53)$$

$$(12)$$

Large U.S. Ground Operations

Even as U.S. forces withdrew from Vietnam, the remaining forces continued to engage in large ground operations of battalion size or larger. Because of the Vietnamization program, one would expect that these U.S. ground operations would have decreased as the number of South Vietnamese ground operations increased. This was not the case however. Empirically, U.S. ground operations were generally independent of those of the South Vietnamese.

One would expect that U.S. ground operations would have increased as North Vietnamese and Viet Cong attacks increased, and decrease after they decreased. The regression equations show that this was the case, even when controlling for the number of South Vietnamese ground operations. This finding is consistent with a pattern of action and reaction: the U.S. engaged in fewer major ground operations in response to fewer North Vietnamese and Viet Cong armed attacks.

$$\underset{(R^2 = .24)}{\textit{U.S. ground operations}} = 67 + \underset{(.03)}{.07}\ \text{N.V.} + \textit{V.C. armed attacks}_{t\text{-}1} \qquad (13)$$

The number of U.S. ground operations was entirely independent of U.S. public opinion, thus indicating that war operations were carried out more in response to the battlefield situation than to the home front during the period following the Tet Offensive.

U.S. Bombing in South Vietnam

United States air attacks in South Vietnam were made primarily to provide close air support for allied troops engaged in combat. The number of U.S. bombing attacks in South Vietnam declined after the Tet offensive, although the Vietnamization policy of the U.S. government included continued American air support for the South Vietnamese forces.

One might hypothesize that as the bombing of North Vietnam was reduced and then halted, more airplanes were available for use in South Vietnam, and therefore there would be more attacks in South Vietnam. This was not the case, however; U.S. bombing in the North and in the South were independent of each other. This independence reflects the different military objectives of bombing the North and bombing the South, as well as different weather patterns in Vietnam.

Bombing attacks were made in support of South Vietnamese as well as American troops; however, the bivariate regressions show that U.S. bombing decreased as South Vietnamese ground operations increased.

$$\textit{U.S. bombing attack sorties in S.V.} = 25{,}000 - \underset{(3.4)}{13.}\ \textit{S.V. ground operations}$$

$(R^2 = .37)$ (14)

United States bombing in South Vietnam was independent of the number of large U.S. ground operations and of the number of North Vietnamese and Viet Cong armed attacks in the previous month. The faster the monthly rate of U.S. troop withdrawals, however, the fewer air attacks there were in South Vietnam.

$$\textit{U.S. bombing attack sorties in S.V.} = 16{,}000 + \underset{(.07)}{.27}\ \textit{monthly change in number of U.S. troops}$$

$(R^2 = .40)$ (15)

It is thus significant that the American air war in South Vietnam was scaled down as U.S. troops were being withdrawn, generally irrespective of large U.S., South Vietnamese, or Communist ground combat operations.

U.S. Helicopter Attack Sorties in South Vietnam

According to the policy of Vietnamization, U.S. helicopter attack sorties in South Vietnam, like U.S. bombing missions, would continue to support the South Vietnamese after U.S. troops were withdrawn. Only Viet Cong terror is found to be associated with increased numbers of helicopter attack sorties, while North Vietnamese and Viet Cong armed attacks, South Vietnamese ground operations, and U.S. ground operations are found to be independent of helicopter attack sorties.

$$\textit{U.S. helicopter attack sorties in S.V.} = 68{,}000 + \underset{(26)}{61}\ \textit{V.C. terrorist incidents}$$

$(R^2 = .19)$ (16)

"PACIFICATION": NORTH VIETNAMESE AND VIET CONG ACTIONS

"Pacification" in South Vietnam above all means the security of the people from attack by the North Vietnamese and Viet Cong. The success of both American withdrawal and Vietnamization was dependent upon the North Vietnamese and Viet Cong's willingness to scale down their own actions as the Americans disengaged or on their inability to continue their hostile actions at a high rate as the South Vietnamese forces were strengthened. Thus, it is important to see to what extent North Vietnamese and Viet Cong actions were affected by U.S. and South Vietnamese actions.

North Vietnamese and Viet Cong Armed Attacks

In the post-Tet period, North Vietnamese and Viet Cong armed attacks declined with the decline of U.S. ground operations in the same month.

$$\textit{N.V. + V.C. armed attacks} = 56 + \underset{(1.3)}{2.9}\ \textit{U.S. ground operations} \quad (R^2 = .18) \qquad (17)$$

Communist armed attacks were systematically independent of these other variables that were thought to be related: South Vietnamese ground operations, the proportion of South Vietnamese to total U.S. and South Vietnamese ground operations, the total of U.S. and South Vietnamese ground operations, the rate of U.S. troop withdrawals, the number of U.S. troops in Vietnam, and the number of bombing attacks in South or North Vietnam. Thus, the North Vietnamese and Viet Cong did seem to deescalate their main force armed attacks as the U.S. deescalated its own major ground combat operations. The motivations for the reductions on the two sides were probably different. Deescalation of U.S. ground combat was motivated by political pressures in the United States. In the aftermath of the unprecedented fighting and losses during the Tet offensive and the following few months, the North Vietnamese and Viet Cong were unable to continue their major ground combat at high levels for some time.

Viet Cong Terrorist Incidents

Viet Cong terrorist incidents were increased by increases in South Vietnamese ground operations in the previous month and decreases in U.S. bombing attack sorties in South Vietnam in the previous month. The Viet Cong apparently reacted to the increased number of South Vietnamese ground operations—the indigenous escalation inherent in the policy of Vietnamization—especially when they were given more freedom to carry out their terrorist attacks as the harassment of U.S. bombing attacks in South Vietnam was reduced.

$$\textit{V.C. terrorist incidents} = 52 + \underset{(.03)}{.07}\ \textit{S.V. ground operations}_{t\text{-}1} \quad (R^2 = .16) \qquad (18)$$

$$V.C.\ terrorist\ incidents = 210 - \underset{(.001)}{.007}\ U.S.\ bombing\ attack\ sorties\ in\ S.V._{t-1} \quad (R^2 = .46) \tag{19}$$

Viet Cong Killing of Civilians

Both the Viet Cong and the South Vietnamese government have over the years sought to eliminate each other's political and administrative leadership. If one hypothesized that Viet Cong political or military defectors were evidence of loss of Viet Cong support, then it might follow that as they lost more political support, the Viet Cong would try to eliminate more Saigon government leaders in an attempt to regain control. This was not the case however: Viet Cong killing of civilians was independent of Viet Cong defectors. It was also independent of U.S. or South Vietnamese ground operations in the previous month.

Viet Cong Abductions of Civilians

The Viet Cong abducted civilians to impress them into service in the Viet Cong army or into temporary local labor for the Viet Cong. These abductions were independent of U.S. or South Vietnamese ground operations in the previous month, and of total Viet Cong defectors.

Summary of Findings on Pacification

In summing up the main findings concerning pacification, it appears that as U.S. ground operations declined, North Vietnamese and Viet Cong armed attacks also declined. Since, in the post-Tet period, North Vietnamese and Viet Cong armed attacks were carried out primarily by regular North Vietnamese units, it appears that the U.S. deescalation was reciprocated by the North Vietnamese and Viet Cong. Viet Cong terrorist incidents, however, increased in the post-Tet period, facilitated by a decrease in U.S. bombing attack sorties in South Vietnam, and to some extent stimulated by the increasing strength and pacification efforts of the South Vietnamese government forces. Terrorism appears to have been the major coercive means used by the Viet Cong in the struggle for political control while trying to rebuild military units and political cadres decimated during the Tet and spring offensives of 1968.

MILITARY CASUALTIES

The number of troops killed is an indicator of the overall intensity of fighting in an armed conflict.[7] Moreover, the United States fought the Vietnam War as a war of attrition, in which one of the strategic objectives was to kill as many Viet Cong and North Vietnamese troops as possible in order to so weaken the Communists' military capabilities that they would be unable to achieve their political objective of overthrowing the South Vietnamese government by force. The North Vietnamese also adopted a policy aimed at increasing the number of Americans killed in order to affect public opinion in the United States.[8]

There was some difference of opinion as to what affected U.S. casualties. The U.S. military command, for example, argued that North Vietnamese and Viet Cong attacks, rather than their own military operations, were the primary determinants of U.S. casualties. Domestic critics of the war in the United States asserted that one way the United States could decrease the number of Americans killed in Vietnam was to stop the large "search and destroy" operations. Others argued that large operations merely send many men out to "beat the bushes" and that relatively few Viet Cong or North Vietnamese were killed in such operations. Others have somewhat cynically asserted that large South Vietnamese ground operations were aimed not really at engaging the Communist forces but at satisfying their American advisers that ARVN forces were making some effort to defend their own country. Contact with the Communist forces would be evidenced by South Vietnamese casualties.

Empirically, North Vietnamese and Viet Cong armed attacks increased South Vietnamese casualties. Surprisingly, the greater the number of South Vietnamese ground operations the fewer South Vietnamese soldiers were killed. One might infer from this finding that the majority of South Vietnamese casualties were suffered not by the ARVN in large ground operations but by the Regional Forces and Popular Forces who made contact with the Viet Cong in small unit actions.

$$\begin{aligned} \textit{S.V. troops killed} &= 2{,}300 - \underset{(.6)}{2.0}\ \textit{S.V. ground operations} \\ (R^2 = .66) \qquad &\quad + \underset{(.8)}{3.5}\ \textit{N.V. + V.C. armed attacks} \end{aligned} \qquad (20)$$

U.S. Troops Killed

Bivariate regressions show that fewer troops were killed as the rate of troop withdrawal increased, and North Vietnamese and Viet Cong armed attacks and large U.S. ground operations decreased. In a multiple regression including all three factors, North Vietnamese and Viet Cong armed attacks and the rate of U.S. troop withdrawals remain significant causes of U.S. troops killed. United States ground operations, however, do not remain a significant factor. Thus, there is some support for the statement that U.S. casualties were primarily determined by Communist attacks rather than U.S. ground operations; of course, casualties were also reduced as U.S. forces were withdrawn.

$$\begin{aligned} \textit{U.S. troops killed} &= 52 + \underset{(3.6)}{3.4}\ \textit{U.S. ground operations} \\ (R^2 = .64) \quad & \quad + \underset{(.5)}{1.9}\ \textit{N.V. + V.C. armed attacks} \\ & \quad + \underset{(.007)}{.019}\ \textit{monthly change in number of U.S. troops} \end{aligned} \tag{21}$$

North Vietnamese and Viet Cong Troops Killed

The bivariate regressions show that Communist casualties were increased by North Vietnamese and Viet Cong armed attacks. Communist casualties were systematically independent of U.S. ground operations, South Vietnamese ground operations, and U.S. bombing attacks in South Vietnam. Thus, North Vietnamese and Viet Cong armed attacks were the primary determinant of casualties on both sides during this post-Tet period. From this we can infer that the Communists generally controlled the intensity of the fighting during this period.

$$\underset{(R^2 = .59)}{\textit{N.V. + V.C. killed}} = 960 + \underset{(7)}{39}\ \textit{N.V. + V.C. armed attacks} \tag{22}$$

POPULAR CONFIDENCE IN THE SOUTH VIETNAMESE GOVERNMENT

In this study, the ratio of the black market value of the South Vietnamese piastre in terms of dollars to the value of the piastre in goods and services, i. e.

$$\left[\left(\frac{\textit{Dollars}}{\textit{Piastre}}\right) \Big/ \left(\frac{\textit{Money Supply}}{\textit{Consumer Price Index}}\right)\right]$$

is used as a measure of the confidence of the South Vietnamese people in their government.[9] (See chapter 2 for the development of this measure.)

After the Tet offensive the primary influence on popular confidence in the South Vietnamese government was U.S. troop withdrawals from South Vietnam. The greater the rate of U.S. troop withdrawals and the smaller the number of remaining U.S. troops, the less confidence the South Vietnamese had in their government. Thus, confidence in the regime was highly dependent upon the presence of U.S. forces, and that confidence was shaken as the rate of withdrawal increased.

$$\underset{(R^2 = .45)}{\textit{Popular Confidence}} = -1.6 + \underset{(14)}{60}\ \textit{Number of U.S. troops} \quad (23)$$

$$\underset{(R^2 = .40)}{\textit{Popular Confidence}} = 15000 + \underset{(.5)}{19}\ \textit{monthly change in number of U.S. troops} \quad (24)$$

Vietnamization negatively affected popular confidence. The smaller the ratio of U.S. troops to South Vietnamese troops killed, the lower was South Vietnamese popular confidence in the following month.

$$\underset{(R^2 = .34)}{\textit{Popular Confidence}} = 8700 + \underset{(3900)}{14000} \left(\frac{\textit{U.S. troops killed}}{\textit{S.V. troops killed}}\right)_{t-1} \quad (25)$$

United States troops killed can be taken as another indicator of the intensity of fighting assumed by the U.S. forces. As the number of U.S. troops killed declined, so did popular confidence in the following month. The confidence of the South Vietnamese in their government depended not only on the presence of U.S. forces but also on the part these forces took in combat.

$$\underset{(R^2 = .39)}{\textit{Popular Confidence}} = 12000 + \underset{(1.0)}{3.8}\ \textit{U.S. troops killed}_{t-1} \quad (26)$$

Popular confidence appeared to be independent of the number of North Vietnamese and Viet Cong armed attacks and the number of terrorist incidents and civilians killed and abducted by the Viet Cong in the previous month.

Thus, we may conclude that as U.S. troops withdrew and Vietnamization increased, popular confidence in the Saigon regime declined.

These findings indicate that one of the major policy objectives of the Vietnamization program was not being achieved between the Tet offensive and Cambodian invasion: popular confidence in the South Vietnamese government. They thus have important significance both for the American and for the South Vietnamese governments: the Vietnamization program and U.S. disengagement weakened the regime politically rather than strengthened it.

VIET CONG POLITICAL SUPPORT: DEFECTORS

If fighting weakened the political position of the South Vietnamese regime, what was its effect on the political support for the Viet Cong? An indicator of *lack* of popular support for the Viet Cong is the number of political and military defectors. Defecting can be viewed as "voting with one's feet," although the behavior of defection may not follow the desire because of mitigating circumstances. Likewise, actual defection may not be politically motivated, but simply an attempt to survive by giving oneself up to government forces who locally or temporarily have military superiority. Defection may often be motivated by the desire to return to one's family or home at harvest time. Past studies have shown that the longer a soldier remained with the Viet Cong, the less likely he was to defect. Most of the defectors did so within a few months of their joining or impressment into the Viet Cong.[10]

A plausible hypothesis is that as the South Vietnamese regime gained support, the Viet Cong would lose support, and vice versa. Empirically, however, in the two and a quarter years following the Tet offensive, popular confidence in the South Vietnamese government declined while the number of political defectors from the Viet Cong increased. It thus appears that both the South Vietnamese regime and the Viet Cong lost political support after the Tet offensive.

The number of defectors was independent of the number of North Vietnamese and Viet Cong troops killed. This finding presents clear evidence that simply "killing Viet Cong" did not change the allegiance of the South Vietnamese people in this war.

The fewer civilians the Viet Cong abducted, the more Viet Cong defectors there were. This finding suggests that when the Viet Cong was less coercive, people took the opportunity and defected more readily.

$$\underset{(R^2 = .19)}{\textit{Total V.C. defectors}} = 3300 - \underset{(.5)}{1.3}\ \textit{civilians abducted by V.C.} \qquad (27)$$

After the Tet offensive, U.S. bombing attack sorties in South Vietnam declined as the total number of Viet Cong defectors increased. As the intensity of the fighting decreased (thus requiring less U.S. air support), more Viet Cong had the opportunity to defect because they were less frequently under attack.

$$\underset{(R^2 = .30)}{\textit{Total V.C. defectors}} = 4600 - \underset{(.04)}{.15}\ \textit{U.S. bombing attack sorties in S.V.} \qquad (28)$$

The Viet Cong's loss of support as the Americans withdrew offers some supporting evidence to the contention that the Viet Cong gained political support by emphasizing their protection of the Vietnamese people against the foreigners who wreaked destruction on their country. As the Americans disengaged, this argument was less relevant, and therefore support for the Viet Cong declined. As voluntary support declined, the Viet Cong increasingly used terror in their attempt to control the population.

Most strongly associated with the total number of Viet Cong defectors is the number of South Vietnamese ground operations.

$$\underset{(R^2 = .76)}{\textit{Total V.C. defectors}} = 1500 + \underset{(.6)}{5.0}\ \textit{S.V. ground operations} \qquad (29)$$

As these large ground operations increased, Viet Cong defected in greater numbers in order to survive when and where government forces showed military superiority and overran Viet Cong areas.

U.S. PUBLIC OPINION: DOMESTIC POLITICAL EFFECTS OF THE WAR

Almost every month the American Institute for Public Opinion (the Gallup Poll) measured the percentage of the U.S. public who approved and disapproved of the way the president (Johnson and Nixon) had been handling the war, as well as his job as president. The responses to those two questions have been highly correlated, especially during the Johnson administration. Since it is translated into votes, public opinion has important consequences, as Lyndon Johnson found out when his public approval was so low that he could not realistically seek reelection. Public approval of President Johnson did increase, however, as the number of bombing missions over North Vietnam the previous month declined. This increased approval near the end of his administration was no doubt related to the implication that peace would finally be achieved.

$$\underset{(R^2 = .40)}{\textit{Percentage U.S. public approval}} = 52 - \underset{(.0003)}{.001}\ \textit{U.S. bombing missions in N.V.}_{t\text{-}1} \qquad (30)$$

The more South Vietnamese ground operations in the previous month, the greater was the public approval for the president and his Vietnam policy.

$$\text{Percentage U.S. public approval} = 31 + \underset{(.006)}{.02}\ \text{S.V. ground operations}_{t\text{-}1} \quad (R^2 = .33) \tag{31}$$

This finding shows that the U.S. public responded positively to the Vietnamization program and to the South Vietnamese assuming more ground combat. The regression analysis supports this conclusion, for the greater the Vietnamization (as measured by the ratio of U.S. to South Vietnamese troops killed), the greater was the public approval for the president's Vietnam policy.

$$\text{Percentage U.S. public approval} = 65 - \underset{(11)}{34}\left(\frac{\text{U.S. troops killed}}{\text{S.V. troops killed}}\right)_{t\text{-}1} \quad (R^2 = .27) \tag{32}$$

The domestic political implications of these findings are clear: since (1) greater public approval for the president and his Vietnam policy depended upon fewer U.S. casualties relative to those of the South Vietnamese; (2) fewer U.S. casualties depended upon fewer North Vietnamese and Viet Cong armed attacks; and (3) fewer North Vietnamese and Viet Cong armed attacks depended upon fewer large U.S. ground operations, then President Nixon's policy of decreasing U.S. involvement in the war was a correct one for his purpose of maintaining his popular support in the United States.

However, the analysis above has shown that the policy of U.S. troop withdrawals and Vietnamization that strengthened the political position of the president in the United States by reducing American involvement and casualties in South Vietnam weakened the political position of the South Vietnamese government. These findings pose a continuing dilemma for the president of the United States. President Johnson faced this dilemma in 1965: whether to intervene in South Vietnam with massive U.S. military power and save the South Vietnamese government from collapse and overthrow by the Viet Cong at the risk of losing popular support in the United States. He intervened, and the subsequent escalation of the war and the massive participation by United States forces that was required to save the South Vietnamese government from overthrow led directly to large numbers of American casualties and other war costs that badly reduced President Johnson's support.

President Nixon apparently faced a similar dilemma. His Vietnamization policy required that there be fewer U.S. troops and fewer U.S. casualties in Vietnam. As this was done, he maintained U.S. public support. However, this very withdrawal of U.S. troops led to a severe loss of popular confidence in the South Vietnamese regime. Thus, both Presidents Johnson and Nixon have faced the same dilemma: whether to achieve domestic political objectives in the United States or international political objectives in Vietnam. Although both presidents obviously preferred to have it both ways, both have had to choose because of the very structure of the war and its political consequences. Each president made a fundamentally different choice. President Nixon's choice was no doubt informed by his predecessor's early retirement. The domestic political success of his choice was evident in his landslide reelection victory.

A SIMPLIFIED MODEL OF THE VIETNAM WAR FROM THE TET OFFENSIVE TO THE CAMBODIAN INVASION

Figure 39 is a simplified model in flow diagram form, i.e., a chain of relationships among the variables. Regression analysis has been used to reveal the simplified structure of relationships that are in reality interwoven into a complex whole.

Figure 39. Major Relationships in the Vietnam War from the Tet Offensive to the Cambodian Invasion

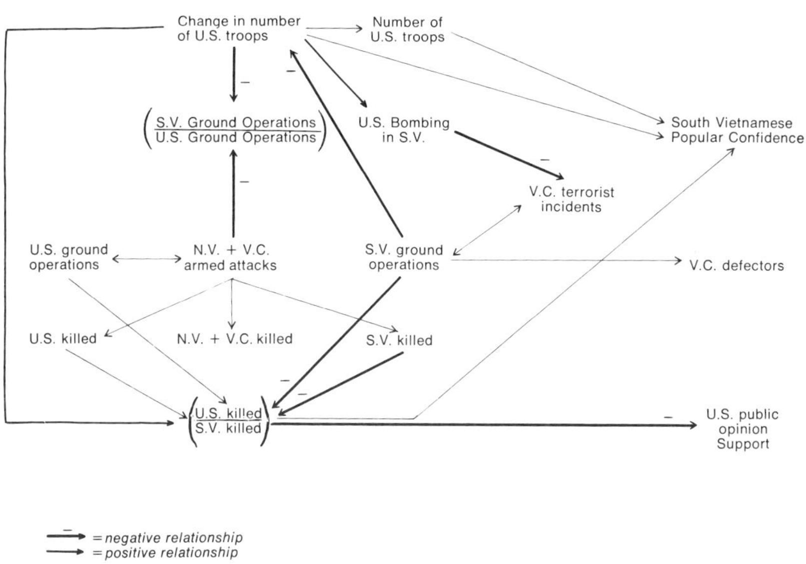

This structure of relationships and the regression equations upon which the structure is based can be used to trace what would have

been the probable consequences of any particular action engaged in by either side during the period from the Tet offensive to the Cambodian invasion. The policy implications of this structure of relationships are clear: one can see the necessary actions or conditions that are linked to certain policy objectives. For example, if the president of the United States was concerned about increasing his popular support, he would find that if he decreased the number of U.S. ground operations, this would lead to decreases in North Vietnamese and Viet Cong armed attacks and to decreases in U.S. troops killed, which in turn would lead to an increase in U.S. public support for the president and his policy.

Like the structure of relationships of the pre–Tet offensive period, the structure represented in the regression equations and in the flow diagram for the period from the Tet offensive to the Cambodian invasion is partly based on time-lagged relationships. Thus, the entire structure can be used to forecast likely outcomes resulting from specified actions. As described in chapters 3 and 6, with a complex structure, this forecasting can be done by means of computer simulation in which the predicted value of each dependent variable is used as the value for that variable when it appears as an independent variable in another regression equation farther along the chain of relationships. As long as there is at least one time-lagged relationship, one can reiterate this procedure to make month-by-month predictions of each variable by boot-strapping from only the initial values of each variable. If the predictions from such a computer simulation prove to be close to the actual values for the period from which these regression equations were derived (i.e., from February 1968 through April 1970), then one has more confidence in the predictions of the value of each variable in the months beyond the last real data point.

Once such a simulation model proves to make valid predictions, one could exercise the model (as demonstrated in chapter 7) to see what the likely outcome in a number of dependent variables would be when one changes the values of manipulable independent variables. For example, one could estimate the magnitude of the likely effect on public approval of the president's Vietnam policy if large U.S. ground operations in Vietnam were increased or decreased by given amounts. Or one could find the likely effect of increasing or decreasing the rate of U.S. troop withdrawals from Vietnam on such variables as South Vietnamese popular confidence, political support for the Viet Cong, or U.S. public opinion.

A simple example of how one can predict the value of a variable (with or without a computer) is as follows: for every additional ten thousand U.S. troops withdrawn from Vietnam each month, the ratio of U.S. to South Vietnamese troops killed would be reduced by approximately .07. (See equation 6.) For every additional monthly reduction of approximately .07 in the ratio of U.S. to South Vietnamese troops killed, there would be an increase of about 2.4 percent in U.S. public approval of the president. (See equation 32.) Following through this chain of relationships, one can thus forecast the probable consequences, measured in numerical terms, of a number of possible actions that a policy-maker is considering and among which he must choose.

This ability to predict consequences of alternative actions is one of the purposes of scientific and quantitative analysis of international relations. Such analysis strengthens our capability for critical evaluation of existing policies, and potentially could enlighten policy-making so that future tragedies can be avoided.

1. In this chapter the newer data for the 1968-70 period are analyzed as individual variables, rather than as weighted composite indices. This approach allows one to use the regression equations to calculate the estimated value of each individual dependent variable.

2. Except for the black market piastre value, money supply, consumer price index, and the public opinion data, all data come from "Unclassified Statistics from Southeast Asia," a table prepared monthly by the Directorate for Information Operations of the U.S. Department of Defense. The public opinion data come from the "Gallup Poll," (the American Institute of Public Opinion in Princeton, N.J.). The monthly data on the black market value of the South Vietnamese piastre come from dealers in Saigon, Hong Kong, and San Francisco.

3. Robert H. Johnson, "Vietnamization: Can It Work?" Committee on Foreign Relations, United States Senate, "Vietnam: December, 1969," section 7, p. 18.

4. All ground operations used as measures in this study are those of battalion size or larger.

5. As described in chapter 3, the structure of relationships set forth in all of the regression equations in this study can be used to estimate the consequences of given actions or conditions. The regression coefficients (b) state (within some stated standard error(SE)) the magnitude of the effect of an independent variable on a dependent variable. These equations can be used to predict the value of a dependent variable given the value of an independent variable, assuming that the value of the independent variable stays within the range of the values it has had in the past and from which these regression equations were derived. The proportional reduction in the error of the prediction of a dependent variable, as compared with the error associated with using the mean value as the predicted value of the dependent variable, is measured by the square of the multiple correlation coefficient, or R^2. Values for all variables in the regression equations are monthly. Values are within the same month except those marked "t-1," which are of the previous month.

6. Clark M. Clifford, "A Vietnam Reappraisal: The Personal History of One Man's View and How It Evolved," and E. W. Kenworthy, "The Tet Offensive and the Turnaround," in *Pentagon Papers*, chap. 10.

7. Rudolph J. Rummel, "Indicators of Cross-National and International Patterns," p. 134.

8. Tad Szulc, "Hanoi Calls for the Infliction of Heavier Combat Losses on U.S.," p. 13.

9. During the period under study the piastre was worth an average of about one-fourth of one cent on the black market.

10. Paul Berman, "The Liberation Armed Forces of the NLF: Compliance and Cohesion in a Revolutionary Army," chap. 4.

The Paradox of Waging War to Achieve Power

A major political paradox emerges from an analysis of the Vietnam War. The war was conducted by each side to increase its own, and to diminish its opponent's, political power in Vietnam. Each side increased its own efforts when it appeared that the other side might prevail. Thus, the escalation of the war.

Yet in seeking political power through the use of increased military force in Vietnam, the leaders of each side tended to lose the political support of their own people. This chapter will seek to analyze both theoretically and empirically this general paradox and what underlies it.

Presidents Johnson and Nixon both faced a dilemma in the Vietnam War. The objective of both administrations, following precedents established by Presidents Truman, Eisenhower, and Kennedy, was to prevent the Communists from achieving power in Indochina, particularly in South Vietnam after 1954. Since this objective was shared by five American presidents, one can infer that it was widely supported by the political, military, and economic elite in the United States.[1] The motivations for this general objective were economic, strategic, and political. Southeast Asian markets and resources were to be kept open to the United States and its allies for trade and investment. Through the use of military bases and alliances, the United States sought to resist the expansion into Southeast Aisa of the spheres of influence of Communist China and of the Soviet Union. In addition, the United States sought to frustrate a Communist-led "war of national liberation" in Vietnam so as to deter similar Communist or nationalist challenges to American hegemony elsewhere in the world, particularly in the underdeveloped areas of Latin America, Asia, and Africa. Finally, the U.S. government repeatedly maintained that unless it honored its commitment to South Vietnam to resist Communist subversion and aggression, U.S. commitments elsewhere in the world would not be credible. Such loss of credibility would weaken or eliminate the deterrent value of American political commitments, thus inviting Communist challenges or accommodations to Communism by other nations.

The Johnson administration sought to prevent the Communists from gaining political control over South Vietnam by a continuing escalation of U.S. troop levels, supplies, military assistance, combat operations in South Vietnam, and bombing in North Vietnam. At enormous monetary expense and with vast destruction and the loss of tens of thousands of American and Vietnamese lives, this massive effort did avert a Communist take-over of South Vietnam during the Johnson administration. However, the American people became greatly frustrated and dissatisfied with the war and with the Johnson administration. As a consequence, President Johnson paid the ultimate political cost of pursuing the international objectives of the American elite: the loss of both his domestic political support and of the office and power of the presidency.

As the Vietnam War progressed during the Nixon administration, U.S. popular support for the war continued to decline, and a majority of Americans came to desire an end to the U.S. role in the war. Aware of both this popular sentiment in the United States and the political costs of President Johnson's experience, President Nixon attempted to avoid similar consequences. During his last nine months in office President Johnson had initiated some leveling-off of U.S. ground commitments in Vietnam and a reduction in, and eventual halt to, the bombing of North Vietnam. President Nixon extended this strategy by withdrawing American ground troops from Vietnam while simultaneously pursuing the Vietnamization policy of improving South Vietnamese ground and air combat capabilities, and supporting the South Vietnamese military effort with massive U.S. air and naval power. President Nixon correctly saw that fewer American ground forces in Vietnam would result in fewer American casualties and lower financial costs of U.S. support of an anti-Communist South Vietnam. With fewer costs and U.S. casualties in Vietnam, President Nixon was able to retain strong political support in the United States for his Vietnam policy.

However, in escaping, through its Vietnamization policy, one horn of the dilemma of the Vietnam War—declining popular support—the Nixon administration risked being caught on the other—losing the U.S. objective in the war. Vietnamization included the withdrawal of U.S. ground troops, their replacement by South Vietnamese ground troops, and the extension of both the air and ground war into Laos and Cambodia, using South Vietnamese ground troops and American air and naval power. This policy constituted, however, a less effective defense against the expansion of Communist power in Indochina—the stated U.S. objective in the war. The withdrawal of the majority of U.S. ground forces in South Vietnam weakened the combined American-South Vietnamese military strength in South Vietnam. The *combined* fighting strength of the South Vietnamese and U.S. troops had been unable to defeat the North Vietnamese and Viet Cong. It was most unlikely that the South Vietnamese army would be able to do so on its own. Indeed, without the help of massive American air power and naval firepower, the South Vietnamese army could not have withstood the major offensive launched by the North Vietnamese in the spring of 1972.

If the Communists were able to take over South Vietnam by military means after American troops were withdrawn from Vietnam, the long history of American commitments and costs in Vietnam would have been futile. Such a defeat of U.S. objectives would likely lead to a questioning of the credibility of U.S. commitments to less powerful nations around the world to help resist Communist aggression or subversion, and to those nations' accommodation to Chinese or Soviet demands. In short, the Nixon administration's Vietnamization policy, though being more likely than the previous policy of escalation to minimize domestic political dissatisfaction with President Nixon, nonetheless risked losing the objective of an anti-Communist South Vietnam. Thus, the Nixon administration, like the Johnson administration, was locked in the dilemma of incompatible domestic and international political objectives.

In Vietnam, too, the pursuit of political power by means of military force by the leaders of South Vietnam on the one hand, and of North Vietnam and the Viet Cong on the other, also had a paradoxical effect. Successive South Vietnamese governments fell as they tried to press the war against the Communists and as the South Vietnamese Army and people halfheartedly continued the struggle. As the Communists intensified their efforts in the war, they lost thousands of both military and civilian defectors. Thus, in Vietnam as well as in the United States, the pursuit of power by political leaders through the use of military force resulted in a lessening of the popular support upon which their political power was based.

The paradox of the Vietnam War, then, is that leaders on both sides were forced to make the trade-off between their own political support and the pursuit of their war objectives. This paradox is represented graphically in figure 40 as an inverse functional relationship.[2]

What underlies this paradox of national leaders' being unable to increase their power over others by waging war without eroding the popular basis of their domestic political power? A theoretical answer can be found in an analysis of the way in which the costs and benefits of the war goals are differently evaluated by elites and masses. Consider the set of expected benefits that the elites of the participating countries may expect to achieve by waging the Vietnam War: having a particular kind of government in South Vietnam; controlling markets,

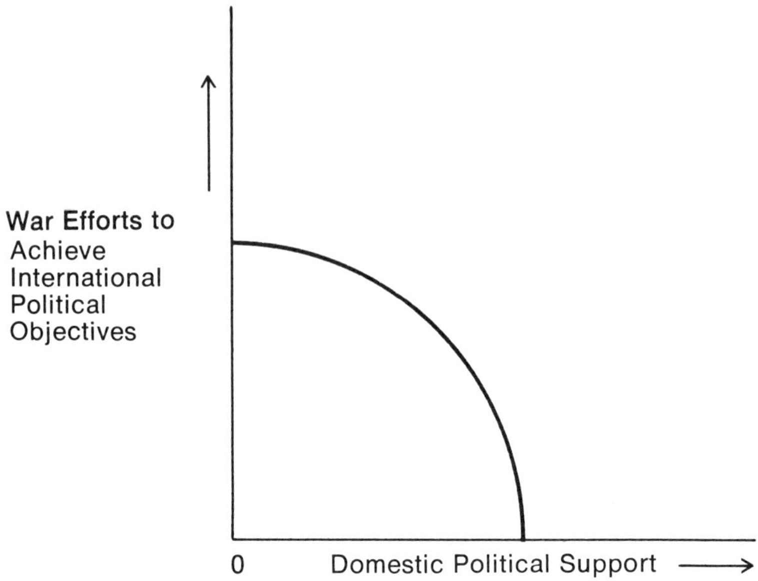

Figure 40. Loss of Political Support in Pursuit of War Objectives

resources, or people in Southeast Asia; using South Vietnam as a precedent-setting example of what happens when guerrilla wars of "national liberation" are attempted and succeed or fail; proving the credibility (or incredibility) of U.S. (or Russian or Chinese) political treaties or military commitments; and so on. Both Communist and anti-Communist leaders are commited to the achievement of these goals, although they may evaluate them differently. Consider further the set of expected costs associated with attempting to achieve these goals by means of war: lives lost, physical destruction, tax dollars spent, families uprooted, people maimed, diminished purchasing power of national currency, psychological fear and frustration, loss of a nation's moral prestige, the general waste of people and resources, and so on.

We can postulate that members of both masses and elites in a country will have some system of preferences regarding the trade-offs between these expected net benefits and expected net costs that are the result of a policy of waging war. These are shown in figure 41.[3]

There we see a family of indifference curves, or equal utility contours. We may postulate that for any individual, there will be some set of associated net expected costs and benefits to which he will be indifferent, i.e., that will yield the same satisfaction to the individual (e.g., points

Figure 41. Trade-offs between Expected Net Benefits and Expected Net Costs of Waging War

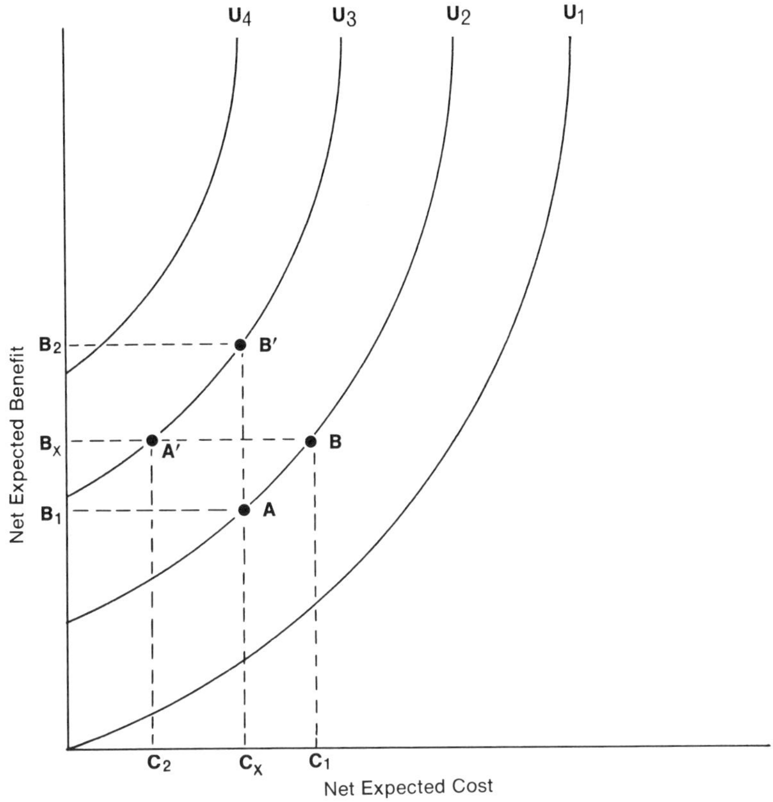

A and *B*).[4] The connection of these points is represented by a single indifference curve, e.g., U_2. Each indifference curve is assumed to be convex upward to represent the psychological fact that as marginal costs become greater, the marginal benefits expected to accrue from them must be still greater for people to be willing to bear them. Each indifference curve in figure 41 is drawn in such a way as to indicate that there is some positive relationship between the expected net costs and benefits of a war policy; i.e., people realize that the more benefits they expect to achieve by a war, the more effort is required and the more costly the war is likely to be.

For any individual we can define a higher indifference curve for the net expected costs and benefits of war, e.g., U_3. For the *same* expected net cost, C_x, any individual would prefer to receive a *larger* net benefit, i.e., B_2 to B_1. Thus, an individual would prefer the combination of net expected costs and benefits represented by point B' to those associated with A. Put another way, if the net expected benefit is to remain constant, e.g., B_x, one would prefer to have *fewer* associated net costs rather than more, i.e., point A' rather than point B. Thus, an individual would prefer C_2 to C_1, and so on.

For any individual we can postulate a large number of such indifference curves, the totality of which is his *preference system* and which we can represent graphically as his indifference map. On this map each indifference curve could be considered a contour line at a constant height on a mountain that is the individual's utility, which we can imagine getting higher as it comes out of the page in the third dimension toward us. As we move from indifference curve U_1 to U_2 to U_3 etc., and cross successive indifference curves we are indicating higher levels of satisfaction or utility.

We know that the major burdens of warfare are usually borne by the mass of people in any country, rather than by the political and economic elites. It is the masses who provide the soldiers who are maimed and killed, the taxes that finance war efforts, and who experience the destruction, dislocation, and terrible fear for their own lives and safety.

We also know that because of their particular social and economic perspectives, the mass of people in any country are usually minimally concerned about many of the international objectives of their governments (Campbell et al., 1960). Because they have less to gain directly than do the political, military, and economic elites, the masses are less concerned with such things as the placement of strategic bases or control of world resources and markets, including competition for such control by different powers in the world. The masses of people are primarily concerned with issues they perceive as directly affecting their own lives. Elites, on the other hand, generally take into account economic, strategic, and political conditions that are more remote temporally and geographically. Moreover, as shown in the "Pentagon Papers," elites base their evaluations of policies on different information than is available to the masses.

Given these facts, we can postulate that elites and masses give different subjective evaluations to the associated net expected benefits and costs of waging war. The sets of trade-offs preferred by elites are different from those preferred by the masses. Specifically, because the masses bear the greater costs of war, we can assume, as shown in figure 42, that they desire a greater marginal benefit (B_4 — B_3) for a given marginal cost (C_2 — C_1) than do the political, military, and economic elites ($B_2 - B_1$). Put another way, the political, military, and economic elites are more willing to have their country assume a greater marginal net cost ($C_4 - C_3$) for a given expected marginal net benefit ($B_4 - B_3$) than are the masses ($C_2 - C_1$), since the costs of war are borne mainly by the masses. Thus, we assume that in the indifference curves of the masses the net expected benefits increase more steeply as a function of the net expected costs than in the indifference curves of members of the political, military, and economic elite.

Figure 42. Trade-offs of Elites and Masses between Expected Net Benefits and Expected Net Costs of Waging War

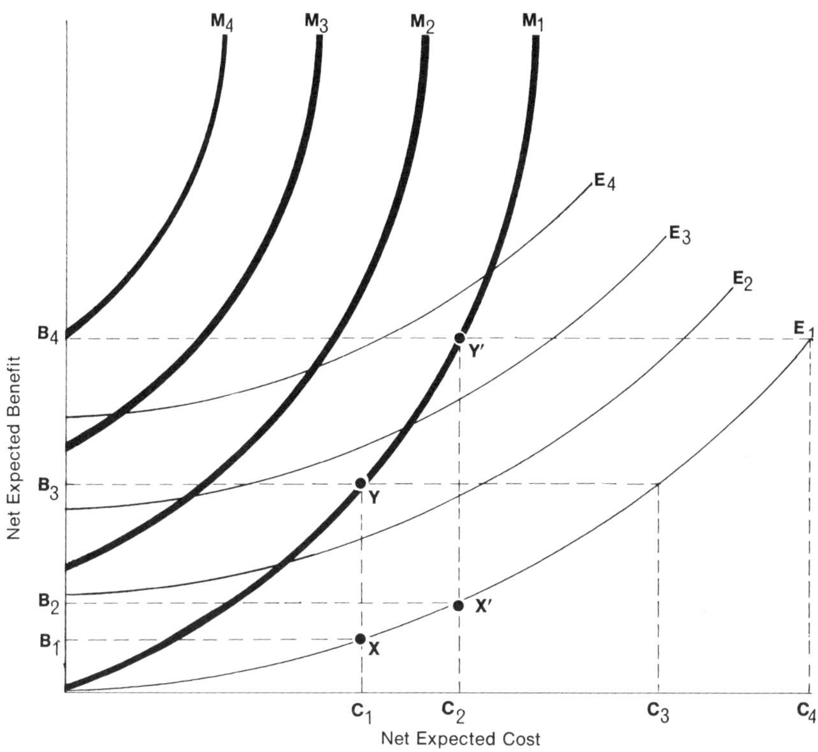

Our discussion so far has considered only the *subjective* preference systems of members of the elites and masses. In waging war, however, there are some *objective* functional relationships between costs and benefits (e.g., the relationship between U.S. casualties and diminishing Communist support in South Vietnam as measured by numbers of defectors). To produce some expected net benefit (e.g., "pacification"

in Vietnam), there are associated real net costs (e.g., lives and money). We can represent this *objective* relationship by the straight line, *OP*, as shown in figure 43.[5]

We can combine our analysis of objective reality and subjective preferences by superimposing the objective price line on an individual's indifference map, as shown in figure 44. If he had the power to decide a trade-off point, this individual would still be constrained by the objective price line *OP*. Since any individual would prefer the greatest possible satisfaction, he would choose the combination in which his highest indifference curve is touched by the objective price line, i.e., the point at which the objective price line is *tangent* to his highest possible indifference curve. In figure 44 that point is *X* on indifference curve U_2. Any other point on *OP* lies on a lower indifference curve than

Figure 43. Expected Net Benefits and Real Net Costs

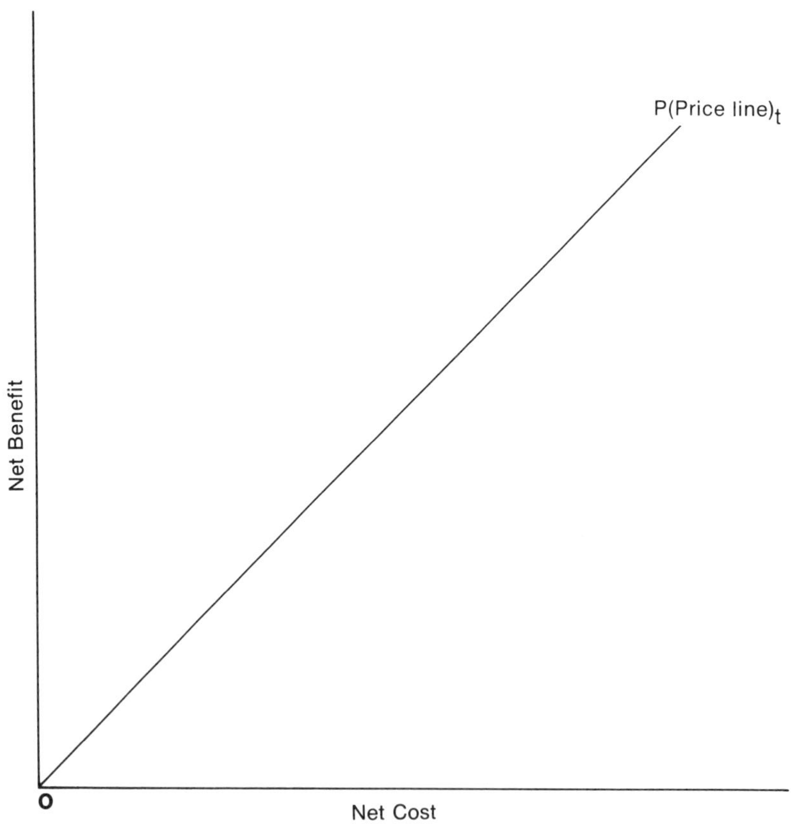

Figure 44. Real Net Costs and Individual's Indifference Map

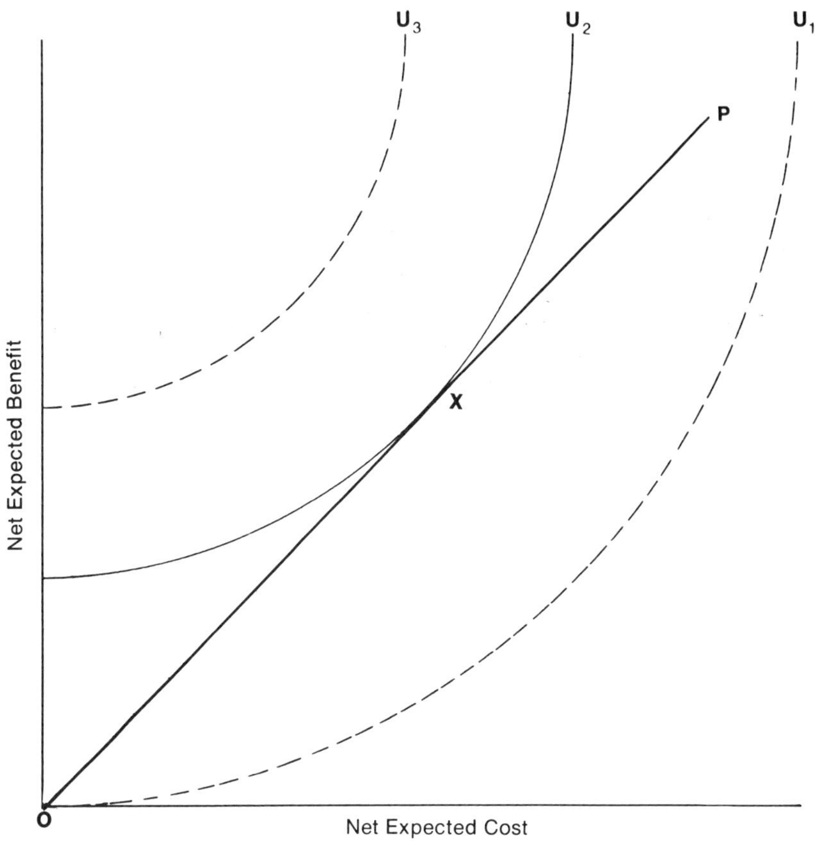

X. At the tangency point *X*, the slope of U_2 is equal to the slope of *OP*, i.e., the rate at which the individual is *willing* to trade-off net expected costs for benefits is the rate at which he *can* do so.

It is the elites who formulate and influence foreign and military policy. They actually have the power to choose trade-off points in a war between such expected costs as tens of thousands of people being killed and tens of billions of dollars being spent in exchange for such expected benefits as military victory, the credibility of political commitments, successful challenge to domination, and open markets and resources. Figure 44 can thus be considered to represent the consensus preference system of those who make war policy.

When we superimpose the objective price line *OP* onto the different consensus preference systems of elites and masses taken from figure

42, we see in figure 45 that the policy combining the optimum trade-off of net expected costs and benefits by the policy-making elites, point X, is actually *less* preferred by the masses than point Y, which is the point at which the objective price line OP is tangent to the highest possible indifference curve of the masses.

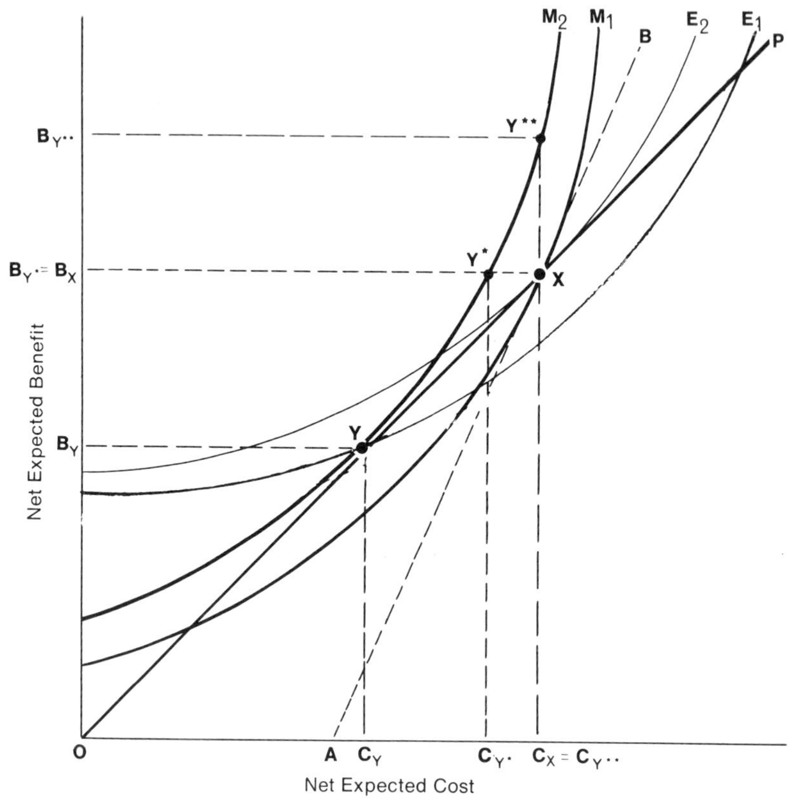

Figure 45. Real Net Costs and Different Preference Systems of Elites and Masses

Point X lies on a *higher* indifference curve for the elites (E_2) than does point Y, which lies on E_1. However, point X lies on a *lower* indifference curve for the masses (M_1) than does point Y, which lies on M_2. Since it is the *elites*, however, who choose the policy, they choose the trade-off point which they most prefer, i.e., point X, even though X is less satisfying to the masses than is point Y, given the difference in preference systems between elites and masses and the objective constraints of the objective price line OP.

The trade-off point the masses would prefer, point Y, has associated with it fewer net expected costs and benefits than does point X. However, we can find a point Y^* on the same mass indifference curve M_2 at which the net expected *benefit* for the mass is *equal* to that at the trade-off point X, i.e. $B_{Y*} = B_X$. The masses would be indifferent in choosing between trade-off points Y and Y^*. However, the net expected *costs* which the mass would be *willing* to pay at the trade-off point Y^* (i.e., C_{Y*}), for the net expected benefit of B_{Y*} (or B_X) is *less* than the net expected costs which they are *forced* to pay by the elites' choice of the trade-off point X (i.e., C_X). This difference in net expected costs $(C_X - C_{Y*})$ is the amount that the elites are *exploiting* the masses by the elites' choice of their most preferred trade-off point X.[6]

From this analysis we can see that given the assumption of different preference systems for elites and masses, the choice of a trade-off point or policy by the elites not only exploits the masses but causes them to be dissatisfied as well, since the masses are forced to accept a trade-off point lying on a lower indifference curve than they would prefer (i.e., a point on M_1 instead of M_2). We shall now analyze how exploitation and dissatisfaction are affected by changing objective costs and by changing preference systems.

First, let us consider what happens when the *objective* marginal costs per unit of benefit increase while the subjective preference systems of masses and elites remain the same as in our previous analysis. An example of this occurring in the Vietnam War is when both sides have escalated their commitments and costs over what they had previously been and both sides are stalemated as before the escalation. Under such circumstances neither side is closer to winning the war, yet the objective costs have increased. We can represent this situation of increased objective costs in figure 46. The objective price line OP represents the lower marginal costs per unit of benefit and the objective price line OP″ represents a higher marginal cost per unit of benefit.

In figure 46 we can see that as the *objective* marginal costs per unit of benefit increase from price line OP to price line OP'', the elites will choose the new trade-off point X'', since it is the point at which the new objective price line is tangent to the highest possible elite indifference curve, which in this case is now E_1. Thus, with the higher objective costs, the elite have had to make a choice less satisfying to them, i.e., they have had to move from point X on elite indifference curve E_2 to point X'' on the lower elite indifference curve E_1.

We will also note that the new price line OP'' intersects the mass utility curve M_1 at X''. Given the new constraints of greater objective

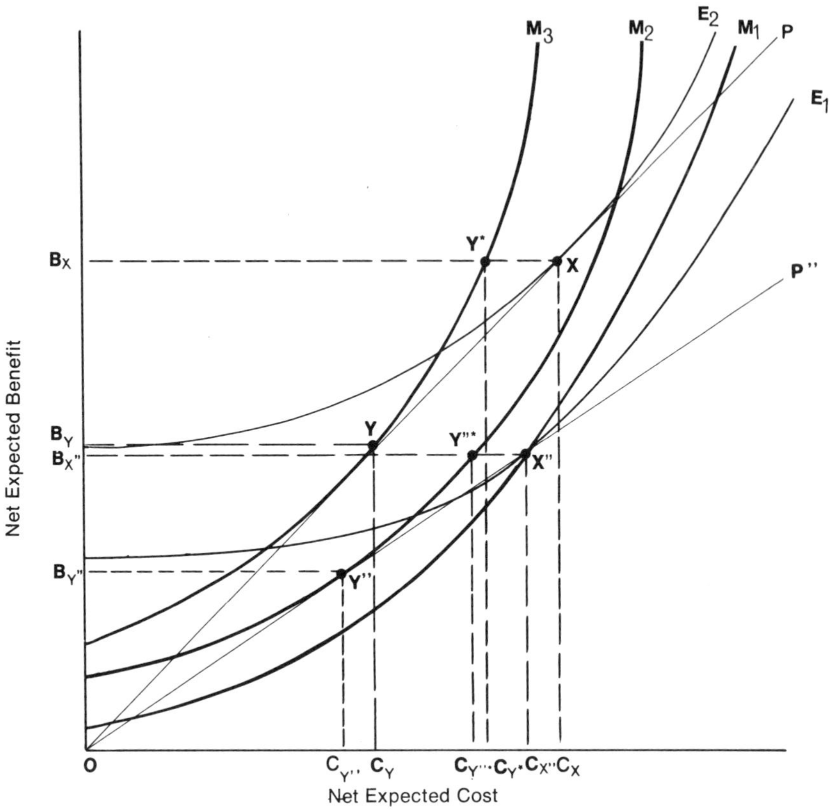

Figure 46. Increasing Real Costs and Consensus Preference Systems of Elites and Masses

costs, however, the masses would most prefer the trade-off associated with point Y'', where OP'' is tangent to the highest possible mass indifference curve M_2.

As in our previous analysis, we can find a trade-off point Y''^* on the mass indifference curve M_2 that represents a net expected benefit equal to that at X'' i.e., $B_{x''}$. However, the net expected costs that the masses would be willing to pay at Y''^* (i.e., $C_{Y''*}$) is again less than the net expected costs $C_{x''}$ that the masses must pay because of the elites' choice of the trade-off point X''.

Thus, the masses continue to be exploited as the objective costs of the war increase. Moreover, we have assumed that the shape of the indifference curves of the masses and elites differ in such a way that the masses would prefer to pay *fewer* net expected costs per unit of net expected benefits than the elites; in proportion to what the masses have to pay as a result of the elites' decision (i.e. exploitation of the masses), the difference between what they are willing to pay and what they actually have to pay increases. Thus, in figure 46, $\frac{(C_X'' - C_Y''^*)}{C_X''}$ is greater than $\frac{(C_X - C_Y^*)}{C_X}$. In effect, then, the more costly the objective net expected benefits become, the more the masses are exploited by elite choices of trade-off points.

We should also note that as the objective costs per unit of net expected benefits increase, and as the masses are more exploited, they become more dissatisfied with the policy choice of the elites; as the objective price line shifts in figure 46 from *OP* to *OP″*, the trade-off points selected by the elites lie on a lower mass indifference curve. (Point *X″* lies on a lower indifference curve than does point *X*.)

We will now consider what happens when dynamic changes in preference systems of elites and masses occur. Although they are determined in part by socialization, education, and persuasion, the preference systems of people do change as a result of their experience. In the Vietnam War, for example, U.S. political elites came to include in their evaluation of the net expected benefits of victory not only the value held early in the war of defeating a Communist attempt to gain control in South Vietnam but also the goal of maintaining American prestige after more than half a million American troops were committed and more than 40,000 American lives were lost in Vietnam. Such values as making good on American political commitments to governments challenged by the Communists and of not losing American "face" were added to the U.S. political elites' net expected benefits of victory in Vietnam.

As value was added to the net expected benefits of the elites, they became willing to permit their country and people to incur greater net expected costs for a given net expected benefit than they had previously. In figure 47 this effect is represented as a flattening-out of the elites' indifference curves. Thus, the slopes of the elites' changed indifference curves E'_1 and E'_2 are less steep than they were before (E_1 and E_2) when victory had relatively less value to them.

The preference system of the masses can also change with their experience. If they perceive themselves to be personally threatened by the enemy, they may become attracted to appeals to national loyalty and may change their preference system to be more like that of the elite, as happened with the American public in World War II. If this occurs, the slopes of the mass indifference curves would also become less steep.

However, in a stalemated war like the Vietnam War, the masses learn that additional objective costs they bear do not increase their net expected benefits; they learn of additional costs previously hidden by official secrecy; the opportunity costs of pursuing the war become more salient (i.e., people become more and more aware of the goods and services they must forgo because of the war effort); and the contagion effect of concern and dissatisfaction occurs (i.e., people communicate their dissatisfaction to each other, influence each other, and reinforce each others' dissatisfaction). In such a war the masses are will-

Figure 47. Changes in Elites' and Masses' Preference Systems Over Time

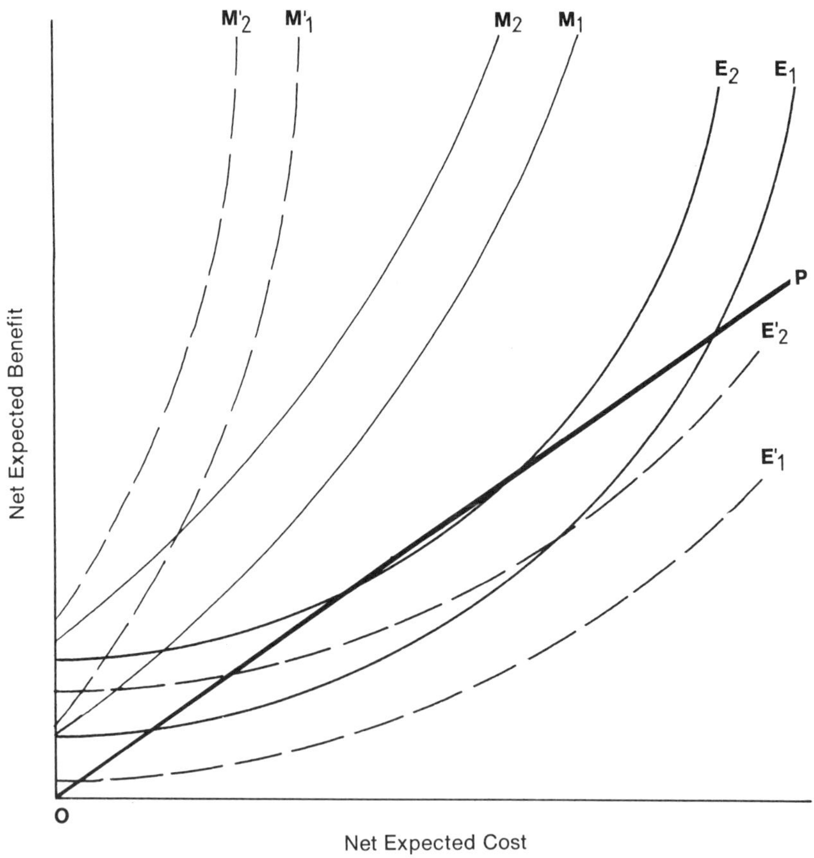

ing to pay fewer net expected costs for any given net expected benefit, and thus, as shown in figure 47, the slopes of the masses changed indifference curves M'_1 and M'_2 become steeper than they were before (M_1 and M_2).

We can see from our previous analysis that as the elites become willing to pay more, and the masses less, for a given net expected benefit, the slopes of the indifference curves of each group become increasingly different,[7] the trade-off point chosen by the elites with any objective price line will exploit the masses more; and the masses become even more dissatisfied with the policy trade-off point chosen by the elites.

The objective costs of waging war increase with the war efforts made. As we have seen in the empirical analysis of the Vietnam War, the war effort of each side increases with the resistance and war effort of the other side. Thus, in a war like that in Vietnam, in which there is a disparity between the preference systems of the policy-making elites and the masses, we can deduce that the greater the war efforts made and the greater the objective costs incurred, the greater mass dissatisfaction there will be with the war policy chosen by the elite.

This then is what underlies the political analyst's paradox and the elites' policy dilemma in the Vietnam War. As the elites increase their efforts to extend their control over others, and as these efforts are resisted and the costs of the efforts increase, the dissatisfaction of the masses in the elites' own polity—who provide the popular basis of the elites' own domestic political power—must bear the disproportionate costs of those efforts.

On the other hand, if the elites decrease their efforts to extend their control over others, the masses in the elites' own polity will be more satisfied, but the elites will be less likely to achieve their war policy goals. Thus, there is an objective inverse functional relationship between, on the one hand, the achievement of international political objectives by waging a war for which elite and mass preference systems are not the same, and, on the other hand, the elites' retention of domestic mass political satisfaction and support (see figure 40).

The basis of this paradox and policy dilemma is that the masses of people are in general less willing to pay the costs of achieving the international political objectives than are the elites, because the masses bear the disproportionate burden of those costs.

This analysis has demonstrated that the amount of exploitation of the masses by the elites and the dissatisfaction of the masses is dependent upon how divergent the preference systems of elites and masses are. An important implication of this point is that in a war, the masses on the side that has a relatively greater consensus of preferences between elites and masses will feel relatively less exploited by, and dissatisfied with, their elites' war policy. In the Vietnam War, whether because of indoctrination or self-interest, there has been evidence from many sources indicating a closer agreement on war policy and the necessity of sacrifice on the part of the North Vietnamese and Viet Cong masses and elites than on the part of the South Vietnamese or American masses and elites. In a test of wills between societies in a protracted war, that side with the least feeling of mass exploitation and dissatisfaction has the greater chance of prevailing.

What *empirical evidence* do we have that would support this general theoretical analysis in the case of the Vietnam War? One of the basic hypotheses deduced in this theoretical analysis is that as the objective costs of achieving a war goal increase, mass dissatisfaction with the policy the elites chose to pursue that goal will also grow. From 1965, with the initial escalation of massive American commitments to the Vietnam War, to 1971 the American people considered the Vietnam War to be the *most* important problem facing the United States (AIPO, 17 March 1971). In repeated surveys by the American Institute of Public Opinion, the American people were asked whether they agreed with this statement: "In view of the developments, it was a mistake for the U.S. to be involved in Vietnam." There is a linear trend upward in the affirmative response to this question that begins with 24 percent in August 1965 and continues to increase to 61 percent in May 1971. In more than twenty such surveys made over time, the increasing linear trend is highly correlated with various cumulated costs of the war in Vietnam, e.g., American casualties in the war (the correlation coefficient is .94),[8] money spent on the war, number of servicemen who have served in Vietnam, and so on.

Even during the Nixon administration, as the costs of the war continued, the American people were dissatisfied with the slow pace at which the administration seemed to be "winding down" American participation in the war. In two public opinion surveys taken by the American Institute of Public Opinion, the following percentages of the nation's adults thought that the United States should follow the four policies listed below; the questions were asked in December 1969 and February 1970.

	Dec. 1969	*Feb. 1970*
A. Withdraw all troops from Vietnam immediately	19%	21%
B. Withdraw all troops by end of 1970 (Withdraw all troops by end of 18 months)	22%	25%

	Dec. 1969	Feb. 1970
C. Withdraw troops but take as many years to do this as are needed to turn the war over to the South Vietnamese	40%	38%
D. Send more troops to Vietnam and step up the fighting	11%	7%
No opinion	8%	9%

(AIPO, 10 Jan. 1970; 14 Mar. 1970)

It is clear that the American public overwhelmingly favored withdrawing American troops from Vietnam: 81 percent of the people supported this viewpoint in December 1969; 84 percent in February 1970. Indeed, a large percentage of the people wanted faster troop withdrawals than was later carried out in the Nixon administration's Vietnamization policy.

This public sentiment was reiterated in the results of two later surveys. In September 1970, 55 percent of the American public stated their support for Congressional approval of the McGovern-Hatfield Senate proposal that would require the U.S. government to withdraw all U.S. troops by the end of 1971. Only 36 percent expressed opposition, and 9 percent had no opinion. In a subsequent poll taken in January 1971, 73 percent favored the above Senate proposal (AIPO, 30 January 1971).

Our analysis so far has shown that increased objective costs increase the dissatisfaction of the masses in the *policy* chosen by the elites. We may further hypothesize that those increased objective costs also increase the dissatisfaction of the mass public with the political elites who choose the policy. The empirical evidence also supports this hypothesis. During the 1965-67 period of escalation in the Vietnam War, the percentage of the American public that disapproved of President Johnson's handling both of the situation in Vietnam and of his job as president was highly correlated with the monthly number of American casualties in Vietnam (the correlation coefficient is .79 for both questions).

The expected continuation of costs implicit in the policy of Vietnamization contributed to some decline in political support for President Nixon and his policy. This long-term policy of gradual transfer of combat responsibility from U.S. to South Vietnamese ground forces in a continuing stalemated war drew a negative response from those Americans favoring a more immediate end to the war. The February 1971 invasion of Laos by South Vietnamese forces supported by American air power, for example, was seen as lengthening the Vietnam War (and continuing the costs) by more than twice as many Americans

(40%) than as who viewed it as shortening the war (19%) (AIPO, 27 February 1971).

This expectation of a lengthened war was followed by some decline in President Nixon's popular approval. In a Gallup Poll taken 19–21 February 1971 the percentage of people who approved of the way President Nixon was handling his job as president was 5 percent lower (51%) than it had been the previous month (56% on 9–10 January), before the Laos invasion began (AIPO, 3 March 1971). The same poll indicated that 69 percent of the people felt that the Nixon administration was not being truthful in telling the American people the facts about the Vietnam War (AIPO, 6 March 1971). It further indicated that 18 percent more Americans disapproved of Nixon's handling of the war in February 1971 than did so in August 1970.

From September 1969 to February 1971 the public's ratings of President Nixon became less positive both in terms of his overall popularity and the public's intensity of feeling. In that time his overall popularity, measured in terms of approval of the way in which he handled his job, dropped from 61 to 51 percent. The percentage of people saying they "strongly approved" of the president dropped from 23 to 14 percent, whereas those who strongly disapproved increased from 8 to 16 percent (AIPO, 3 March 1971). Finally, the percentage of Americans who agreed with the statement, "In view of the developments since we entered in Vietnam, do you think the U.S. made a mistake sending troops to Vietnam?", rose from 52 percent in March 1969 to 61 percent in May 1971 (AIPO, July 1971).[9]

The Nixon administration thus appeared to be caught in a similar political dilemma as faced by the Johnson administration. In continuing the costs of the Vietnam War, even with diminished U.S. ground involvement and fewer American casualties, the Nixon administration lost some political support from an increasingly dissatisfied American people.

In Vietnam, too, there is evidence that the masses of people became more dissatisfied with the war policies of the ruling elites as the objective costs of pursuing those policies increased. As the terrible costs of war in Vietnam rose, the elites lost mass support. In the pre-Tet period, for example, defections from the Viet Cong are significantly correlated with North Vietnamese and Viet Cong attrition ($r = .54$), and in the post-Tet period, defections from the Communists are highly correlated with South Vietnamese military ground operations ($r = .86$). Vietnamese peasants, including those who support the Viet Cong, have shown themselves to be committed primarily to their own safety and the protection of their loved ones. When caught in a South Vietnamese military operation where the Viet Cong cannot protect them, they defect to save their own lives.

In South Vietnam in the post-Tet period, as American troops withdrew and the war continued, there was less popular political support given the South Vietnamese government, as indicated by the measure of popular confidence given in chapter 2. (The correlation between the number of U.S. troops and popular confidence in South Vietnam is .90.) Without U.S. military support the war became more costly to the South Vietnamese, who had to assume greater combat and casualties and who were less well protected.

In summary, the general theoretical analysis presented in this chapter is that ruling elites and mass publics have different subjective values regarding the trade-offs between the net expected costs and benefits of waging war. The implications of this assumption explain the observed objective trade-off in the ability of political elites both to extend their power over others and to retain the political support of their own people. In Vietnam the mass of people who were most vulnerable to physical danger placed more value on their own safety and less value on the outcome of the military and political struggle between the Communists and anti-Communists than did the elites who chose the war policies.

In the United States, too, the mass public felt more than did the elite U.S. policy-makers that the costs of the Vietnam War outweighed the expected benefits of the stated objectives of the war. The U.S. public and the U.S. policy-makers had different preference systems regarding the trade-offs between the lives of American soldiers and tens of billions of additional tax dollars on the one hand and the expected benefits of keeping South Vietnam within the American sphere of influence and retaining the credibility of American political commitments on the other hand.

Mass dissatisfaction has grown in the United States as the American people have begun to experience and realize the growing *indirect* costs as well as the direct objective costs not only of the Vietnam War but of excessively high military expenditures in general. Manpower, resources, and skills have been diverted from activities that enhance production and general welfare in the United States into generally nonproductive military and war expenditures. The consequences—especially for members of the lower social strata—have included inadequate housing, medical care, education, mass transportation, and general social services, as well as unemployment, underemployment, and decaying and polluted environments. The resultant lack of opportunity, crowding, and sense of frustration—combined with a sense of powerlessness regarding either the war policy or the allocation of resources—have contributed to alienation and asocial behavior. Domestic violence has increased, and the use of hard drugs as an escape has grown to epidemic proportions. These have not only weakened the social fabric of the country by leading to a breakdown of family life and further asocialization of the young, but have led also to alarmingly rapid increases in crime rates against both persons and property, particularly in the cities where the lack of resources has been most severely felt. High crime rates have contributed to a growing fear and further alienation of people from each other.[10] Moreover, the response of political elites to this personal fear has been a call for "law and order." This sentiment, combined with the vast purchase of private arms, has produced the beginnings of a militarization of the domestic society. Thus, conducted in the cause of "national security" and strength, the Vietnam War and the excessive military spending that has accompanied it have instead contributed to a weakening of American society internally and to what truly can be called *national insecurity*.

The Vietnam War has also contributed directly to the weakening of the international economic position of the United States. Deficit financing and the resource and production requirements of the war initially placed an excessive demand on the U.S. economy. A steep rise in inflation and an extremely unfavorable balance of payments followed, partly because of the inability of American-manufactured goods with their inflated prices to compete with foreign products. Thus, the international economic position of the United States has weakened with regard to its industrial competitors in the world—particularly Japan and West Germany—as a direct consequence of the U.S. involvement in the Vietnam War. Moreover, the moral prestige of the United States has fallen throughout the world because of the devastating U.S. policy in Vietnam.

Thus, there is an appropriateness and rationality in the dissatisfaction of the mass public with both the policy-makers and the policy that have involved the United States in the Vietnam War, for that involvement has weakened the United States in political, economic, social, and moral ways, both domestically and internationally. This is the greatest paradox of the Vietnam War.

1. The term *elite* in this chapter refers to the political, military, and bureaucratic leaders who formulated and executed policy in Vietnam, and to those corporate and financial owners and executives whose interests were served by that policy. It does *not* refer simply to the above-average, e.g., to those in the U.S. population with incomes over $12,000 or who have a college education.

2. The functional curve is assumed to be convex to reflect the assumption that domestic political support falls faster the more that national energies and resources are allocated to the achievement of international objectives.

3. Indifference curves between *positively* valued goods are assumed to be convex to the origin. Because the net expected *costs* in figure 40 and in the other figures in this chapter can be considered *negatively* valued goods, we have shifted the origin of the horizontal axis from the righthand to the lefthand side of the figures.

4. Indifference curve analysis is explained in detail in Paul A. Samuelson, *Economics: An Introductory Analysis*, pp. 429-34; and in Lloyd G. Reynolds, *Economics: A General Introduction*, pp. 329-39.

5. This objective function is similar to the price line or consumption-possibility line in economics.

6. We can state this exploitation in terms of net expected benefits forgone by the masses, rather than additional costs they are forced to pay. On the same mass indifference curve M_2 on which Y lies, we can find another trade-off point Y^{**} at which the net expected costs, $C_Y{}^{**}$, are equal to those at the trade-off point X, i.e., C_X. The masses would be indifferent in choosing among the trade-off points Y, Y^*, and Y^{**}. However, the net expected *benefit* $B_Y{}^{**}$ that the masses would *want* in exchange for net expected costs as high as $C_Y{}^{**}$ (or C_X) is *greater* than the smaller net expected benefit B_X, which is the amount they get because of the elites' choice of the trade-off point X. The difference $(B_Y{}^{**} - B_X)$ is the amount of net expected benefit desired but forgone by the masses because of the elites' choice of X.

We can combine these two different ways of thinking about exploitation by noting that the ratio of additional net expected benefits forgone to the additional net expected costs borne by the masses at the trade-off point X, i.e. $[(B_Y{}^{**} - B_X)/(C_X - C_Y{}^{*})]$, is the slope of the mass indifference curve M_1 where it is intersected by the objective price line OP at point X. This slope is the same as that of the line AB tangent to M_1 at X. Comparing the slopes of AB and OP, we can see that the masses are forced by the elites' choice of the trade-off point X to exchange net expected costs for net expected benefits at a greater *rate* than they would prefer. The *ratio* of the slope of AB to the slope of OP is both the ratio of the marginal net expected benefits desired by the masses to those that can actually be expected to be forthcoming for a given marginal net expected cost and the ratio of the marginal net expected costs that must actually be borne by the masses to the marginal net expected costs that the masses would be willing to pay for a given marginal net expected benefit.

7. I.e., as the angle BXP in figure 45 widens.

8. Controlling for the linear trend over time, the partial correlation between U.S. troops killed in the previous month and agreement with this statement is .50.

9. The percentage of Americans who agreed with this statement had been as low as 24 percent in August 1965.

10. In a national survey in December 1972, the Gallup Poll found that in a randomly selected sample of the population 18 years of age and older, 21 percent had been victims of one or more crimes surveyed during the previous 12 months. Seven percent had had their homes broken into or an attempt made to do so; 2 percent had been mugged or assaulted; 8 percent had money or property stolen from their person or from some other member of their household; 8 percent had had their home, car, or other personal property vandalized; and 2 percent had had their car or the car owned by a member of their household stolen. The incidence of crime in the inner city is 33 percent—far higher than in the suburbs (19 percent) and smaller communities or rural areas (13 percent).

Moreover, the high incidence of crime has made people fearful: 49 percent of the national population are afraid to walk alone at night in their neighborhoods (an increase from 31 percent in 1968); 61 percent of women are afraid to go out alone in their neighborhoods at night; and 17 percent of the people do not even feel safe and secure in their own homes at night (George Gallup, "One in Three Is City Crime Victim," *Washington Post*, 14 January 1973).

10

United States Policy in Vietnam: Calculated or Miscalculated?

Successful action in international relations requires an accurate understanding of past and present events and an ability to predict realistically future events. In foreign policy-making, where experimentation can be especially costly and perilous, reasonably accurate prediction of the consequences of alternative policies is particularly desirable. This research has focused on the specification and testing of models that represent the interrelationships between policy choices and their military and political consequences in the Vietnam War. These models include those based on social and behavioral theories and observed empirical relationships as well as the "folk theories," or assumptions and hypotheses, of principal policy-makers. The former, interrelating key variables, permitted, through computer simulation, more reliable and systematic prediction than the latter. These models facilitated an analysis of military and political behavior and consequences in the war under actual and assumed alternative policies.

The importance of valid and reliable models can be appreciated when contrasted with negative examples. In chapter 4 it was demonstrated that many of the crucial assumptions upon which U.S. policy and actions in Vietnam were based were empirically invalid. Military escalation to achieve military victory and to retain political control in South Vietnam resulted instead in counterescalation by the Communists, and the war was stalemated at higher levels of violence and human and material costs. The escalated and stalemated war that took the lives of tens of thousands of American men and tens of billions of American dollars was repudiated by the American people. Policy-makers seemed to believe that by their unilateral decisions and actions they could control military and political outcomes and achieve their policy objectives; they appeared to ignore the interdependence of decisions made and actions taken by *both* sides in the war.

Had principal policy-makers consciously explicated their own assumptions and hypotheses about actions and outcomes in the war, tested them systematically against the available facts, and modified their objectives and actions accordingly, they would have enhanced their ability both to predict the consequences of their actions and perhaps to formulate and implement less costly policies.

As cited in chapter 4, there is ample documentary evidence from the "Pentagon Papers" that many important agencies and advisers in the U.S. government repeatedly analyzed Vietnam policy alternatives and their expected effects at the time that policy was being formulated, demonstrated to the principal U.S. policy-makers the invalidity of crucial policy assumptions, and argued against policy and actions based upon those invalid assumptions. Yet, policies were made and actions taken by the U.S. government that were based on these invalid assumptions and the predictions derived from them.

A major question then arises: Why were the invalid assumptions acted upon as though they were true when there were arguments, evidence, and analysis presented to the principal policy-makers at the time to demonstrate that they were in fact not true? Two different answers to this question will be discussed in this chapter, and they have vastly different implications about the nature of the making of foreign policy in the United States. The first characterizes U.S. policy in Vietnam as having been directed through miscalculation, inadvertence, ignorance, and misjudgment; i.e., the principal U.S. policy-makers honestly disagreed with the consequences accurately predicted by some of their advisers and decided instead to follow their own judgments. The second characterizes U.S. policy in Vietnam as having been calculated and carefully orchestrated by policy-makers who were cognizant of the probable consequences of their policies, but decided to risk those consequences rather than those they predicted would result from alternative policies.

The question of whether U.S. policy in Vietnam was a result of calculation or miscalculation hinges on the accuracy of the various forecasts made concerning the consequences that would follow from policy choices and actions and the extent to which those forecasts were considered by principal policy-makers. We have already seen that accurate forecasts depend upon valid models. We have also seen that many of the crucial assumptions and hypotheses held by key policy-makers were empirically false. We shall now look at the "miscalculation" and "calculation" theses in more detail in order to understand their components and implications.

U.S. VIETNAM POLICY AS MISCALCULATION

United States policy in Vietnam has been described as the result of miscalculation and inadvertence (Schlesinger, 1968, p. 47). This interpretation characterizes the U.S. leadership as having been ignorant of the potential consequences of American involvement in Vietnam.

From this point of view, U.S. involvement in Vietnam occurred as the result of a series of blunders within the entire governmental structure and in all American administrations from President Truman on.

Many explanations have been offered as to why U.S. policy in Vietnam was one of blunder and miscalculation. First of all, there was a significant lack of Vietnam or Indochina expertise among U.S. policy-makers (Thomson, 1968). This lack of area expertise permitted the acceptance, distortion, and misapplication of historical analogies, including the Munich "sellout," (i.e., the failure to challenge small aggressions that would "inevitably" result in more serious ones), the containment of the Soviet Union, and North Korean aggression.

Miscalculation occurred through the interplay of various objective and subjective factors. Optimistic predictions about the success of various U.S. policies and actions were based partially on information derived from field reports and intelligence sources that were biased to show the positive progress of U.S. efforts. Field reports were often biased because the evaluation and promotion of field personnel within their own military or civilian bureaucracies were to a large extent based on their job performance as measured by their own progress reports. They also knew that their superiors wanted to see "progress." Positive evaluations of this already-biased information led to reinforced optimism and self-deception. Thus, General Maxwell Taylor concluded: "The intelligence upon which we based our judgments or, for that matter, the intelligence supporting the government decisions . . . was very poor" (Public Broadcasting Service discussion with Martin Agronsky, 27 June 1971, quoted in Schlesinger, *New York Review of Books* 21 October 1971, p. 32).

The realities of the military and political situation in Vietnam were distant from the principal policy-makers in Washington. Information was no doubt selectively passed up the chain of command in the military and civilian bureaucracies. At each step the information was reassessed and reinterpreted according to a particular bias that combined personal and bureaucratic interests with the national interest, protecting and advancing personal and bureaucratic investments in particular policies and programs. The memoranda written and read at the highest levels of the U.S. government semantically interpreted the bullets, bombs, blood, terror, death, and destruction of the war in Vietnam as movements in a lofty and romantic symphony (Thomson, 1968). An example of this semantic blurring of reality is a paper drafted by Assistant Secretary of Defense McNaughton on 6 November 1964, entitled "Action for South Vietnam":

> OPTION C. Progressive squeeze-and-talk. Present policies plus an orchestration of communications with Hanoi and a crescendo of additional military moves against infiltration targets, first in Laos and then in the DRV, and then against other targets in North Vietnam. The scenario would be designed to give the U.S. the option at any point to proceed or not, to escalate or not, and to quicken the pace or not. The decision in these regards would be made from time to time in view of all relevant factors. (NYT, *PP*, p. 366)

The evaluation of current progress, the predictions of the anticipated effects of policies and actions, and the advice, warnings, and recommendations the principal policy-makers received were of mixed optimism and pessimism. Different advisers and agencies (e.g., the commanding generals in the field and the Central Intelligence Agency) often gave contradictory assessments. This raised the problem for the principal policy-makers, particularly the president, of deciding whose predictions and advice to believe. Given this ambiguity, the president was able to draw any conclusion that suited his purposes (Schlesinger, 1971).

Among the principal policy-makers, however, certain fundamental assumptions were rarely questioned. Those within the inner circle of policy-making usually chose to pose questions and alternatives in such a way as to remain within the general consensus. Questioning of fundamental assumptions usually led to exclusion from the inner circle of real influence on policy. Thus, the pressure to retain some influence led to a mutual reinforcement of mistaken fundamental assumptions. Policy-makers usually dealt with tactical rather than fundamental arguments (Gelb, 1971).

The self-reinforcing optimism characterizing President Johnson's circle of closest advisers derived not only from the ambiguity of mixed evaluations and advice but also from deeply held beliefs about the omnipotence of American power. Principal policy-makers felt that they were guaranteed success in solving their difficulties in Vietnam if they applied superior American military and technological power. A memorandum from Walt Rostow to Secretary of State Dean Rusk written in the fall of 1964 illustrates this faith in American power:

> I know well the anxieties and complications on our side of the line. But there may be a tendency to underestimate both the anxieties and complications on the other side and also to underestimate that limited but real margin of influence on the outcome that flows from the simple fact that we are the greatest power in the world—if we behave like it. (NYT, *PP*, p. 256)

The principal policy-makers met difficulties from many sources: fear of escalating the war to such an extent that Communist China or the

Soviet Union would directly intervene; frustration with the weakness of the South Vietnamese government and fear of its defeat by the Viet Cong in spite of U.S. commitments; fear of declining U.S. prestige should the South Vietnamese government be defeated, of future challenges to U.S. influence throughout the world, and of political defeat at home should the Communists win in Vietnam.

Fatigued, anxious, frustrated, not wishing to appear impotent, principal U.S. policy-makers repeatedly turned to the use of increasing levels of military force, rather than to political or diplomatic solutions (Thomson, 1968). In particularly frustrating times, actions were undertaken just for the sake of "doing something," or just to encourage the South Vietnamese, rather than because they were expected to be effective in defeating the Communists. According to the "Pentagon Papers": "But in the end, the decision to go ahead with the strikes [against North Vietnam] seems to have resulted as much from the lack of alternative proposals as from any compelling logic in their favor" (NYT, *PP*, p. 344). Men accustomed to gambling and winning in their respective climbs to positions of power led themselves to believe that policies based on a whole chain of optimistic assumptions about risky outcomes would somehow work out to their advantage (Gelb, 1971).

Optimistic expectations of policies led to their adoption; once adopted, the policies acquired a bureaucratic momentum of their own. People in the military and civilian bureaucracies tended to ask *what* they should do next, rather than *whether* they should be doing anything in Vietnam at all (Gelb, 1971). Means became ends in themselves, and concern about the magnitude of U.S. commitments to South Vietnam was answered by self-fulfilling prophecies of success, as the war was escalated to avoid rendering meaningless what had already been lost (Thomson, 1968). The marginal cost of each new commitment was perceived as being less costly than total disengagement.

The policies actually implemented were the results of numerous compromises among competing international and domestic political objectives of the president and among conflicting factions, interests, and bureaucracies. International and domestic political goals—assuaging the hawks and doves in American politics, avoiding Soviet or Chinese intervention, maintaining an anti-Communist South Vietnam, and avoiding defeat by the North Vietnamese and Viet Cong—led to the compromise of gradual escalation. But that compromise policy itself was flawed by its own internal contradictions. The North Vietnamese adapted to gradual escalation, rather than being broken by it. The South Vietnamese had the Americans to defend them, and so were less motivated to defend themselves.

According to the "miscalculation" thesis, then, U.S. policy in Vietnam was a series of miscalculations. Even though some within the government had accurately forecast the poor results of policies and actions, that knowledge was not adequately taken into account as U.S. policy in Vietnam was being made. As a result, according to this view, the United States became entrapped more and more deeply in the quagmire of the Vietnam War.

The "miscalculation" thesis explicates U.S. policy in Vietnam as the ultimate product of incorrect albeit conscientiously held assumptions and predictions made by principal policy-makers. The contradictory advice given by other governmental agencies and advisers was not followed because the principal policy-makers genuinely had greater faith in the reports that supported their initial convictions. These convictions led to military, economic, and political commitments that became self-sustaining. As the war progressed, U.S. leaders were faced with a choice between admitting failure (and accepting all the negative political consequences they believed would accrue from such an admission) or declaring a self-fulfilling prophecy of success (and undertaking the concomitant increase in military commitments that such an attitude required). The latter course was chosen, and each successive step seemed to lead inevitably to a network of human and material costs that had to be further justified to domestic and international critics.

If U.S. policy in Vietnam was indeed the result of a long series of miscalculations by each administration since Truman's, there is, at least theoretically, a remedy for the future. If principal policy-makers become misinformed or over-optimistic about the effectiveness of their means or the feasibility of their ends, a detailed government-wide prescription for the future is suggested: collect better information; have experts analyze it with better empirical methods; ensure more frank communication in governmental organizations, particularly between advocates of conflicting positions; reveal the limitations of military means to accomplish political ends; fully consider how the counteractions of opposing parties will affect conditions and events; enforce the pursuit of only clearly defined national goals on each bureaucracy; test policymakers own models against the facts; develop valid models that allow more accurate forecasting of the likely consequences of alternative policies under consideration; and demonstrate the truth of the situation to the national leaders. They should act accordingly, choosing more effective and less costly policies.

These remedies are based on the liberal tradition of political thought, dating from at least Locke and Hume, that assumes that good leaders, if they recognize the truth about good means and good ends, will choose them. Thus, from the point of view of the "miscalculation" thesis, the barriers to good policy are mainly technical; better organization, information collection, and analysis can act to overcome them.

A major implication of viewing U.S. policy in Vietnam as a result of miscalculation is that the "fault" of U.S. policy-makers over five administrations was simply that of insufficient wisdom and understanding. In this view such a fault is forgivable, particularly since expert technical knowledge had not yet been sufficiently developed to be applied to U.S. policies and actions in Vietnam (Ellsberg, 1971). The implications are very different, however, if U.S. policy in Vietnam is viewed as the result of calculation rather than miscalculation.

U.S. VIETNAM POLICY AS CALCULATED

The thesis that U.S. policy in Vietnam was calculated and informed by accurate predictions of the consequences that would follow from that policy has been articulated in two forms. The first emphasizes the domestic political motivations, and the second the interplay between international and domestic political motivations of principal U.S. policy-makers. The man who has most strongly asserted the thesis incorporating calculation of Vietnam policy for domestic political reasons is Daniel Ellsberg, who was also the person who released the "Pentagon Papers" to the press.

The major point of this "calculation" thesis is that principal U.S. policy-makers since the Truman administration were aware that their policies and actions were not and would not be adequate to achieve their main policy objective of defeating the Communists in South Vietnam, and that other actions would have to be undertaken subsequently (Ellsberg, 1971).

According to this thesis, the evidence that policy-makers were acutely aware of the faults of their own actions is that they were presented with remarkably accurate forecasts of the likely consequences of the policies they considered, and remarkably accurate evaluations of the limited effectiveness of the policies and actions they actually took. For the Johnson administration, many analyses were done by the intelligence agencies and other analytic groups, and even by members of President Johnson's close circle of top policy advisers (in particular Undersecretary of State George Ball). These studies showed, for example, the futility of bombing North Vietnam in order to defeat the Communists in the South, and warned against increasing the commitment of U.S. ground forces in South Vietnam because it would increase the U.S. stake in the outcome of the war. (See, for example, the assessment on the bombing done by the Institute for Defense Analysis, quoted in chapter 4.)

The second form of the "calculation" thesis, as developed most clearly by Leslie Gelb, who also had overall direction of the "Pentagon Papers" project in the Department of Defense, emphasizes the interplay between the international and domestic political objectives of the principal U.S. policy-makers (Gelb, 1972). If U.S. policy-makers had accurate forecasts and analyses that warned of the impending dangers of U.S. entanglement in Vietnam, of the ineffectiveness of U.S. efforts, and of the necessary future commitments of lives and resources that would entangle the U.S. still further, why did they proceed with increased U.S. commitments to Vietnam? The answer, according to this second form of the "calculation" thesis, is that principal U.S. policy-makers wanted to achieve simultaneously their international and domestic political objectives. These objectives were to maintain an anti-Communist South Vietnam and to retain political power in the United States. The dilemma of trying to achieve both at the same time (as analyzed in chapter 9) led to the policy of gradual escalation, a policy that, according to this view, was the result of planning rather than inadvertance.

Over the years Southeast Asia in general and Vietnam in particular had come to be defined as being of vital strategic importance to the United States. A "Statement of Policy" made by the National Security Council in early 1952 noted the various economic, political, military, and psychological stakes the U.S. had in Southeast Asia. Excerpts from this policy statement include the following:

> 2. Communist domination, by whatever means, of all Southeast Asia would seriously endanger in the short term, and critically endanger in the long term, United States security interest.
>
> a. The loss of any of the countries of Southeast Asia to communist aggression would have critical psychological, political and economic consequences. In the absence of effective and timely counteraction, the loss of any single country would probably lead to relatively swift submission to or an alignment with communism by the remaining countries of this group. Furthermore, an alignment with communism of the rest of Southeast Asia and India, and in the longer term, of the Middle East (with the probable exceptions of at least Pakistan and Turkey) would in all probability progressively follow: such widespread alignment would endanger the stability and security of Europe.
>
> b. Communist control of all of Southeast Asia would render the U.S. position in the Pacific offshore island chain precarious and would seriously jeopardize fundamental U.S. security interests in the Far East.

> c. Southeast Asia, especially Malaya and Indonesia, is the principal world source of natural rubber and tin, and a producer of petroleum and other strategically important commodities. The rice exports of Burma and Thailand are critically important to Malaya, Ceylon and Hong Kong and are of considerable significance to Japan and India, all important areas of free Asia.
>
> d. The loss of Southeast Asia, especially of Malaya and Indonesia, could result in such economic and political pressures in Japan as to make it extremely difficult to prevent Japan's eventual accommodation to communism. (NYT, *PP*, pp. 27-28)

Given these general considerations, the stated U.S. objective for Southeast Asia according to the "Statement of Policy" was: "To prevent the countries of Southeast Asia from passing into the communist orbit, and to assist them to develop will and capability to resist communism from within and without and to contribute to the strengthening of the free world" (NYT, *PP*, p. 27).

This statement of policy clearly demonstrates the official view of the continuing international interests and objectives of the United States in Southeast Asia, and therefore in Indochina and Vietnam: the economic advantage of the natural resources and food produced in the area; the military advantage of allies and bases on the periphery of Communist China; the political advantage of keeping Southeast Asia from Communist domination so as to avoid political accommodation with the Communists by the remaining Asian countries (particularly Japan and India); and finally, the fear that if Southeast Asia "went Communist," not only would the rest of the countries in Asia topple like dominoes but so would those in the Middle East and Europe.

Thus, the prevention of a Communist take-over in South Vietnam was a major motivation for the escalation of U.S. commitments in South Vietnam, not only for the material resources to be gained there, but also for the real psychological advantage to be gained against the Communists in the cold war. If the U.S. were successful in defeating the Communist challenge in South Vietnam, the credibility of U.S. commitments would be enhanced around the world, and the Communists would be less likely to mount subversive or aggressive challenges to the United States elsewhere in the world. Thus, issues of international prestige and power and the deterrence of future conflict motivated U.S. policy-makers in Vietnam.

Former President Johnson stated this motivation in his memoirs:

> . . . Our allies . . . throughout the world would conclude that our word was worth little or nothing. . . . [Moscow and Peking] could

> not resist the opportunity to expand their control into the vacuum of power. . . . With Moscow and Peking . . . moving forward, we would return to a world role to prevent their full takeover of Europe, Asia, and the Middle East—after they had committed themselves. (Quoted in Gelb, 1972)

The commitment of the U.S. political, military, and economic elites to prevent the spread of communism in Asia had become in official rhetoric over the years an ideology of anticommunism that went back at least as far as the Russian Revolution; this ideology made its greatest domestic political impression in the wake of the Communist assumption of power in mainland China in 1949. The political reaction in the United States to this event was so severe—with right-wing McCarthyites accusing the Truman administration of treason, with thousands of government officials losing their jobs, and with most of the rest intimidated—that, according to the "calculation" thesis, no U.S. president after Truman dared allow another country to be "lost to Communism" while he was in office. Each president believed that he could expect his own and his party's electoral defeat at the hands of an outraged public if that should occur. Indeed, no president wished to show any evidence of being "soft on Communism" lest that evidence be used against him politically (Ellsberg, 1971).

Thus, according to the "calculation" thesis, each U.S. president felt he could not afford politically to lose South Vietnam to the Communists, especially after initial commitments to South Vietnam were made that publicly gave America's word that it would help defeat Communist subversion and aggression. The presidents feared a loss of political power in the United States and a loss of international power for the United States relative to the Communists.

President Johnson wrote in his memoirs:

> I know our people well enough to realize that if we walked away from Vietnam and let Southeast Asia fall, there would follow a divisive and destructive debate in our country. . . . A divisive debate about "who lost Vietnam" would be, in my judgment, even more destructive to our national life than the argument over China had been. . . . (Quoted in Gelb, 1972, p. 461)

There were, on the other hand, particularly during the Johnson administration, countervailing political pressures in favor of decreasing U.S. involvement in Vietnam. These pressures came from left-wing doves who viewed U.S. policy in Vietnam as a moral outrage. Ironically, it was Secretary McNamara who voiced these concerns late in the escalation of the war (19 May 1967):

> The picture of the world's greatest superpower killing or seriously injuring 1000 noncombatants a week, while trying to pound a tiny backward nation into submission on an issue whose merits are hotly disputed, is not a pretty one. It could conceivably produce a costly distortion in the American national consciousness and in the world image of the United States—especially if the damage to North Vietnam is complete enough to be "successful." (*New York Times*, 4 July 1971, p. E1)

Another pressure that mitigated against further U.S. commitments in Vietnam was the public's opposition to an unending land war in Asia. Further, the fear that the Soviet Union and Communist China could be provoked into direct intervention in the Vietnam War led U.S. policy-makers to limit their attacks on North Vietnam and to refrain from attacking Soviet or Chinese military supplies en route to North Vietnam.

According to the "calculation" thesis, then, U.S. policy-makers felt they could not "lose" South Vietnam to the Communists; yet they also knew that politically feasible policies and actions would not allow them to win. They therefore decided to take the minimum actions necessary to maintain the status quo until after the next U.S. presidential election (Ellsberg, 1971). That necessary minimum, given the international and domestic military and political considerations, was the policy of gradual escalation of U.S. military commitments and activities in Vietnam (Gelb, 1971).

Thus, making "incremental" decisions over a long period of time, U.S. policy-makers attempted to do just enough to balance domestic, bureaucratic, and international pressures. Each decision became a small experiment to balance those pressures; as new imbalances developed, further decisions and actions were made and taken. This behavior is characteristic of many decisions on U.S. troop levels and bombing made during the escalatory phase of the war under President Johnson and during the deescalatory and Vietnamization phase under President Nixon. This kind of decision-making suggests that policy-makers were acting like those described by stress theory (see chapter 1), i.e., responding to pressures and tensions when events and conditions upset their equilibria.

Insofar as the pressures policy-makers perceived were related to their domestic and international goals, their decisions and actions did exhibit a type of rationality—that of minimizing pressures. However, policy-makers learned to cope successfully with only some of their pressures; the Johnson administration failed to prevent public disaffection with its Vietnam policy even though that policy did prevent the Communists from taking over South Vietnam during that administration.

The "calculation" thesis provides one possible explanation of why the Johnson administration lost public support for its Vietnam policy: the "credibility gap." According to this explanation, U.S. policy-makers, in order to retain their domestic political support, deliberately misled the public about the probable success of the various holding actions it was implementing to achieve U.S. objectives in Vietnam (Ellsberg, 1971). For example, President Johnson said in his public speech at Johns Hopkins University on 7 April 1965: "In recent months attacks on South Vietnam were stepped up. Thus, it became necessary for us to increase our response and to make attacks by air. . . . We do this in order to slow down aggression." He implied that the bombing would at least be effective in slowing down the Communist infiltration and attacks. However, his own chief assistant for national security, McGeorge Bundy, wrote about sustained bombing in a memorandum to President Johnson on 7 February 1965:

> We cannot assert that a policy of sustained reprisal will succeed in changing the course of the contest in Vietnam. It may fail, and we cannot estimate the odds of success with any accuracy—they may be somewhere between 25% and 75%. What we can say is that even if it fails, the policy will be worth it. At a minimum it will damp down the charge that we did not do all that we could have done, and this charge will be important in many countries, including our own. Beyond that, a reprisal policy—to the extent that it demonstrates U.S. willingness to employ this new norm in counter-insurgency—will set a higher price for the future upon all adventures of guerrilla warfare, and it should therefore somewhat increase our ability to deter such adventures. We must recognize, however, that that ability will be gravely weakened if there is failure for any reason in Vietnam. (NYT, *PP*, p. 426)

This private Bundy memorandum shows far less optimism about the effectiveness of bombing in slowing down the North Vietnamese than did President Johnson's public statement. The optimistic public statements of the principal policy-makers were soon belied by events that became obvious to the public. The public gradually came to doubt the veracity of the statements made by policy-makers; this loss of faith became known as the "credibility gap." According to the "calculation" thesis, the policy-makers knew ahead of time that their actions would be ineffective in defeating the Communists in Vietnam; they were intended instead to cope with and to balance domestic and international political pressures. The Bundy memorandum, for example, does indicate that the sustained bombing of the North was calculated to cope with domestic political pressures from the military and civilian hawks who called upon the administration to do more in Vietnam, and with international political pressures concerning the need to demonstrate U.S. determination not to let Communist insurgencies go unchecked.

The "calculation" thesis views the principal policy-makers' decisions to escalate U.S. commitments and actions in Vietnam as leading to ill-founded optimism (Ellsberg, 1971). The "miscalculation" thesis, on the other hand, maintains that initial optimistic expectations for success led to the adoption of the actions taken (Schlesinger, 1971). The policy-makers themselves may well have become optimistic through self-deception based on the psychological principal of cognitive consistency. Lower-ranking members of the military and civilian bureaucracies could have become optimistic because they were uninformed about the variety of domestic and international pressures and interests the principal policy-makers were trying to balance; they were subject also to the process of cognitive consistency when their own jobs, career functions, and interests were concerned. The public was persuaded to be optimistic, until events belied official optimism.

If the "calculation" thesis is correct, it would be naïve to believe that policy-makers would have acknowledged their error and stopped the war if only they had been informed of the inadequacy of their policies. Rather, they would have used whatever means they had to achieve their goals, because the stakes of international and domestic power were so high. This is true for policy-makers on both sides of the war. United States leaders would only most reluctantly give up their goals of retaining the U.S. sphere of influence over Southeast Asia and its resources, of strengthening the credibility of U.S. commitments elsewhere, or of keeping political power in the United States. It is equally unlikely that North Vietnamese and Viet Cong leaders would give up their goal of political power in all of Vietnam.

Thus, if the "calculation" thesis is correct, the policy that led to such bloody consequences in Vietnam could not have been remedied by better information and analysis. The only information and analysis that would have been used by the policy-makers is that which indicated how they might achieve their interests more efficiently and effectively.

UNITED STATES POLICY IN VIETNAM AS BOTH CALCULATED AND MISCALCULATED

In reviewing the assertions of both the "calculation" and "miscalculation" theses of U.S. policy in Vietnam, one can extract and synthesize those aspects that appear to be commonly valid in both. Only theoretical analysis is possible because, at this writing (early 1973), the complete empirical truth about U.S. policy-making in Vietnam cannot be known. The presidential papers from the Johnson and Nixon administrations, in particular, are still not publicly available.

The "miscalculation" thesis suggests many plausible reasons why U.S. policy-makers chose to escalate their use of force in Vietnam: misinformation; a poor understanding of the interactive dynamics of the war; bad models and analysis; bureaucracies seeking their own interests; and anxieties, frustrations, and over-optimism. The "miscalculation" thesis asserts the proposition that U.S. policy-makers escalated military commitments in the war because less force was found ineffective and because they did not realize that marginal increments of force would also be ineffective.

This thesis does not, however, explain the motive forces behind the escalating use of force; it offers no insight into the original objectives for which force was initially employed. The "calculation" thesis provides an explanation of those objectives: to prevent the fall of South Vietnam to the Communists and the consequences presumed to be entailed in that fall—a decline in the international credibility and influence of the United States, the loss of international power relative to the Communists, and the loss of political power in the United States.

The incremental decision-making of U.S. policy-makers characterized by the "miscalculation" thesis is a kind of calculation over time, even though it was not a comprehensive and simultaneous calculation of costs, benefits, and probabilities of all possible alternatives. According to the "calculation" thesis, the policy-makers did have a goal for their incremental force commitments, i.e., to balance various international and domestic political pressures.

In chapter 4, we saw that the principal U.S. policy-makers were wrong in several of their assumptions: that U.S. bombing of North Vietnam and commitment of combat troops in South Vietnam would defeat the Communists, strengthen popular confidence in the South Vietnamese government, and win the support of the American public. But they apparently thought they could begin to move in the direction of achieving these goals and reduce, at least temporarily, the international and domestic pressures they sought to balance.

The "calculation" and "miscalculation" theses can be further synthesized. In defining the focus of U.S. policy-makers' goals as maintaining both their political power in the United States and U.S. influence in the world, the "calculation" thesis overlooks the fact that the policy-makers did miscalculate the effects of U.S. military commitments in Vietnam on the achievement of these goals. In general, U.S. military commitments in Vietnam had the opposite of the desired effect. Because of the war, for example, President Johnson lost the public support on which his political power was based. The military stalemate in Vietnam had a divisive political effect in the United States, producing great public resistance to any similar interventions by the United States in the future. The war had a very great inflationary effect on the U.S. economy and weakened its world trade and monetary positions. American influence and the credibility of U.S. commitments throughout the world declined. And these effects of the Vietnam War have probably encouraged rather than deterred future challenges to U.S. hegemony in the world. After Vietnam, the United States seems less omnipotent.

It is therefore the conclusion of this analysis that the making of U.S. Vietnam policy was in part calculated and in part miscalculated. The "calculation" thesis is correct in identifying some of the major domestic and international political motivations of the principal U.S. policy-makers. Thus, actions were taken with the hope of simultaneously satisfying different domestic and international political objectives despite forecasts warning that these actions might not be adequate to defeat the Communists in Vietnam. The "miscalculation" thesis is correct in its analysis of the policy-makers' failure to choose effective means to achieve those different objectives, particularly that of defeating the Communists in Vietnam.

11

Afterword: The 1973 Cease-Fire Agreement

The cease-fire in Vietnam and the withdrawal of U.S. troops from that country is a long-hoped-for achievement. However fragile and incomplete, the cease-fire was made possible only because of a constellation of international and domestic U.S. political and economic conditions. Until the diplomatic record becomes fully available, we can only trace the outlines of what brought about the cease-fire, what its terms are and what they imply, the degree of compliance with those terms, what the consequences of the cease-fire are likely to be, and what the future possibilities for real peace in Vietnam might be.

INTERNATIONAL FACTORS CONTRIBUTING TO THE CEASE-FIRE

Among the factors that contributed to the cease-fire were the enormous accumulated political and economic costs of the war to the United States. Political division in this country over the issue of the Vietnam War and U.S. policy in Vietnam was as great as any since the Civil War and needed to be healed. The domestic U.S. economy and international economic position of the United States had been weakened by the war and needed to be strengthened.

Internationally, the bipolar system of a Communist bloc versus an anti-Communist bloc had changed. The Sino-Soviet split deepened into mutual hostility between these two Communist giants. President Nixon and his administration began a significant rapprochement with the People's Republic of China, and moved away from cold war confrontation with the Soviet Union by negotiating important agreements in the control of strategic weapons and on economic issues. The *Östpolitik* of the West Germans moved Western European-Soviet détente ahead. Meanwhile, conflicting economic interests strained relations between the United States and the Japanese and the United States and the Western Europeans.

Thus, the global system had changed from the post-World War II confrontation of the two mutually hostile blocs of Communists and anti-Communists to a multipolar system of crosscutting interests among the major powers.

The leaders of the United States, the Soviet Union, and the People's Republic of China now recognize that their larger self-interests and mutual interests are far more important than the distribution of power among the Vietnamese, or among the Indo-Chinese in general. United States leaders wanted to cut the domestic and international political and economic costs of direct U.S. military involvement in Vietnam. Chinese leaders wanted to be on better terms with the United States as problems with the Soviet Union grew more serious. Soviet leaders wanted more cooperation with the United States, both because of problems with China—e.g., Chinese claims on Soviet territory in Asia—and because the Soviet Union wants American grain and technology to feed itself and to develop its own economy.

Thus, the leaders of the United States, the Soviet Union, and the People's Republic of China all had good self-interested reasons to influence the contending Vietnamese parties to agree to a cease-fire so that the United States could get its troops out of Vietnam and its prisoners of war returned, and the Vietnamese could start working out their own accommodation with each other.

TERMS OF THE CEASE-FIRE IN VIETNAM

The "Agreement on Ending the War and Restoring Peace in Vietnam"[1] was initialed in Paris on 23 January 1973 by the principals who worked out the Agreement, Dr. Henry Kissinger on behalf of the United States and Special Adviser Le Duc Tho on behalf of the Democratic Republic of Vietnam. The Agreement was signed in Paris on 27 January 1973 by Secretary of State William P. Rogers for the United States, Minister for Foreign Affairs Nguyen Duy Trinh for the government of the Democratic Republic of Vietnam, Minister for Foreign Affairs Tran Van Lam for the government of the Republic of Vietnam, and Minister for Foreign Affairs Nguyen Thi Binh for the Provisional Revolutionary Government of the Republic of South Vietnam. The agreement was acknowledged and supported by the participants in the International Conference on Vietnam on 2 March 1973 by the above four parties plus the foreign ministers of France, Hungary, Indonesia, Poland, the United Kingdom, the Soviet Union, Canada, and the People's Republic of China. The secretary general of the United Nations also attended the conference.

The Agreement includes four protocols specifying the means by which the Agreement should be implemented. These focus on the return of prisoners of war, the International Commission of Control and Supervision (the ICCS), the Joint Military Commissions, and the deactivation and removal of mines in North Vietnam.

The provisions of the Agreement are contained in nine chapters.

The first chapter affirms the Vietnamese national rights of independence, sovereignty, unity, and territorial integrity, as well as the 1954 Geneva Agreements on Vietnam, which established two zones divided by a military demarcation line.

The second chapter calls for a cease-fire in place in South Vietnam and the withdrawal of American and all other foreign combat forces from the country, a prohibition against introduction of additional forces, and a prohibition against the introduction of new military equipment except as replacement on a one-to-one basis of existing military equipment that might be used up.

The third chapter specifies the internationally supervised release of all military prisoners and foreign civilians, and civilian prisoners within South Vietnam.

Chapter four is concerned with the self-determination rights of the South Vietnamese people. It calls for free elections to be decided by the two South Vietnamese parties, organized by a National Council for National Reconciliation and Concord. It also calls for a reduction of the armed forces of both South Vietnamese parties.

The fifth chapter of the Agreement repeats the existence of the provisional demarcation line along the Seventeenth Parallel, as stated in the 1954 Geneva accords, restricts military movement through the Demilitarized Zone, and leaves the reunification of the country up to future negotiation between the leaders of North and South Vietnam.

The sixth chapter specifies the international organizations that are to recognize or supervise the cease-fire. These include the Four-Party Joint Military Commission and the Two-Party Joint Military Commission. These have the task of ensuring joint action by the parties to the conflict to implement the provisions of the cease-fire. The Agreement established the International Commission of Control and Supervision (consisting of Canada, Indonesia, Hungary, and Poland), including 1,160 members to supervise the implementation of the Agreement's provisions. The International Conference, consisting of the participants in the war, the participants in the ICCS, the remaining permanent members of the Security Council of the United Nations, and the secretary general of the United Nations, is also established to contribute to and guarantee peace in Indochina.

Chapter seven is concerned with Cambodia and Laos. It affirms the national rights of these two countries as specified in the 1954 Geneva Agreement on Cambodia and the 1962 Geneva Agreements on Laos. It prohibits the use of Laos and Cambodia for military and any other operations against any of the signatories of the Paris Agreement or against any other country. It also requires that foreign troops be withdrawn from the two countries, including North Vietnamese troops. It also notes that the internal affairs of Cambodia and Laos shall be settled by the people of these two countries without foreign interference.

The eighth chapter announces the intent of the governments of the United States and the Democratic Republic of Vietnam to normalize their relations with each other, and for the United States to aid in the postwar reconstruction of North Vietnam as well as reconstruction throughout Indochina.

The ninth chapter puts the Agreement into legal force with the signatures of the parties participating in the Paris Conference on Vietnam.

DISCUSSION OF THE CEASE-FIRE AGREEMENT

The provisions of the cease-fire agreement have brought about the withdrawal of U.S. combat forces from Vietnam, a reduction in the fighting, the return of prisoners of war, and have prevented the imposition of a Communist-dominated government in South Vietnam. These significant results have achieved some of the most important objectives of the Nixon administration's Vietnam policy, and were the prerequisites for an "honorable" settlement from the point of view of the United States government.

The provisions of the cease-fire, however, still leave unresolved some of the most central issues of the entire Vietnam conflict. These include the questions of whether Vietnam is one or two countries and the corollary question of whether North Vietnamese forces have a right to intervene in the South; whether the government of the Republic of Vietnam is the sole legitimate sovereign power in all of South Vietnam; and the related question of whether the Provisional Revolutionary Government (the Viet Cong) has a legitimate political role in South Vietnam.

Article 15 of chapter five of the Agreement states: "Pending Reunification: (a) The military demarcation line between the two zones at the 17th parallel is only provisional and not a political or territorial boundary, as provided for in paragraph 6 of the Final Declaration of the 1954 Geneva Conference." The same article states: "The reunification of Vietnam shall be carried out step by step through peaceful means on the basis of discussions and agreements between North and South Vietnam, without coercion or annexation by either party, and without foreign interference. The time for reunification will be agreed upon by North and South Vietnam."

Thus, the agreement recognizes the existence of South as well as North Vietnam, but also the fact that their separateness is provisional and depends on negotiations and agreement on reunification among the North and South Vietnamese sometime in the future. Furthermore, article 15 of chapter five clearly denies either North or South Vietnam the right to use military force against the other to achieve reunification. Thus, the Agreement leaves Vietnam with a dual status: it is recognized as being one country in principle, but there are in fact two zones now and until such time as the North and South Vietnamese agree to reunite.

The militarily, and thus politically, significant question of the 145,000 North Vietnamese troops estimated to be in South Vietnam at the time of the cease-fire is also left to the Vietnamese to settle among themselves. Article 13 of chapter four states: "The question of Vietnamese armed forces in Sourth Vietnam shall be settled by the two South Vietnamese parties in a spirit of national reconciliation and concord, equality and mutual respect, without foreign interference, in accordance with the postwar situation." The presence of the North Vietnamese troops in South Vietnam obviously adds to the military power of the Communists in South Vietnam, and therefore to their viability as a political power.

Throughout the Agreement, "the two South Vietnamese parties" are referred to in both political and military contexts. Although neither is designated until the signature pages of the Agreement, the Agreement clearly recognizes the two contending South Vietnamese political and military forces. Indeed, chapter four of the Agreement seems to legitimate both parties by referring to their future behavior. Article 10 states: "The two South Vietnamese parties undertake to respect the cease-fire and maintain peace in South Vietnam, settle all matters of contention through negotiations, and avoid all armed conflict." Article 12 states: "Immediately after the cease-fire, the two South Vietnamese parties shall hold consultations in a spirit of national reconciliation and concord, mutual respect, and mutual non-elimination to set up a National Council of National Reconciliation and Concord of three equal segments." It further states: "The National Council of National Reconciliation and Concord shall have the task of promoting the two South Vietnamese parties' implementation of this Agreement, achievement of national reconciliation and concord and ensurance of democratic liberties." The Provisional Revolutionary Government is thus given a legitimate political role in the post-cease-fire period in South Vietnam. That role is central to the "South Vietnamese people's right to self-determination," the right explicitly recognized in article 9 of chapter four of the Agreement. Thus, a central theme of the Agreement is that the political resolution of the Vietnamese conflict is to be left to the Vietnamese to work out among themselves.

Notwithstanding the language of the Agreement, in the months immediately following the cease-fire the government of the Republic of Vietnam has behaved as though it were the only legitimate political authority in South Vietnam, and has sought to deny the legitimacy of the representatives of the Provisional Revolutionary Government, e.g., in isolating the PRG representatives in the Four-Party Joint Military Commission from other people in Saigon. Moreover, in his very announcement of the cease-fire agreement, President Nixon declared: "The United States will continue to recognize the Government of the Republic of Vietnam as the sole legitimate government of South Vietnam."[2] Thus, the central question of whether the Viet Cong has a legitimate political role and power in South Vietnam—one of the key issues contributing to the entire Vietnam War—in fact remained an unresolved issue after the signing of the Agreement.

DEGREE OF COMPLIANCE WITH TERMS OF THE CEASE-FIRE AND STATUS OF THE VIETNAM CONFLICT

Immediately after the initialing of the cease-fire agreement on 23 January 1973, but before the Agreement was formally signed and given legal status on 27 January 1973, each side in South Vietnam sought to bolster its military and political control over the South Vietnamese people, and to avoid losing whatever control it had. Each side sought to raise its flag and assert its control, however nominal, over as many people, hamlets, villages, towns, and cities as possible. Military activity increased before and during this "land grab" period.

Prior to the cease-fire, South Vietnamese President Thieu declared a state of martial law, and authorized his police and armed forces commanders to shoot people who incited riots, "applauded the Communists," or used or distributed currency issued by the Communists. The martial law also authorized commanders to arrest summarily anyone who distributed Communist propaganda, flew a Communist flag, interfered with government officials attempting to maintain order, urged people to move to Communist-controlled areas, or engaged in neutralist or pro-Communist political activities.[3] The Viet Cong similarly used coercion to bolster their political control in South Vietnam immediately before and after the Agreement.

Indeed, the cease-fire agreement did not achieve a real cease-fire. Fighting within Vietnam continued, although at a lower level. Generally, fewer and smaller military units fought for shorter periods of time. However, in the first three months following the signing of the Agreement, the respective statements by the two delegations to the Two-Party Joint Military Commission cited some 12,000 violations of the cease-fire, with the resultant deaths of some 25,000 soldiers and civilians.[4] These events are clear evidence that the Agreement did not achieve its objective of "national reconciliation and concord," at least in the short run.

Both sides expected and prepared for continued fighting after the Agreement. The United States gave the South Vietnamese government billions of dollars worth of military equipment and bases either immediately before the cease-fire or during the sixty-day period following the signing, when U.S. military forces withdrew from Vietnam. The South Vietnamese government was left so much equipment by the United States that it had to hire thousands of civilian technicians, including American civilians, to maintain it.

On their side, the North Vietnamese reequipped and resupplied their troops in the South with considerable military power. Thus, following the Agreement, both sides prepared themselves militarily for renewed hostilities. In many cases, these very preparations precipitated preemptive violence that violated the cease-fire.

The significant achievements of the cease-fire agreement were the withdrawal of U.S. and allied foreign military forces from Vietnam, the halt in the bombing of North Vietnam, and the return of the prisoners of war. Moreover, the South Vietnamese government was not removed by force of arms; indeed, it has been given the military means to defend itself while it engages in the continuing political struggle with the Communists.

The Agreement did not formally settle the conflicts in Laos and Cambodia, which, although spillovers from the Vietnam War, took on a character and dynamic of their own. In Laos, soon after the signing of the Vietnam cease-fire agreement, the Communist Pathet Lao and the Royal Laotian Government did reach a basis for their own agreement and resolution of their conflict. After this agreement, only a very small amount of fighting occurred in Laos; and Communists and non-Communists appeared willing to stay within the geographical areas each controls, without attacking areas the other side controls.

The Cambodians fared worse. Although a de facto cease-fire had been hoped for there, the Communist forces in Cambodia were under the command of different political factions. From 1970 to 1973, the indigenous forces (both Communist and non-Communist) had grown to be a formidable military power, especially when backed by the North Vietnamese army forces.

The military forces of the Cambodian government, headed by Lon Nol, showed themselves to be quite weak; and by May of 1973, these forces required American bombing of the Communist forces attacking them to stave off defeat, the siege of the capital city Phnom Penh, and the fall of the Lon Nol government.

The original target of American bombing within Cambodia was the North Vietnamese troops who supported the war in South Vietnam. According to a Senate Foreign Relations Committee staff report, however, by April 1973 the mission of the U.S. bombing and strafing within Cambodia had shifted from interdiction of North Vietnamese troops to support for the military forces of the government headed by Lon Nol. In the first two weeks of April, the daily average bombing was fifty-eight B-52 sorties (of 65,000 pounds each) and about 180 fighter-bomber and gunship bombing and strafing missions.[5]

The Nixon administration, having extricated itself from direct military involvement in Vietnam, seemed to be involving itself in a situation in Cambodia that has an unfortunately strong resemblance to the situation in which the United States government found itself in late 1964 and early 1965: having to use U.S. bombers in Vietnam to stave off the military defeat and political overthrow of a weak anti-Communist government by strong Communist-led forces. One would hope that U.S. leaders will learn from their past mistakes in Vietnam and avoid a repetition of the tragic policy of military entanglement in Indochina.[6]

IMPLICATIONS OF THE CEASE-FIRE AGREEMENT FOR THE FUTURE

One of the greatest concessions by the Communists in the January cease-fire agreement was their accession to demands by the United States that the military issues in Vietnam be separated from the political issues. The Agreement spells out in considerable detail proscriptions against the use of military force. It is much more vague on the political issues, and generally leaves their resolution to the Vietnamese to determine sometime in the future.

The separation of the military from the political issues was of great benefit to the non–South Vietnamase parties to the Vietnam War, the United States and the North Vietnamese. It halted the bombing of North Vietnam, allowed the withdrawal of U.S. troops, and accomplished the return of prisoners of war. The South Vietnamese Communists, however, gave up considerable bargaining ground when they finally agreed to this separation. Their position prior to the Agreement had been to tie military and political issues together. They had demanded that, before they would cease fighting, there would have to be a new government in Saigon that included the Communists and excluded President Thieu. The cease-fire agreement finally signed, however, does not impose this condition. Thus, the Communists in South Vietnam are left in the position of having to continue to struggle to achieve power at the national level as well as at the local level.

Since the signing of the Agreement, representatives of the Provisional

Revolutionary Government and of the government of Vietnam have been meeting in Paris to talk about their differences and possibly to move to some kind of political accommodation as stipulated by the Agreement. One would hope that some kind of reconciliation will be achieved through these talks.

At the same time, however, the South Vietnamese government has not allowed the Communists to participate politically at either the national level or local levels not already under Viet Cong control. Instead, the thousands of cease-fire violations are clear evidence that each side has sought to increase its political power by means of force and to prevent the other side from doing the same. Thus, even though there are some local military and political accommodations being made between Communists and non-Communists in South Vietnam, political conflict and guerrilla war continues at this writing.

The situation of the South Vietnamese people is thus one of neither war nor peace. This situation might continue indefinitely. It has within it, however, the seeds for the resumption and reescalation of the war. Dr. Kissinger and Le Duc Tho held additional meetings in Paris in May and June 1973 to talk about this continuing conflict in South Vietnam. They reached and signed an additional agreement along with the Provisional Revolutionary Government and the government of the Republic of Vietnam on 13 June 1973. Their fourteen-point communiqué is designed to improve observance of the original cease-fire agreement of 27 January 1973.

As long as President Thieu has reason to feel that the United States will continue to support his government and country with economic aid, and will come to his rescue militarily should he ever be faced with the possibility of military defeat by the Communist forces in Vietnam, he has little incentive to reach a political accommodation with the Provisional Revolutionary Government. However, the less accommodating President Thieu is, the more incentive the Communists have for reverting to the use of large-scale military forces, including the main-force units of the 145,000 North Vietnamese army troops still in South Vietnam, to try to gain political power, as was their policy prior to the Agreement.

Such a military reescalation by the Viet Cong and North Vietnamese could reinvolve the United States in the war militarily to save the South Vietnamese government from a military defeat. One possible form that U.S. military involvement might take would be through the use of bombing from U.S. aircraft that continue to be stationed in Southeast Asia and off the shores of Vietnam. Whether the United States Congress would allow such reintervention by U.S. armed forces is questionable at this point. Thus, the North Vietnamese and Viet Cong may not be deterred by the threat of resumed U.S. bombing.

The United States, the Soviet Union, and the People's Republic of China can continue to play a positive role in moving the Vietnamese toward political accommodation and reconciliation. The United States could visibly tie its offer to North Vietnam of economic aid for reconstruction to North Vietnamese military restraint in South Vietnam. At the same time, in the interests of their respective bilateral relationships with the United States, the governments of the Soviet Union and the People's Republic of China could separately persuade the North Vietnamese (by control of military and economic aid, for example) to restrain their military behavior in South Vietnam.

In return for such restraint by the North Vietnamese and Viet Cong, the United States government could firmly make it known to the South Vietnamese government that continued U.S. economic and political support is contingent upon the Republic of Vietnam government's reaching some political accommodation with the Provisional Revolutionary Government. Moreover, the U.S. government can make it clearly known to the South Vietnamese government that the United States will not be reinvolved in Vietnam militarily. This would give the South Vietnamese government the incentive to make a reasonable political accommodation with the Communists in South Vietnam and thus avoid provoking the Communists to reescalate the war militarily to gain political power.

Such a policy by the the government of the United States, as well as by the governments of the Soviet Union and the People's Republic of China, could give to all Vietnamese the hope for a real peace.

1. The complete documentation on the Vietnam Agreement, including President Nixon's 23 January 1973 address, Dr. Henry Kissinger's 24 January 1973 press conference, and the texts of the Agreement and the protocols concerning the cease-fire, the return of prisoners, the ICCS, and the deactivation of mines can be found in the *Weekly Compilation of Presidential Documents*, Monday, 29 January 1973, vol. 9, no. 4, pp. 43-74.

The statement and news conference of Secretary of State William Rogers and the text of the Act of the International Conference on Vietnam can be found in the *Department of State Bulletin*, vol. 67, no. 1761, 26 March 1973, pp. 337-47.

2. Richard M. Nixon, "Ending the War and Restoring Peace in Vietnam," (The President's Address to the Nation Announcing the Conclusion of an Agreement), 23 January 1973, in *Weekly Compilation of Presidential Documents*, p. 43.

3. "Saigon Puts All Troops on Full Alert to Counter Expected Drive by Enemy," *New York Times*, 23 January 1973, p. 6.

4. "3 Months after the Truce, No Let-up in the Charges," *New York Times,* 28 April 1973, p. 3.

5. "U.S. Data on Cambodia Raids Show Shift to a Support Role," *New York Times,* 28 April 1973, p. 3.

6. The U.S. Congress did learn a lesson from the Vietnam experience. It passed a law prohibiting the use of *any* U.S. military forces in, from offshore, or over Indochina effective 15 August 1973.

Appendixes

APPENDIX A

Content Analysis of Communications

For purposes of this study the communication data were aggregated into the eight indices described in Appendix B. Messages about the specific referents included within each index were coded to pick up two characteristics: one, how frequently the referent was mentioned, and two, whether the referent was perceived or preferred to be increasing or decreasing. The following code was used:

Blank = referent not in statement.
Perceptions of referent as:
 0 = certainly decreasing
 1 = possibly decreasing
 2 = unchanging
 3 = possibly increasing
 4 = certainly increasing
Preferences for referent:
 5 = for decreasing
 7 = for continuing unchanged
 9 = for increasing.

Thus, all policy-makers' communications about any of the specific referents were reduced to a single digit on one of two ordinal scales. A statement by President Johnson that domestic dissension weakened the United States' posture of firmness in Vietnam would be coded "9" in column 36 (specific referent: U.S. domestic support of Johnson administration's Vietnam policy; popularity of Johnson and his Vietnam policy; determination, will, patience, of U.S. public for continuing war). It is hypothesized that the sums of the numerical values of each specific referent comprising an index is related to the behavior of the policy-makers who communicate.

Coding Sheet for Public Communications and Diplomatic Contacts

IBM Columns	
2	Communication code = 1
3	*New York Times Index* code: 1 = annual; 0 = semimonthly
4-7	*New York Times Index* page number
8	*New York Times Index* column number (1,2,3)
9-11	*New York Times Index* line number
12-13	Date published in *New York Times*: Month
14-15	Day
16	Year

17-18 Week number within year (01-52)

19 *Source of message:*
1 = United States
2 = North Vietnam
3 = Viet Cong (National Liberation Front)
4 = South Vietnam

20-21 *Speaker (highest ranking if more than one from single source involved):*
(United States)
00 = Other
01 = President L. B. Johnson
02 = Secretary of Defense R. S. McNamara
03 = Secretary of State D. Rusk
04 = U.S. ambassadors in Saigon: H. C. Lodge; M. Taylor; U. A. Johnson; W. Porter; E. Bunker; E. Locke
05 = Field Commander Gen. W. C. Westmoreland
06 = Joint Chiefs of Staff: Gen. E. Wheeler et al.
07 = Other U.S. military officials
08 = Vice President H. H. Humphrey
09 = Presidential assistants and advisers: McG. Bundy; B. D. Moyers; W. W. Rostow; R. W. Komer; G. Christian; T. Johnson; J. Califano; R. Kinter; Bryant; M. Taylor; C. Clifford; A. Fortas; D. Acheson; J. Gardner; CIA Directors W. F. Raborn, J. McCone, R. Helms
10 = Assistant and deputy secretaries and other inner elites: Undersecretaries of State G. W. Ball, N. Katzenback, E. V. Rostow; Assistant Secretary of State for East Asia W. P. Bundy; Deputy Assistant Secretary of State for East Asia L. Unger; Deputy Secretaries of Defense C. Vance, P. Nitze; Assistant Secretary of Defense for International Security Affairs J. T. McNaughton; Deputy Director of AID W. S. Gaud; Ambassador-at-Large A. Harriman; USIA Director L. Marks
11 = UN Ambassadors A. Goldberg, A. Stevenson
12 = "Unidentified spokesmen" from executive branch of U.S. government
13 = Other special U.S. envoys and ambassadors
(North Vietnam)
14 = President Ho Chi Minh
15 = Premier Pham Van Dong
16 = Defense Minister Vo Nguyen Giap
17 = Vice Premier Truong Chinh
18 = Other inner North Vietnamese elites: Foreign Minister Nguyen Duy Trinh; Le Duan, [North] Vietnamese Workers' [Communist] Party head; Ton Duc Thang, president of Vietnam Fatherland Front; Le Duc Tho, Politburo member and leader of Committee for Supervision of the South
19 = Official North Vietnamese media: *Quan Doi Nhan Dan, Hoc Tap, Tien Phong*, Hanoi Radio
(National Liberation Front)
20 = Official spokesmen Nguyen Huu Tho, president of Presidium of NFLSV Central Committee; Nguyen Van Tien, permanent representative of NLF in Hanoi
21 = Official media: clandestine Liberation Radio
(South Vietnam)

22 = President Nguyen Van Thieu; heads of government N. Khanh, T. V. Huong, X. N. Oanh, P. H. Quat
23 = Vice President (formerly Premier) Nguyen Cao Ky
24 = Other South Vietnamese government spokesmen
25 = Official South Vietnamese media

22-23 *Audience directly receiving message:*

00 = Other
01 = Executive branch of U.S. government
02 = U.S. Congress
03 = General U.S. domestic public
04 = North Vietnamese government or public
05 = Viet Cong leadership or public
06 = South Vietnamese government or public
07 = Government or public of nation supporting United States (not South Vietnam)
08 = Government or public of nation supporting North Vietnam and Viet Cong
09 = Government or public of neutral nation, or a neutral figure (e.g., the pope)
10 = International organization (e.g., UN), its leadership, membership, and committees
11 = General world audience
12 = Unknown or none

24-25 *Target audience of action within message:*

(Primary sources: those capable of enacting policy; target is their enemy. Secondary sources: those who can only hope to influence primary sources; target is their own government's executive.)

00 = Other
01 = Executive branch of U.S. government
03 = General U.S. domestic public
04 = North Vietnamese government or public
05 = Viet Cong leadership or public
06 = South Vietnamese government or public
07 = Government or public of nation supporting United States (not South Vietnam)
08 = Government or public of nation supporting North Vietnam and Viet Cong
09 = Government or public of neutral nation, or neutral figure (e.g., the pope)
10 = International organization (e.g., UN), its leadership, membership, and committees
11 = General world audience
12 = Unknown or none

26-27 *Medium:*

00 = Other
01 = Diplomatic note or letter
02 = Government communiqué, press release, or message from official media

03 = International conference (three or more parties)
04 = Domestic speech, public television interviews
05 = Foreign speech
06 = News conference
07 = Background briefing; unidentified source; "reportedly"
08 = Private interview; ambassadorial and diplomatic personal contacts
09 = Congressional hearing or address
10 = Quote or paraphrased quote (code source as person quoted; target is target in original quoted statement.)
11 = Unknown

Specific Referents

Code: Blank = Referent not in statement

Perceptions:
- 0 = Certainly decreasing
- 1 = Possibly decreasing
- 2 = Unchanging
- 3 = Possibly increasing
- 4 = Certainly increasing

Preferences:
- 5 = For decreasing
- 7 = For continuing unchanged
- 9 = For increasing

29 U.S. bombing, shelling, mining, invading, blockading, and other armed hostilities against North Vietnam; effects and effectiveness of U.S. hostilities in North Vietnam; destruction in North Vietnam; military, economic, industrial, and agricultural costs to North Vietnam

30 U.S. troop strength, bases, weapons, firepower, mobility, and other military capabilities in South Vietnam

31 U.S. bombing, armed hostilities, and effectiveness in South Vietnam

32 U.S. aid to, alliance with, commitments to, shield for, interest in, influence on, support for, strengthening of, South Vietnam; S.V. dependence on United States

33 U.S. casualties

34 U.S. plane losses

35 U.S. dollar, economic, and material costs of war

36 U.S. domestic public support of Johnson administration's Vietnam policy; popularity of Johnson and his Vietnam policy; determination, will, patience of U.S. public for continuing war

37 World opinion, prestige, support of United States in Vietnam

38 ARVN military activity and effectiveness in South Vietnam and in North Vietnam

39 ARVN casualties

40 ARVN morale, determination, motivation, will to continue war, confidence, optimism, lack of defections

41 Civilian casualties in South Vietnam

42 North Vietnamese and Viet Cong infiltration, troop strength, supplies, mu-

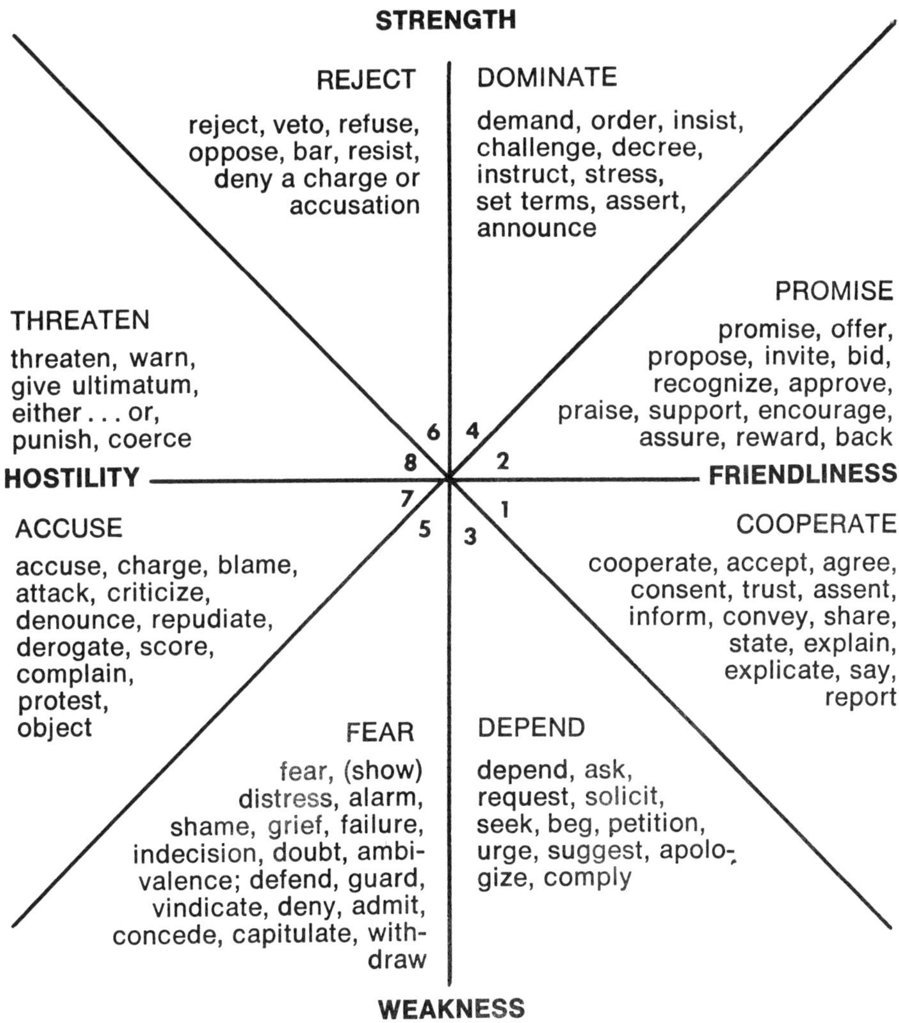

9 = Unclassifiable communication or other
0 = Conspicuous absence of response

Figure 48. Primary Message Types

nitions, recruitment in South Vietnam and in DMZ; other military capabilities

43 North Vietnamese and Viet Cong armed hostilities and effectiveness in South Vietnam

44 North Vietnamese and Viet Cong morale, determination, motivation, will to continue war, confidence, optimism, lack of defections

45 North Vietnamese and Viet Cong casualties

46 Civilian casualties in North Vietnam

47 Extension, spillover of war into neighboring countries (e.g., Laos, Cambodia, Thailand)

48 Extension of communism into Southeast Asian countries; extension (lack of containment) of China and Chinese influence in Southeast Asia; lack of security in Southeast Asia; spreading of other wars of national liberation

49 Communist Chinese participation in war, aid to North Vietnam and Viet Cong; "volunteers"; threats to U.S. security and interests; likelihood of U.S. war with China, U.S. (nuclear) bombing of China; North Vietnamese dependence on China

50 Soviet participation in war, aid to North Vietnam and Viet Cong; "volunteers"; protection of North Vietnam, likelihood of U.S. war with U.S.S.R.; tensions between United States and U.S.S.R. over Vietnam; North Vietnamese dependence on U.S.S.R.

51 North Vietnamese control of NLF (Viet Cong); Viet Cong dependence on North Vietnam

52 GVN control of, and support from, South Vietnamese population; stability of GVN; degree of pacification

53 Viet Cong political activities, effectiveness, strength, structure, influence; implementation of NLF program; political and administrative control in South Vietnam; popular support for Viet Cong in South Vietnam

54 Reciprocity in military deescalation

55 Stalement, standoff, standstill militarily and politically; each side controls only part of South Vietnam, de facto territorial division or partition of South Vietnam; enclaves

56 Victory, winning war militarily; defeating, destroying enemy; enemy capitulation, withdrawal, retreat, fade-out

57 Diplomatic contacts and communications of unknown content (Code 8 = present)

58 Third party (e.g., UN, nonbelligerents) mediation in achieving peace negotiations and settlement, and in supervision of settlement

59 Talks or negotiations between United States and North Vietnam; new international conference at Geneva or elsewhere

60 Talks or negotiations between United States and Viet Cong; recognized Viet Cong role in negotiations

61 Sincerity, trustworthiness, honesty, seriousness of U.S. peace proposals and moves

62 Sincerity, trustworthiness, honesty, seriousness of North Vietnamese and Viet Cong peace proposals and moves

63 Cease-fire, truce, armistice, temporary cessation of warfare

64 Permanent cessation of warfare, peace, settlement, negotiated compromise, end of aggression and hostilities; international order and security

65 Reunification; independence, sovereignty, territorial integrity, democratic freedom of reunified Vietnam; implementation of 1954 Geneva accords

66 Neutralization, nonalignment of South Vietnam; coalition government including Viet Cong and non-Viet Cong

67 Buddhist or other South Vietnamese third political party's activity and strength

68 Independence, sovereignty, democracy, and territorial integrity and security of South Vietnam; political self-determination, absence of foreign interference

69 Material and economic reconstruction, development, modernization in South Vietnam; prosperity, better living conditions; land reform; economic reform, sharing wealth; price stability

APPENDIX B

Components of the Eight Communications Indices

1. *North Vietnamese and Viet Cong (NV + VC) Preferences for Their Own Military and Political Activities.* This index is a sum composed of (a) the product of the preference value times the frequency of NV + VC statements concerning NV + VC troop infiltration, troop strength, supplies, munitions, recruitment, and other military capabilities in South Vietnam and in the De-Militarized Zone; plus (b) the product of the preference value times the frequency of NV + VC statements concerning NV + VC armed hostilities (terrorism, conventional and guerrilla operations) and effectiveness (military control) in South Vietnam; plus (c) the sum of the frequency of NV + VC preference statements plus the frequency of NV + VC perception statements referring to NV + VC morale, determination, motivation, confidence, optimism, lack of defections, and will to continue the war; plus (d) the frequency of NV + VC preference statements referring to Viet Cong political activities, effectiveness, strength, structure, influence, popular support, political and administrative control, and implementation of the NLF program in South Vietnam. This index of statements is so constructed that high values should correspond to greater NV + VC military and political activity.

2. *North Vietnamese and Viet Cong (NV + VC) Perceptions of United States and South Vietnamese (US + SV) Military and Political Activities.* This index is composed of the sum of the frequencies of NV + VC statements concerning (a) NV + VC perceptions of U.S. bombing, shelling, mining, invading, blockading, and other armed hostilities against North Vietnam, including the effects and effectiveness of these hostilities, destruction in North Vietnam, and military, economic, industrial, and agricultural costs to North Vietnam; (b) NV + VC preferences concerning U.S. troop strength, bases, weapons, firepower, mobility, and other military capabilities in South Vietnam; (c) NV + VC perception of U.S. domestic public support of the Johnson administration's Vietnam policy, the popularity of President Johnson and his Vietnam policy, and the determination, patience, and will of the U.S. public for continuing the war; (d) NV + VC perceptions of ARVN military activity and effectiveness; (e) NV + VC perceptions of civilian casualties in North Vietnam; plus (f) the value of NV + VC perceptions of the South Vietnamese government's stability and its control of and support from the people of South Vietnam. This index of *statements* is so constructed that higher values should correspond to greater US + SV military and political *activity.*

3. *North Vietnamese and Viet Cong (NV + VC) Preferences for Negotiations.* This index is composed of the sum of (a) the product of the preference value times the frequency of NV + VC statements concerning third party (e.g., UN, nonbelligerents) mediation for achieving peace negotiations and a settlement, and for supervision of a settlement; minus (b) the frequency of NV + VC preference statements concerning reciprocity in military deescalation; plus (c) the product of the preference value times the frequency of NV + VC statements concerning talks or negotiations between the United States and/or the South Vietnamese on the one hand and the North Vietnamese on the other, including a new international conference at Geneva or elsewhere, plus the frequency of NV + VC statements

the frequency of preferences, plus the frequency of perceptions concerning military victory in the war, defeat or destruction of the enemy, enemy capitulation, withdrawal, retreat, or fade-out; minus (e) the perception value times the frequency of perceptions, plus the frequency of preferences concerning peace, permanent cessation of the war, settlement, negotiated compromise, end of aggression and hostilities, and international order and security; plus (f) the frequency of preferences by *South Vietnamese* speakers concerning neutralization or nonalignment of South Vietnam, or a coalition government that would include Viet Cong and non-Viet Cong elements; plus (g) the frequency of US + SV preferences concerning the independence, sovereignty, political self-determination, territorial integrity, absence of foreign interference, and security of South Vietnam; plus (h) the frequency of US + SV preferences for material and economic reconstruction, development, and modernization in South Vietnam, including land and economic reform, price stability, and the sharing of wealth.

APPENDIX C

Time Plots of Composite Indices and Individual Variables

On each of the following plots, "MON" is the *month* (month 1 = January 1965, month 36 = December 1967, month 69 = September 1970, etc.). "VALUE" (plotted with 0's) is the *amount* of the variable in each month. "1ST D" (plotted with 1's) is the *difference* in the amount from the previous month, i.e., the *rate* of change. "2ND D" (plotted with 2's) is the difference in the rate from the previous month, i.e., the acceleration.

For N.V. + V.C. Armed Attacks, V.C. Terrorist Incidents, and Combined U.S. + S.V. Ground Operations, 0's in 1965 and 1966 indicate *missing data,* not zero amounts.

In the following charts, successive months in the war run from top to bottom; increasing values run from left to right.

U.S. Troops in S.V.

ION	VALUE	1ST D	2ND D
1	24.0	0.0	0.0
2	25.0	1.0	0.0
3	27.0	2.0	1.0
4	29.0	2.0	0.0
5	42.0	13.0	11.0
6	54.0	12.0	-1.0
7	80.0	26.0	14.0
8	90.0	10.0	-16.0
9	132.0	42.0	32.0
10	148.0	16.0	-26.0
11	166.0	18.0	2.0
12	184.0	18.0	0.0
13	197.0	13.0	-5.0
14	201.0	4.0	-9.0
15	231.0	30.0	26.0
16	255.0	24.0	-6.0
17	255.0	0.0	-24.0
18	267.0	12.0	12.0
19	285.0	18.0	6.0
20	303.0	18.0	0.0
21	313.0	10.0	-8.0
22	345.0	32.0	22.0
23	361.0	16.0	-16.0
24	389.0	28.0	12.0
25	403.0	14.0	-14.0
26	414.0	11.0	-3.0
27	421.0	7.0	-4.0
28	436.0	15.0	8.0
29	443.0	7.0	-8.0
30	449.0	6.0	-1.0
31	458.0	9.0	3.0
32	466.0	8.0	-1.0
33	460.0	-6.0	-14.0
34	467.0	7.0	13.0
35	470.0	3.0	-4.0
36	486.0	16.0	13.0
37	498.0	12.0	-4.0
38	506.0	8.0	-4.0
39	515.0	9.0	1.0
40	520.0	5.0	-4.0
41	536.0	16.0	11.0
42	536.0	0.0	-16.0
43	537.0	1.0	1.0
44	537.0	0.0	-1.0
45	538.0	1.0	1.0
46	534.0	-4.0	-5.0
47	538.0	4.0	8.0
48	537.0	-1.0	-5.0
49	542.0	5.0	6.0
50	541.0	-1.0	-6.0
51	538.0	-3.0	-2.0
52	543.0	5.0	8.0
53	540.0	-3.0	-8.0
54	539.0	-1.0	2.0
55	537.0	-2.0	-1.0
56	510.0	-27.0	-25.0
57	510.0	0.0	27.0
58	495.0	-15.0	-15.0
59	480.0	-15.0	-0.0
60	474.0	-6.0	9.0
61	473.0	-1.0	5.0
62	467.0	-6.0	-5.0
63	439.0	-28.0	-22.0
64	428.0	-11.0	17.0
65	414.0	-14.0	-3.0
66	415.0	1.0	15.0
67	390.0	-25.0	-26.0
68	387.0	-3.0	22.0
69	390.0	3.0	6.0

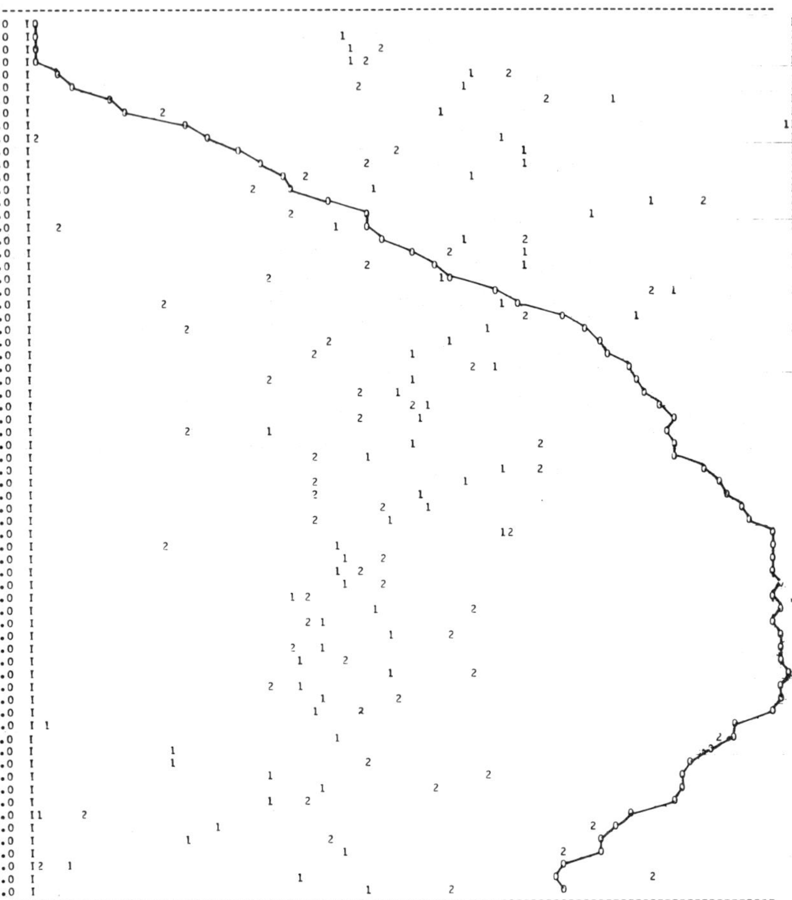

BOUNDS ON VALUES ARE 24.00 543.00
BOUNDS ON FIRST DIFFERENCES ARE -28.00 42.00
BOUNDS ON SECOND DIFFERENCES ARE -25.00 32.00
0 VALUE 1 FIRST DIFFERENCE 2 SECOND DIFFERENCE

U.S. Ground Operations of Battalion Size or Larger

MON	VALUE	1ST D	2ND D
1	0.0	0.0	0.0
2	0.0	0.0	0.0
3	0.0	0.0	0.0
4	0.0	0.0	0.0
5	0.0	0.0	0.0
6	4.0	4.0	4.0
7	12.0	8.0	4.0
8	21.0	9.0	1.0
9	19.0	-2.0	-11.0
10	55.0	36.0	38.0
11	38.0	-17.0	-53.0
12	42.0	4.0	21.0
13	40.0	-2.0	-6.0
14	70.0	30.0	32.0
15	65.0	-5.0	-35.0
16	74.0	9.0	14.0
17	78.0	4.0	-5.0
18	105.0	27.0	23.0
19	91.0	-14.0	-41.0
20	89.0	-2.0	12.0
21	104.0	15.0	17.0
22	93.0	-11.0	-26.0
23	85.0	-8.0	3.0
24	85.0	0.0	8.0
25	105.0	20.0	20.0
26	125.0	20.0	0.0
27	111.0	-14.0	-34.0
28	120.0	9.0	23.0
29	118.0	-2.0	-11.0
30	121.0	3.0	5.0
31	114.0	-7.0	-10.0
32	121.0	7.0	14.0
33	111.0	-10.0	-17.0
34	120.0	9.0	19.0
35	140.0	20.0	11.0
36	125.0	-15.0	-35.0
37	125.0	0.0	15.0
38	119.0	-6.0	-6.0
39	125.0	6.0	12.0
40	104.0	-21.0	-27.0
41	93.0	-11.0	10.0
42	81.0	-12.0	-1.0
43	88.0	7.0	19.0
44	63.0	-25.0	-32.0
45	70.0	7.0	32.0
46	82.0	12.0	5.0
47	89.0	7.0	-5.0
48	81.0	-8.0	-15.0
49	81.0	0.0	8.0
50	106.0	25.0	25.0
51	93.0	-13.0	-38.0
52	101.0	8.0	21.0
53	108.0	7.0	-1.0
54	111.0	3.0	-4.0
55	107.0	-4.0	-7.0
56	108.0	1.0	5.0
57	103.0	-5.0	-6.0
58	91.0	-12.0	-7.0
59	88.0	-3.0	9.0
60	87.0	-1.0	2.0
61	85.0	-2.0	-1.0
62	62.0	-23.0	-21.0
63	54.0	-8.0	15.0
64	48.0	-6.0	2.0
65	54.0	6.0	12.0
66	64.0	10.0	4.0
67	66.0	2.0	-8.0
68	71.0	5.0	3.0
69	92.0	21.0	16.0

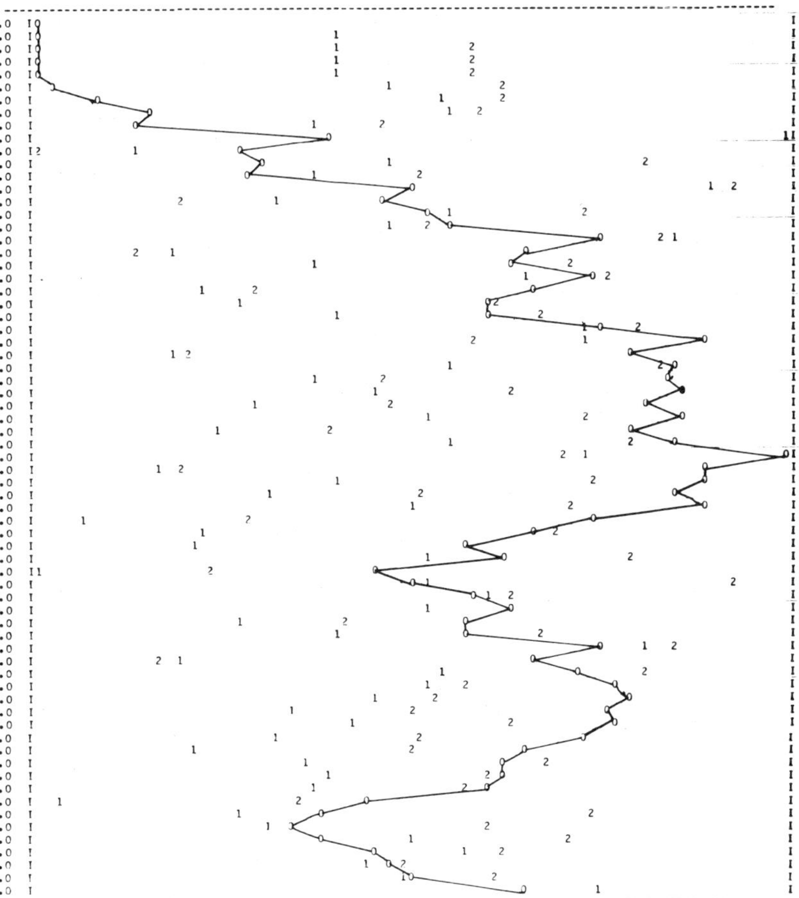

BOUNDS ON VALUES ARE 0.00 140.00
BOUNDS ON FIRST DIFFERENCES ARE -25.00 36.00
BOUNDS ON SECOND DIFFERENCES ARE -53.00 38.00
0 VALUE 1 FIRST DIFFERENCE 2 SECOND DIFFERENCE

U.S. Bombing of S.V.

MON	VALUE	1ST D	2ND D
1	0.0	0.0	0.0
2	28.0	28.0	0.0
3	419.0	391.0	363.0
4	966.0	547.0	156.0
5	[illegible]	-102.0	-649.0
6	5047.0	4183.0	4285.0
7	7197.0	2150.0	-2033.0
8	6698.0	-499.0	-2649.0
9	6094.0	-604.0	-105.0
10	7928.0	1834.0	2438.0
11	8133.0	205.0	-1629.0
12	7946.0	-187.0	-392.0
13	9039.0	1093.0	1280.0
14	10572.0	1533.0	440.0
15	12636.0	2064.0	531.0
16	9871.0	-2765.0	-4829.0
17	10071.0	200.0	2965.0
18	10799.0	728.0	528.0
19	13613.0	2814.0	2086.0
20	10293.0	-3320.0	-6134.0
21	12288.0	1995.0	5315.0
22	11781.0	-507.0	-2502.0
23	12643.0	862.0	1369.0
24	11310.0	-1333.0	-2195.0
25	12192.0	882.0	2215.0
26	13149.0	957.0	75.0
27	14395.0	1246.0	289.0
28	14092.0	-303.0	-1549.0
29	16366.0	2274.0	2577.0
30	15106.0	-1260.0	-3534.0
31	16023.0	917.0	2177.0
32	14536.0	-1487.0	-2404.0
33	15624.0	1088.0	2575.0
34	14492.0	-1132.0	-2220.0
35	14437.0	-55.0	1077.0
36	13517.0	-920.0	-865.0
37	15371.0	1854.0	2774.0
38	18757.0	3386.0	1532.0
39	18682.0	-75.0	-3461.0
40	18447.0	-235.0	-150.0
41	21213.0	2766.0	3001.0
42	21486.0	273.0	-2493.0
43	18389.0	-3097.0	-3370.0
44	20237.0	1848.0	4945.0
45	18463.0	-1774.0	-3622.0
46	14972.0	-3491.0	-1717.0
47	15815.0	843.0	4334.0
48	16373.0	558.0	-285.0
49	15003.0	-1370.0	-1928.0
50	15480.0	477.0	1847.0
51	16485.0	1005.0	528.0
52	16370.0	-115.0	-1120.0
53	16800.0	430.0	545.0
54	17186.0	386.0	-44.0
55	14916.0	-2270.0	-2656.0
56	15259.0	343.0	2613.0
57	11632.0	-3627.0	-3970.0
58	9246.0	-2386.0	1241.0
59	9638.0	392.0	2778.0
60	8822.0	-816.0	-1208.0
61	8936.0	114.0	930.0
62	7942.0	-994.0	-1108.0
63	8324.0	382.0	1376.0
64	10034.0	1710.0	1328.0
65	8795.0	-1239.0	-2949.0
65	7774.0	-1021.0	218.0
67	7979.0	205.0	1226.0
68	7102.0	-877.0	-1082.0
69	5985.0	-1117.0	-240.0

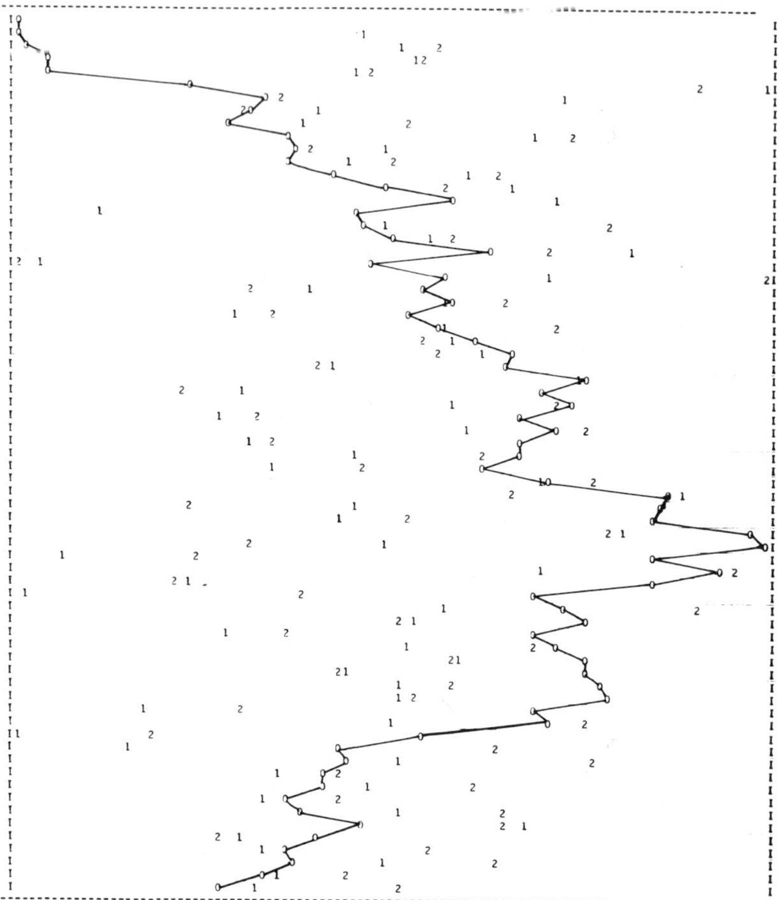

BOUNDS ON VALUES ARE 0.00 21486.00
BOUNDS ON FIRST DIFFERENCES ARE -3627.00 4183.00
BOUNDS ON SECOND DIFFERENCES ARE -6134.00 5315.00
0 VALUE 1 FIRST DIFFERENCE 2 SECOND DIFFERENCE

U.S. Commitments

MON	VALUE	1ST D	2ND D
1	771.0	0.0	0.0
2	918.6	147.6	0.0
3	1086.5	167.9	20.3
4	2144.6	1058.1	890.2
5	2489.9	345.3	-712.8
6	3715.5	1225.6	880.4
7	5255.5	1540.0	314.3
8	6806.9	1551.5	11.5
9	7837.9	1031.0	-520.5
10	10033.4	2195.5	1164.6
11	8602.1	-1431.3	-3626.8
12	8701.9	99.7	1531.0
13	8297.0	-404.8	-504.6
14	11333.1	3036.0	3440.8
15	13221.4	1888.4	-1147.6
16	15210.3	1988.9	100.5
17	14945.2	-265.2	-2254.1
18	18460.0	3514.9	3780.1
19	19970.0	1510.0	-2004.9
20	21631.3	1661.2	151.2
21	22837.7	1206.5	-454.8
22	22439.8	-397.9	-1604.4
23	20669.2	-1770.6	-1372.7
24	21021.7	352.5	2123.1
25	22419.4	1397.7	1045.2
26	23368.5	949.1	-448.6
27	24776.2	1407.7	459.6
28	26620.3	1844.1	436.4
29	27109.7	489.4	-1354.7
30	27952.1	842.4	353.0
31	27793.3	-158.8	-1001.2
32	30029.8	2236.6	2395.3
33	27484.0	2545.9	-4782.4
34	27974.0	490.1	3035.9
35	30232.2	2258.2	1769.2
36	27464.2	-2768.0	-5026.2

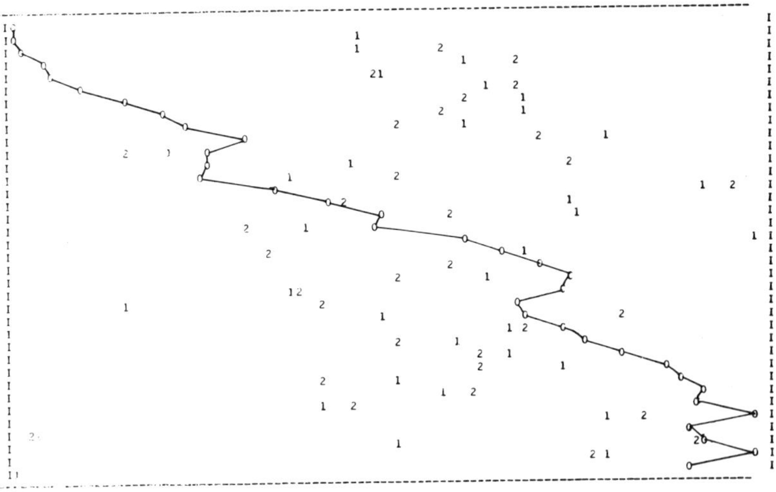

BOUNDS ON VALUES ARE 771.00 30232.23
BOUNDS ON FIRST DIFFFFENCES ARE -2768.03 3514.87
BOUNDS ON SECOND DIFFEFELNCES ARE -5026.44 3780.06
0 VALUE 1 FIRST DIFFERENCE 2 SECOND DIFFERENCE

U.S. Bombing of N.V.

MON	VALUE	1ST D	2ND D
1	0.0	0.0	0.0
2	177.0	177.0	0.0
3	253.0	76.0	-101.0
4	1377.0	1124.0	1048.0
5	958.0	-419.0	-1543.0
6	2150.0	1192.0	1611.0
7	2041.0	-109.0	-1301.0
8	2279.0	238.0	347.0
9	2364.0	85.0	-153.0
10	2120.0	-244.0	-329.0
11	1942.0	-178.0	66.0
12	1461.0	-481.0	-303.0
13	12.0	-1449.0	-958.0
14	915.0	903.0	2352.0
15	3432.0	2517.0	1614.0
16	4302.0	870.0	-1647.0
17	3945.0	-357.0	-1227.0
18	6306.0	2361.0	2718.0
19	8706.0	2400.0	39.0
20	10275.0	1569.0	-831.0
21	10713.0	438.0	-1131.0
22	9246.0	-1457.0	-1905.0
23	6660.0	-2586.0	-1119.0
24	6219.0	-441.0	2145.0
25	6132.0	-87.0	354.0
26	4879.0	-1253.0	-1166.0
27	7554.0	2675.0	3928.0
28	8775.0	1221.0	-1454.0
29	9398.0	623.0	-598.0
30	10821.0	1423.0	800.0
31	11087.0	266.0	-1157.0
32	13552.0	2465.0	2199.0
33	10188.0	-3364.0	-5829.0
34	10306.0	118.0	3482.0
35	12069.0	1763.0	1645.0
36	8460.0	-3609.0	-5372.0
37	7836.0	-624.0	2985.0
38	6610.0	-1226.0	-602.0
39	7705.0	1095.0	2321.0
40	10236.0	2531.0	1436.0
41	10431.0	195.0	-2336.0
42	11376.0	945.0	750.0
43	11128.0	-248.0	-1193.0
44	9810.0	-1318.0	-1070.0
45	9753.0	-57.0	1261.0
46	10860.0	1107.0	1164.0
47	0.0	-10860.0	-11967.0
48	0.0	0.0	10860.0
49	0.0	0.0	0.0
50	0.0	0.0	0.0
51	0.0	0.0	0.0
52	0.0	0.0	0.0
53	0.0	0.0	0.0
54	0.0	0.0	0.0
55	0.0	0.0	0.0
56	0.0	0.0	0.0
57	0.0	0.0	0.0
58	0.0	0.0	0.0
59	0.0	0.0	0.0
60	0.0	0.0	0.0
61	0.0	0.0	0.0
62	0.0	0.0	0.0
63	0.0	0.0	0.0
64	0.0	0.0	0.0
65	0.0	0.0	0.0
66	0.0	0.0	0.0
67	0.0	0.0	0.0
68	0.0	0.0	0.0
69	0.0	0.0	0.0

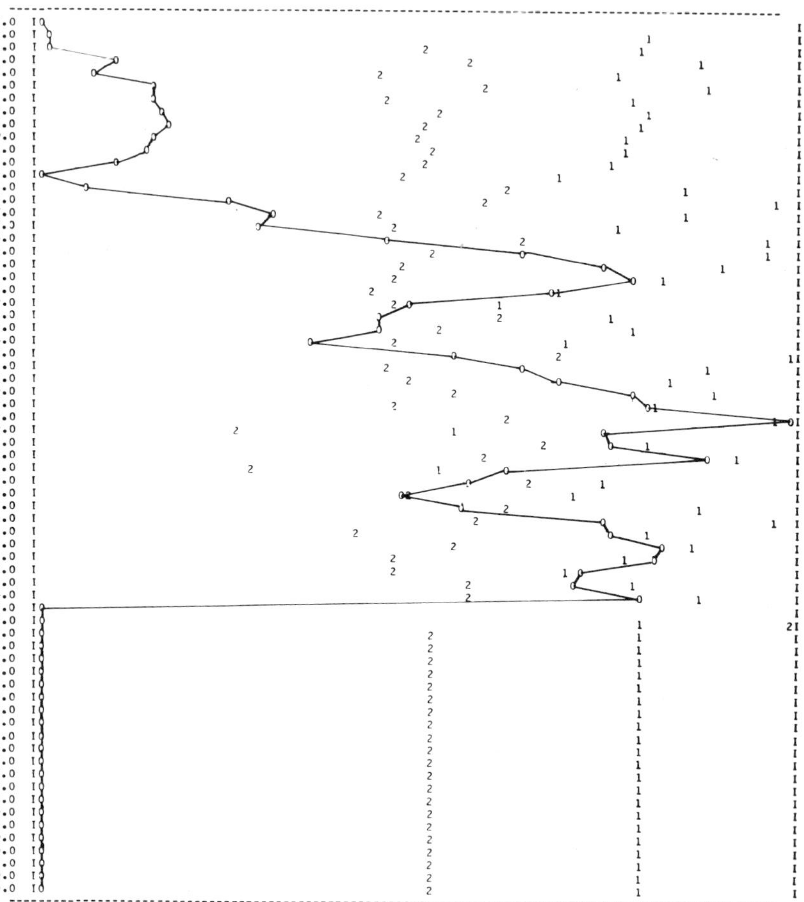

BOUNDS ON VALUES ARE 0.00 13552.00
BOUNDS ON FIRST DIFFERENCES ARE -10860.00 2675.00
BOUNDS ON SECOND DIFFEREENCES ARE -11967.00 10860.00
0 VALUE 1 FIRST DIFFERENCE 2 SECOND DIFFERENCE

Combined U.S. + S.V. Ground Operations of Battalion Size or Larger

MON	VALUE	1ST D	2ND D
1	0.0	0.0	0.0
2	0.0	0.0	0.0
3	0.0	0.0	0.0
4	0.0	0.0	0.0
5	0.0	0.0	0.0
6	0.0	0.0	0.0
7	0.0	0.0	0.0
8	0.0	0.0	0.0
9	0.0	0.0	0.0
10	0.0	0.0	0.0
11	0.0	0.0	0.0
12	0.0	0.0	0.0
13	0.0	0.0	0.0
14	0.0	0.0	0.0
15	0.0	0.0	0.0
16	0.0	0.0	0.0
17	0.0	0.0	0.0
18	0.0	0.0	0.0
19	0.0	0.0	0.0
20	0.0	0.0	0.0
21	0.0	0.0	0.0
22	0.0	0.0	0.0
23	0.0	0.0	0.0
24	0.0	0.0	0.0
25	16.0	16.0	16.0
26	19.0	3.0	-13.0
27	9.0	-10.0	-13.0
28	11.0	2.0	12.0
29	12.0	1.0	-1.0
30	8.0	-4.0	-5.0
31	14.0	6.0	10.0
32	8.0	-6.0	-12.0
33	10.0	2.0	8.0
34	10.0	0.0	-2.0
35	11.0	1.0	1.0
36	5.0	-6.0	-7.0
37	3.0	-2.0	4.0
38	0.0	-3.0	-1.0
39	13.0	13.0	16.0
40	80.0	67.0	54.0
41	27.0	-53.0	-120.0
42	41.0	14.0	67.0
43	37.0	-4.0	-18.0
44	58.0	21.0	25.0
45	40.0	-18.0	-39.0
46	41.0	1.0	19.0
47	47.0	6.0	5.0
48	46.0	-1.0	-7.0
49	72.0	26.0	27.0
50	45.0	-27.0	-53.0
51	37.0	-8.0	19.0
52	18.0	-19.0	-11.0
53	30.0	12.0	31.0
54	26.0	-4.0	-16.0
55	49.0	23.0	27.0
56	44.0	-5.0	-28.0
57	61.0	17.0	22.0
58	40.0	-21.0	-38.0
59	7.0	-33.0	-12.0
60	10.0	3.0	36.0
61	14.0	4.0	1.0
62	15.0	1.0	-3.0
63	11.0	-4.0	-5.0
64	4.0	-7.0	-3.0
65	3.0	-1.0	6.0
66	7.0	4.0	5.0
67	5.0	-2.0	-6.0
68	4.0	-1.0	1.0
69	5.0	1.0	2.0

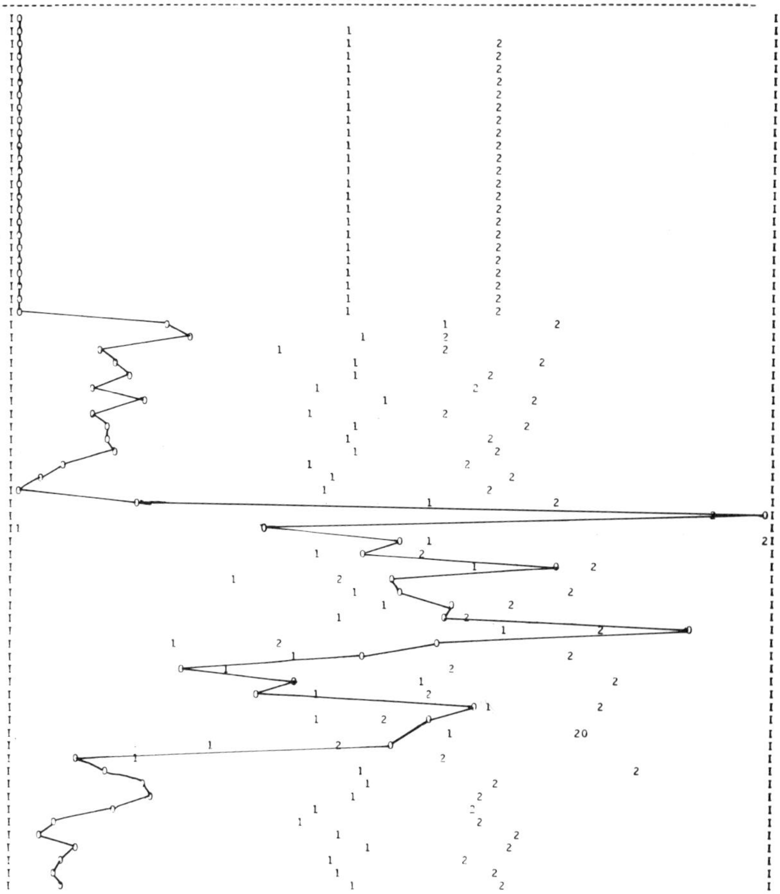

BOUNDS ON VALUES ARE 0.00 80.00
BOUNDS ON FIRST DIFFERENCES ARE -53.00 67.00
BOUNDS ON SECOND DIFFERENCES ARE -120.00 67.00
0 VALUE 1 FIRST DIFFERENCE 2 SECOND DIFFERENCE

N.V. + V.C. Troops

MON	VALUE	1ST D	2ND D
1	113.0	0.0	0.0
2	117.0	4.0	0.0
3	138.0	21.0	17.0
4	165.0	27.0	6.0
5	165.0	0.0	-27.0
6	165.0	0.0	0.0
7	187.0	22.0	22.0
8	210.0	23.0	1.0
9	213.0	3.0	-20.0
10	221.0	8.0	5.0
11	228.0	7.0	-1.0
12	230.0	2.0	-5.0
13	238.0	8.0	6.0
14	239.0	1.0	-7.0
15	239.0	0.0	-1.0
16	250.0	11.0	11.0
17	267.0	17.0	6.0
18	271.0	4.0	-13.0
19	277.0	6.0	2.0
20	282.0	5.0	-1.0
21	283.0	1.0	-4.0
22	279.0	-4.0	-5.0
23	280.0	1.0	5.0
24	280.0	0.0	-1.0
25	284.0	4.0	4.0
26	284.0	0.0	-4.0
27	287.0	3.0	3.0
28	286.0	-1.0	-4.0
29	292.0	6.0	7.0
30	296.0	4.0	-2.0
31	297.0	1.0	-3.0
32	297.0	0.0	-1.0
33	297.0	0.0	0.0
34	297.0	0.0	0.0
35	297.0	0.0	0.0
36	297.0	0.0	0.0

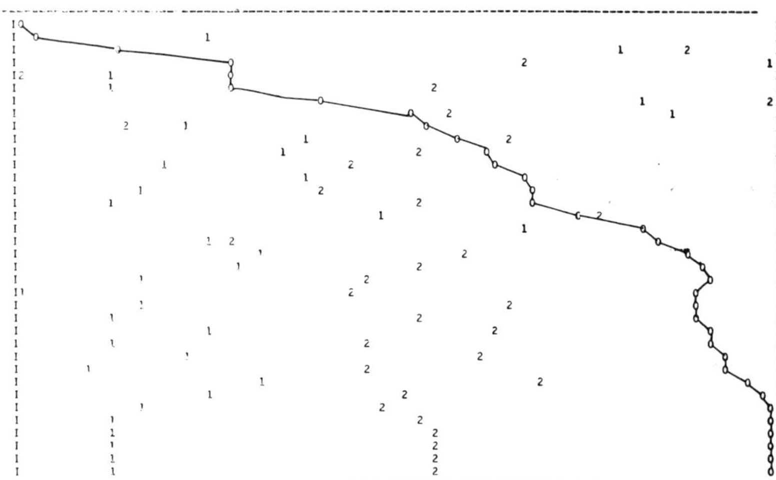

BOUNDS ON VALUES ARE 113.00 297.00
BOUNDS ON FIRST DIFFERENCES ARE -4.00 27.00
BOUNDS ON SECOND DIFFEREENCES ARE -27.00 22.00
0 VALUE 1 FIRST DIFFERENCE 2 SECOND DIFFERENCE

N.V. + V.C. Armed Attacks

MON	VALUE	1ST D	2ND D
1	0.0	0.0	0.0
2	0.0	0.0	0.0
3	0.0	0.0	0.0
4	0.0	0.0	0.0
5	0.0	0.0	0.0
6	0.0	0.0	0.0
7	0.0	0.0	0.0
8	0.0	0.0	0.0
9	0.0	0.0	0.0
10	0.0	0.0	0.0
11	0.0	0.0	0.0
12	0.0	0.0	0.0
13	0.0	0.0	0.0
14	0.0	0.0	0.0
15	0.0	0.0	0.0
16	0.0	0.0	0.0
17	0.0	0.0	0.0
18	0.0	0.0	0.0
19	0.0	0.0	0.0
20	0.0	0.0	0.0
21	0.0	0.0	0.0
22	0.0	0.0	0.0
23	0.0	0.0	0.0
24	0.0	0.0	0.0
25	137.0	137.0	137.0
26	125.0	-12.0	-149.0
27	212.0	87.0	99.0
28	162.0	-50.0	-137.0
29	187.0	25.0	75.0
30	168.0	-19.0	-44.0
31	191.0	23.0	42.0
32	197.0	6.0	-17.0
33	260.0	63.0	57.0
34	255.0	-5.0	-68.0
35	264.0	9.0	14.0
36	277.0	13.0	4.0
37	396.0	119.0	106.0
38	590.0	194.0	75.0
39	540.0	-50.0	-244.0
40	391.0	-149.0	-99.0
41	569.0	178.0	327.0
42	288.0	-281.0	-459.0
43	133.0	-155.0	126.0
44	234.0	101.0	256.0
45	215.0	-19.0	-120.0
46	140.0	-75.0	-56.0
47	184.0	44.0	119.0
48	188.0	4.0	-40.0
49	208.0	20.0	16.0
50	331.0	123.0	103.0
51	446.0	115.0	-8.0
52	316.0	-130.0	-245.0
53	444.0	128.0	258.0
54	454.0	10.0	-118.0
55	198.0	-256.0	-266.0
56	237.0	39.0	295.0
57	309.0	72.0	33.0
58	186.0	-123.0	-195.0
59	339.0	153.0	276.0
60	307.0	-32.0	-185.0
61	318.0	11.0	43.0
62	231.0	-87.0	-98.0
63	224.0	-7.0	80.0
64	472.0	248.0	255.0
65	480.0	8.0	-240.0
66	340.0	-140.0	-148.0
67	247.0	-93.0	47.0
68	307.0	60.0	153.0
69	295.0	-12.0	-72.0

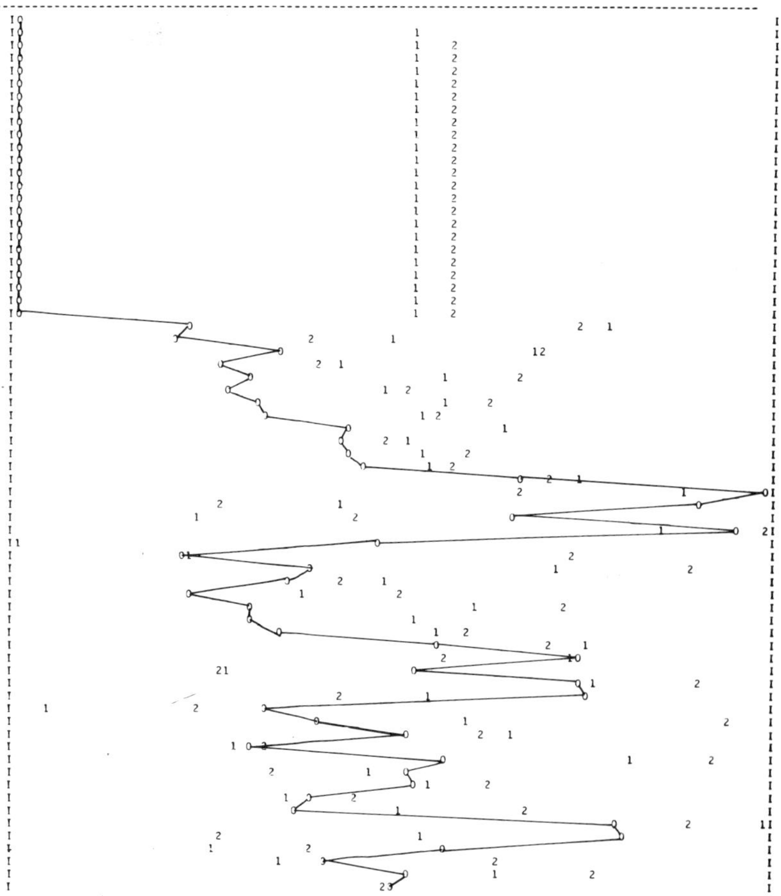

BOUNDS ON VALUES ARE 0.00 590.00
BOUNDS ON FIRST DIFFERENCES ARE -281.00 248.00
BOUNDS ON SECOND DIFFEREENCES ARE -459.00 327.00
O VALUE 1 FIRST DIFFERENCE 2 SECOND DIFFERENCE

V.C. Terrorist Incidents

MON	VALUE	1ST D	2ND D
1	0.0	0.0	0.0
2	0.0	0.0	0.0
3	0.0	0.0	0.0
4	0.0	0.0	0.0
5	0.0	0.0	0.0
6	0.0	0.0	0.0
7	0.0	0.0	0.0
8	0.0	0.0	0.0
9	0.0	0.0	0.0
10	0.0	0.0	0.0
11	0.0	0.0	0.0
12	0.0	0.0	0.0
13	0.0	0.0	0.0
14	0.0	0.0	0.0
15	0.0	0.0	0.0
16	0.0	0.0	0.0
17	0.0	0.0	0.0
18	0.0	0.0	0.0
19	0.0	0.0	0.0
20	0.0	0.0	0.0
21	0.0	0.0	0.0
22	0.0	0.0	0.0
23	0.0	0.0	0.0
24	0.0	0.0	0.0
25	130.0	130.0	130.0
26	132.0	2.0	-128.0
27	107.0	-25.0	-27.0
28	200.0	93.0	118.0
29	195.0	-5.0	-98.0
30	158.0	-37.0	-32.0
31	175.0	17.0	54.0
32	212.0	37.0	20.0
33	209.0	-3.0	-40.0
34	136.0	-73.0	-70.0
35	123.0	-13.0	60.0
36	157.0	34.0	47.0
37	135.0	-22.0	-56.0
38	70.0	-65.0	-43.0
39	130.0	60.0	125.0
40	75.0	-55.0	-115.0
41	109.0	34.0	89.0
42	61.0	-48.0	-82.0
43	58.0	-3.0	45.0
44	57.0	-1.0	2.0
45	99.0	42.0	43.0
46	73.0	-26.0	-68.0
47	73.0	0.0	26.0
48	88.0	15.0	15.0
49	98.0	0.0	-15.0
50	109.0	21.0	21.0
51	118.0	9.0	-12.0
52	138.0	20.0	11.0
53	132.0	-6.0	-26.0
54	111.0	-21.0	-15.0
55	74.0	-37.0	-16.0
56	108.0	34.0	71.0
57	123.0	15.0	-19.0
58	118.0	-5.0	-20.0
59	122.0	4.0	9.0
60	116.0	-6.0	-10.0
61	117.0	1.0	7.0
62	129.0	12.0	11.0
63	200.0	71.0	59.0
64	224.0	24.0	-47.0
65	185.0	-39.0	-63.0
66	185.0	0.0	39.0
67	160.0	-25.0	-25.0
68	117.0	-43.0	-18.0
69	132.0	15.0	58.0

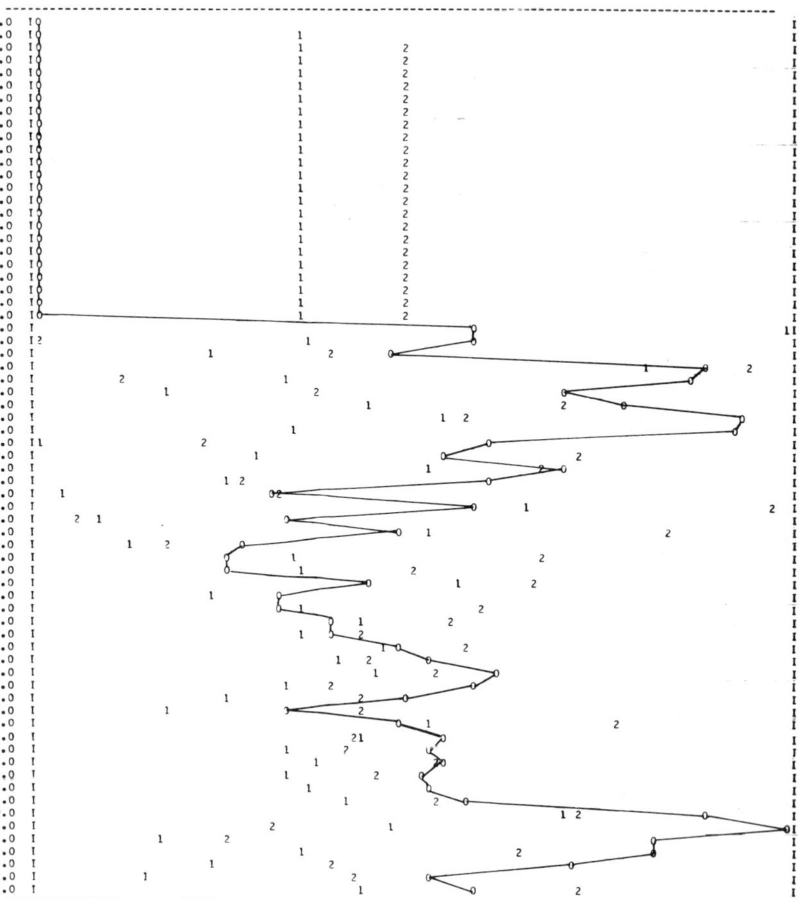

BOUNDS ON VALUES ARE 0.00 224.00
BOUNDS ON FIRST DIFFERENCES ARE -73.00 130.00
BOUNDS ON SECOND DIFFERENCES ARE -128.00 130.00
0 VALUE 1 FIRST DIFFERENCE 2 SECOND DIFFERENCE

V.C. Abductions of Civilians

MON	VALUE	1ST D	2ND D
1	500.0	0.0	0.0
2	392.0	-108.0	0.0
3	672.0	280.0	388.0
4	867.0	195.0	-85.0
5	600.0	-267.0	-462.0
6	1632.0	1032.0	1299.0
7	1072.0	-560.0	-1592.0
8	370.0	-702.0	-142.0
9	480.0	110.0	812.0
10	676.0	196.0	86.0
11	504.0	-172.0	-368.0
12	441.0	-63.0	109.0
13	241.0	-200.0	-137.0
14	556.0	315.0	515.0
15	408.0	-148.0	-463.0
16	180.0	-228.0	-80.0
17	181.0	1.0	229.0
18	334.0	153.0	152.0
19	41.0	-293.0	-446.0
20	293.0	252.0	545.0
21	219.0	-74.0	-326.0
22	473.0	254.0	328.0
23	503.0	30.0	-224.0
24	345.0	-158.0	-188.0
25	315.0	-30.0	128.0
26	358.0	43.0	73.0
27	203.0	-155.0	-198.0
28	218.0	15.0	170.0
29	333.0	115.0	100.0
30	429.0	96.0	-19.0
31	225.0	-204.0	-300.0
32	452.0	227.0	431.0
33	967.0	515.0	288.0
34	242.0	-725.0	-1240.0
35	587.0	345.0	1070.0
36	973.0	386.0	41.0
37	833.0	-140.0	-526.0
38	1823.0	990.0	1130.0
39	1096.0	-727.0	-1717.0
40	828.0	-268.0	459.0
41	843.0	15.0	283.0
42	588.0	-255.0	-270.0
43	512.0	-76.0	179.0
44	415.0	-97.0	-21.0
45	952.0	537.0	634.0
46	1384.0	432.0	-105.0
47	430.0	-954.0	-1386.0
48	685.0	255.0	1209.0
49	1342.0	657.0	402.0
50	659.0	-683.0	-1340.0
51	1178.0	519.0	1202.0
52	628.0	-550.0	-1069.0
53	313.0	-315.0	235.0
54	504.0	191.0	506.0
55	220.0	-284.0	-475.0
56	415.0	195.0	479.0
57	288.0	-127.0	-322.0
58	187.0	-101.0	26.0
59	282.0	95.0	196.0
60	149.0	-133.0	-228.0
61	257.0	108.0	241.0
62	596.0	339.0	231.0
63	889.0	293.0	-46.0
64	889.0	0.0	-293.0
65	1035.0	146.0	146.0
66	740.0	-295.0	-441.0
67	517.0	-223.0	72.0
68	372.0	-145.0	78.0
69	337.0	-35.0	110.0

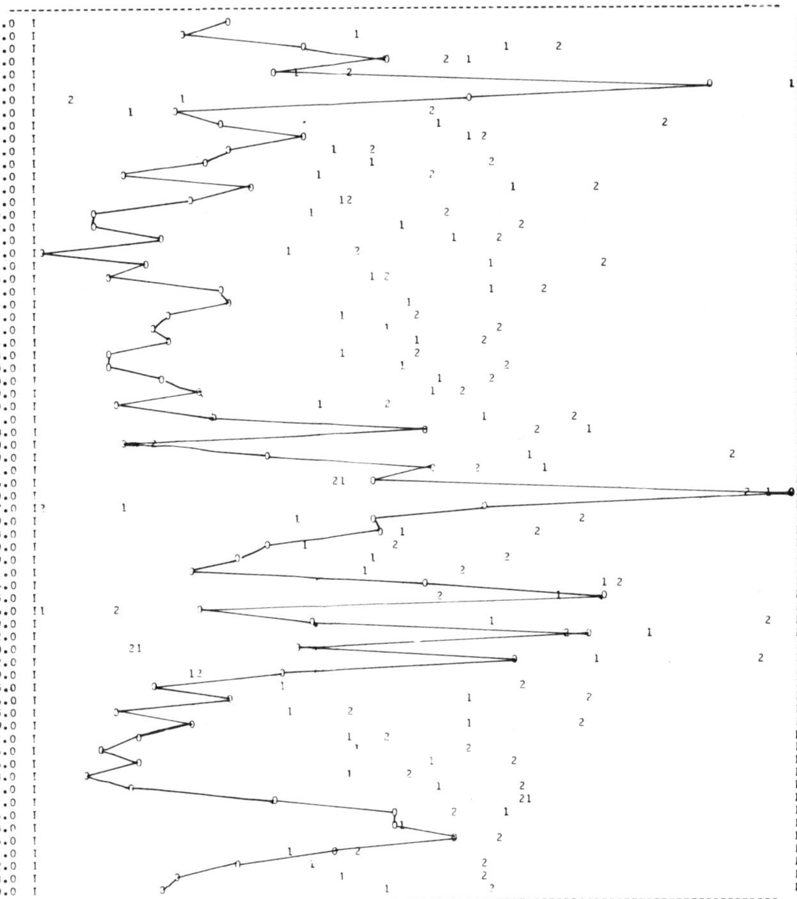

BOUNDS ON VALUES ARE 41.00 1823.00
BOUNDS ON FIRST DIFFERENCES ARE -954.00 1032.00
BOUNDS ON SECOND DIFFERENCES ARE -1717.00 1299.00
0 VALUE 1 FIRST DIFFERENCE 2 SECOND DIFFERENCE

U.S. Casualties

MON	VALUE	1ST D	2ND D
1	200.5	0.0	0.0
2	638.0	437.5	0.0
3	209.0	-429.0	-866.5
4	503.0	294.0	723.0
5	446.0	-57.0	-351.0
6	912.5	466.5	523.5
7	1010.0	97.5	-369.0
8	1276.5	266.5	169.0
9	1361.5	85.0	-181.5
10	2286.0	924.5	839.5
11	5770.5	3484.5	2560.0
12	3536.5	-2234.0	-5718.5
13	3777.5	241.0	2475.0
14	6252.0	2474.5	2233.5
15	7217.0	965.0	-1509.5
16	4970.0	-2247.0	-3212.0
17	6727.5	1757.5	4004.5
18	7085.5	358.0	-1399.5
19	6031.5	-1054.0	-1412.0
20	5745.0	-296.5	767.5
21	6105.5	360.5	647.0
22	4986.0	-1119.5	-1480.0
23	6928.5	1942.5	3062.0
24	6084.0	-844.5	-2787.0
25	7745.0	1661.0	2505.5
26	9462.5	1717.5	56.5
27	14098.0	4635.5	2918.0
28	10763.0	-3335.0	-7970.5
29	18534.0	7771.0	11106.0
30	11950.5	-6583.5	-14354.5
31	11864.0	-86.5	6497.0
32	8755.5	-3108.5	-3022.0
33	13116.5	4361.0	7469.5
34	10313.5	-2803.0	-7164.0
35	11750.0	1436.5	4239.5
36	11267.0	-483.0	-1919.5

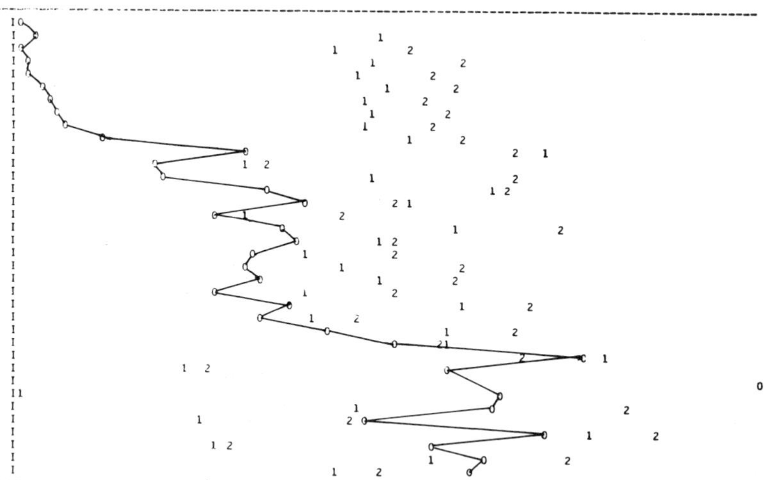

BOUNDS ON VALUES ARE 200.50 18534.00
BOUNDS ON FIRST DIFFERENCES ARE -6583.50 7771.00
BOUNDS ON SECOND DIFFEREENCES ARE -14354.50 11106.00
0 VALUE 1 FIRST DIFFERENCE 2 SECOND DIFFERENCE

U.S. Troops Killed in Action

MON	VALUE	1ST D	2ND D
1	12.0	0.0	0.0
2	48.0	36.0	0.0
3	15.0	-33.0	-69.0
4	41.0	26.0	59.0
5	31.0	-10.0	-36.0
6	71.0	40.0	50.0
7	74.0	3.0	-37.0
8	85.0	11.0	8.0
9	97.0	12.0	1.0
10	164.0	67.0	55.0
11	469.0	305.0	238.0
12	246.0	-223.0	-528.0
13	273.0	27.0	250.0
14	466.0	193.0	166.0
15	491.0	25.0	-168.0
16	316.0	-175.0	-200.0
17	449.0	133.0	308.0
18	507.0	58.0	-75.0
19	421.0	-86.0	-144.0
20	383.0	-38.0	48.0
21	419.0	36.0	74.0
22	329.0	-90.0	-126.0
23	475.0	146.0	236.0
24	418.0	-57.0	-203.0
25	503.0	85.0	142.0
26	709.0	206.0	121.0
27	914.0	205.0	-1.0
28	710.0	-204.0	-409.0
29	1193.0	483.0	687.0
30	830.0	-363.0	-846.0
31	756.0	-74.0	289.0
32	518.0	-238.0	-164.0
33	775.0	257.0	495.0
34	709.0	-56.0	-323.0
35	881.0	172.0	238.0
36	749.0	-132.0	-304.0
37	1163.0	414.0	546.0
38	2197.0	1034.0	620.0
39	1493.0	-704.0	-1738.0
40	1410.0	-83.0	621.0
41	2099.0	689.0	772.0
42	1146.0	-953.0	-1642.0
43	787.0	-359.0	594.0
44	1052.0	265.0	624.0
45	1053.0	1.0	-264.0
46	581.0	-472.0	-473.0
47	703.0	122.0	594.0
48	723.0	20.0	-102.0
49	769.0	46.0	26.0
50	1150.0	381.0	335.0
51	1274.0	124.0	-257.0
52	847.0	-427.0	-551.0
53	1170.0	323.0	750.0
54	1100.0	-70.0	-393.0
55	617.0	-483.0	-413.0
56	769.0	152.0	635.0
57	477.0	-292.0	-444.0
58	365.0	-112.0	180.0
59	446.0	81.0	193.0
60	330.0	-116.0	-197.0
61	332.0	2.0	118.0
62	415.0	83.0	81.0
63	434.0	19.0	-64.0
64	526.0	92.0	73.0
65	729.0	203.0	111.0
66	418.0	-311.0	-514.0
67	321.0	-97.0	214.0
68	308.0	-13.0	84.0
69	219.0	-89.0	-76.0

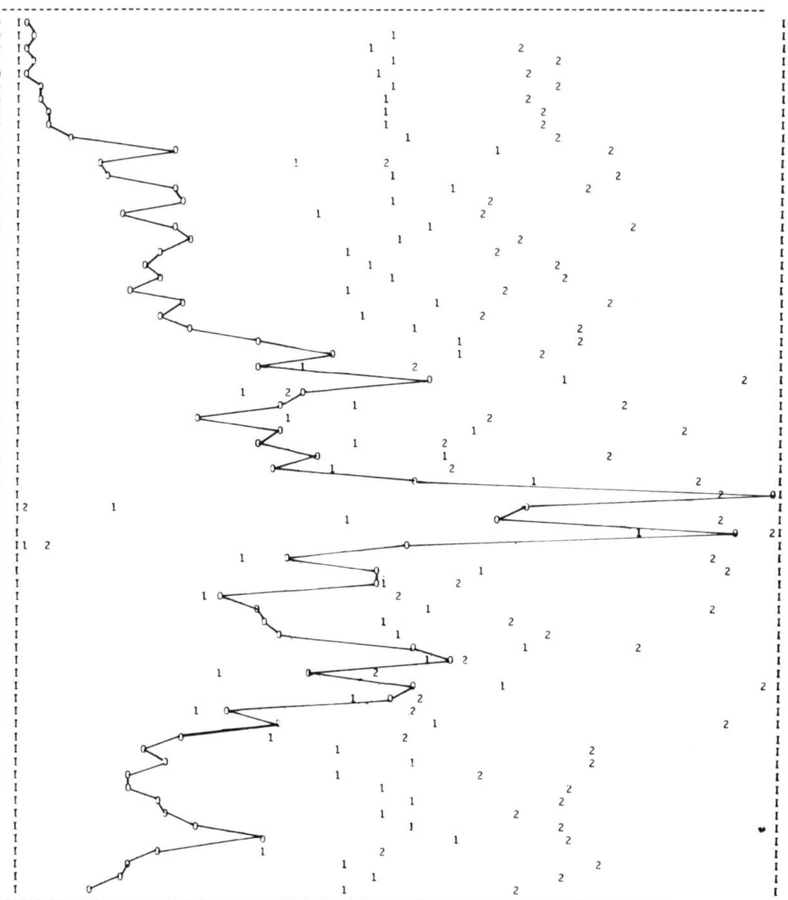

BOUNDS ON VALUES ARE 12.00 2197.00
BOUNDS ON FIRST DIFFERENCES ARE -953.00 1034.00
BOUNDS ON SECOND DIFFEREENCES ARE -1738.00 772.00
0 VALUE 1 FIRST DIFFERENCE 2 SECOND DIFFERENCE

S.V. Troops Killed in Action

MON	VALUE	1ST D	2ND D
1	875.0	0.0	0.0
2	943.0	68.0	0.0
3	727.0	-216.0	-284.0
4	591.0	-136.0	80.0
5	1015.0	424.0	560.0
6	1211.0	196.0	-228.0
7	1123.0	-88.0	-284.0
8	782.0	-341.0	-253.0
9	655.0	-127.0	214.0
10	930.0	275.0	402.0
11	1034.0	104.0	-171.0
12	1199.0	165.0	61.0
13	723.0	-476.0	-641.0
14	1089.0	366.0	842.0
15	908.0	-181.0	-547.0
16	574.0	-334.0	-153.0
17	640.0	66.0	400.0
18	860.0	220.0	154.0
19	832.0	-28.0	-248.0
20	699.0	-133.0	-105.0
21	566.0	-133.0	-0.0
22	877.0	311.0	444.0
23	804.0	-73.0	-384.0
24	789.0	-15.0	58.0
25	885.0	96.0	111.0
26	948.0	63.0	-33.0
27	1255.0	307.0	244.0
28	1057.0	-198.0	-505.0
29	1146.0	89.0	287.0
30	981.0	-165.0	-254.0
31	654.0	-327.0	-162.0
32	1034.0	380.0	707.0
33	1090.0	56.0	-324.0
34	1032.0	-58.0	-114.0
35	1299.0	267.0	325.0
36	1160.0	-139.0	-406.0
37	2811.0	1651.0	1790.0
38	5198.0	2387.0	736.0
39	2487.0	-2711.0	-5098.0
40	1922.0	-565.0	2146.0
41	3355.0	1433.0	1998.0
42	1974.0	-1381.0	-2814.0
43	1364.0	-610.0	771.0
44	2316.0	952.0	1562.0
45	2164.0	-152.0	-1104.0
46	1131.0	-1033.0	-881.0
47	1408.0	277.0	1310.0
48	1460.0	52.0	-225.0
49	1610.0	150.0	98.0
50	2220.0	610.0	460.0
51	2115.0	-105.0	-715.0
52	1710.0	-405.0	-300.0
53	2178.0	468.0	873.0
54	1867.0	-311.0	-779.0
55	1408.0	-459.0	-148.0
56	1540.0	132.0	591.0
57	1014.0	-526.0	-658.0
58	1545.0	531.0	1057.0
59	2068.0	523.0	-8.0
60	1017.0	-1051.0	-1574.0
61	1437.0	420.0	1471.0
62	886.0	-551.0	-971.0
63	1559.0	673.0	1224.0
64	1602.0	43.0	-630.0
65	2497.0	895.0	852.0
66	1998.0	-499.0	-1394.0
67	1572.0	-426.0	73.0
68	1280.0	-292.0	134.0
69	974.0	-306.0	-14.0

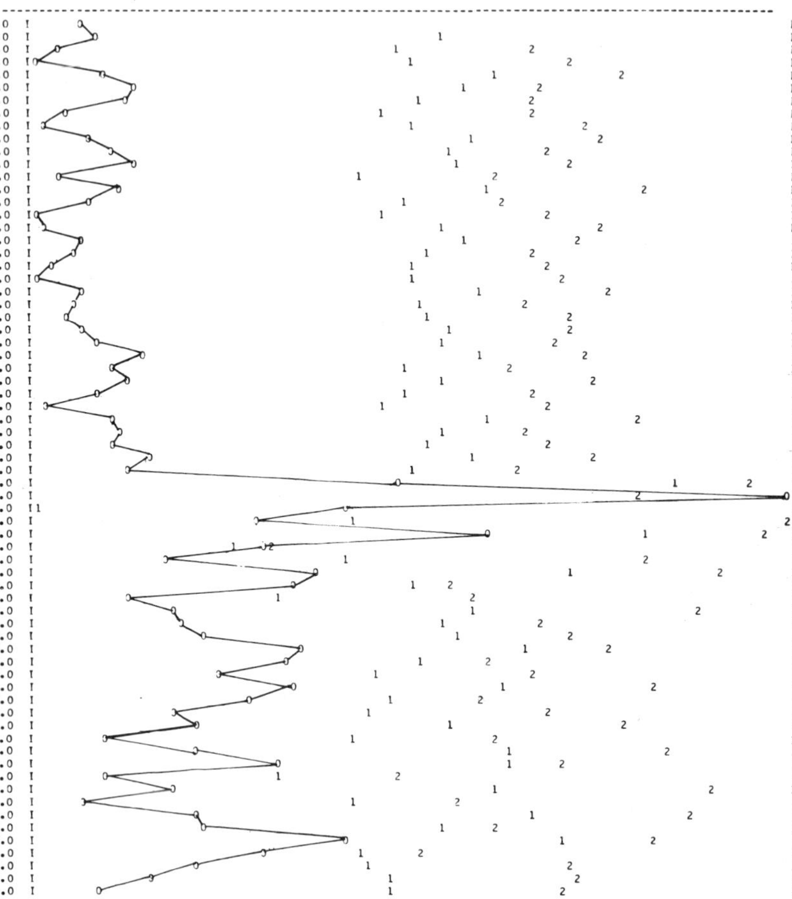

BOUNDS ON VALUES ARE 566.00 5198.00
BOUNDS ON FIRST DIFFERENCES ARE -2711.00 2387.00
BOUNDS ON SECOND DIFFEREENCES ARE -5098.00 2146.00
0 VALUE 1 FIRST DIFFERENCE 2 SECOND DIFFERENCE

S.V. Casualties

MON	VALUE	1ST D	2ND D
1	1174.0	0.0	0.0
2	1150.0	-24.0	0.0
3	976.0	-174.0	-150.0
4	846.0	-130.0	44.0
5	1319.0	473.0	603.0
6	1556.0	237.0	-236.0
7	1400.0	-156.0	-393.0
8	1108.0	-292.0	-136.0
9	955.0	-153.0	139.0
10	1291.0	336.0	489.0
11	1364.0	73.0	-263.0
12	1494.0	130.0	57.0
13	980.5	-513.5	-643.5
14	1330.2	349.7	863.2
15	1232.1	-98.1	-447.8
16	802.3	-429.8	-331.7
17	879.1	76.6	506.6
18	1130.0	250.9	174.1
19	1105.8	-24.2	-275.1
20	945.6	-160.2	-136.0
21	799.1	-146.5	13.7
22	1223.7	424.6	571.1
23	1093.9	-129.8	-554.4
24	1092.6	-1.3	128.5
25	1192.2	99.6	100.9
26	1089.7	-102.5	-202.1
27	1535.9	446.2	548.7
28	1308.5	-227.4	-673.6
29	1450.5	142.0	369.4
30	1088.7	-361.8	-503.8
31	956.2	-132.5	229.3
32	1194.1	237.9	370.4
33	1102.4	-91.7	-329.6
34	1106.2	3.8	95.5
35	1559.3	453.1	449.3
36	1713.2	153.9	-299.2

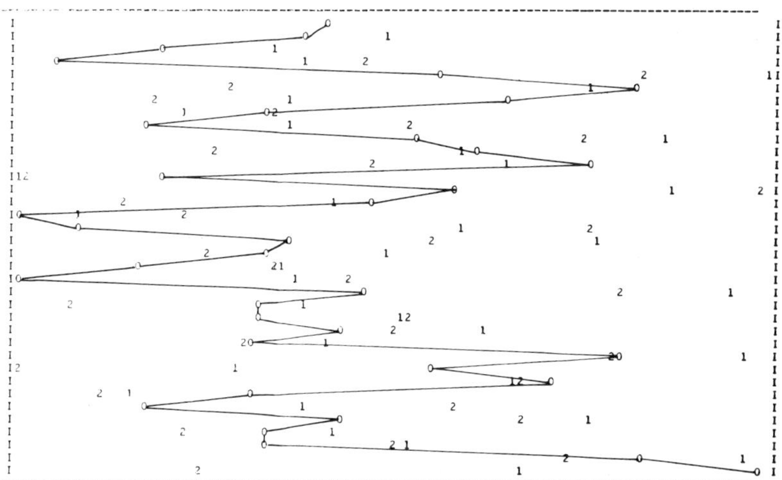

BOUNDS ON VALUES ARE 799.10 1713.20
BOUNDS ON FIRST DIFFERENCES ARE -513.50 473.00
BOUNDS ON SECOND DIFFERENCES ARE -673.60 863.20
0 VALUE 1 FIRST DIFFERENCE 2 SECOND DIFFERENCE

"Vietnamization" (U.S. KIA/S.V. KIA)

MON	VALUE	1ST D	2ND D
1	137.0	0.0	0.0
2	509.0	372.0	0.0
3	206.0	-303.0	-675.0
4	694.0	488.0	791.0
5	305.0	-389.0	-877.0
6	586.0	281.0	670.0
7	659.0	73.0	-208.0
8	1087.0	428.0	355.0
9	1481.0	394.0	-34.0
10	1763.0	282.0	-112.0
11	4536.0	2773.0	2491.0
12	2052.0	-2484.0	-5257.0
13	3776.0	1724.0	4208.0
14	4283.0	507.0	-1217.0
15	5407.0	1124.0	617.0
16	5505.0	98.0	-1026.0
17	7016.0	1511.0	1413.0
18	5895.0	-1121.0	-2632.0
19	5056.0	-839.0	282.0
20	5479.0	423.0	1262.0
21	7403.0	1924.0	1501.0
22	3751.0	-3652.0	-5576.0
23	5908.0	2157.0	5809.0
24	5298.0	-610.0	-2767.0
25	5684.0	386.0	996.0
26	7449.0	1765.0	1379.0
27	7293.0	-156.0	-1931.0
28	6717.0	-556.0	-400.0
29	10410.0	3693.0	4259.0
30	8461.0	-1949.0	-5642.0
31	11560.0	3099.0	5048.0
32	5010.0	-6550.0	-9649.0
33	7110.0	2100.0	8650.0
34	6870.0	-240.0	-2340.0
35	6782.0	-88.0	152.0
36	6457.0	-325.0	-237.0
37	4137.0	-2320.0	-1995.0
38	4227.0	90.0	2410.0
39	6003.0	1776.0	1686.0
40	7336.0	1333.0	-443.0
41	6256.0	-1080.0	-2413.0
42	5805.0	-451.0	629.0
43	5770.0	-35.0	416.0
44	4542.0	-1228.0	-1193.0
45	4866.0	324.0	1552.0
46	5137.0	271.0	-53.0
47	4993.0	-144.0	-415.0
48	4952.0	-41.0	103.0
49	4776.0	-176.0	-135.0
50	5180.0	404.0	580.0
51	6024.0	844.0	440.0
52	4953.0	-1071.0	-1915.0
53	5372.0	419.0	1490.0
54	5892.0	520.0	101.0
55	4382.0	-1510.0	-2030.0
56	4994.0	612.0	2122.0
57	4704.0	-290.0	-902.0
58	2362.0	-2342.0	-2052.0
59	2157.0	-205.0	2137.0
60	3245.0	1088.0	1293.0
61	2310.0	-935.0	-2023.0
62	4684.0	2374.0	3309.0
63	2784.0	-1900.0	-4274.0
64	3283.0	499.0	2399.0
65	2912.0	-371.0	-870.0
65	2091.0	-821.0	-450.0
67	2042.0	-49.0	772.0
68	2406.0	364.0	413.0
69	2249.0	-157.0	-521.0

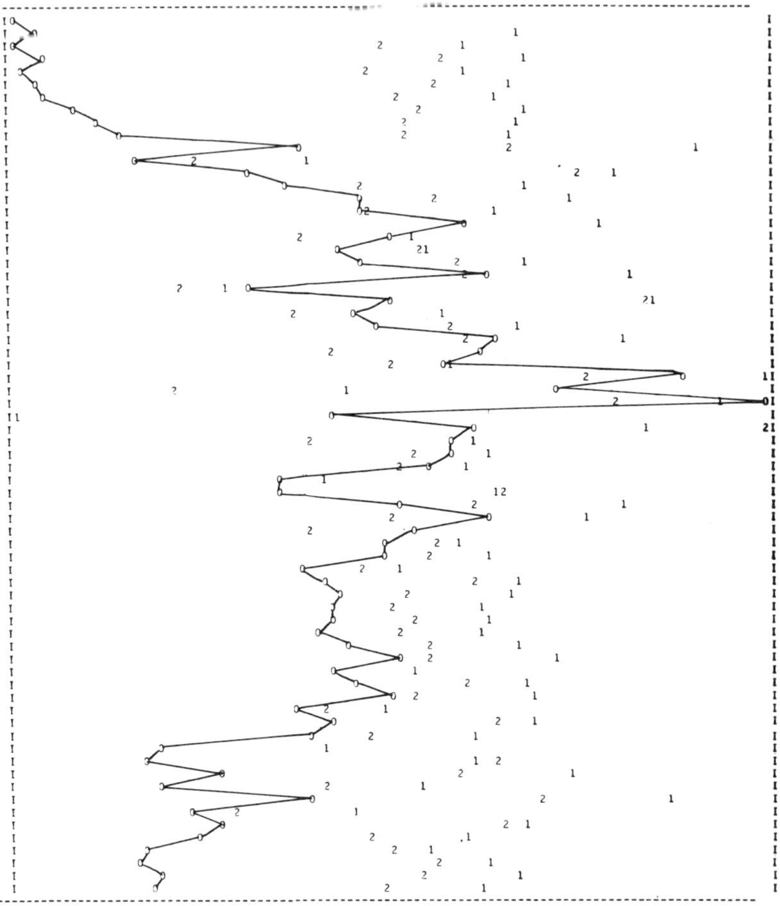

BOUNDS ON VALUES ARE 137.00 11560.00
BOUNDS ON FIRST DIFFERENCES ARE -6550.00 3693.00
BOUNDS ON SECOND DIFFEREENCES ARE -9649.00 8650.00
0 VALUE 1 FIRST DIFFERENCE 2 SECOND DIFFERENCE

N.V. + V.C. Troops Killed in Action

MON	VALUE	1ST D	2ND D
1	2131.0	0.0	0.0
2	1675.0	-456.0	0.0
3	1956.0	281.0	737.0
4	1909.0	-47.0	-328.0
5	1911.0	2.0	49.0
6	2208.0	297.0	295.0
7	2883.0	675.0	378.0
8	3507.0	624.0	-51.0
9	3485.0	-22.0	-646.0
10	3749.0	264.0	286.0
11	5516.0	1767.0	1503.0
12	3944.0	-1572.0	-3339.0
13	2562.0	-1382.0	190.0
14	5064.0	2502.0	3884.0
15	5501.0	437.0	-2065.0
16	2818.0	-2683.0	-3120.0
17	4102.0	1284.0	3967.0
18	4815.0	713.0	-571.0
19	5126.0	311.0	-402.0
20	5570.0	544.0	233.0
21	4459.0	-1211.0	-1755.0
22	5482.0	1023.0	2234.0
23	5447.0	-35.0	-1058.0
24	3739.0	-1708.0	-1673.0
25	5868.0	2129.0	3837.0
26	7865.0	1997.0	-132.0
27	9049.0	1184.0	-813.0
28	6227.0	-2822.0	-4006.0
29	9491.0	3264.0	6086.0
30	7354.0	-2137.0	-5401.0
31	7667.0	313.0	2450.0
32	5622.0	-2045.0	-2358.0
33	6354.0	732.0	2777.0
34	6069.0	-285.0	-1017.0
35	7662.0	1593.0	1878.0
36	7681.0	19.0	-1574.0
37	14726.0	7045.0	7026.0
38	41241.0	26515.0	19470.0
39	16762.0	-24479.0	-50994.0
40	12215.0	-4547.0	19932.0
41	23309.0	11094.0	15641.0
42	10319.0	-12990.0	-24084.0
43	6438.0	-3881.0	9109.0
44	14978.0	9540.0	12421.0
45	12535.0	-2443.0	-10983.0
46	7904.0	-4631.0	-2188.0
47	9632.0	1728.0	6359.0
48	9290.0	-342.0	-2070.0
49	10601.0	1311.0	1653.0
50	15092.0	4491.0	3180.0
51	19166.0	4074.0	-417.0
52	14539.0	-4627.0	-8701.0
53	16880.0	2341.0	6968.0
54	16825.0	-55.0	-2396.0
55	9906.0	-6919.0	-6864.0
56	11973.0	2057.0	8986.0
57	10369.0	-1604.0	-3671.0
58	8465.0	-1904.0	-300.0
59	11639.0	3174.0	5078.0
60	9615.0	-2024.0	-5198.0
61	8891.0	-724.0	1300.0
62	9459.0	568.0	1292.0
63	10001.0	542.0	-26.0
64	13063.0	3062.0	2520.0
65	16699.0	3636.0	574.0
66	7861.0	-8838.0	-12474.0
67	6951.0	-910.0	7928.0
68	6237.0	-714.0	196.0
69	6139.0	-99.0	615.0

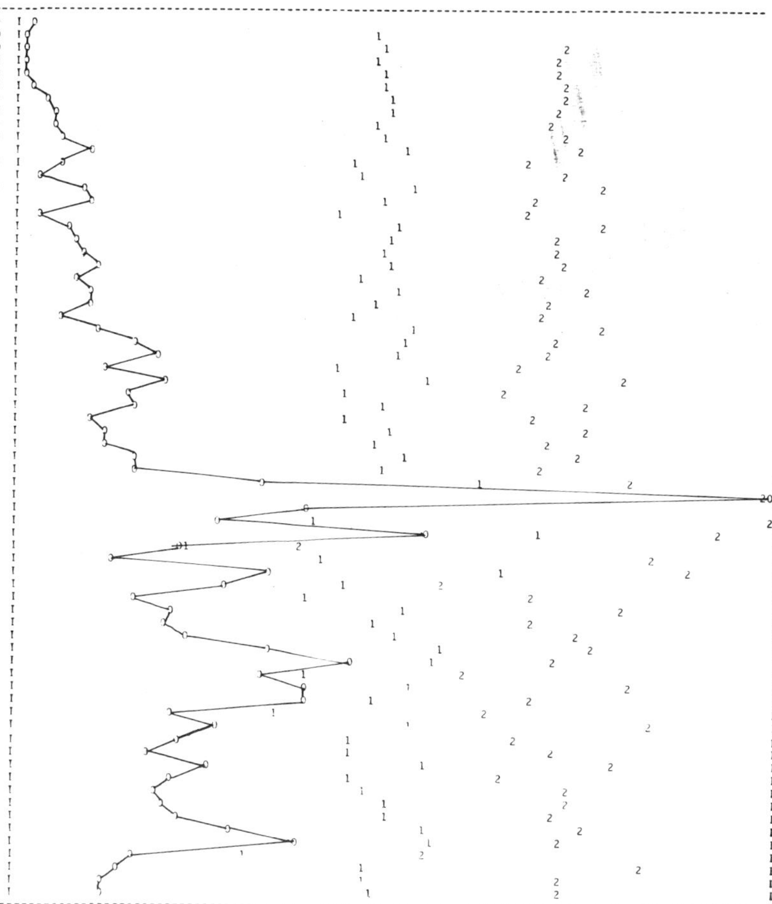

OUNDS ON VALUES ARE 1675.00 41241.00
OUNDS ON FIRST DIFFERENCES ARE -24479.00 26515.00
OUNDS ON SECOND DIFFERENCES ARE -50994.00 19932.00
0 VALUE 1 FIRST DIFFERENCE 2 SECOND DIFFERENCE

N.V. + V. C. Attrition

MON	VALUE	1ST D	2ND D
1	8248.0	0.0	0.0
2	6174.0	-2074.0	0.0
3	7276.0	1102.0	3176.0
4	8552.0	1276.0	174.0
5	7949.0	-603.0	-1879.0
6	7932.0	-17.0	586.0
7	10516.0	2584.0	2601.0
8	12752.0	2236.0	-348.0
9	12111.0	-641.0	-2877.0
10	13441.0	1330.0	1971.0
11	20916.0	7475.0	6145.0
12	14078.0	-6838.0	-14313.0
13	10547.0	-3531.0	3307.0
14	15718.0	5171.0	8702.0
15	20876.0	5158.0	-13.0
16	10258.0	-10618.0	-15776.0
17	14555.0	4297.0	14915.0
18	24303.0	9748.0	5451.0
19	17793.0	-6510.0	-16258.0
20	19847.0	2054.0	8564.0
21	16439.0	-3408.0	-5462.0
22	22558.0	6119.0	9527.0
23	18592.0	-3966.0	-10085.0
24	15230.0	-3362.0	604.0
25	23257.0	8027.0	11389.0
26	26259.0	3002.0	-5025.0
27	38687.0	12428.0	9426.0
28	25302.0	-13385.0	-25813.0
29	37854.0	12552.0	25937.0
30	30445.0	-7409.0	-19961.0
31	38693.0	8248.0	15657.0
32	25482.0	-13211.0	-21459.0
33	25995.0	513.0	13724.0
34	31025.0	5030.0	4517.0
35	32110.0	1085.0	-3945.0
36	32379.0	269.0	-816.0

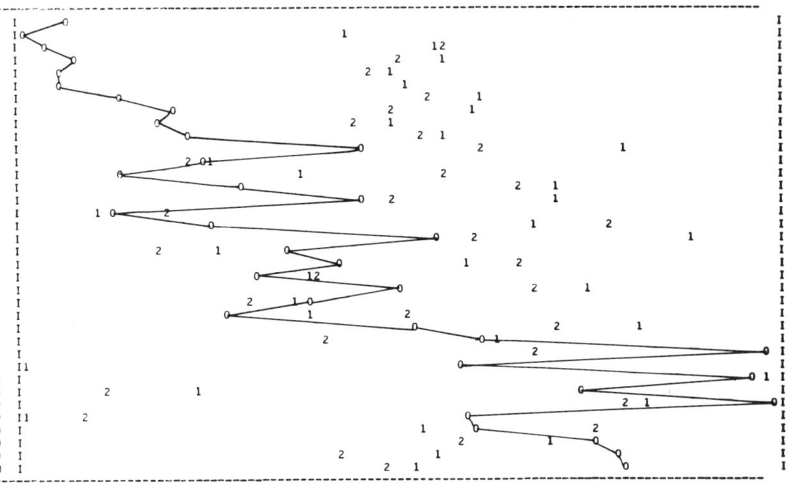

BOUNDS ON VALUES ARE 6174.00 38693.00
BOUNDS ON FIRST DIFFERENCES ARE -13385.00 12552.00
BOUNDS ON SECOND DIFFEREENCES ARE -25813.00 25937.00
0 VALUE 1 FIRST DIFFERENCE 2 SECOND DIFFERENCE

Kill Ratio (U.S. + S.V./N.V. + V.C.) x 10

MON	VALUE	1ST D	2ND D
1	24.0	0.0	0.0
2	16.9	-7.1	0.0
3	26.4	9.5	16.6
4	30.2	3.8	-5.7
5	18.3	-11.9	-15.7
6	17.2	-1.0	10.9
7	24.1	6.9	7.9
8	40.4	16.3	9.4
9	46.3	5.9	-10.4
10	34.3	-12.1	-18.0
11	36.7	2.4	14.5
12	27.3	-9.4	-11.8
13	25.7	-1.6	7.8
14	32.6	6.8	8.4
15	39.3	6.8	-0.1
16	31.7	-7.7	-14.4
17	37.7	6.0	13.7
18	35.2	-2.5	-8.5
19	40.9	5.7	8.1
20	52.4	11.5	5.8
21	45.3	-7.1	-18.7
22	45.5	0.2	7.3
23	42.6	-2.9	-3.1
24	31.0	-11.6	-8.7
25	43.1	12.1	23.7
26	51.2	8.1	-4.0
27	45.3	-5.9	-14.0
28	37.9	-7.5	-1.6
29	43.4	5.6	13.1
30	45.9	2.5	-3.0
31	54.8	8.8	6.3
32	41.9	-12.9	-21.7
33	41.9	0.1	12.9
34	42.2	0.3	0.2
35	38.4	-3.8	-4.0
36	39.2	0.8	4.6

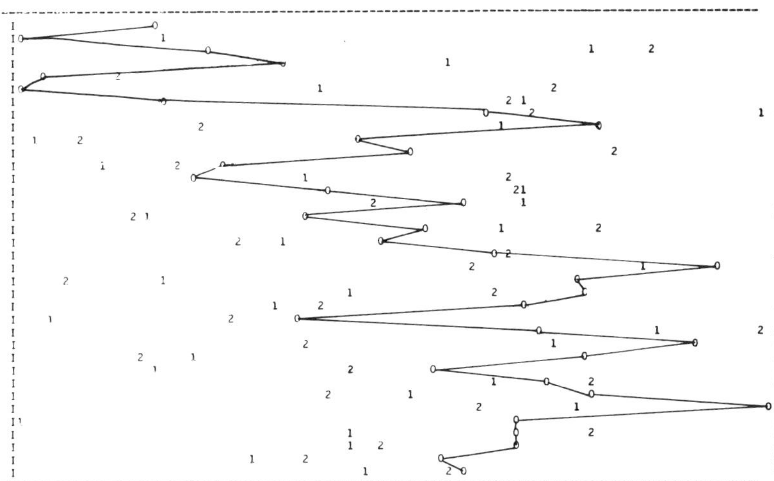

BOUNDS ON VALUES ARE 16.91 54.76
BOUNDS ON FIRST DIFFERENCES ARE -12.87 16.34
BOUNDS ON SECOND DIFFEREENCES ARE -21.69 23.71
0 VALUE 1 FIRST DIFFERENCE 2 SECOND DIFFERENCE

N.V. + V.C. Weapons Captured

MON	VALUE	1ST D	2ND D
1	700.0	0.0	0.0
2	701.0	1.0	0.0
3	589.0	-112.0	-113.0
4	1088.0	499.0	611.0
5	795.0	-293.0	-792.0
6	725.0	-70.0	223.0
7	845.0	120.0	190.0
8	995.0	150.0	30.0
9	855.0	-140.0	-290.0
10	999.0	144.0	284.0
11	2178.0	1179.0	1035.0
12	1088.0	-1090.0	-2269.0
13	1077.0	-11.0	1079.0
14	1212.0	135.0	146.0
15	1955.0	743.0	608.0
16	910.0	-1045.0	-1788.0
17	1066.0	156.0	1201.0
18	3838.0	2772.0	2616.0
19	1325.0	-2513.0	-5285.0
20	1380.0	55.0	2568.0
21	1482.0	102.0	47.0
22	1922.0	440.0	338.0
23	1397.0	-525.0	-965.0
24	1571.0	174.0	699.0
25	2284.0	713.0	539.0
26	2566.0	282.0	-431.0
27	3703.0	1137.0	855.0
28	2118.0	-1585.0	-2722.0
29	2691.0	573.0	2158.0
30	1979.0	-712.0	-1285.0
31	3395.0	1416.0	2128.0
32	2001.0	-1394.0	-2810.0
33	1877.0	-124.0	1270.0
34	3196.0	1319.0	1443.0
35	2579.0	-617.0	-1936.0
36	2326.0	-253.0	364.0
37	4052.0	1726.0	1979.0
38	8976.0	4924.0	3198.0
39	4485.0	-4491.0	-9415.0
40	5351.0	356.0	5357.0
41	8395.0	3044.0	2178.0
42	5259.0	-3136.0	-6180.0
43	2642.0	-2617.0	519.0
44	5600.0	2958.0	5575.0
45	4643.0	-957.0	-3915.0
46	3793.0	-850.0	107.0
47	3906.0	113.0	963.0
48	3983.0	77.0	-36.0
49	5423.0	1440.0	1363.0
50	6501.0	1078.0	-362.0
51	7498.0	997.0	-81.0
52	7290.0	-208.0	-1205.0
53	6826.0	-464.0	-256.0
54	6149.0	-677.0	-213.0
55	4445.0	-1704.0	-1027.0
56	4217.0	-228.0	1476.0
57	3698.0	-519.0	-291.0
58	3924.0	226.0	745.0
59	3835.0	-89.0	-315.0
60	4192.0	357.0	446.0
61	3830.0	-362.0	-719.0
62	5746.0	1916.0	2278.0
63	4189.0	-1557.0	-3473.0
64	5932.0	1743.0	3300.0
65	18503.0	12571.0	10828.0
66	10623.0	-7880.0	-20451.0
67	4080.0	-6543.0	1337.0
68	3453.0	-627.0	5916.0
69	2478.0	-975.0	-348.0

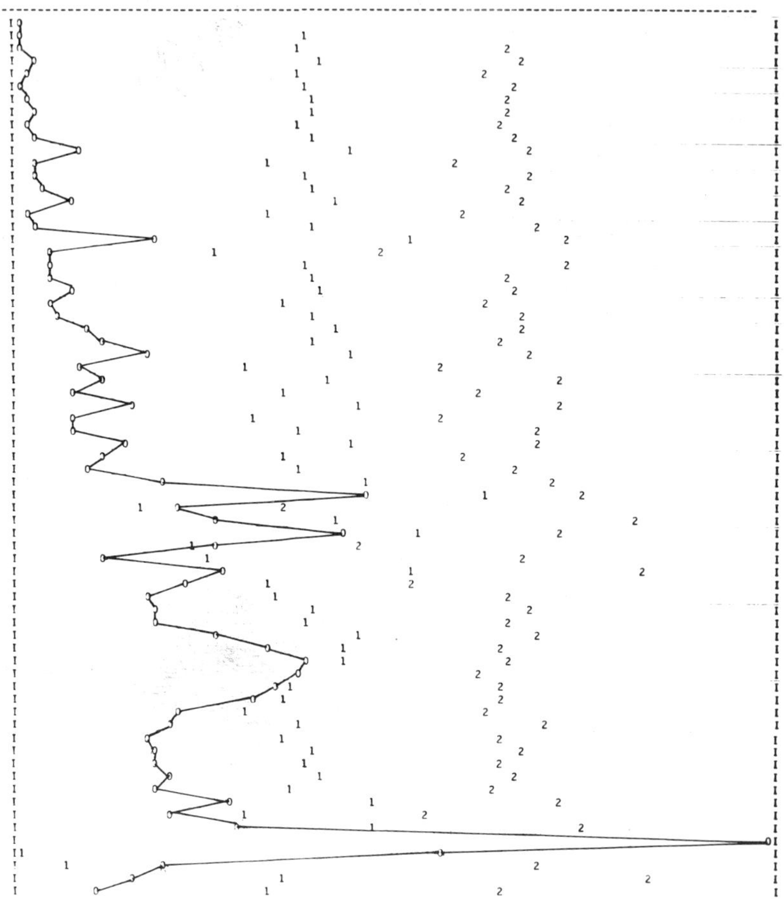

BOUNDS ON VALUES ARE 589.00 18503.00
BOUNDS ON FIRST DIFFERENCES ARE -7880.00 12571.00
BOUNDS ON SECOND DIFFEREENCES ARE -20451.00 10828.00
0 VALUE 1 FIRST DIFFERENCE 2 SECOND DIFFERENCE

U.S. Public Disapproval of the President

MON	VALUE	1ST D	2ND D
1	16.0	0.0	0.0
2	15.0	-1.0	0.0
3	21.0	6.0	7.0
4	22.0	1.0	-5.0
5	22.0	0.0	-1.0
6	18.0	-4.0	-4.0
7	19.0	1.0	5.0
8	20.0	1.0	0.0
9	22.0	2.0	1.0
10	24.0	2.0	0.0
11	22.0	-2.0	-4.0
12	22.0	0.0	2.0
13	26.0	4.0	4.0
14	27.0	1.0	-3.0
15	28.0	1.0	0.0
16	28.0	0.0	-1.0
17	33.0	5.0	5.0
18	33.0	0.0	-5.0
19	30.0	-3.0	-3.0
20	38.0	8.0	11.0
21	38.0	0.0	-8.0
22	42.0	4.0	4.0
23	41.0	-1.0	-5.0
24	42.0	1.0	2.0
25	37.0	-5.0	-6.0
26	37.0	0.0	5.0
27	42.0	5.0	5.0
28	38.0	-4.0	-9.0
29	39.0	1.0	5.0
30	35.0	-4.0	-5.0
31	35.0	0.0	4.0
32	47.0	12.0	12.0
33	47.0	0.0	-12.0
34	50.0	3.0	3.0
35	49.0	-1.0	-4.0
36	41.0	-8.0	-7.0
37	39.0	-2.0	6.0
38	39.0	0.0	2.0
39	52.0	13.0	13.0
40	40.0	-12.0	-25.0
41	45.0	5.0	17.0
42	45.0	0.0	-5.0
43	48.0	3.0	3.0
44	52.0	4.0	1.0
45	52.0	0.0	-4.0
46	51.0	-1.0	-1.0
47	44.0	-7.0	-6.0
48	43.0	-1.0	6.0
49	5.0	-38.0	-37.0
50	6.0	1.0	39.0
51	10.0	4.0	3.0
52	11.0	1.0	-3.0
53	12.0	1.0	0.0
54	16.0	4.0	3.0
55	17.0	1.0	-3.0
56	20.0	3.0	2.0
57	23.0	3.0	0.0
58	29.0	6.0	3.0
59	19.0	-10.0	-16.0
60	23.0	4.0	14.0
61	23.0	0.0	-4.0
62	27.0	4.0	4.0
63	30.0	3.0	-1.0
64	31.0	1.0	-2.0
65	29.0	-2.0	-3.0
66	31.0	2.0	4.0
67	28.0	-3.0	-5.0
68	32.0	4.0	7.0
69	30.0	-2.0	-6.0

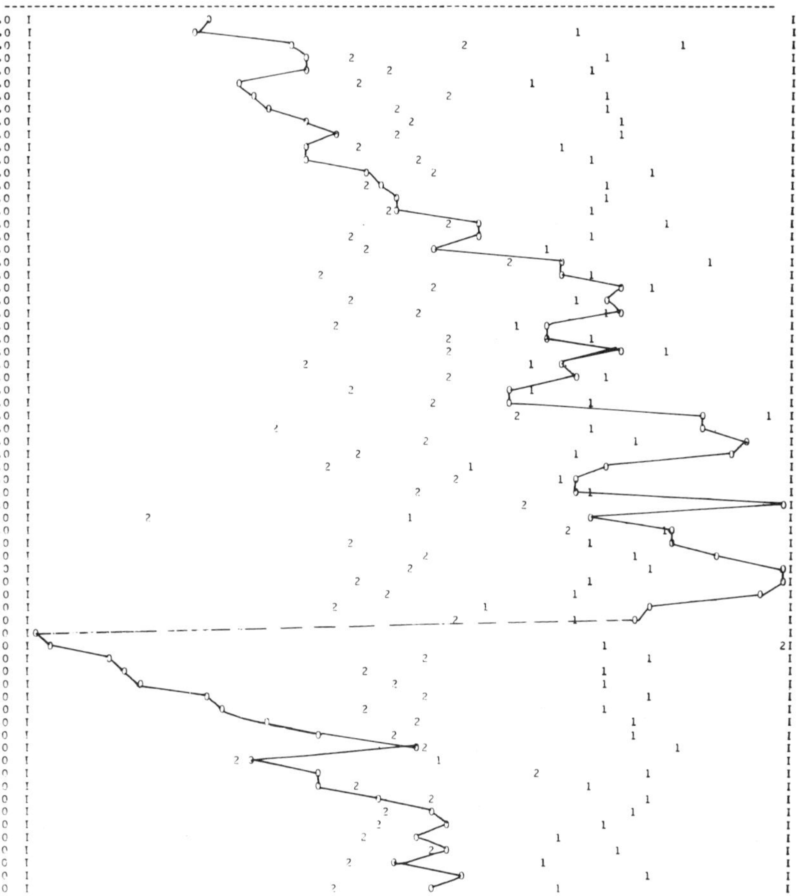

BOUNDS ON VALUES ARE 5.00 52.00
BOUNDS ON FIRST DIFFERENCES ARE -38.00 13.00
BOUNDS ON SECOND DIFFERENCES ARE -37.00 39.00
0 VALUE 1 FIRST DIFFERENCE 2 SECOND DIFFERENCE

U.S. Public Approval of the President

MON	VALUE	1ST D	2ND D
1	71.0	0.0	0.0
2	71.0	0.0	0.0
3	69.0	-2.0	-2.0
4	67.0	-2.0	-0.0
5	64.0	-3.0	-1.0
6	70.0	6.0	9.0
7	69.0	-1.0	-7.0
8	65.0	-4.0	-3.0
9	65.0	0.0	4.0
10	63.0	-2.0	-2.0
11	64.0	1.0	3.0
12	62.0	-2.0	-3.0
13	63.0	1.0	3.0
14	61.0	-2.0	-3.0
15	58.0	-3.0	-1.0
16	57.0	-1.0	2.0
17	54.0	-3.0	-2.0
18	50.0	-4.0	-1.0
19	56.0	6.0	10.0
20	51.0	-5.0	-11.0
21	48.0	-3.0	2.0
22	44.0	-4.0	-1.0
23	44.0	0.0	4.0
24	46.0	2.0	2.0
25	47.0	1.0	-1.0
26	46.0	-1.0	-2.0
27	45.0	-1.0	-0.0
28	46.0	1.0	2.0
29	45.0	-1.0	-2.0
30	52.0	7.0	8.0
31	52.0	0.0	-7.0
32	39.0	-13.0	-13.0
33	39.0	0.0	13.0
34	38.0	-1.0	-1.0
35	41.0	3.0	4.0
36	46.0	5.0	2.0
37	48.0	2.0	-3.0
38	48.0	0.0	-2.0
39	36.0	-12.0	-12.0
40	49.0	13.0	25.0
41	41.0	-8.0	-21.0
42	42.0	1.0	9.0
43	40.0	-2.0	-3.0
44	35.0	-5.0	-3.0
45	35.0	0.0	5.0
46	42.0	7.0	7.0
47	43.0	1.0	-6.0
48	44.0	1.0	0.0
49	59.0	15.0	14.0
50	61.0	2.0	-13.0
51	63.0	2.0	0.0
52	61.0	-2.0	-4.0
53	65.0	4.0	6.0
54	63.0	-2.0	-6.0
55	65.0	2.0	4.0
56	62.0	-3.0	-5.0
57	58.0	-4.0	-1.0
58	56.0	-2.0	2.0
59	68.0	12.0	14.0
60	59.0	-9.0	-21.0
61	66.0	7.0	16.0
62	56.0	-10.0	-17.0
63	53.0	-3.0	7.0
64	56.0	3.0	6.0
65	59.0	3.0	0.0
66	55.0	-4.0	-7.0
67	61.0	6.0	10.0
68	55.0	-6.0	-12.0
69	56.0	1.0	7.0

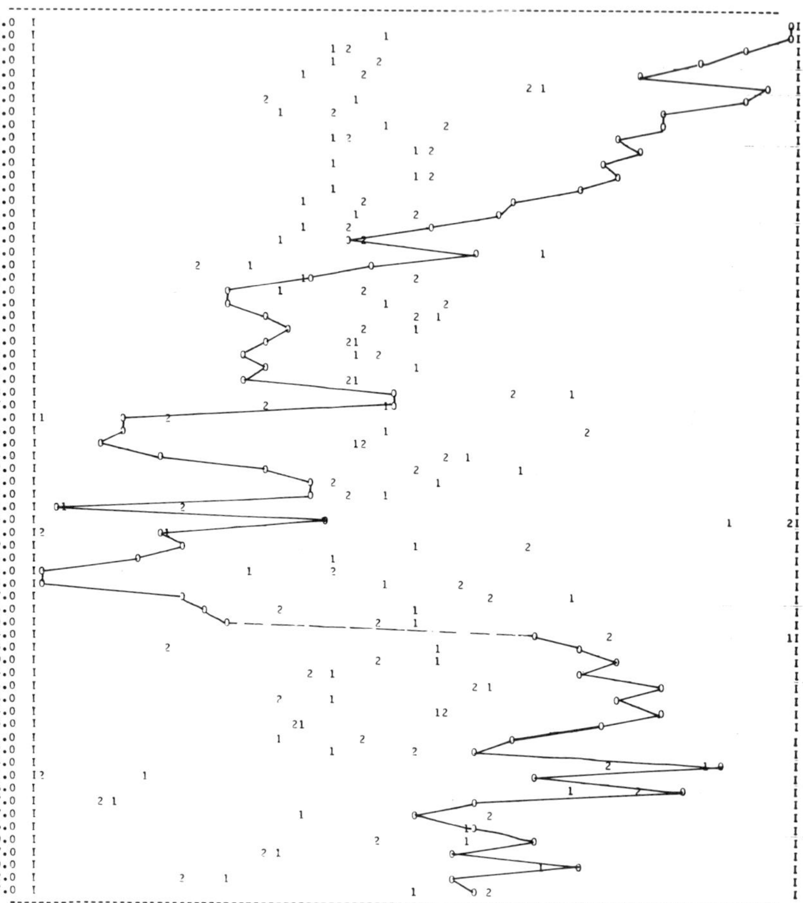

BOUNDS ON VALUES ARE 35.00 71.00
BOUNDS ON FIRST DIFFERENCES ARE -13.00 15.00
BOUNDS ON SECOND DIFFERENCES ARE -21.00 25.00
0 VALUE 1 FIRST DIFFERENCE 2 SECOND DIFFERENCE

S.V. Popular Confidence

MON	VALUE	1ST D	2ND D
1	28664.1	0.0	0.0
2	24996.6	-3557.5	0.0
3	23611.9	-1384.7	2282.8
4	23219.0	-392.9	991.8
5	23320.0	101.0	493.9
6	23056.0	-264.0	-365.0
7	25668.8	2612.8	2876.8
8	24223.4	-1445.4	-4058.2
9	22822.4	-1401.0	44.4
10	19127.3	-3695.1	-2294.1
11	18701.5	-425.7	3269.4
12	17481.8	-1219.8	-794.0
13	18239.7	758.0	1977.7
14	17547.2	-692.5	-1450.5
15	17006.8	-540.3	152.2
16	16869.1	-137.8	402.6
17	15608.2	-1260.9	-1123.2
18	16013.1	405.0	1665.9
19	17701.4	1638.3	1283.3
20	21630.4	3929.1	2240.8
21	20377.8	-1252.6	-5181.7
22	19740.3	-637.5	615.1
23	20492.3	752.0	1389.5
24	21216.0	723.7	-28.3
25	20657.7	-558.3	-1282.0
26	20839.0	191.3	739.6
27	22554.1	1715.1	1533.8
28	23304.5	750.4	-964.8
29	23448.5	144.0	-606.4
30	24423.3	974.8	830.8
31	25959.1	1535.8	561.0
32	27046.8	1037.7	-448.1
33	26693.9	-352.9	-1440.5
34	24540.7	-2153.2	-1800.4
35	23860.7	-680.0	1473.2
36	21543.8	-2316.9	-1636.9
37	20350.0	-1193.8	1123.1
38	24087.1	3737.1	4930.9
39	16470.6	-7616.5	-11353.7
40	18899.9	2419.3	10035.8
41	18541.0	-348.9	-2768.2
42	17058.4	-1482.6	-1133.7
43	17032.9	-25.5	1457.1
44	15683.2	-1349.7	-1324.2
45	14647.7	-1035.5	314.1
46	15276.4	628.7	1664.2
47	15183.9	-92.5	-721.2
48	15504.6	320.7	413.2
49	15282.6	-222.0	-542.7
50	15295.9	13.3	235.3
51	15263.3	-32.7	-46.0
52	15820.3	557.1	589.7
53	16188.8	368.5	-188.6
54	16386.3	197.5	-171.0
55	15843.9	-542.4	-739.8
56	16116.5	272.6	815.0
57	15155.8	-960.7	-1233.4
58	15385.9	230.1	1190.8
59	13450.9	-1934.9	-2165.0
60	12094.4	-1356.5	578.4
61	10731.5	-1362.9	-6.4
62	10460.9	-270.6	1092.3
63	9809.5	-651.4	-380.8
64	8947.0	-862.5	-211.1
65	9450.6	503.5	1366.1
66	10526.5	1075.9	572.4
67	10666.1	139.6	-936.4
68	10596.5	-69.5	-209.1
69	9891.8	-704.7	-635.2

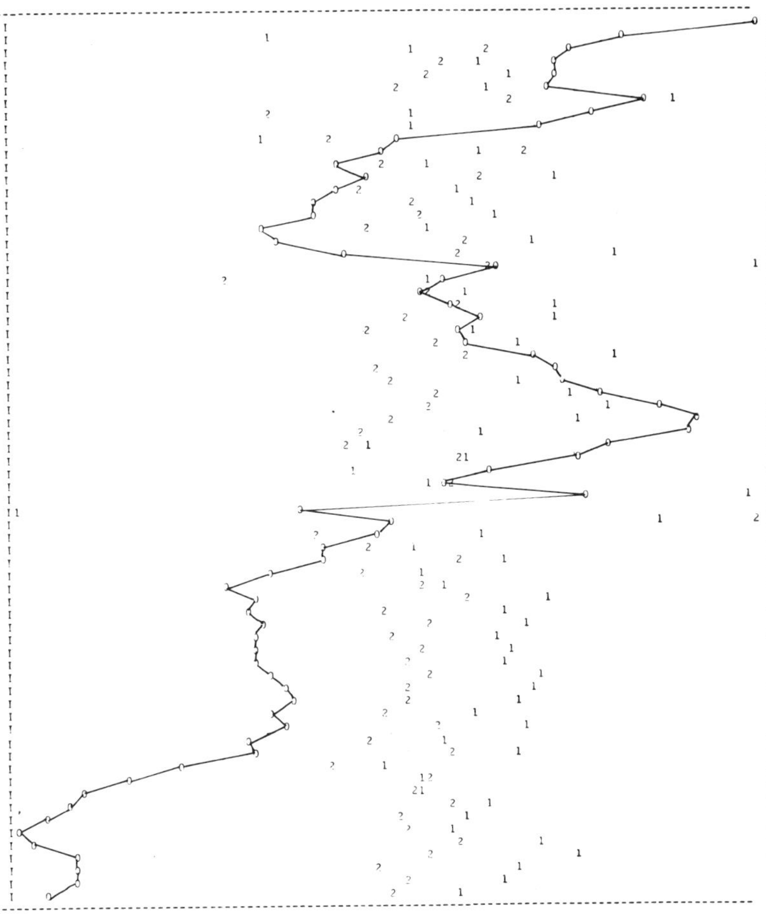

BOUNDS ON VALUES ARE 8947.01 28664.11
BOUNDS ON FIRST DIFFERENCES ARE -7616.53 3929.05
BOUNDS ON SECOND DIFFERENCES ARE -11353.66 10035.84
0 VALUE 1 FIRST DIFFERENCE 2 SECOND DIFFERENCE

END OF FILE READING UNIT05

S.V. Piastre Value in Saigon Black Market

MON	VALUE	1ST D	2ND D
1	7233.0	0.0	0.0
2	7242.0	9.0	0.0
3	7196.0	-46.0	-55.0
4	7161.0	-35.0	11.0
5	7208.0	47.0	82.0
6	7205.0	-3.0	-50.0
7	7637.0	432.0	435.0
8	7545.0	-92.0	-524.0
9	7132.0	-413.0	-321.0
10	6184.0	-948.0	-535.0
11	6188.0	4.0	952.0
12	5868.0	-320.0	-324.0
13	5925.0	57.0	377.0
14	6000.0	75.0	18.0
15	5996.0	-4.0	-79.0
16	5899.0	-97.0	-93.0
17	5449.0	-450.0	-353.0
18	5280.0	-169.0	281.0
19	4966.0	-314.0	-145.0
20	6251.0	1285.0	1599.0
21	5889.0	-362.0	-1647.0
22	5913.0	24.0	386.0
23	5920.0	7.0	-17.0
24	6022.0	102.0	95.0
25	5890.0	-132.0	-234.0
26	5966.0	76.0	208.0
27	6003.0	37.0	-39.0
28	6540.0	537.0	500.0
29	6478.0	-62.0	-599.0
30	6465.0	-13.0	49.0
31	6764.0	299.0	312.0
32	6830.0	66.0	-233.0
33	6740.0	-90.0	-156.0
34	6484.0	-256.0	-166.0
35	6415.0	-59.0	187.0
36	6004.0	-411.0	-342.0
37	6105.0	101.0	512.0
38	5931.0	-174.0	-275.0
39	5000.0	-931.0	-757.0
40	6013.0	1013.0	1944.0
41	5897.0	-116.0	-1129.0
42	5719.0	-178.0	-62.0
43	5646.0	-73.0	105.0
44	5328.0	-318.0	-245.0
45	4989.0	-339.0	-21.0
46	5189.0	200.0	539.0
47	5115.0	-74.0	-274.0
48	5141.0	26.0	100.0
49	5147.0	6.0	-20.0
50	5189.0	42.0	36.0
51	5232.0	43.0	1.0
52	5287.0	55.0	12.0
53	5356.0	69.0	14.0
54	5228.0	-128.0	-197.0
55	5031.0	-197.0	-69.0
56	4864.0	-167.0	30.0
57	4504.0	-360.0	-193.0
58	4470.0	-34.0	326.0
59	3789.0	-681.0	-647.0
60	3459.0	-330.0	351.0
61	3166.0	-293.0	37.0
62	3056.0	-110.0	183.0
63	2808.0	-248.0	-138.0
64	2449.0	-359.0	-111.0
65	2562.0	113.0	472.0
66	2750.0	188.0	75.0
67	2724.0	-26.0	-214.0
68	2692.0	-32.0	-6.0
69	2457.0	-235.0	-203.0

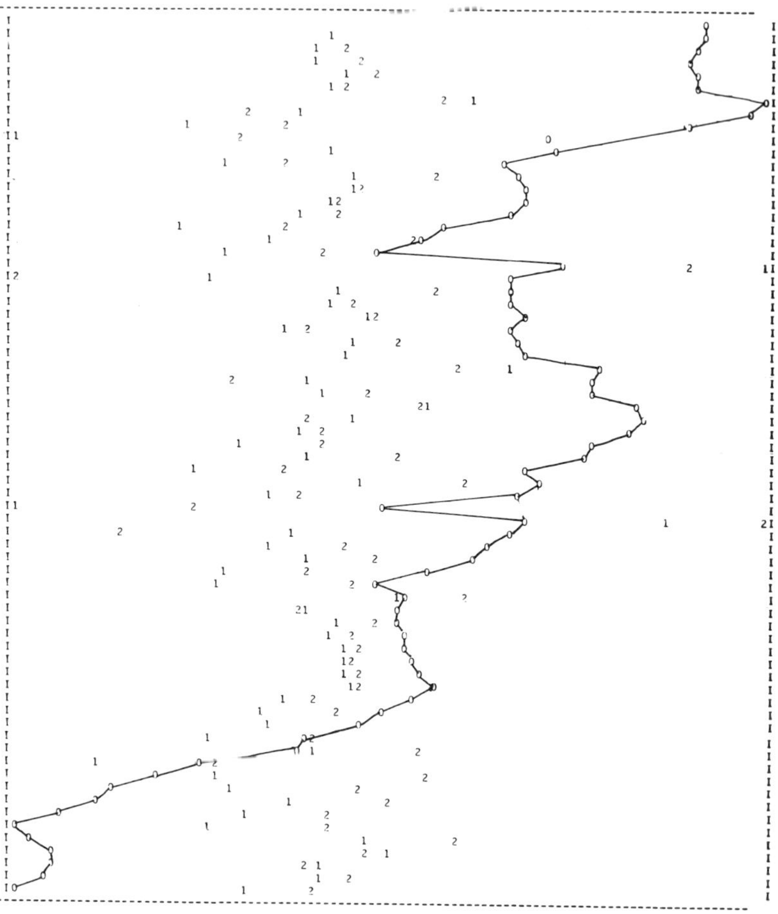

BOUNDS ON VALUES ARE 2449.00 7637.00
BOUNDS ON FIRST DIFFERENCES ARE -948.00 1285.00
BOUNDS ON SECOND DIFFERENCES ARE -1647.00 1944.00
0 VALUE 1 FIRST DIFFERENCE 2 SECOND DIFFERENCE

S.V. Money Supply

MON	VALUE	1ST D	2ND D
1	27.0	0.0	0.0
2	31.0	4.0	0.0
3	32.0	1.0	-3.0
4	33.0	1.0	0.0
5	34.0	1.0	0.0
6	35.0	1.0	0.0
7	36.0	1.0	0.0
8	38.0	2.0	1.0
9	40.0	2.0	0.0
10	43.0	3.0	1.0
11	45.0	2.0	-1.0
12	48.0	3.0	1.0
13	51.0	3.0	0.0
14	53.0	2.0	-1.0
15	55.0	2.0	0.0
16	57.0	2.0	0.0
17	59.0	2.0	0.0
18	61.0	2.0	0.0
19	62.0	1.0	-1.0
20	63.0	1.0	0.0
21	63.0	0.0	-1.0
22	65.0	2.0	2.0
23	65.0	0.0	-2.0
24	65.0	0.0	0.0
25	69.0	4.0	4.0
26	71.0	2.0	-2.0
27	70.0	-1.0	-3.0
28	71.0	1.0	2.0
29	71.0	0.0	-1.0
30	72.0	1.0	1.0
31	74.0	2.0	1.0
32	75.0	1.0	-1.0
33	76.0	1.0	0.0
34	79.0	3.0	2.0
35	82.0	3.0	0.0
36	85.0	3.0	0.0

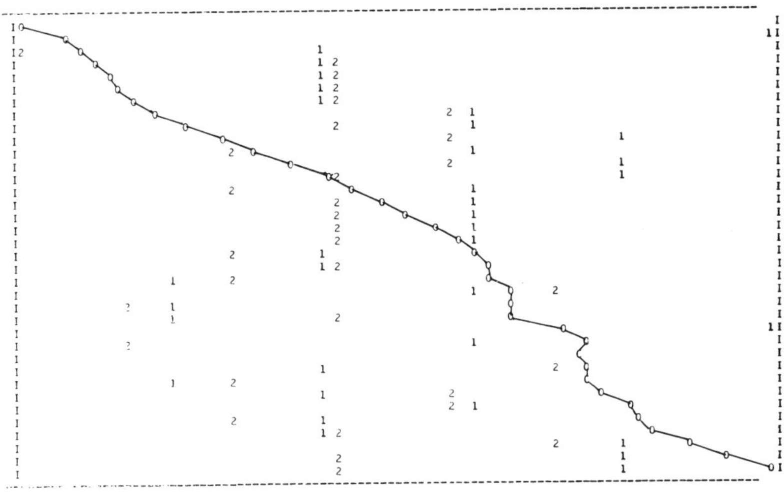

BOUNDS ON VALUES ARE 27.00 85.00
BOUNDS ON FIRST DIFFERENCES ARE -1.00 4.00
BOUNDS ON SECOND DIFFERENCES ARE -3.00 4.00
0 VALUE 1 FIRST DIFFERENCE 2 SECOND DIFFERENCE

S.V. Cost of Living

MON	VALUE	1ST D	2ND D
1	107.0	0.0	0.0
2	107.0	0.0	0.0
3	105.0	-2.0	-2.0
4	107.0	2.0	4.0
5	110.0	3.0	1.0
6	112.0	2.0	-1.0
7	121.0	9.0	7.0
8	122.0	1.0	-8.0
9	128.0	6.0	5.0
10	133.0	5.0	-1.0
11	136.0	3.0	-2.0
12	143.0	7.0	4.0
13	157.0	14.0	7.0
14	155.0	-2.0	-16.0
15	156.0	1.0	3.0
16	163.0	7.0	6.0
17	169.0	6.0	-1.0
18	185.0	16.0	10.0
19	221.0	36.0	20.0
20	218.0	-3.0	-39.0
21	218.0	0.0	3.0
22	217.0	-1.0	-1.0
23	225.0	8.0	9.0
24	229.0	4.0	-4.0
25	242.0	13.0	9.0
26	248.0	6.0	-7.0
27	263.0	15.0	9.0
28	253.0	-10.0	-25.0
29	257.0	4.0	14.0
30	272.0	15.0	11.0
31	284.0	12.0	-3.0
32	297.0	13.0	1.0
33	301.0	4.0	-9.0
34	299.0	-2.0	-6.0
35	305.0	6.0	8.0
36	305.0	0.0	-6.0

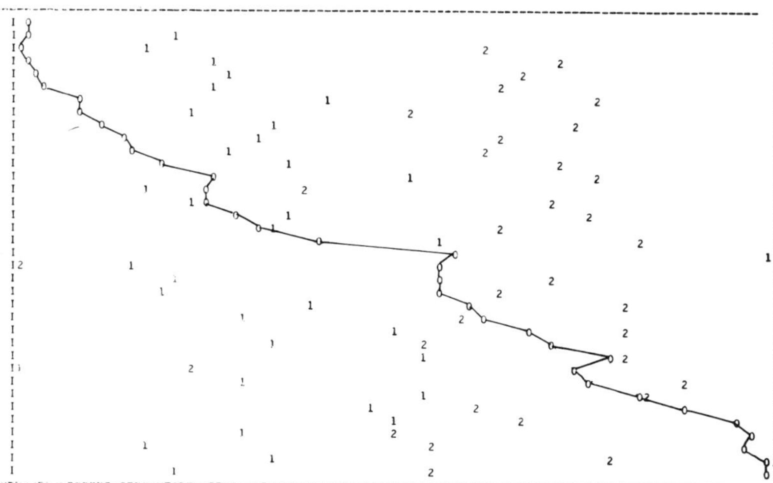

BOUNDS ON VALUES ARE 105.00 305.00
BOUNDS ON FIRST DIFFERENCES ARE -10.00 36.00
BOUNDS ON SECOND DIFFERENCES ARE -39.00 20.00
0 VALUE 1 FIRST DIFFERENCE 2 SECOND DIFFERENCE

N.V. + V.C. Defectors

MON	VALUE	1ST D	2ND D
1	393.0	0.0	0.0
2	500.0	107.0	0.0
3	473.0	-27.0	-134.0
4	532.0	59.0	85.0
5	982.0	450.0	391.0
6	1089.0	107.0	-343.0
7	666.0	-423.0	-530.0
8	1520.0	854.0	1277.0
9	1068.0	-452.0	-1306.0
10	1172.0	104.0	556.0
11	1482.0	310.0	206.0
12	1070.0	-412.0	-722.0
13	1067.0	-3.0	409.0
14	2231.0	1164.0	1167.0
15	2260.0	29.0	-1135.0
16	1510.0	-750.0	-779.0
17	1446.0	-64.0	686.0
18	1314.0	-132.0	-68.0
19	1140.0	-174.0	-42.0
20	1216.0	76.0	250.0
21	885.0	-331.0	-407.0
22	1995.0	1110.0	1441.0
23	2505.0	510.0	-600.0
24	2435.0	-70.0	-580.0
25	2440.0	5.0	75.0
26	3395.0	955.0	950.0
27	4755.0	1360.0	405.0
28	3018.0	-1737.0	-3097.0
29	2274.0	-744.0	993.0
30	2105.0	-169.0	575.0
31	1978.0	-127.0	42.0
32	1863.0	-115.0	12.0
33	1543.0	-320.0	-205.0
34	1518.0	-25.0	295.0
35	1070.0	-448.0	-423.0
36	920.0	-150.0	298.0
37	1261.0	341.0	491.0
38	745.0	-516.0	-857.0
39	501.0	-244.0	272.0
40	1168.0	667.0	911.0
41	873.0	-295.0	-962.0
42	1133.0	260.0	555.0
43	1559.0	436.0	176.0
44	1581.0	12.0	-424.0
45	1501.0	-80.0	-92.0
46	2047.0	546.0	626.0
47	2408.0	351.0	-185.0
48	3046.0	638.0	277.0
49	3045.0	-1.0	-639.0
50	2560.0	-485.0	-484.0
51	4188.0	1628.0	2113.0
52	4213.0	25.0	-1603.0
53	3799.0	-414.0	-439.0
54	3156.0	-643.0	-229.0
55	4927.0	1771.0	2414.0
56	4167.0	-760.0	-2531.0
57	3924.0	-243.0	517.0
58	4802.0	878.0	1121.0
59	4306.0	-496.0	-1374.0
60	3170.0	-1136.0	-640.0
61	2271.0	-899.0	237.0
62	2562.0	291.0	1190.0
63	3131.0	569.0	278.0
64	2373.0	-758.0	-1327.0
65	3538.0	1165.0	1923.0
66	2409.0	-1129.0	-2294.0
67	2752.0	343.0	1472.0
68	3222.0	470.0	127.0
69	2801.0	-421.0	-891.0

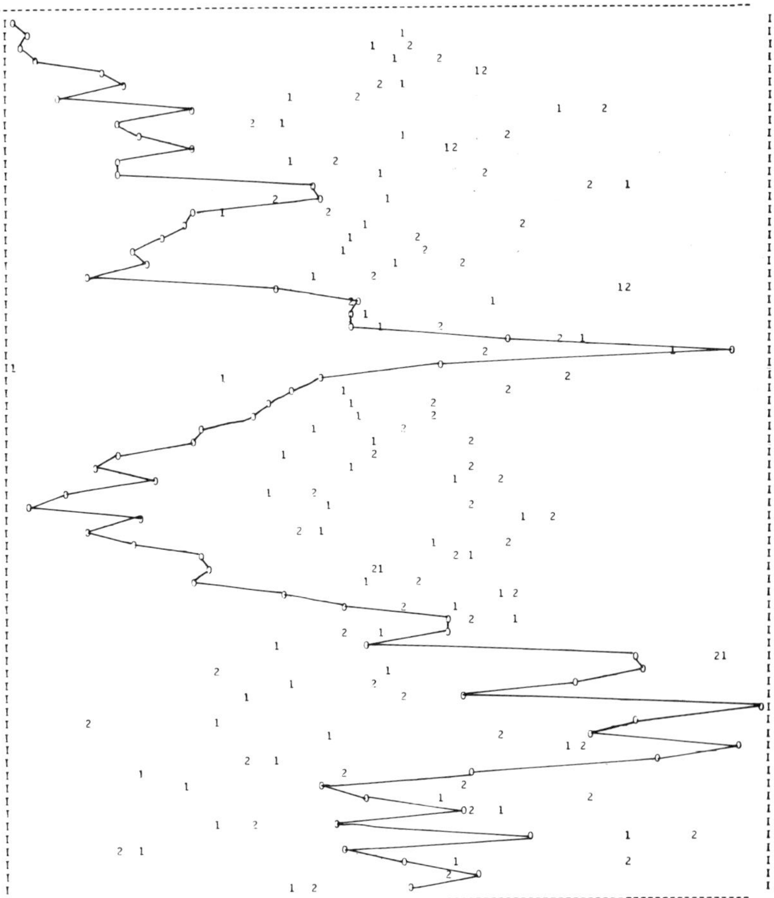

BOUNDS ON VALUES ARE 393.00 4927.00
BOUNDS ON FIRST DIFFERENCES ARE -1737.00 1771.00
BOUNDS ON SECOND DIFFEREENCES ARE -3097.00 2414.00
0 VALUE 1 FIRST DIFFERENCE 2 SECOND DIFFERENCE

N.V. + V.C. Preference for Own Actions

MON	VALUE	1ST D	2ND D
1	5.0	0.0	0.0
2	4.0	-1.0	0.0
3	7.0	3.0	4.0
4	6.0	-1.0	-4.0
5	3.0	-3.0	-2.0
6	0.0	-3.0	-0.0
7	3.0	3.0	6.0
8	3.0	0.0	-3.0
9	1.0	-2.0	-2.0
10	1.0	0.0	2.0
11	2.0	1.0	1.0
12	4.0	2.0	1.0
13	11.0	7.0	5.0
14	-16.0	-27.0	-34.0
15	2.0	18.0	45.0
16	0.0	-2.0	-20.0
17	-19.0	-19.0	-17.0
18	-14.0	5.0	24.0
19	7.0	21.0	16.0
20	4.0	-3.0	-24.0
21	-12.0	-16.0	-13.0
22	1.0	13.0	29.0
23	1.0	0.0	-13.0
24	14.0	13.0	13.0
25	8.0	-6.0	-19.0
26	7.0	-1.0	5.0
27	3.0	-4.0	-3.0
28	1.0	-2.0	2.0
29	3.0	2.0	4.0
30	1.0	-2.0	-4.0
31	2.0	1.0	3.0
32	-18.0	-20.0	-21.0
33	14.0	32.0	52.0
34	-14.0	-28.0	-60.0
35	5.0	19.0	47.0
36	5.0	0.0	-19.0

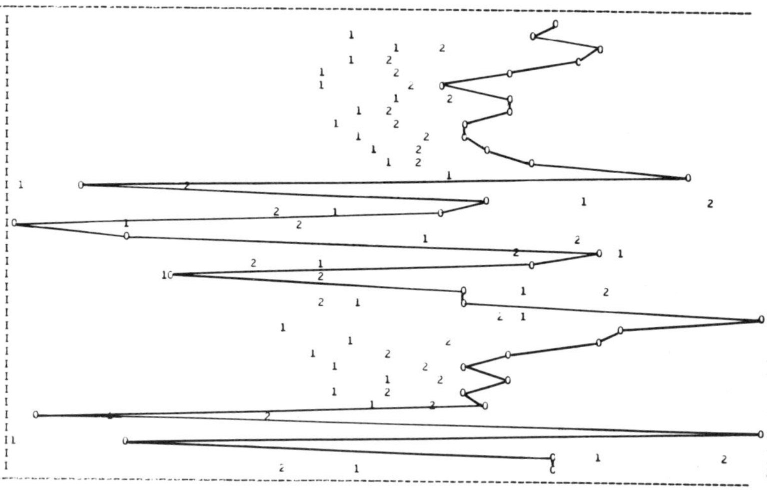

BOUNDS ON VALUES ARE -19.00 14.00
BOUNDS ON FIRST DIFFERENCES ARE -28.00 32.00
BOUNDS ON SECOND DIFFERENCES ARE -60.00 52.00
0 VALUE 1 FIRST DIFFERENCE 2 SECOND DIFFERENCE

N.V. + V.C. Perceptions of U.S. + S.V. Actions

MON	VALUE	1ST D	2ND D
1	0.0	0.0	0.0
2	0.0	0.0	0.0
3	1.0	1.0	1.0
4	21.0	20.0	19.0
5	1.0	-20.0	-40.0
6	0.0	-1.0	19.0
7	1.0	1.0	2.0
8	16.0	15.0	14.0
9	2.0	-14.0	-29.0
10	0.0	-2.0	12.0
11	1.0	1.0	3.0
12	5.0	4.0	3.0
13	15.0	10.0	6.0
14	11.0	-4.0	-14.0
15	2.0	-9.0	-5.0
16	2.0	0.0	9.0
17	0.0	-2.0	-2.0
18	15.0	15.0	17.0
19	16.0	1.0	-14.0
20	6.0	-10.0	-11.0
21	2.0	-4.0	6.0
22	2.0	0.0	4.0
23	9.0	7.0	7.0
24	2.0	-7.0	-14.0
25	4.0	2.0	9.0
26	1.0	-3.0	-5.0
27	0.0	-1.0	2.0
28	1.0	1.0	2.0
29	0.0	-1.0	-2.0
30	0.0	0.0	1.0
31	0.0	0.0	0.0
32	2.0	2.0	2.0
33	3.0	1.0	-1.0
34	9.0	6.0	5.0
35	5.0	-4.0	-10.0
36	11.0	6.0	10.0

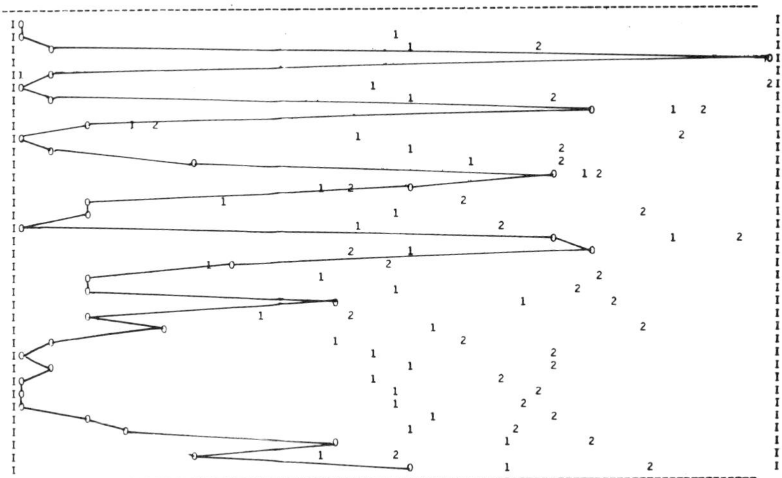

BOUNDS ON VALUES ARE 0.00 21.00
BOUNDS ON FIRST DIFFERENCES ARE -20.00 20.00
BOUNDS ON SECOND DIFFEREENCES ARE -40.00 19.00
0 VALUE 1 FIRST DIFFERENCE 2 SECOND DIFFERENCE

N.V. + V.C. Preferences for Negotiation

MON	VALUE	1ST D	2ND D
1	0.0	0.0	0.0
2	4.0	4.0	0.0
3	0.0	-4.0	-8.0
4	-10.0	-10.0	-6.0
5	-5.0	5.0	15.0
6	-8.0	-3.0	-8.0
7	-4.0	4.0	7.0
8	-2.0	2.0	-2.0
9	0.0	2.0	0.0
10	-5.0	-5.0	-7.0
11	-9.0	-4.0	1.0
12	6.0	15.0	19.0
13	4.0	-2.0	-17.0
14	-1.0	-5.0	-3.0
15	-6.0	-5.0	-0.0
16	-9.0	-3.0	2.0
17	0.0	9.0	12.0
18	-4.0	-4.0	-13.0
19	-19.0	-15.0	-11.0
20	-13.0	6.0	21.0
21	-7.0	6.0	0.0
22	-8.0	-1.0	-7.0
23	-7.0	1.0	2.0
24	-10.0	-3.0	-4.0
25	3.0	13.0	16.0
26	18.0	15.0	2.0
27	-18.0	-36.0	-51.0
28	-4.0	14.0	50.0
29	-8.0	-4.0	-18.0
30	2.0	10.0	14.0
31	4.0	2.0	-8.0
32	-1.0	-5.0	-7.0
33	-17.0	-16.0	-11.0
34	-26.0	-9.0	7.0
35	-3.0	23.0	32.0
36	6.0	9.0	-14.0

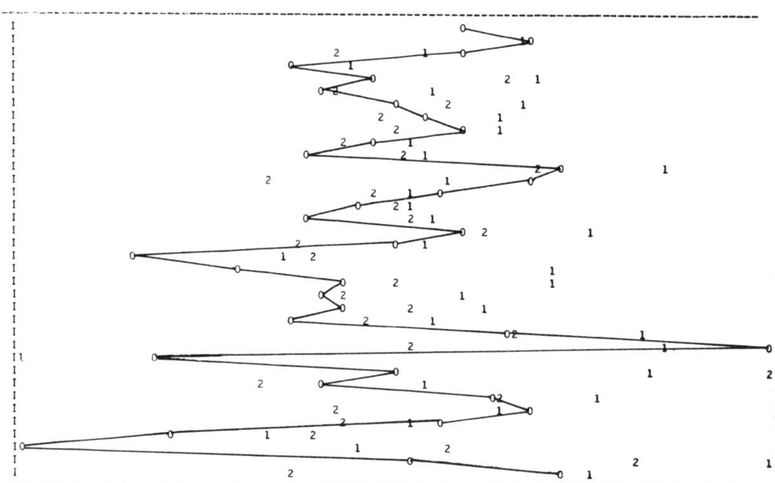

BOUNDS ON VALUES ARE -26.00 18.00
BOUNDS ON FIRST DIFFERENCES ARE -36.00 23.00
BOUNDS ON SECOND DIFFEREENCES ARE -51.00 50.00
0 VALUE 1 FIRST DIFFERENCE 2 SECOND DIFFERENCE

N.V. + V.C. Preferences for Favorable Outcomes

MON	VALUE	1ST D	2ND D
1	0.0	0.0	0.0
2	0.0	0.0	0.0
3	-1.0	-1.0	-1.0
4	8.0	9.0	10.0
5	0.0	-8.0	-17.0
6	0.0	0.0	8.0
7	0.0	0.0	0.0
8	1.0	1.0	1.0
9	6.0	5.0	4.0
10	1.0	-5.0	-10.0
11	2.0	1.0	6.0
12	-1.0	-3.0	-4.0
13	8.0	9.0	12.0
14	13.0	5.0	-4.0
15	5.0	-8.0	-13.0
16	11.0	6.0	14.0
17	0.0	-11.0	-17.0
18	1.0	1.0	12.0
19	11.0	10.0	9.0
20	4.0	-7.0	-17.0
21	3.0	-1.0	6.0
22	1.0	-2.0	-1.0
23	0.0	-1.0	1.0
24	4.0	4.0	5.0
25	17.0	13.0	9.0
26	3.0	-14.0	-27.0
27	16.0	13.0	27.0
28	9.0	-7.0	-20.0
29	5.0	-4.0	3.0
30	-2.0	-7.0	-3.0
31	3.0	5.0	12.0
32	5.0	2.0	-3.0
33	10.0	5.0	3.0
34	1.0	-9.0	-14.0
35	0.0	-1.0	8.0
36	5.0	5.0	6.0

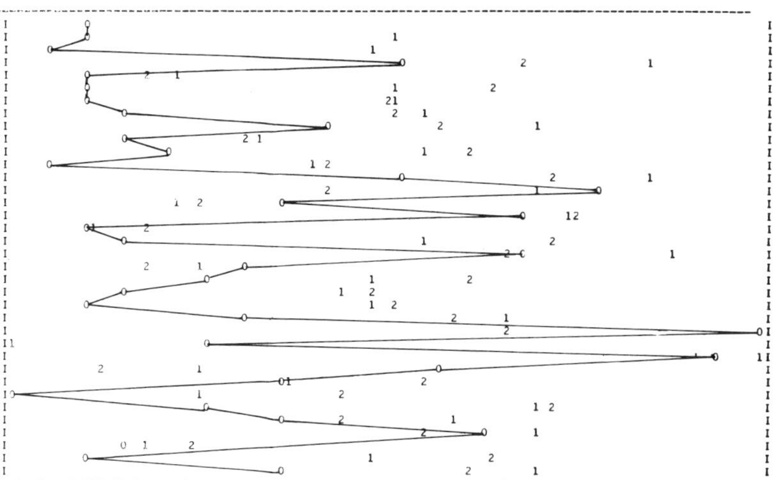

BOUNDS ON VALUES ARE -2.00 17.00
BOUNDS ON FIRST DIFFERENCES ARE -14.00 13.00
BOUNDS ON SECOND DIFFEREENCES ARE -27.00 27.00
0 VALUE 1 FIRST DIFFERENCE 2 SECOND DIFFERENCE

U.S. + S.V. Perceptions of N.V. + V.C. Actions

MON	VALUE	1ST D	2ND D
1	4.0	0.0	0.0
2	7.0	3.0	0.0
3	3.0	-4.0	-7.0
4	7.0	4.0	8.0
5	-2.0	-9.0	-13.0
6	2.0	4.0	13.0
7	-8.0	-10.0	-14.0
8	-1.0	7.0	17.0
9	0.0	1.0	-6.0
10	-2.0	-2.0	-3.0
11	-2.0	-0.0	2.0
12	18.0	20.0	20.0
13	30.0	12.0	-8.0
14	-2.0	-32.0	-44.0
15	-1.0	1.0	33.0
16	-14.0	-13.0	-14.0
17	-11.0	3.0	16.0
18	1.0	12.0	9.0
19	-5.0	-6.0	-18.0
20	2.0	7.0	13.0
21	16.0	14.0	7.0
22	-8.0	-24.0	-38.0
23	12.0	20.0	44.0
24	9.0	-3.0	-23.0
25	1.0	-8.0	-5.0
26	4.0	3.0	11.0
27	6.0	2.0	-1.0
28	-2.0	-8.0	-10.0
29	7.0	9.0	17.0
30	3.0	-4.0	-13.0
31	10.0	7.0	11.0
32	-5.0	-15.0	-22.0
33	17.0	22.0	37.0
34	-1.0	-18.0	-40.0
35	16.0	17.0	35.0
36	1.0	-15.0	-32.0

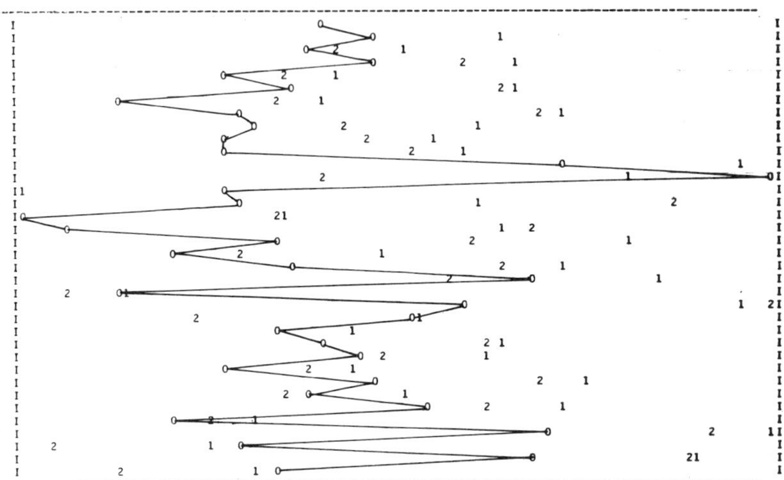

BOUNDS ON VALUES ARE -14.00 30.00
BOUNDS ON FIRST DIFFERENCES ARE -32.00 22.00
BOUNDS ON SECOND DIFFFREENCES ARE -44.00 44.00
0 VALUE 1 FIRST DIFFERENCE 2 SECOND DIFFERENCE

U.S. + S.V. Preferences for Own Actions

MON	VALUE	1ST D	2ND D
1	4.0	0.0	0.0
2	46.0	42.0	0.0
3	28.0	-18.0	-60.0
4	6.0	-22.0	-4.0
5	8.0	2.0	24.0
6	28.0	20.0	18.0
7	22.0	-6.0	-26.0
8	-8.0	-30.0	-24.0
9	-4.0	4.0	34.0
10	10.0	14.0	10.0
11	52.0	42.0	28.0
12	14.0	-38.0	-80.0
13	13.0	-1.0	37.0
14	9.0	-4.0	-3.0
15	4.0	-5.0	-1.0
16	0.0	-4.0	1.0
17	10.0	10.0	14.0
18	18.0	8.0	-2.0
19	-35.0	-53.0	-61.0
20	14.0	49.0	102.0
21	15.0	1.0	-48.0
22	14.0	-1.0	-2.0
23	24.0	10.0	11.0
24	8.0	-16.0	-26.0
25	-15.0	-23.0	-7.0
26	17.0	32.0	55.0
27	30.0	13.0	-19.0
28	18.0	-12.0	-25.0
29	-5.0	-23.0	-11.0
30	8.0	13.0	36.0
31	-2.0	-10.0	-23.0
32	8.0	10.0	20.0
33	4.0	-4.0	-14.0
34	0.0	-4.0	-0.0
35	-15.0	-15.0	-11.0
36	-13.0	2.0	17.0

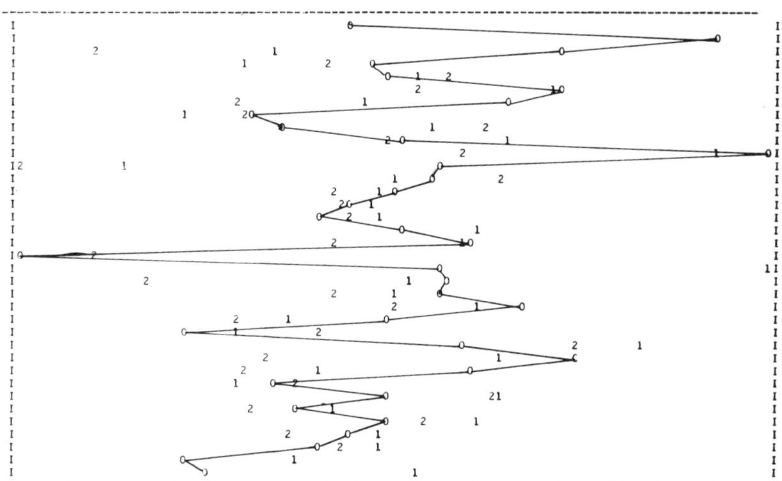

BOUNDS ON VALUES ARE -35.00 52.00
BOUNDS ON FIRST DIFFERENCES ARE -53.00 49.00
BOUNDS ON SECOND DIFFEREENCES ARE -80.00 102.00
0 VALUE 1 FIRST DIFFERENCE 2 SECOND DIFFERENCE

U.S. + S.V. Preferences for Negotiation

MON	VALUE	1ST D	2ND D
1	-4.0	0.0	0.0
2	1.0	5.0	0.0
3	-5.0	-6.0	-11.0
4	5.0	10.0	16.0
5	1.0	-4.0	-14.0
6	-11.0	-12.0	-8.0
7	11.0	22.0	34.0
8	-25.0	-36.0	-58.0
9	4.0	29.0	65.0
10	-3.0	-7.0	-36.0
11	-12.0	-9.0	-2.0
12	5.0	17.0	26.0
13	22.0	17.0	0.0
14	-19.0	-41.0	-58.0
15	-6.0	13.0	54.0
16	-13.0	-7.0	-20.0
17	6.0	19.0	26.0
18	13.0	7.0	-12.0
19	3.0	-10.0	-17.0
20	4.0	1.0	11.0
21	20.0	16.0	15.0
22	21.0	1.0	-15.0
23	26.0	5.0	4.0
24	5.0	-21.0	-26.0
25	23.0	18.0	39.0
26	12.0	-11.0	-29.0
27	-2.0	-14.0	-3.0
28	-3.0	-1.0	13.0
29	12.0	15.0	16.0
30	1.0	-11.0	-26.0
31	2.0	1.0	12.0
32	-10.0	-12.0	-13.0
33	-2.0	8.0	20.0
34	-4.0	-2.0	-10.0
35	17.0	21.0	23.0
36	7.0	-10.0	-31.0

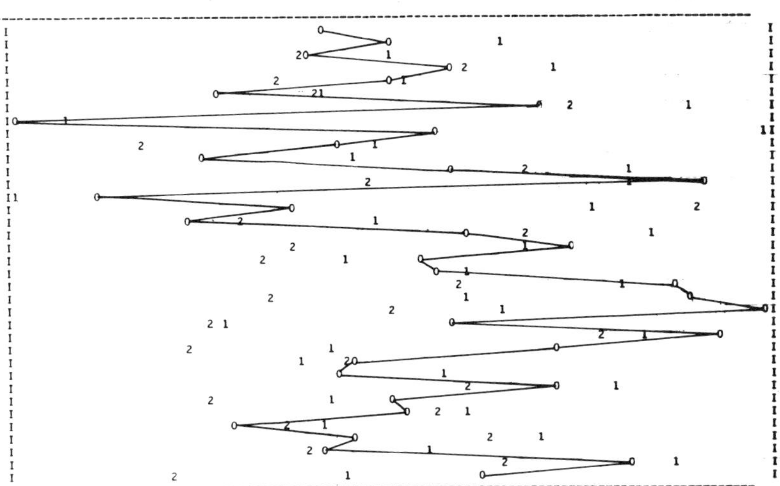

BOUNDS ON VALUES ARE -25.00 26.00
BOUNDS ON FIRST DIFFERENCES ARE -41.00 29.00
BOUNDS ON SECOND DIFFEREENCES ARE -58.00 65.00
0 VALUE 1 FIRST DIFFERENCE 2 SECOND DIFFERENCE

U.S. + S.V. Preferences for Favorable Outcomes

MON	VALUE	1ST D	2ND D
1	1.0	0.0	0.0
2	1.0	0.0	0.0
3	21.0	20.0	20.0
4	3.0	-18.0	-38.0
5	7.0	4.0	22.0
6	16.0	9.0	5.0
7	7.0	-9.0	-18.0
8	6.0	-1.0	8.0
9	6.0	0.0	1.0
10	30.0	24.0	24.0
11	16.0	-14.0	-38.0
12	17.0	1.0	15.0
13	10.0	-7.0	-8.0
14	23.0	13.0	20.0
15	-2.0	-25.0	-38.0
16	7.0	9.0	34.0
17	20.0	13.0	4.0
18	8.0	-12.0	-25.0
19	19.0	11.0	23.0
20	16.0	-3.0	-14.0
21	0.0	-16.0	-13.0
22	-12.0	-12.0	4.0
23	5.0	17.0	29.0
24	-3.0	-8.0	-25.0
25	-2.0	1.0	9.0
26	-16.0	-14.0	-15.0
27	20.0	36.0	50.0
28	21.0	1.0	-35.0
29	-2.0	-23.0	-24.0
30	5.0	7.0	30.0
31	28.0	23.0	16.0
32	19.0	-9.0	-32.0
33	17.0	-2.0	7.0
34	11.0	-6.0	-4.0
35	30.0	19.0	25.0
36	38.0	8.0	-11.0

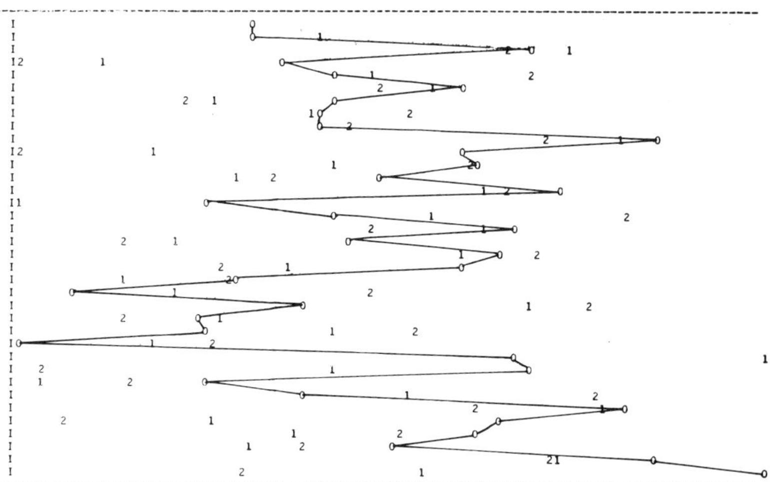

BOUNDS ON VALUES ARE -16.00 38.00
BOUNDS ON FIRST DIFFERENCES ARE -25.00 36.00
BOUNDS ON SECOND DIFFEREENCES ARE -38.00 50.00
0 VALUE 1 FIRST DIFFERENCE 2 SECOND DIFFERENCE

Bibliography

Allison, G. T. "Conceptual Models and the Cuban Missile Crisis." *American Political Science Review* 63, no. 3 (1969): 689-718.

Ayres, B. Drummond, Jr. "The Grim and Inaccurate Casualty Numbers Game." *New York Times*, 1 June 1969, sec. 4, p. 3.

Berman, Paul. "The Liberation Armed Forces of the NLF: Compliance and Cohesion in a Revolutionary Army." Ph.D. dissertation, Massachusetts Institute of Technology, 1970.

Blalock, Hubert M., Jr. *Causal Inferences in Nonexperimental Research*. Chapel Hill: University of North Carolina Press, 1964.

Boulding, Kenneth E. *Conflict and Defense: A General Theory*. New York: Harper & Bros., 1962.

———. *The Image: Knowledge in Life and Society*. Ann Arbor: University of Michigan Press, 1956.

Brody, Richard A. "Cognition and Behavior: A Model of Inter-State Relations." In *Experience, Structure, and Adaptability*, ed. O. J. Harvey. New York: Springer Publishing, 1966.

———, Alexandra H. Benham, and Jeffrey S. Milstein. "Hostile International Communication, Arms Production, and Perception of Threat: A Simulation Study." *Peace Research Society (International) Papers* 7 (1967): 15–40.

Bronowski, J. *The Common Sense of Science*. New York: Random House, 1960.

Campbell, Angus, et al. *The American Voter*. New York: John Wiley & Sons, 1960.

Campbell, Donald T., and Keith N. Clayton. *Avoiding Regression Effects in Panel Studies of Communication Impact*. Studies in Public Communication, No. 3. Chicago: Department of Sociology, University of Chicago, 1961.

———, and Julian C. Stanley. "Experimental and Quasi-Experimental Designs for Research on Teaching." In *Handbook of Research on Teaching*, ed. N. L. Gage. Chicago: Rand McNally, 1963, pp. 171–246.

CBS News Public Opinion Survey. "The People of South Vietnam: How They Feel about the War." Princeton, N.J.: Opinion Research Corporation, 13 March 1967.

Clifford, Clark M. "A Vietnam Reappraisal: The Personal History of One Man's View and How It Evolved." *Foreign Affairs* 47, no. 4 (July 1969).

Committee on Foreign Relations, U.S. Senate. *Vietnam: December, 1969*. Washington: U.S. Government Printing Office, 2 February 1970. Staff Report, Committee Print, 91st Cong., 2d Sess.

Conn, Richard W., and Richard E. von Holdt. "An Outline Display for the Study of Approximating Functions." *Journal of the Association for Computing Machinery* 12, no. 2 (June 1965): 326–49.

Dixon, W. J., ed. *Biomedical Computer Programs*. Los Angeles: Los Angeles Health Science Computing Facility, Department of Preventive Medicine and Public Health, School of Medicine, University of California at Los Angeles, 1964.

Dollard, John R., et al. *Frustration and Aggression*. New Haven, Conn.: Yale University Press, 1939.

Due, John F., and Robert W. Clower. *Intermediate Economic Analysis: Resource Allocation, Factor Pricing, and Welfare*. Homewood, Ill.: Richard D. Irwin, 1961, pp. 73–99.

Ellsberg, Daniel. "The Quagmire Myth and the Stalemate Machine." *Public Policy* 19, no. 2 (Spring 1971): 217–74.

"Excerpts from Talk by Westmoreland." *New York Times*, 22 November 1967, p. 2.

Fanfani, Amintore. "Texts of Letters from Fanfani and Rusk." *New York Times*, 18 December 1965, p. 3.

Friedheim, R. L., and J. B. Kadane. "Quantitative Content Analysis of the United Nations Seabed Debates: Methodology and a Continental Shelf Case Study." *International Organization* 29, no. 3 (Summer 1970): 479–502.

Friedman, Milton. "Money: Quantity Theory." In *International Encyclopedia of the Social Sciences*, ed. Davis L. Sills. New York: Macmillan Co. and The Free Press, 10:432–47.

Gallup, George. "One in Three Is City Crime Victim." *Washington Post*, 14 January, 1973.

Gallup Poll Index: Political, Social, and Economic Trends. Report no. 55 (January 1970); Report no. 57 (March 1970); Report no. 73 (July 1971). Princeton, N.J.: American Institute of Public Opinion.

Gelb, Leslie H. "The Essential Dominoe: American Politics and Vietnam." *Foreign Affairs* 50, no. 3 (July 1971).

———. "Vietnam: The System Worked." *Foreign Policy*, No. 3 (Summer 1971), pp. 140–67.

Gravel, Michael. *The Pentagon Papers: The Defense Department History of United States Decision-making on Vietnam*. Vols. 1–9. Boston: Beacon Press, 1971.

Gullahorn, John T., and Jeanne E. Gullahorn. "A Computer Model of Elementary Social Behavior." In *Computers and Thought*, ed. E. A. Feigenbaum and J. Feldman. New York: McGraw-Hill Book Co., 1963.

Hall, D. J., et al. "PROMENADE—An Interactive Graphics Pattern-Recognition System." Unpublished paper. Menlo Park, Calif.: Stanford Research Institute, 14 June 1968.

Hays, William L. *Statistics for Psychologists*. San Francisco: Holt, Rinehart & Winston, 1963.

"Ho Chi Minh Asks Vietcong Step-up." *New York Times*, 2 January 1966, p. 22.

Holsti, Ole R., Robert C. North, and Richard A. Brody. "Perception and Action in the 1914 Crisis." In *Quantitative International Politics: Insights and Evidence*, ed. J. D. Singer. New York: The Free Press, 1968.

Howard, A., and R. A. Scott. "A Proposed Framework for the Analysis of Stress in the Human Organism." *Behavioral Science* 10, no. 2 (April 1965): 141–60.

"Index of Victory." *Wall Street Journal*, 27 Oct. 1967, p. 1.

International Monetary Fund. *International Financial Statistics*. Washington, D.C.: Statistics Bureau, IMF. Monthly issues, 1965–72.

Johnson, Lyndon B. "Message from President Johnson to Taylor, Envoy in Saigon." Text of 10 May 1965 cable. *New York Times*, 28 June 1972, p. 18.

———. "Pattern for Peace in Southeast Asia." Speech at Johns Hopkins University, Baltimore, Md., 7 April 1965. *Department of State Bulletin* 52 (26 April 1965): 606–10.

Johnson, Robert H. "Vietnamization: Can It Work?" *Foreign Affairs* 18, no. 4 (July 1970).

Johnston, J. *Econometric Methods.* New York: McGraw-Hill Book Co., 1964.

Kreps, Clifton F., Jr., and Olin S. Pugh. *Money, Banking, and Monetary Policy.* New York: Ronald Press Co., 1967, pp. 395–413.

Lagerstrom, Richard P. "An Anticipated-Gap, Mathematical Model of International Dynamics." Unpublished paper. Stanford, Calif.: Institute of Political Studies, 8 February 1968.

Lasswell, Harold D. *Power and Personality.* New York: W. W. Norton and Co., 1948.

March, James G., and Herbert A. Simon. *Organizations.* New York: John W. Wiley & Sons, 1958.

Maslow, Abraham. *Motivation and Personality.* New York: Harper & Bros., 1954.

McNamara, Robert. "Text of McNamara Statement to Senate Subcommittee on Bombing in Vietnam." *New York Times,* 26 August 1967, p. 4.

The New York Times Index. Vols. 53, 54, 55. New York: The New York Times Company, 1965, 1966, 1967.

North, Robert C. "Decision-making in Crisis: An Introduction." *Journal of Conflict Resolution* 6, no. 3 (September 1962): 197–200.

———, Richard A. Brody, and Ole R. Holsti. "Some Empirical Data on the Conflict Spiral." *Peace Research Society (International) Papers* 1 (1964): 1–14.

Olson, Mancur, Jr., and Richard Zeckhauser. "An Economic Theory of Alliances." In *Economic Theories of International Politics,* ed. B. M. Russett. Chicago: Markham Publishing Co., 1968, pp. 25–45.

Osgood, Charles E. *An Alternative to War or Surrender.* Urbana: University of Illinois Press, 1962.

———, and Robert C. North. "From Individual to Nation: An Attempt to Make Explicit the Usually Implicit Process of Personifying International Relations." Unpublished manuscript. Urbana, Ill. and Stanford, Calif.:

Patchen, Martin. "Decision Theory in the Study of National Action: Problems and a Proposal." *Journal of Conflict Resolution* 9, no. 2 (June 1965): 164–76.

Rapoport, Anatol. *Fights, Games, and Debates.* Ann Arbor: University of Michigan Press, 1960.

———, and Albert Chammah. *Prisoner's Dilemma.* Ann Arbor: University of Michigan Press, 1965.

Reynolds, Lloyd. *Economics: A General Introduction.* 3d ed. Homewood, Ill.: Richard D. Irwin, 1969, pp. 340–63.

Richardson, Lewis F. *Arms and Insecurity.* Chicago: Quadrangle Books, 1960.

Rummel, Rudolph J. "Indicators of Cross-National and International Patterns." *American Political Science Review* 63, no. 1 (March 1969).

Salisbury, Harrison E. "Hanoi Premier Tells View: Some in U.S. Detect a Shift." *New York Times,* 4 January 1967, pp. 1, 2.

Samuelson, Paul. *Economics: An Introductory Analysis.* 7th ed. New York: McGraw-Hill Book Co., 1967, pp. 425–31.

Schlesinger, Arthur, Jr. "Eyeless in Indochina." *New York Review of Books* 17, no. 6 (21 October 1971): 23-32.

———. *The Bitter Heritage: Vietnam and American Democracy, 1941–1968.* Rev. ed. Greenwich, Conn.: Fawcett Publication, 1968.

Scott, Howard A., and R. A. Scott. "A Proposed Framework for the Analysis of Stress in the Human Organism." *Behavioral Science* 10, no. 2 (April 1965): 141–60.

Sharp, E. S. G., and W. C. Westmoreland. *Report on the War in Vietnam (As of 30 June 1968),* Washington: Government Printing Office, [1969].

Sheehan, Neil, et al. *The Pentagon Papers.* New York: Bantam Books, 1971.

Skinner, Burrhus F. *Beyond Freedom and Dignity.* New York: Alfred A. Knopf, 1971.

———. *Science and Human Behavior.* New York: Macmillan Co., 1956.

Smith, Adam. *An Inquiry into the Nature and Causes of the Wealth of Nations.* 5th ed. London: Methuen, 1934.

Snyder, Richard C., H. W. Bruck, and Burton Sapin, eds. *Foreign Policy Decision Making.* New York: The Free Press, 1962.

Staats, Arthur W., and Carolyn K. Staats. *Complex Human Behavior.* New York: Holt, Rinehart & Winston, 1964.

Szulc, Tad. "Hanoi Calls for the Infliction of Heavier Combat Losses on U.S." *New York Times,* 21 April 1970.

"Texts of Remarks by U.S. and North Vietnamese Envoys at Second Paris Session." *New York Times,* 16 May 1968, pp. 16–17.

Thomas, W. I., and F. Znaniecki. "The Definition of the Situation." In *Readings in Social Psychology,* ed. T. M. Newcomb and E. L. Hartley. New York: Henry Holt & Co., 1947.

Thomson, James C., Jr. "How Could Vietnam Happen?" *Atlantic Monthly* 221, no. 4 (April 1968), 47–53.

U.S. Department of Defense. *Unclassified Statistics on Southeast Asia,* Table 6. Washington: Office of Assistant Secretary (Comptroller), Directorate for Information Operations.

Verba, Sidney, et al. "Public Opinion and the War in Vietnam." *American Political Science Review* 61, no. 2 (June 1967): 317–33.

Webb, Eugene J., et al. *Unobtrusive Measures.* Chicago: Rand McNally Co., 1966.

Westmoreland, William C. Interview on *Meet the Press.* Washington, D.C.: Merkle Press, 11, 47 (19 November 1967), p. 17.

White, Ralph K. "Misperception and the Vietnam War." *Journal of Social Issues* 22, no. 3 (July 1966): 1–164.

Wolfers, Arnold. "The Pole of Power and the Pole of Indifference." *World Politics* 4 (1951): 39–63.

Wright, Quincy. *The Study of War.* Chicago: University of Chicago Press, 1942, pp. 644, 1541.

Zinnes, Dina A., Robert C. North, and Howard E. Koch, Jr. "Capability, Threat, and the Outbreak of War." In *International Politics and Foreign Policy: A Reader in Research and Theory,* ed. James N. Rosenau. New York: The Free Press, 1961.

———. "The Expression and Perception of Hostility in Prewar Crisis: 1914." In *Quantitative International Politics: Insights and Evidence,* ed. J. D. Singer. New York: The Free Press, 1968.

Index

Bombing of North Vietnam, 41-47, 135-36; assumed effect of, 41; and bombing of Laos, 52; doubts about, 42; halt of, by President Johnson, 47; hawkish critique of, 47; ineffectiveness of, 44-47; initiation of, 43; objective of, 43-44; and popular confidence in South Vietnamese government, 50-53; and risk of Chinese intervention, 48; study of, by Institute for Defense Analysis, 45-46, 56 n; as test of wills, 41

Calculation in U.S. Vietnam policy, 117-83; and accurate forecasts of policy consequences, 177; and anticommunism, 180; and domestic political motivations, 177-78, 180-81, 184-85; and gradual escalation, 178, 181; and incremental decision-making, 181; of international goals, 184-85; and interplay between international and domestic political motivations, 178-81; and morality, 180-81; and optimism, 183; and role of information and analysis, 183; and U.S. objectives, 184

Cambodia: invasion of, 129; war in, 192-93

Casualties, xiii, 138-40; as strategic objective, 139

Cease-fire agreement, 186-96; achievements of, 192; Communist concessions in, 193-94; and continuing conflict, 194-95; degree of compliance with, 191-93; and hope for a real peace, 195; international conditions for, 186-87; and military aid, 192, 195; terms of 187-89; and unresolved issues, 189-91

Communist armed attacks, 137

Communist terriorism, 137-38

Components of communications indices, 207-10

Computer simulation, 34-38, 78-105; accuracy of, 82-86; and autocorrelation, 80; and bootstrapping predictions, 34-35, 84; and concurrent hierarchy of variables, 36, 79; of escalation, 81-87, 90-97 fig.; as evidence of kind of U.S. influence in South Vietnam, 110-11; exercises of experimental changes in, 37, 106-27; to explore alternative policies, 106-11; graphs of dovish policy alternative, 114-20 figs.; graphs of hawkish policy alternative, 121-27 figs.; hawk and dove policy alternatives, 106-27; to inform decisions, 106; and use of exogenous variable, 106-7; and explained variance, 79-80; and feedback, 79-81; and numerical analysis, 38 n; of post-Tet period, 84-89, 98-105 fig.; as predictive technique, 34-35, 37, 78-89; and predictive validity of model, 35-37, 84; of President Johnson's popular support, 86-87; and regression equations, 34-35, 37, 78-81; and system change, 86-88; time trend and phase in, 81-82; time-lagged relationships and, 34-35, 79-81

Conflict spiral, 9

Content analysis of public statements, 199-205

Correlation, 29-32; and cause, 30; outlying values and, 30-31; serial, 30; and statistical significance tests, 31-32; time lags and leads in, 29-30; visual inspection and, 31

Credibility gap, 77 n, 182

Crime in U.S., 168-69 n

Data: requests for copies, 28 n

Democratic Republic of Vietnam. *See* North Vietnam

Domino theory, 39-40; and People's Republic of China, 40

Dove policy model, 11-16; as folk theory, xiv, 3; basic assumptions of, 13; as behavioral theory, 3-7; and critique of hawk model, 14-15; empirical test of, 16; policy prescription of, 13-14

Effective policy: requirements for, xiii
Elites: different evaluation than masses of war's costs and benefits, 151-70 passim; and exploitation of masses, 159-61, 169 n; as policy-makers, 157
Escalation of Vietnam War, xiii, 61. *See also* Mutual escalation
Exchange theory, 5-7

Folk theory, xiv; of policy-makers, 38, 57
Forecasting. *See* Prediction

Government of the Republic of Vietnam, xiii n
Graphs: use of in analysis, 29

Hawk policy model, 11-16; as behavioral theory, 3-7; critique of dove model, 14-15; empirical test of, 16; as folk theory, xiv, 3; policy prescription of, 11, 13; view of deescalation, 14

Indifference curves, 152-54; and changes in preferences, 161; and exploitation, 163-64; and mass dissatisfaction, 159-66; and optimum trade-off point of elites, 157-59; and preferences, 152-55
Indirect economic costs of war to U.S., 168
Indirect social costs of war to U.S., 166-69 n
Inflation in U.S.: as result of war, 168
Institute for Defense Analysis, 45-46, 56 n

Laos: resolution of conflict in, 192
Learning theory, 5-7
Linked mediated stimulus-response models, 10-12; prisoner's dilemma as, 10; Richardson equations as, 10-11. *See also* Mediated stimulus-response models

Masses: dissatisfaction of, 159-66; and decline in political support, 165-66; empirical evidence of dissatisfaction, 164-67; and major burdens of war, 154
Mediated stimulus-response models, 8-10; bureaucratic commitments in, 9-10; definition of the situation in, 8, 12; definition of policy in, 8, 12; misperception in, 9; perceptions in, 10; preferences in, 10. *See also* Linked mediated stimulus-response models
Military outcomes, 130; operational measures of, 130
Miscalculation in U.S. Vietnam policy, 172-77; and beliefs about U.S. power, 174; and biased field reporting, 173; and bureaucratic interests, 173, 175; and compromise, 175; and desire for influence, 174; and disuse of existing knowledge, 174; and general consensus, 174; and lack of expertise, 173, 177; of means and their consequences, 184-85; and mixture of optimism and pessimism, 174; and nonrational decision-making, 174-75; and reasons for escalation, 184; remedies for, 176-77; and self-fulfilling prophecy, 176; and semantic distortion, 173-74
Model of the war after Tet offensive, 145-47
Multiple regression equations: as form of representing relationships, xiv. *See also* Regression analysis
Mutual escalation, 57-61; of casualties, 60-61, 65; and North Vietnamese troops, 57-60; and U.S. bombing of North Vietnam, 58-60; and political losses, 65; reversed by Tet offensive, 67; and U.S. troop commitments, 60. *See also* Escalation

National Liberation Front. *See* Viet Cong
North Vietnam, xiii n

Objective war costs and benefits, 155-56, 159-61; and mass dissatisfaction, 163

Pacification, 130-31, 136-38; operational measure of, 130; summary of, 138
Peace offensives, 67-76; and bombing pause, 68; and call for capitulation, 70, 73-75; and distrust, 75-76; exploitation of, 71; and holidays, 70; and mixed rhetoric, 72-73; and public opinion, 68; and subsequent escalation, 74
People's Republic of China: as supplier of North Vietnam, xiii, 195
Policy-makers: lack of empirical testing by, 45; principal ones in U.S. Vietnam

policy, 42, 56 n; as theorizers, 3; and use of invalid models, 57, 172
Political conditions in South Vietnam, 50-52
Political dilemma: cause of, 163; of U.S. leaders, xiv-xv, 62-63, 111-12, 144-45; for Viet Cong, 65. *See also* Political paradox
Political paradox, 149-70; cause of, 163; for Communists in South Vietnam, 151; during Johnson administration, 149-50; during Nixon administration, 150-51; and evaluation of war's costs and benefits, 151-53; of losing power while seeking to extend it, 149; for South Vietnamese government, 151. *See also* Political dilemma
Politics: definition of, 3
Popular confidence of South Vietnamese in Government of Vietnam, 65, 130-31, 140-41, 167; and Vietnamization, 132, 141; and U.S. troop withdrawal, 140-41
Popular support for Viet Cong, 63-65, 142-43, 166-67; and defectors, 63-64, 77 n, 130, 142-43, 166-67
Prediction: accuracy of American, 172; based on empirical patterns, 78, 145-47, 171; implications of U.S. policy makers', xiv, 171-72; and need for valid model, 57; of policy consequences, xiii, 171-72; as purpose of scientific inquiry, 78
Power: definition of, 3
Preventing Communist power in Indochina, 149-52; U.S. motivations for, 149-52
Prisoner's dilemma model: of Vietnam War, 107-8
Provisional Revolutionary Government. *See* Viet Cong
Public statements of policy-makers, 67-76; and credibility gap, 77 n; and military actions, 71

Quantitative indices, 18-28; of casualties, 20-21; differences as, 19; of military efforts, 19-20; of political support, 21-23; proportional differences as, 19; of public policy statements, 23-25; reliability and validity of, 25-28; of seasons, 23

Rational theories, 5-7, 181. *See also* Exchange theory
Regression analysis, 32-34, 76 n; and autocorrelation, 76 n; and multicollinearity, 33; and multiple correlation coefficient, 33-34, 76 n, 147 n; and predictive models, 33; and regression coefficient, 76 n, 147 n

Serial correlation. *See* Correlation
Soviet Union: as supplier of North Vietnam, xiii, 195
Stimulus-response models, 7. *See also* Linked mediated stimulus-response models and Mediated stimulus-response models
Stress theory, 5-7, 181

Tet offensive of 1968, 128-29; and change in the war, 129; costs to Communists, 128; leading indicator of, 129; success for Communists, 128
Theory, xiii; use of in prediction, xiii-xiv, 3. *See also* Dove policy model; Exchange theory; Folk theory; Hawk policy model; Learning theory; Linked mediated stimulus-response models; Mediated stimulus-response models; Model; Prediction; Prisoner's dilemma model; Rational theories; Stimulus-response models; Stress theory
Time plots: of composite indices and individual variables, 211-45

U.S. ground forces in South Vietnam, 47-50, 133-34; and casualties, 76 n; and Communist counterescalation, 49-50; and ineffectiveness of bombing of North Vietnam, 48; purpose of, 48-49; and U.S. public opinion, 53-55
U.S. helicopter attacks, 136-37
U.S. military actions, 130, 135; operational measures of, 130
U.S. public opinion, 53-55, 60-63, 77 n, 130, 143-45; and anticommunism, 53-54; as affected by Korean War, 54; and Chinese revolution, 53; and government secrecy, 54; and President Johnson's chances for reelection, 62; as strategic target of North Vietnamese, 62; and U.S. casualties, 55; and U.S. troop commitments, 55, 62; and Vietnamization, 143-44

Viet Cong, xiii n

Vietnamization, 112, 128-33; and abductions by Viet Cong, 131; and Communist armed attacks, 131-32; and Communist terriorism, 132; operational measure of, 130; and rate of U.S. troop withdrawal, 131

War costs: effect of in U.S. 77 n